W9-DJP-247

Dear **NFT**™ User:

Needless to say, it's been quite a year in New York. We're still totally shocked at the events of September 11, which we witnessed and filmed from our fire escape in Chinatown. We're also deeply saddened by the death of someone in the NFT family, Stephen Wilcox, who died in early 2002. Stephen was one of the first people we weren't sleeping with who believed (or said they believed!) in NFT, and came on very early to try and help sell it to potential customers. Stephen: it was a pleasure.

We are, however, extremely excited to be releasing NFT-Chicago. We debuted NFT-Manhattan 2000 at Book Expo America in May of 2000, at McCormick Convention Center in Chicago. The burning question then was, "That's great…when's Chicago coming out?" Well, it took a little over two years, but here it finally is!

It was at McCormick Place in 2001 where we first met Kit Bernardi, a lifelong Chicago native and writer, who has subsequently become our City Editor. Kit— thanks for caring so much and for being so eager to join in our madness. Kit diligently researched and wrote while marshaling an army of dedicated neighborhood editors who helped us paint a Chicagoan's portrait of their city. We say thank you to them as well as Diana Pizzari for her help on NFT-Chicago.

To all the New York folks—Diana, John, Scot, Aaron, Anny, Kim, Donna, Gabe, Alli, Eric, Jodie, Carol, Justin and Kerrie etc.—thanks for playing. Hope to see you all again next year.

As always, we can be found on the web at www.notfortourists.com. We'd love to hear from you—questions, complaints, additions, desires, polemic—anything.

Here's hoping you find what you need.

Jane & Rob

Table of Contents

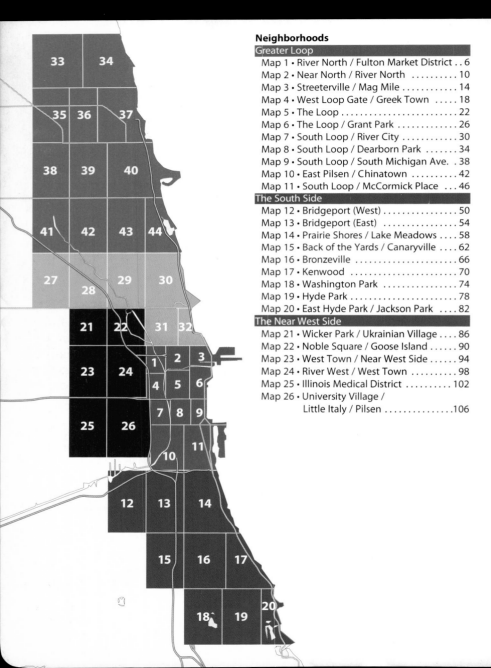

Neighborhoods

Greater Loop
Map 1 • River North / Fulton Market District . . 6
Map 2 • Near North / River North 10
Map 3 • Streeterville / Mag Mile 14
Map 4 • West Loop Gate / Greek Town 18
Map 5 • The Loop 22
Map 6 • The Loop / Grant Park 26
Map 7 • South Loop / River City 30
Map 8 • South Loop / Dearborn Park 34
Map 9 • South Loop / South Michigan Ave. . 38
Map 10 • East Pilsen / Chinatown 42
Map 11 • South Loop / McCormick Place . . . 46

The South Side
Map 12 • Bridgeport (West) 50
Map 13 • Bridgeport (East) 54
Map 14 • Prairie Shores / Lake Meadows 58
Map 15 • Back of the Yards / Canaryville 62
Map 16 • Bronzeville 66
Map 17 • Kenwood 70
Map 18 • Washington Park 74
Map 19 • Hyde Park 78
Map 20 • East Hyde Park / Jackson Park 82

The Near West Side
Map 21 • Wicker Park / Ukrainian Village 86
Map 22 • Noble Square / Goose Island 90
Map 23 • West Town / Near West Side 94
Map 24 • River West / West Town 98
Map 25 • Illinois Medical District 102
Map 26 • University Village /
          Little Italy / Pilsen 106

The Near North Side
Map 27 • Logan Square 110
Map 28 • Bucktown 114
Map 29 • DePaul/Wrightwood/Sheffield ... 118
Map 30 • Lincoln Park 122
Map 31 • Old Town / Near North 126
Map 32 • Gold Coast / Mag Mile 130

The North Side
Map 33 • West Rogers Park 134
Map 34 • East Rogers Park 138
Map 35 • Arcadia Terrace / Peterson Park .. 142
Map 36 • Bryn Mawr 146
Map 37 • Edgewater / Andersonville 150
Map 38 • Ravenswood / Albany Park 154
Map 39 • Ravenswood / North Center 158
Map 40 • Uptown 162
Map 41 • Avondale / Logan Square 166
Map 42 • North Center / West Lakeview ... 170
Map 43 • Wrigleyville / East Lakeview 174
Map 44 • East Lakeview 178

Parks & Places
Grant Park 182
Millennium Park 184
Lincoln Park 186
Jackson Park 188
Museum Campus 190
Garfield Park 192
Navy Pier 194
Chicago Cultural Center 196
Harold Washington Library Center 197
McCormick Place 198
Evanston 200
Oak Park 202
Beverly 204
Historic Pullman 206

Colleges & Universities
University of Illinois Chicago 208
University of Chicago 210
DePaul University 212
Northwestern University 214
Loyola University (Rogers Park/Downtown) . 216

Transit
O'Hare Airport 218
Midway Airport 222
Bus Lines: CTA Bus, PACE Bus, Greyhound .. 224
Metra Train Lines 226

South Shore Train Lines xxx
Train Stations 228
Amtrak 230
The El 232
Free Trolleys 234
Pedway 235

Sports
Recreational Paths 236
Bike Information 238
Skate Information 239
Golf 240
Tennis Courts & Volleyball Courts 241
Swimming & Bowling 242
Memorial Stadium 243
United Center 244
Soldier Field 245
Wrigley Field 246
Comiskey Park 247

General Information
Police Precincts 248
Firehouses 248
Post Offices & Zip Codes 249
Hospitals 250
Libraries 251
Fed Ex Locations 252
Gay & Lesbian Information 254
Landmarks 256
Dog Parks / Runs / Beaches 261
Hotels 262
24-Hour Services 264

Arts & Entertainment
Art Galleries 266
Museums 267
Bookstores 268
Clubs & Cabarets 270
Movie Theaters 272
Shopping 273
Restaurants 278
Theaters 286

Essential Phone Numbers 288
Street Index 289

Driving & Parking .... fold-out in back
Highway Map .... fold-out in back

Map 1 · **River North / Fulton Market District** (N)

W Locust St

W Iowa St

W Chestnut St

W Chestnut St

W Chestnut St

N Larrabee St

W Pearson St

N Cambridge Ave

N Mohawk St

N Cleveland Ave

N Hudson Ave

N Sedgwick St

W Institute Pl

31

800N

P

W Chicago Ave

A W Superior St

700N

N Halsted St

N Green St

N Peoria St

W Huron St

W Superior St

700N

W Huron St

P

N Orleans St

W Ancona St

400W

W Erie St

W Erie St

W Erie St

P

W Ontario St

$

Connector 90

2 ▶

600W

800W

W Ohio St

W Ohio St

P

◀ **14**

B Grand

N Union Ave

W Grand Ave

N Kingsbury St

← **W Grand Ave**

P

W Illinois St

500N

North Branch Chicago River

W Ohio St

Milwaukee Ave

W Hubbard St

W Hubbard St

90

94

○ The Blommer
Chocolate Co.

W Kinzie St

P

N 400N

W Kinzie St

N Orleans St

John F Kennedy Expressway

N Green St

W Kinzie St

P

N Union Ave

N Des Plaines St

N Jefferson St

N Clinton St

N Canal St

W Carroll Ave

W Wayman St

C 800W

N Halsted St

P

W Fulton St

600W

500W

P

5 ▶

W Walnut St

W Walnut St

28

N Peoria St

N Green St

Lake St

W Lake St

Clinton

○

W Couch Pl

W Couch Pl

W Randolph Dr ←

1

2

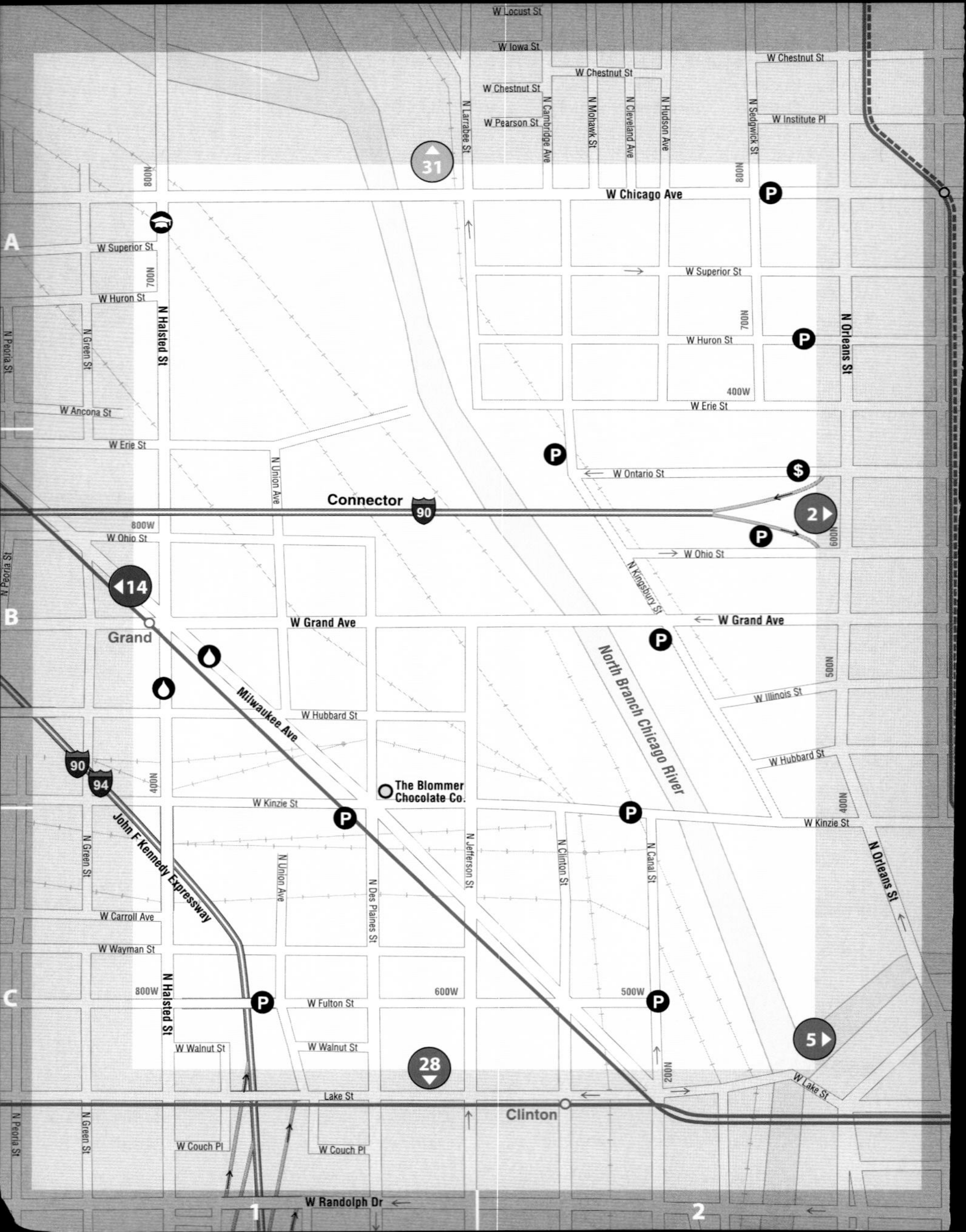

Crisscrossed by rail tracks, I-90/94 and the Chicago River, this area is transitioning from industrial to residential as the loft conversion craze in River North, Greek Town and West Loop Gate expands. The Bloomer Chocolate Company pumps sweet, chocolate-coated air into the streets all day. If you're watching your weight, breathing it in is the next best thing.

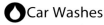## Bank

• **New Century Bank** • 363 W Ontario St

Car Washes

• **River West Hand Car Wash** •
478 N Milwaukee Ave
• **We Wash III** • 453 N Halsted St

Landmark

• **The Blommer Chocolate Co** • 600 W Kinzie St

Parking

• 300 N Canal St
• 631 W Kinzie St
• corner of Canal St & Fulton St
• 367 W Huron St
• 527 W Kinzie St
• 430 W Ohio St
• 530 N Kingsbury St
• 630 N Kingsbury St
• 656 W Fulton St

School

• **Northeastern Illinois University** •
770 N Halsted St

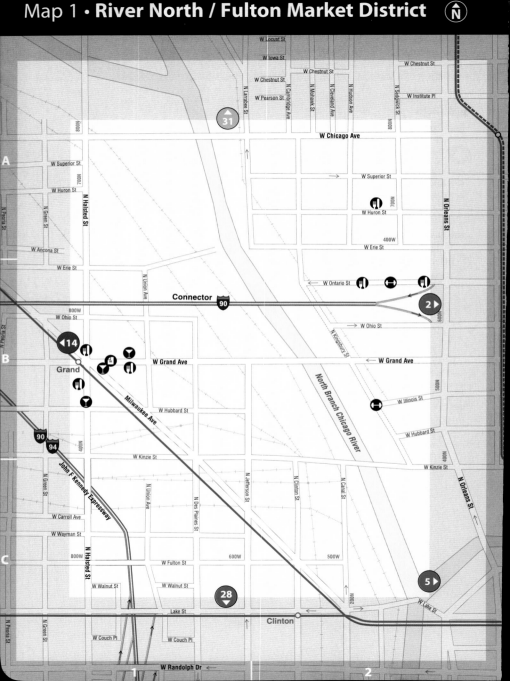

Sundries / Entertainment

Too bad, but the word has spread to the 'burbs about La Scarola serving whopping big bowls of home-made pasta for smallish prices. Go during the week to avoid the double dates. Reza's kebabs are killer. At Funky Buddha Lounge and Scoozi!, look for the buffed and beautiful from East Bank Club. Real people drink at Emmit's Pub.

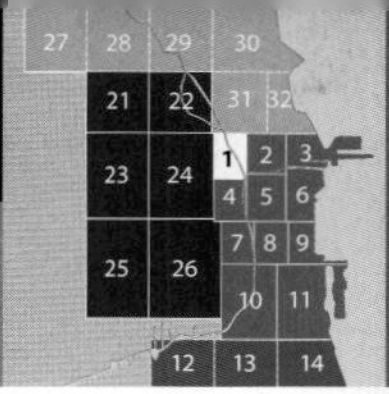

Bars

- **Emmit's Irish Pub & Eatery** • 495 N Milwaukee Ave
- **Funky Buddha Lounge** • 728 W Grand Ave
- **Rednofive** • 440 N Halsted St

Copy Shop

- **Quick Printing** • 730 Grand Ave

Gyms

- **East Bank Club** • 500 N Kingsbury St
- **Sharper Fitness** • 401 W Ontario St

Restaurants

- **Chilpancingo Restaurante** • 358 W Ontario St
- **Iguana Café** • 517 Halsted St
- **La Scarola** • 721 W Grand Ave
- **Reza's Restaurant** • 432 W Ontario St
- **Scoozi!** • 410 W Huron St
- **Thyme** • 464 N Halsted St

Map 2 · **Near North / River North**

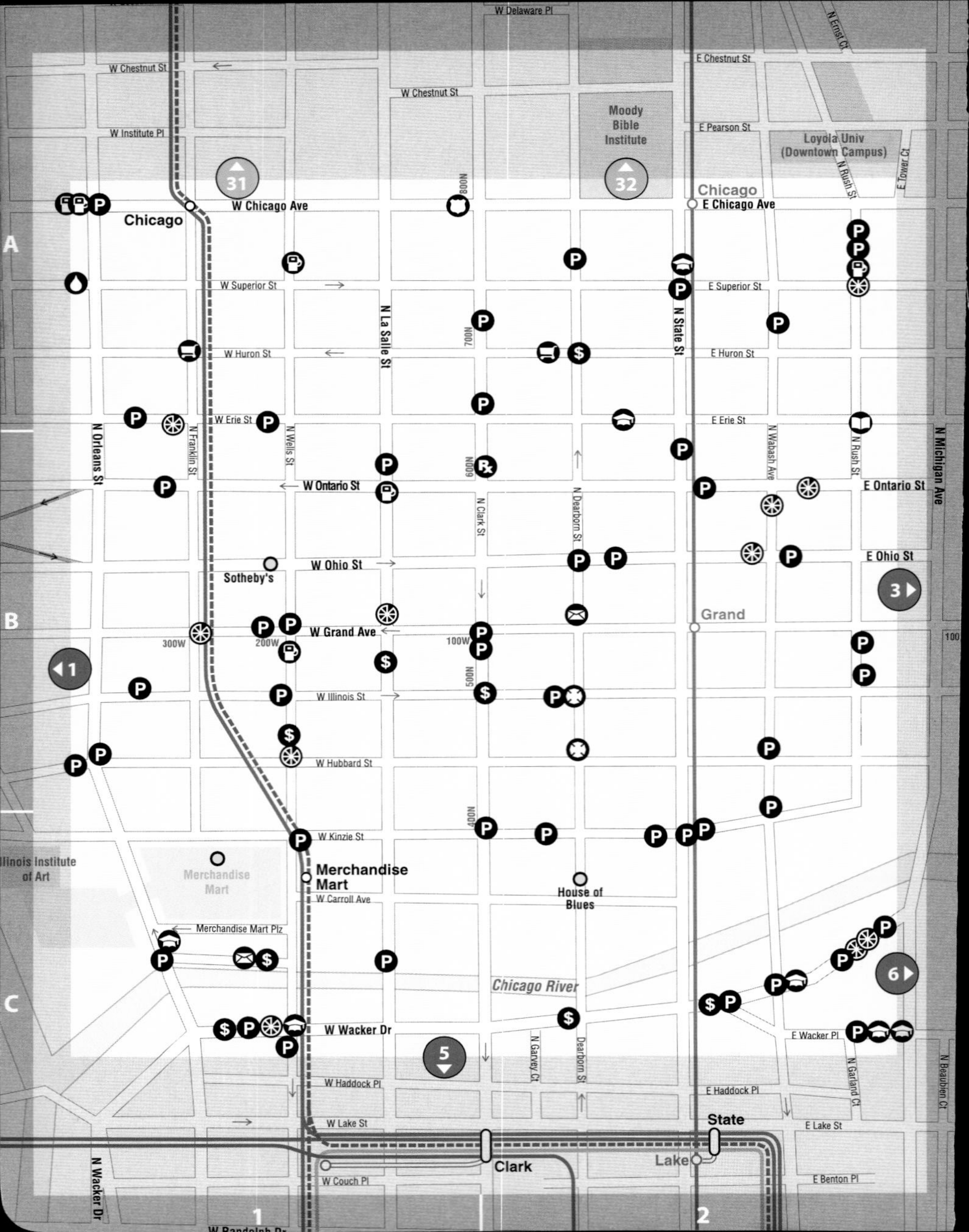

W Delaware Pl

W Chestnut St

E Chestnut St

W Chestnut St

W Institute Pl

E Pearson St

Moody
Bible
Institute

Loyola Univ
(Downtown Campus)

31

W Chicago Ave

Chicago

32

Chicago

E Chicago Ave

Chicago

A

W Superior St

W Superior St

E Superior St

W Huron St

E Huron St

W Erie St

E Erie St

N Franklin St

N Orleans St

N La Salle St

N Wells St

N Clark St

N Dearborn St

N State St

N Wabash St

N Rush St

N Michigan Ave

W Ontario St

E Ontario St

Sotheby's

W Ohio St

E Ohio St

3

B

W Grand Ave

Grand

300W

200W

100W

500N

600N

1

W Illinois St

W Hubbard St

W Kinzie St

600N

500N

W Kinzie St

Merchandise
Mart

W Carroll Ave

House of
Blues

Illinois Institute
of Art

Merchandise
Mart

Merchandise Mart Plz

6

C

Chicago River

W Wacker Dr

E Wacker Pl

5

W Haddock Pl

N Garvey Ct

Dearborn St

E Haddock Pl

W Lake St

State

E Lake St

W Couch Pl

Clark

Lake

E Benton Pl

N Wacker Dr

N Garland Ct

N Beaubien Ct

1

2

W Randolph Dr

Essentials

$ Banks
- **La Salle Bank** · 515 N La Salle Dr
- **Lakeside Bank** · 55 W Wacker Dr
- **Mid-City National Bank** · 1 E Wacker Dr
- **North Bank** · 501 N Clark St
- **North Community Bank** · 448 N Wells St
- **Oak Brook Bank** · 33 W Huron St
- **Old Kent Bank** · 222 Merchandise Mart Plz
- **Wells Fargo Bank** · 225 W Wacker Dr

Car Wash
- **River North Hand Car Wash** · 356 W Superior St

Fire Department
- **Chicago Fire Prevention Bureau** · 444 N Dearborn St

Gas Stations
- **Amoco** · 631 N Lasalle St
- **Chicago Orleans Shell** · 350 W Chicago Ave
- **Downtown Citgo** · 750 N Wells St

Hospital
- **Shaare Zedek Medical Center** · 101 W Grand Ave

Landmarks
- **House of Blues** · 329 N Dearborn St
- **Merchandise Mart** · 222 Merchandise Mart Plz
- **Sotheby's** · 215 W Ohio St

P Parking
- 308 W Ontario St
- 35 E Wacker Dr
- 355 W Chicago Ave
- 57 E Wacker Pl
- 71 E Wacker Dr
- 9 W Kinzie St
- 350 N Orleans St
- 750 N Dearborn St
- 671 N Clark St
- 300 N La Salle Dr
- 401 N State St
- 205 W Wacker Dr
- 212 W Illinois St
- 320 W Illinois St
- 401 N Wells St
- 437 N Orleans St
- 49 E Ohio St
- 506 N Rush St
- 519 N Rush St
- 521 N Clark St
- 600 N Dearborn St
- 640 N State St
- 737 N Rush St
- 750 N Rush St
- 530 N Wells St
- 350 W Hubbard St
- 711 N Wabash Ave
- 225 W Wacker Dr
- 440 N Wabash Ave
- 22 W Ohio St
- 224 W Erie St
- 320 W Erie St
- 222 W Grand Ave
- 85 E Wacker Dr
- 56 W Illinois St
- 1 W Superior St
- 10 E Ontario St
- 401 N Clark St
- 405 N Wabash Ave
- 61 W Kinzie St
- 714 N Clark St
- 1 E Wacker Dr

Pharmacy
- **Walgreens** · 641 N Clark St

Pizza
- **Bacino's** · 75 E Wacker Dr
- **Bravo Restaurants Inc** · 205 W Wacker Dr
- **Gino's East of Chicago** · 62 E Ontario St
- **Giordano's** · 730 N Rush St
- **Lou Malnati's Pizzeria** · 439 N Wells St
- **Pizzeria Due** · 619 N Wabash Ave
- **Pizzeria Ora** · 545 N La Salle Dr
- **Pizzeria Uno** · 29 E Ohio St
- **Rizzata's Pizzeria** · 300 W Grand Ave

Police
- **Chicago District Station 18** · 113 W Chicago Ave

Post Offices
- 222 Merchandise Mart Plz
- 540 N Dearborn St

Schools
- **Associated Colleges-Midwest** · 205 W Wacker Dr
- **Feltre School** · 22 W Erie St
- **Frances Xavier Ward School** · 751 N State St
- **Illinois Institute of Art** · 350 N Orleans St
- **Institute of Clinical Social Work** · 68 E Wacker Pl
- **Marquette University** · 35 E Wacker Dr
- **Urban Youth Program Alternative** · 65 E Wacker Pl

Supermarket
- **Whole Foods Market** · 50 W Huron St

11

Map 2 · **Near North / River North**

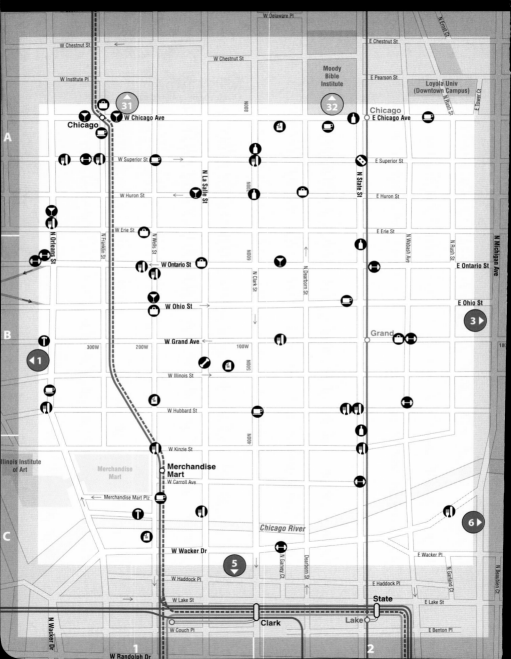

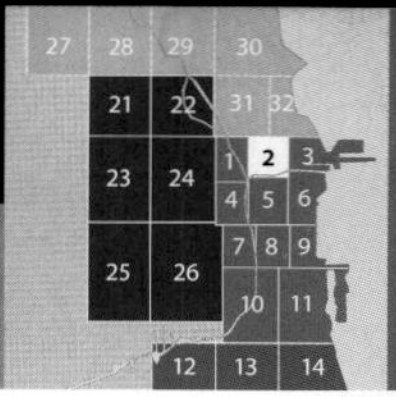

River North is Chicago's largest gallery district. Take several of them in during the Friday night champagne receptions. Clark & Barlow Hardware has the biggest selection of drawer pulls in the City. Zinfandel actually makes American food taste and feel gourmet. Club Lago takes only cash for Italian basics. Bar Louie and Green Door Tavern are good for post-work cocktails. Martini Ranch stirs it up into the a.m.

Map 2

Bars
- **Bar Louie** · 226 W Chicago Ave
- **Blue Frog Bar & Grill** · 676 N Lasalle Dr
- **Cyrano's Bistrot & Wine Bar** · 546 N Wells St
- **Green Door Tavern** · 678 N Orleans St
- **Martini Ranch** · 311 W Chicago Ave
- **Red Head Piano Bar** · 16 W Ontario St

Coffee
- **Dunkin Donuts** · 20 E Chicago Ave
- **Seattle's Best** · 42 E Chicago Ave
- **Seattle's Best** · 701 N Wells St
- **Starbucks** · 222 Merchandise Mart Plz
- **Starbucks** · 414 N Orleans St
- **Starbucks** · 600 N State St
- **Starbucks** · 750 N Franklin St
- **Starbucks** · 430 N Clark St

Copy Shops
- **Chicago Print** · 71 W Chicago Ave
- **The Ink Well** · 112 W Illinois St
- **Kinko's** · 444 N Wells St
- **Mail Boxes Etc** · 446 N Wells St

Gyms
- **Crunch Fitness** · 350 N State St
- **Executive Sports & Fitness Center** · 77 W Wacker Dr
- **Gorilla Sports** · 38 E Grand Ave
- **Lakeshore Athletic Club** · 441 N Wabash Ave
- **Ontario Place Fitness Club** · 10 E Ontario St
- **Sharper Fitness** · 401 N Ontario St

Hardware Stores
- **Clark & Barlow Hardware Co** · 353 W Grand Ave
- **Hinges & Handles** · 222 Merchandise Mart Plz

Liquor Stores
- **Binny's Beverage Depot** · 213 W Grand Ave
- **Copperfield's** · 70 W Huron St
- **Holiday Wines & Spirits** · 6 W Chicago Ave
- **Rossi's Liquors** · 412 N State St
- **Superior Liquor Corp** · 750 N Clark St
- **White Hen Pantry** · 645 N State St

Pet Shop
- **Anti-Cruelty Society** · 510 N La Salle St

Restaurants
- **Ace Grill** · 71 E Wacker Dr
- **Bob Chinn's Crab House** · 321 N La Salle St
- **Brett's Kitchen** · 233 W Superior St
- **Club Lago** · 331 W Superior St
- **Erawan** · 729 N Clark St
- **Hubbard St Grill** · 351 W Hubbard St
- **Kevin** · 9 W Hubbard St
- **Kinzie Chophouse** · 400 N Wells St
- **Linos** · 222 W Ontario St
- **Mr. Beef** · 666 N Orleans St
- **Naniwa** · 607 N Wells St
- **Redfish** · 400 N State St
- **Vong's Thai Kitchen** · 6 W Hubbard St
- **Zinfandel** · 59 W Grand Ave

Shopping
- **Mary Wolf Gallery** · 705 Dearborn St
- **Mig and Tig Furniture** · 549 N Wells St
- **Montauk** · 223 W Erie St
- **Nordstrom** · 55 E Grand Ave
- **Paper Source** · 232 W Chicago Ave
- **Sportmart** · 620 N La Salle St

Video Rental
- **Blockbuster Video** · 1 W Superior St

Map 3 • **Streeterville / Mag Mile**

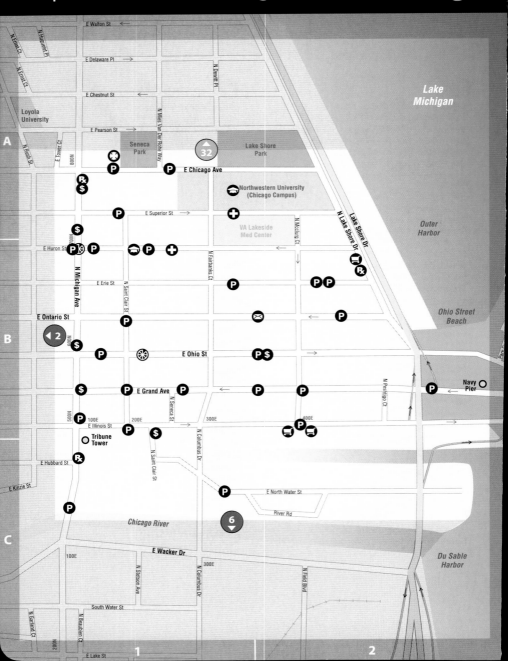

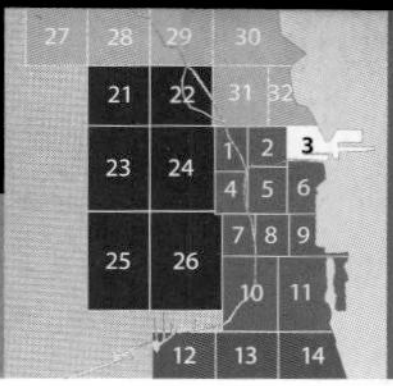

Compact and packed, Streeterville and Mag Mile residents are some of the City's wealthiest living in high-rise homes just steps from the Michigan Ave. and lakefront action. With Navy Pier and shopping galore, these densely populated blocks swarm with conventioneers and tourists. As the labyrinthine Northwestern University Medical Campus expands, construction rules the streets. Rush hour traffic can get as congested as Michigan Ave's sidewalks at Christmas.

Map 3

Banks

- **Banco Popular** • 717 N Michigan Ave
- **BankOne** • 605 N Michigan Ave
- **Citibank** • 539 N Michigan Ave
- **Harris Bank** • 455 N Cityfront Plaza Dr
- **North Bank** • 360 E Ohio St

Fire Department

- **Chicago Fire Department** • 202 E Chicago Ave

⊕Hospitals

- **Northwestern Memorial Hospital** •
  251 E Huron St
- **Prentice Women's Hospital** • 333 E Superior St

Landmarks

- **Navy Pier** • 600 E Grand Ave
- **Tribune Tower** • 435 N Michigan Ave

ⓟParking

- 201 E Illinois St
- 351 E Grand Ave
- 401 E Grand Ave
- 511 E Grand Ave
- 200 E Superior St
- 211 E Ohio St
- 215 E Chicago Ave
- 245 E Grand Ave
- 625 N Saint Clair St
- 350 E Ohio St
- 300 E North Water St
- 161 E Chicago Ave
- 535 N Saint Clair St
- 159 E Ohio St
- 150 E Huron St
- 222 E Huron St
- 321 E Erie St
- 441 E Erie St
- 700 N Michigan Ave

Pharmacies

- **Parkway Drugs** • 680 N Lake Shore Dr
- **Walgreens** • 430 N Michigan Ave
- **Walgreens** • 757 N Michigan Ave

Pizza

- **A Slice of Italy Pizzeria** • 435 E Illinois St
- **Suparossa Restaurant** • 210 E Ohio St

⊠Post Office

- 227 E Ontario St

School

- **Northwestern University** • 205 E Huron St

⊟Supermarkets

- **Fox & Obel Food Store** • 401 E Illinois St
- **Market Place Food Store** • 393 E Illinois St
- **Treasue Island** • 680 N Lake Shore Dr (entrance on Huron St)

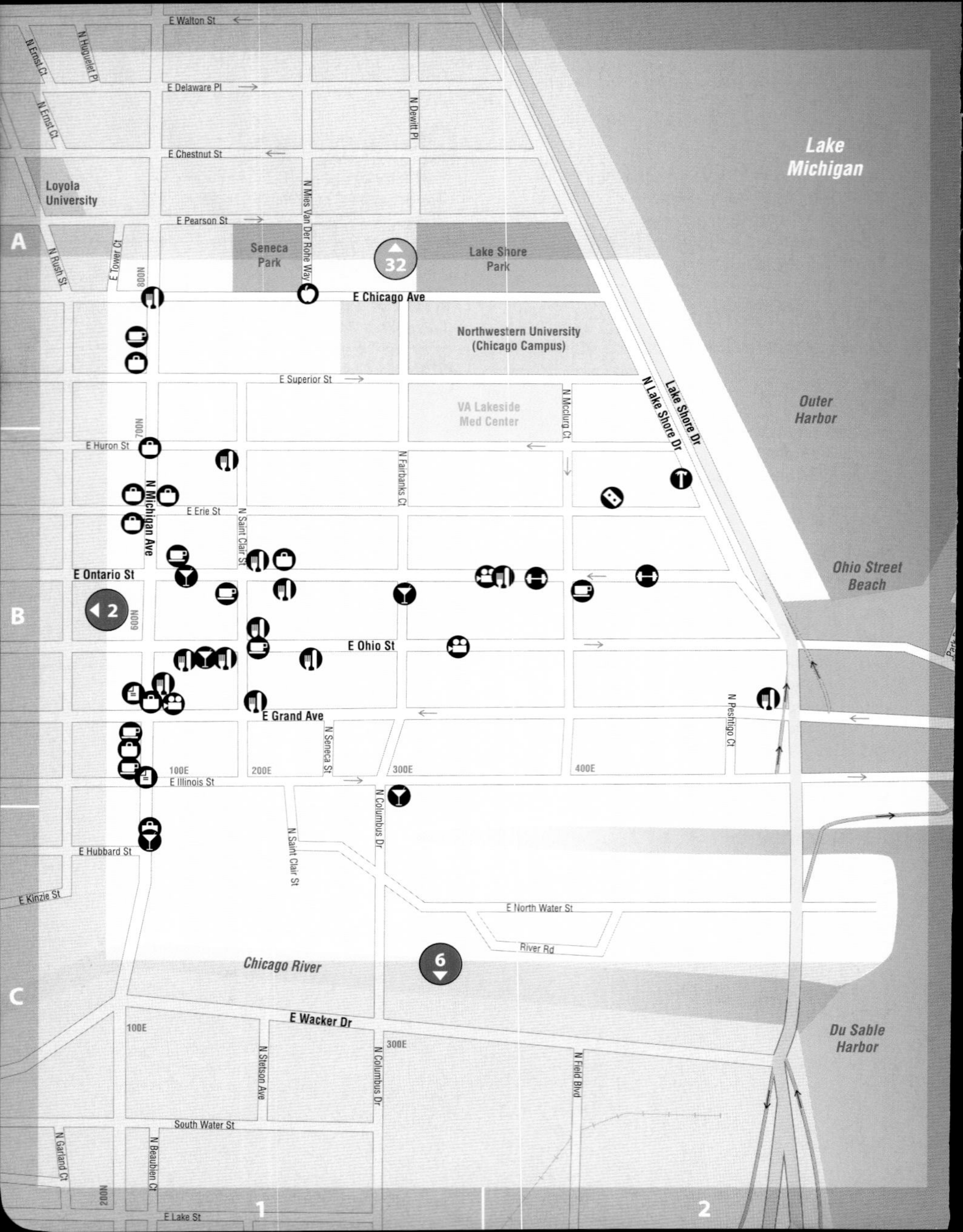

Map 3 · **Streeterville / Mag Mile**

N

Lake
Michigan

E Walton St

E Delaware Pl

E Chestnut St

N Ernst Ct

N Husplels Pl

N Ernst Ct

N DeWitt Pl

N Mies Van Der Rohe Way

E Pearson St

**Loyola
University**

N Rush St

E Tower Ct

A

**Seneca
Park**

▲
32

**Lake Shore
Park**

E Chicago Ave

**Northwestern University
(Chicago Campus)**

**Outer
Harbor**

E Superior St

VA Lakeside
Med Center

N McClurg Ct

N Lake Shore Dr

Lake Shore Dr

E Huron St

N 700E

N Fairbanks Ct

T

E Erie St

N Michigan Ave

N 600E

N Saint Clair St

B

E Ontario St

◄ **2**

Y

E Ohio St

**Ohio Street
Beach**

E Grand Ave

N Seneca St

100E

200E

300E

400E

N Peshtigo Ct

E Illinois St

Y

E Hubbard St

N Saint Clair St

N Columbus Dr

E North Water St

E Kinzie St

River Rd

Chicago River

6
▼

C

E Wacker Dr

100E

N Stetson Ave

300E

N Columbus Dr

N Field Blvd

**Du Sable
Harbor**

South Water St

N Garland Ct

N Beaubien Ct

2000

E Lake St

1

2

Map 3

Escape from the shopping bag-toting throngs at comfy Timothy O'Tooles Pub on Fairbanks or go underground on lower Michigan Ave. to Billy Goat Tavern, a Chicago institution. Indian Garden's lunch buffet is an office worker's fave. Bandera brings in the after-work ad. execs for roast chicken and also makes great takeout. If you've got bucks to blow and months to wait for a weekend reservation, Tru is for you.

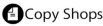Bars
- **Billy Goat Tavern** · 430 N Michigan Ave
- **Bozwog's Second Story Bar** · 157 E Ohio St
- **Dick's Last Resort** · 435 E Illinois St
- **O'Neill's Bar & Grill** · 152 E Ontario St
- **Timothy O'Tooles Pub** · 622 N Fairbanks Ct

Coffee
- **Capra's Coffee** · 205 E Ohio St
- **Starbucks** · 440 N Michigan Ave
- **Starbucks** · 670 N Michigan Ave
- **Starbucks** · 401 E Ontario St
- **Starbucks** · 435 E Illinois St

Copy Shops
- **Kinko's** · 540 N Michigan Ave, 2nd Fl
- **Kwik Kopy** · 500 N Michigan Ave

Farmer's Market
- **Museum of Contemporary Art/Streeterville** · Chicago Ave and Mies Van der Rohe Way

Gyms
- **Lakeshore Athletic Club** · 333 E Ontario St
- **Onterie Fitness Center** · 446 E Ontario St

Hardware Store
- **Ace Hardware** · 680 N Lake Shore Dr

Movie Theaters
- **Cineplex Odeon** · 600 N Michigan Ave
- **McClurg Court Theatre** · 330 E Ohio St

Restaurants
- **Bandera** · 535 N Michigan Ave, 2nd fl
- **Cambridge House Grill** · 162 E Ohio St
- **Capital Grille** · 633 N St Clair St
- **Cite** · Lake Point Tower, 70th fl 505 N Lake Shore Dr
- **Hot Diggity Dogs** · 251 E Ohio St
- **Indian Garden** · 247 E Ontario St, 2nd fl
- **Les Nomades** · 222 E Ontario St
- **NoMI at the Hyatt Hotel** · 800 N Michigan Ave
- **Sayat Nova** · 157 E Ohio St
- **Tru** · 676 N St Clair St
- **Volare** · 201 E Grand Ave

Shopping
- **Chicago Place** · 700 N Michigan Ave
- **Crate & Barrel** · 646 N Michigan Ave
- **Decoro** · 224 E Ontario St
- **Eddie Bauer** · 600 N Michigan Ave
- **Garrett Popcorn Shop** · 670 N Michigan Ave
- **Niketown** · 669 N Michigan Ave
- **Rand McNally Store** · 444 N Michigan Ave
- **Virgin Megastore** · 540 N Michigan Ave

Video Rental
- **Hollywood Video** · 680 N Lake Shore Dr

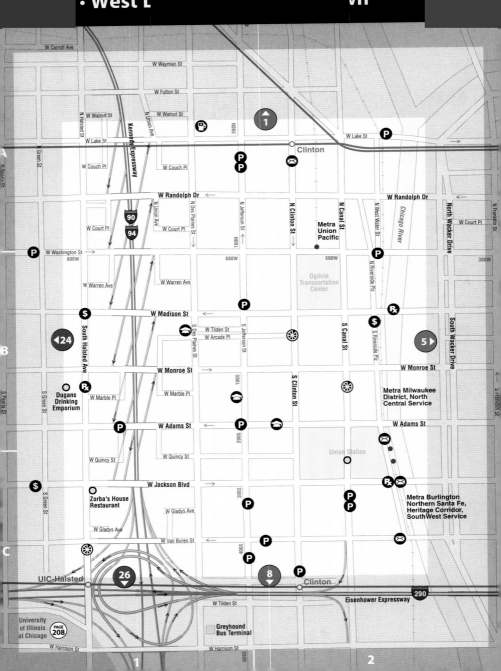

Trains, buses and gyros define this once warehouse district, which is now loft residences and office spaces. The gateway for suburbanites into the City, West Loop is the address for the Richard B. Ogilvie Transportation Center (just call it Northwestern Train Station, please), grand Union Station, where Amtrak is based, and the downtown Greyhound Bus Terminal.

$Banks

- **Cole Taylor Bank** · 850 W Jackson Blvd
- **Corus Bank** · 10 S Riverside Plz
- **Mid-City National Bank** · 801 W Madison St

Gas Station

- **Fulton & Des Plaines Sinclair** ·
  225 N Des Plaines St

Landmarks

- **Dugans Drinking Emporium** · 128 S Halsted St
- **Union Station** · Jackson Blvd & Canal St
- **Zorba's House Restaurant** · 301 S Halsted St

Parking

- 175 N Jefferson St
- 180 N Jefferson St
- 765 W Adams St
- 320 S Canal St
- 850 W Washington Blvd
- 430 S Jefferson St
- 328 S Jefferson St
- 568 W Van Buren St
- 430 S Clinton St
- 440 W Lake St
- 100 N Riverside Plz
- 623 W Adams St

Pharmacies

- **Osco Drug** · 400 W Madison St
- **Walgreens** · 111 S Halsted St

Pizza

- **Bacino's** · 118 S Clinton St
- **Connie's Pizza Inc** · 225 S Canal St
- **Giordano's** · 815 W Van Buren St

Post Offices

- 168 N Clinton St
- 222 S Riverside Plz
- 300 S Riverside Plz
- 433 W Van Buren St

Schools

- **Chicago-Kent College Law Office** ·
  565 W Adams St
- **Frances Xavier Ward School** ·
  122 S Des Plaines St

Map 4 · **West Loop Gate / Greek Town**

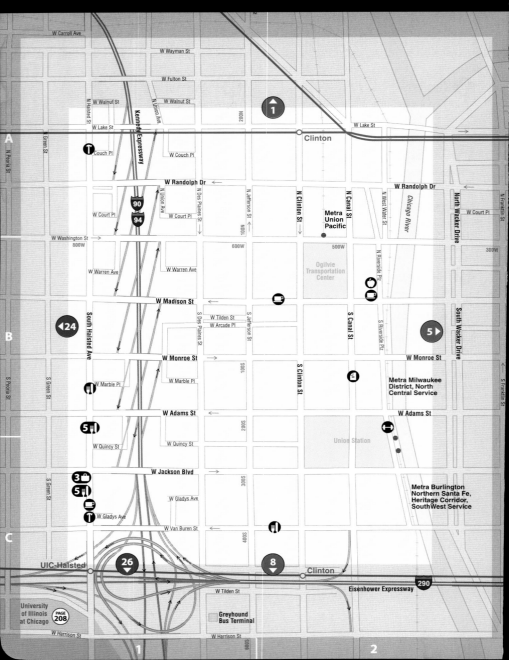

Sundries / Entertainment

"Oompa!" is all you need to say. But say it with gusto around here where the blue and white striped flags wave along Halsted St. Flaming saganaki was introduced by Greek sea captains who cast permanent anchor in Chicago in the 1900s.

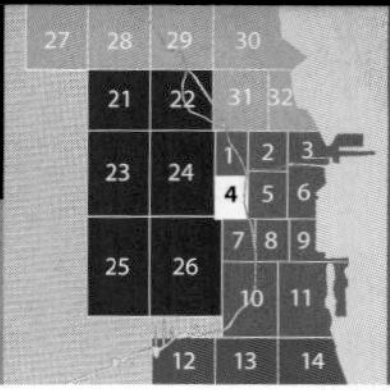

Map 4

Coffee
- **Atruro Express** · 555 W Madison St
- **Grind House Coffee** · 307 S Halsted St
- **Starbucks** · 2 N Riverside Plz

Copy Shop
- **Kinko's** · 128 S Canal St

Farmer's Market
- **On the Plaza** · 2 N Riverside Plz

Gym
- **Union Station Multiplex** · 222 S Riverside Plz

Hardware Stores
- **Chicago Wholesale Hardware Co** ·
  171 N Halsted St
- **Turek & Sons** · 333 S Halsted St

Restaurants
- **Artopolis Cafe and Agora** · 306 S Halsted St
- **Athena** · 212 S Halsted St
- **Byzantium** · 232 S Halsted St
- **Costas** · 340 S Halsted St
- **Greek Islands** · 200 S Halsted St
- **J and C Inn** · 558 W Van Buren St
- **Nine Muses** · 315 S Halsted St
- **Parthenon** · 314 S Halsted St
- **Pegasus Restaurant and Taverna** ·
  130 S Halsted St
- **Roditys** · 222 S Halsted St
- **Santorini** · 800 W Adams St

Shopping
- **Athenian Candle Co** · 300 S Halsted St
- **Athens Jewelry** · 310 S Halsted St
- **Greek Town Gifts** · 330 S Halsted St

Map 5 · **The Loop**

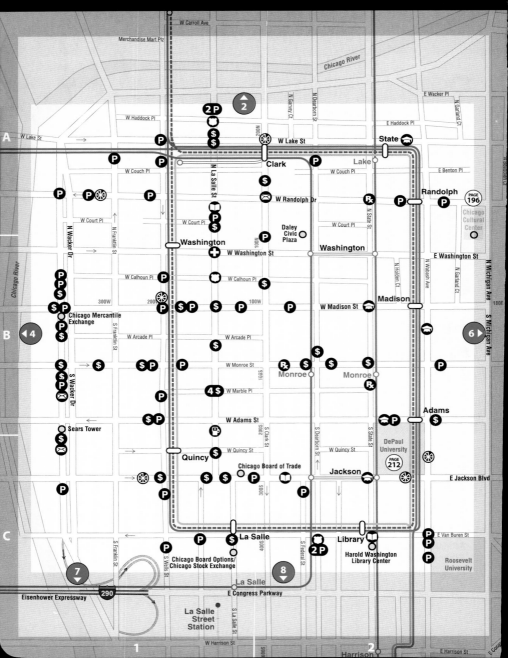

It all starts here, where money changes hands at the CBOT, CBOE, CSE and CME. The Loop, named after the El tracks lassoing Chicago's heart, is the bustling business and financial district. With all the banks, finding an ATM is much easier than a metered parking space, although pricey parking garages abound. The intersection of State and Madison Streets is the point from which Chicago's simple and efficient street number grid system starts making navigation pretty easy.

💲 Banks
- **ABN Amro Bank** · 135 S La Salle St
- **ABN Amro Bank** · 120 S La Salle St
- **Amalgamated Bank Of Chicago** · 1 W Monroe St
- **American National Bank & Trust** · 120 S La Salle St
- **American National Bank & Trust** · 30 S Wacker Dr
- **Associated Bank Chicago** · 200 N La Salle St
- **Banco Popular** · 415 N La Salle St
- **Bank of America** · 231 S La Salle St
- **Bank of Montreal-Harris Bank** · 115 S La Salle St
- **Bank of New York** · 209 W Jackson Blvd
- **CIB Bank** · 161 N Clark St
- **Citibank** · 222 W Adams St
- **Cole Taylor Bank** · 111 W Washington St
- **First American Bank** · 33 W Monroe St
- **First American Bank** · 50 E Adams St
- **First Bank** · 20 N Wacker Dr
- **First Bankers Trust Co** · 225 W Washington St
- **First National Bank Of Chicago** · 55 W Monroe St
- **Harris Trust & Savings Bank** · 311 W Monroe St
- **Harris Trust & Savings Bank** · 141 W Jackson Blvd
- **Harris Trust & Savings Bank** · 99 W Washington St
- **International Commercial Bank** · 2 N La Salle St
- **La Salle Bank** · 120 N La Salle St
- **La Salle Bank** · 203 N La Salle St
- **La Salle Bank** · 100 S Wacker Dr
- **La Salle Bank** · 77 S Dearborn St
- **La Salle Capital Markets** · 181 W Madison St
- **Lakeside Bank** · 141 W Jackson Blvd
- **Manufacturers Bank** · 20 N Clark St
- **Manufacturers Bank** · 2 S LaSalle
- **Mid-City National Bank** · 1 S Wacker Dr
- **Northern Trust Bank** · 125 S Wacker Dr
- **Northern Trust Bank** · 50 S La Salle St
- **Old Kent Bank** · 233 S Wacker Dr
- **Wells Fargo Bank** · 230 W Monroe St

ⓟ Gas Station
- **United Cities Gas Co** · 208 S La Salle St

➕ Hospital
- **National Jewish Center** · 100 N La Salle St

Landmarks
- **Chicago Board of Trade** · 141 W Jackson Blvd
- **Chicago Board Options Exchange** · 400 S La Salle St
- **Chicago Cultural Center** · 78 E Washington St
- **Chicago Mercantile Exchange** · 20-30 S Wacker Dr
- **Chicago Stock Exchange** · 440 S La Salle St
- **Daley Civic Plaza** · 50 W Washington
- **Harold Washington Library Center** · 400 S State St
- **Sears Tower** · 233 S Wacker Dr

📖 Libraries
- **Chicago Public Library** · 400 S State St
- **Municipal Reference Library** · 121 N La Salle St
- **US Library** · 77 W Jackson Blvd

Ⓟ Parking
- 319 W Randolph St
- 430 S Wabash Ave
- 133 S Wacker Dr
- 221 N La Salle St
- 181 W Monroe St
- 30 N Wells St
- 410 S Wabash Ave
- 20 N Wacker Dr
- 180 N Franklin St
- 318 S Federal St
- 401 S Wabash Ave
- 112 N Clark St
- 145 S Wells St
- 211 W Adams St
- 218 W Randolph St
- 29 N Wacker Dr
- 326 S Wells St
- 215 W Washington St
- 177 N Wells St
- 1 S Wacker Dr
- 111 W Jackson Blvd
- 222 N La Salle St
- 55 E Monroe St
- 415 S Financial Pl
- 407 S Dearborn St
- 215 W Lake St
- 200 N Wells St
- 120 W Madison St
- 150 S Wacker Dr
- 172 W Madison St
- 181 N Dearborn St
- 201 W Madison St
- 30 S Wacker Dr
- 321 S Wacker Dr
- 412 S Dearborn St
- 120 N La Salle St
- 17 E Adams St
- 227 W Monroe St
- 60 E Randolph St
- 230 W Washington St
- 70 W Madison St
- 30 E Randolph St
- 425 S Wells St

℞ Pharmacies
- **Osco Drug** · 137 S State St
- **Walgreens** · 151 N State St
- **Walgreens** · 79 W Monroe St

🍊 Pizza
- **Giordano's Pizzeria** · 225 W Jackson Blvd
- **Giordano's Pizzeria** · 236 S Wabash Ave
- **Giordano's** · 310 W Randolph St
- **Giordano's Restaurant** · 28 E Jackson Blvd
- **Little Pompei Bakery** · 218 W Washington St
- **Mama Falco's** · 5 N Wells St
- **Milanos Italian Eatery** · 201 N Clark St
- **Ultimate Pizza** · 69 W Washington St

🚔 Police
- **Chicago Law Dept Investigation** · 30 N La Salle St
- **Chicago Police Pension Board** · 221 N La Salle St
- **Chicago Police-Gun Registration** · 50 W Washington St
- **EAP** · 407 S Dearborn St

✉ Post Offices
- 100 W Randolph St
- 150 S Wacker Dr
- 233 S Wacker Dr

🎓 Schools
- **Career Colleges Of Chicago** · 11 E Adams St
- **De Paul University** · 1 E Jackson Blvd
- **Harold Washington College** · 30 E Lake St
- **International Academy of Design and Technology** · 1 N State St
- **Keller Graduate School Of Management** · 225 W Washington St
- **Loop Laboratory School** · 11 E Adams St
- **School of the Art Institute** · 37 S Wabash Ave

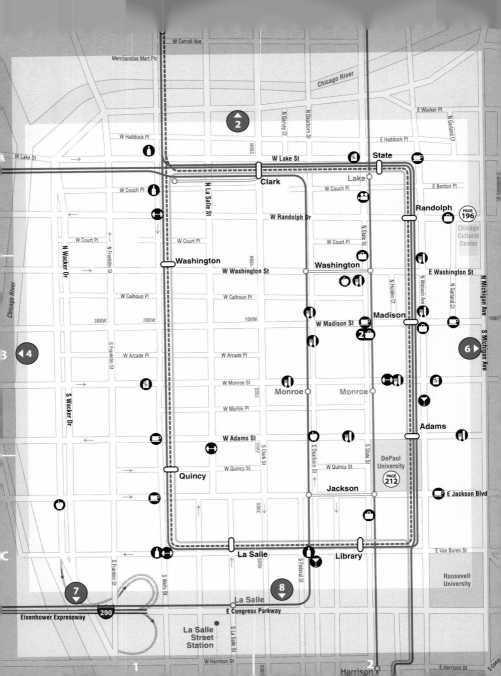

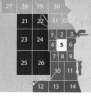

Map 5

Retail giants Marshall Field's and Carson Pirie Scott anchor State St. What was once a great street that went downhill, it's now making a comeback with new retail blood, renovated hotels and revitalized theaters. Armies of lawyers and loyal civil servants march among dozens of government buildings located within blocks of each other. Everest Room is easily the biggest expense report restaurant in the Loop. For decades, spicy Heaven On Seven has drawn Loop workers for Creole home cookin'.

Bars
- **Manhattans** · 415 S Dearborn St
- **Miller's Pub** · 134 S Wabash Ave

Coffee
- **Java Java** · 2 N State St
- **Starbucks** · 200 W Adams St
- **Starbucks** · 209 W Jackson Blvd
- **Starbucks** · 55 E Jackson Blvd
- **Starbucks** · 68 E Madison St
- **The Coffee Grounds** · 203 N Wabash Ave

Copy Shops
- **Kinko's** · 227 W Monroe St
- **Kinko's** · 55 E Monroe St
- **Kinko's** · 6 W Lake St

Farmer's Markets
- **Daley Center Plaza** · 50 W Washington St
- **Federal Plaza** · Adams St & Dearborn St
- **The Park at Jackson & Wacker** · 311 S Wacker Dr at Sears Tower

Gyms
- **Bally's** · 400 S Wells St
- **Executive Fitness Center** · 17 E Monroe St
- **Randolph Athletic Club** · 188 W Randolph St
- **Women's Workout World** · 208 S La Salle St

Liquor Stores
- **Cal's Liquor Store** · 400 S Wells St
- **G & J Gifts & Liquor** · 167 N Wells St
- **Lake & Wells Food & Liquor Inc** · 201 W Lake St
- **Rothschild Liquor Marts** · 55 W Van Buren St

Movie Theater
- **Gene Siskel Film Center** · 164 N State St

Restaurants
- **Atwood Cafe** · 1 W Washington St
- **Berghoff Restaurant** · 17 W Adams St
- **Everest Room** · 440 S LaSalle St
- **Heaven On Seven** · 111 N Wabash Ave
- **Italian Village** · 71 W Monroe St
- **Nick's Fishmarket & Grill** · Clark St & Dearborn St
- **Oasis Restaurant** · 21 N Wabash Ave
- **Russian Tea Time** · 77 E Adams St
- **The French Quarter/Palmer House Hilton** · 17 E Monroe St
- **Trattoria #10** · 10 N Dearborn St

Shopping
- **American Music World** · 333 S State St
- **Carson Pirie Scott** · 1 S State St
- **Gallery 37 Store** · 66 E Randolph St
- **Jeweler's Mall** · 7 S Wabash Ave
- **Marshall Field's** · 111 N State St
- **Sears** · 2 N State St

Map 6 · **The Loop / Grant Park**

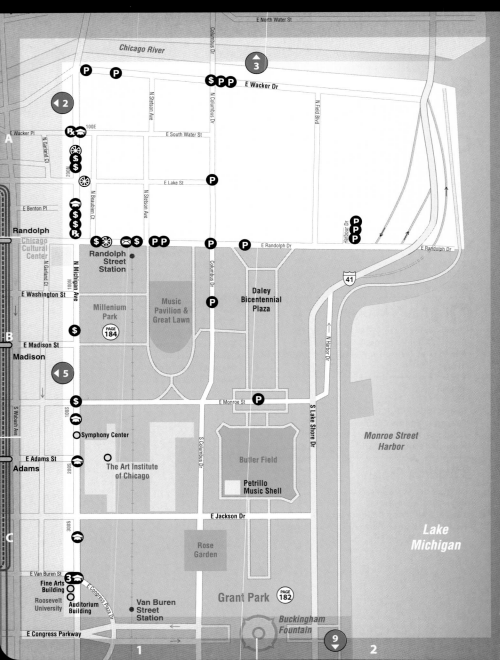

Grant Park is Chicago's front lawn where glass meets grass. The 319-acre park, designed by architect Daniel Burnham, is Chicagoans' favorite place to promenade, party, play and protest. At Buckingham Fountain, turn back towards the City and survey the sparkling, stalwart stretch of skyscrapers representative of world renowned Chicago architectural styles. Millennium Park on the northwest corner promises to deliver more greenery and outdoor entertainment venues by the 21st Century's end.

Banks

- **Altantic Bank of NY - Chicago** ·
  168 N Michigan Ave
- **Associated Bank Chicago** · 130 E Randolph St
- **Associated Bank Chicago** · 200 E Randolph St
- **Associated Bank Chicago** · 225 N Michigan Ave
- **Chicago Community Bank** · 180 N Michigan Ave
- **Citibank** · 104 S Michigan Ave
- **Citibank** · 233 N Michigan Ave
- **Mid-City National Bank** · 303 E Wacker Dr

Landmarks

- **Art Institute of Chicago** · 111 S Michigan Ave
- **Auditorium Building** · 430 S Michigan Ave
- **Fine Arts Building** · 410 S Michigan Ave
- **Symphony Center** · 22 S Michigan Ave

Parking

- 111 E Wacker Dr
- 151 E Wacker Dr
- 200 N Columbus Dr
- 300 E Randolph St
- 323 E Wacker Dr
- 200 E Randolph St
- 350 E Monroe St
- 155 N Harbor Dr
- Columbus Drive, between Washington St & Madison St
- 175 N Harbor Dr
- 195 N Harbor Dr
- 360 E Randolph St
- 303 E Wacker Dr

 Pharmacies

- **Osco Drug** · 150 N Michigan Ave
- **Walgreens** · 300 N Michigan Ave

Pizza

- **Giordano's** · 130 E Randolph St
- **Sbarro** · 233 N Michigan Ave

Post Offices

- 200 E Randolph St

Schools

- **American Academy of Art** · 332 S Michigan Ave
- **American English Academy** ·
  180 N Michigan Ave
- **Aurora University** · 300 N Michigan Ave
- **Harrington Institute-Interior** ·
  410 S Michigan Ave
- **National Louis University** · 122 S Michigan Ave
- **Roosevelt University** · 430 S Michigan Ave

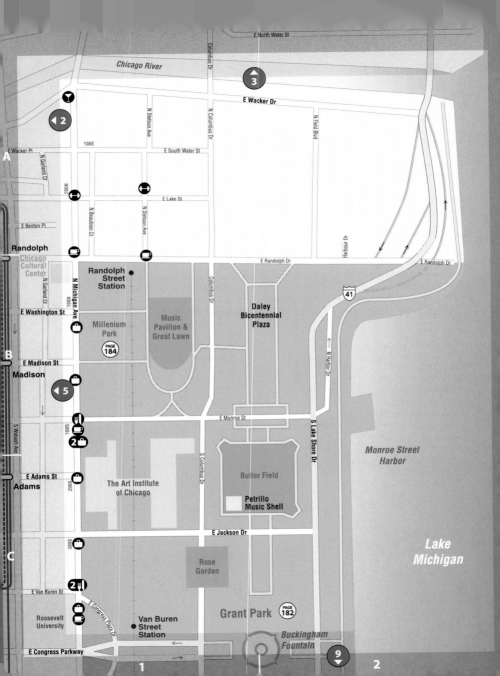

From classical music and Blues to Monet, take it all in along S. Michigan Ave. Spend lunch hours feeding your brain at the Art Institute on Tuesday, when admission is waived. While there is no view, the acoustics are grand in the Chicago Symphony Center's nosebleed section. Savvy Traveler is the globetrotter's choice for good reads. In summer, head down to Grant Park for free music concerts and at least one of the Summer Festivals.

Map 6

Bar

- **Houlihan's** · 111 E Wacker Dr

Coffee

- **Cosi** · 116 S Michigan Ave
- **Rain Dog Books & Cafe** · 408 S Michigan Ave
- **Seattle's Best** · 150 N Michigan Ave
- **Starbucks** · 200 E Randolph St

Gyms

- **Athletic Club at Illinois Center** ·
  211 N Stetson Ave
- **Powerhouse Jim** · 200 N Michigan Ave

Restaurants

- **Art Institute Restaurant on the Park** ·
  111 S Michigan Ave
- **Artist's Cafe** · 412 S Michigan Ave
- **Bennegin's** · 150 S Michigan Ave
- **Rain Dog Books & Cafe** · 408 S Michigan Ave

Shopping

- **Art & Artisians** · 108 S Michigan Ave
- **Museum Shop of the Art Institute** ·
  111 S Michigan
- **Poster Plus** · 200 S Michigan Ave
- **Precious Possessions** · 28 N Michigan Ave
- **Rain Dog Books & Cafe** · 408 S Michigan Ave
- **The Savvy Traveller** · 310 S Michigan Ave

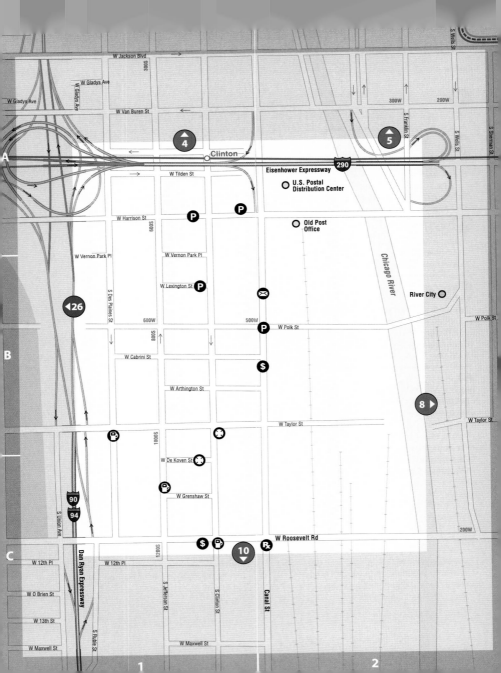

Map

Banks
- **Northern Trust Bank** · 840 S Canal St
- **South Central Bank** · 555 W Roosevelt Rd

Fire Departments
- **Chicago Fire Department Public Ed** · 1010 S Clinton St
- **Chicago Fire Department Academy** · 558 W De Koven St

Gas Stations
- **BP Amoco** · 534 W Roosevelt Rd
- **Citgo** · 1004 S Des Plaines St
- **Marathon** · 1121 S Jefferson St

Landmarks
- **Old Post Office** · 404 W Harrison St
- **River City** · 800 S Wells St
- **US Postal Distribution Center** · 433 W Harrison St

Parking
- 506 W Harrison St
- 801 S Canal St
- 555 W Harrison St
- 550 W Lexington St

Pharmacy
- **Walgreens** · 501 W Roosevelt St

Post Office
- 740 S Canal St

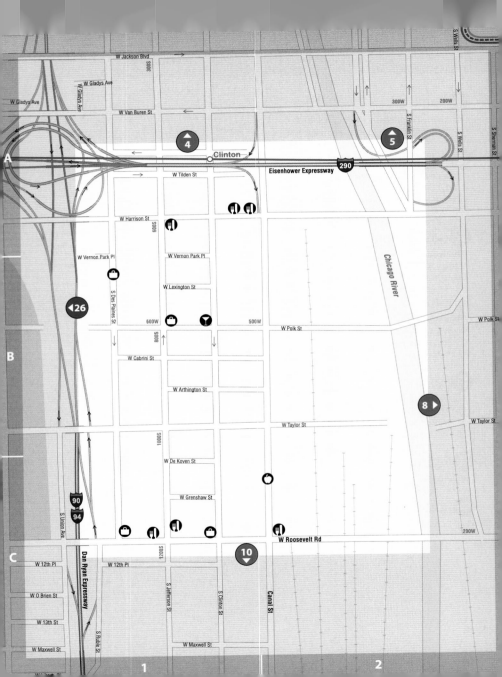

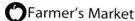

Map 7

The Maxwell Sunday Market is a shadow of its former self. Sadly, the colorful flea market lost its vibe in the move to Roosevelt Rd. to make way for UIC's expansion. The Chicago Fire Department Academy on DeKoven St. sits on the spot where Mrs. O'Leary's lantern-booting bovine started the Great Chicago Fire of 1871. For kicks, see the fire exhibit and watch the recruits' rappelling exercises.

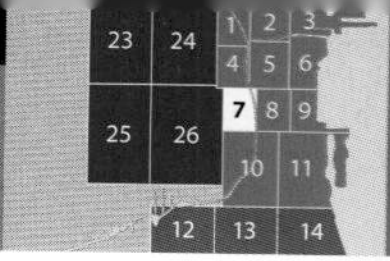

Bar

- **Scarlett's Gentleman's** · 750 S Clinton St

Farmer's Market

- **Maxwell Sunday Market** · Canal St between Taylor St & Roosevelt Rd

Restaurants

- **Bake for Me** · 608 W Roosevelt Rd
- **Harrison Red Hot** · 565 W Harrison St
- **Harrison St Grill** · 506 W Harrison St
- **Manny's Coffee Shop** · 1141 S Jefferson St
- **Nick's Grill** · 518 W Harrison St
- **White Palace Grill** · 1159 S Canal St

Shopping

- **Chicago Vintage Motor Carriage** · 700 S Des Plaines St
- **Fishman's Fabrics** · 1101 S Des Plaines St
- **Joseph Adam's Hats** · 544 W Roosevelt Rd
- **Lee's Foreign Car Service** · 727 S Jefferson St

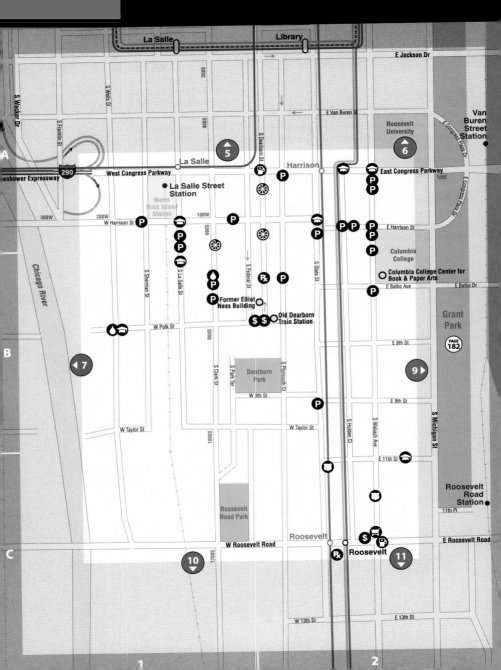

You can tell that this is one of Chicago's fastest growing neighborhoods southwest of Loop by the spruced up Roosevelt Rd El station, the growing presence of Columbia College and the development of single family homes. Parts of this area exude a small community charm, especially at Printer's Row on Dearborn St., around the old Dearborn Train Station. Industrial spaces turned into lofts house stock traders and creative types.

Banks

- **BankOne** · 47 W Polk St
- **Chicago Community Bank** · 47 W Polk St
- **TCF Bank** · 1224 S Wabash Ave

⬤Car Washes

- **Custom Car Wash** · 800 S Wells St
- **Custom Hand Car Wash** · 700 S Clark St

⬤Gas Stations

- **Amoco** · 50 W Congress Pkwy
- **BP** · 1201 S Wabash Ave

Landmarks

- **Columbia College Center for Book & Paper Arts** · 1104 S Wabash Ave, 2nd floor
- **Former Elliot Ness Building** · 618 S Dearborn St
- **Old Dearborn Train Station** · 47 W Polk St

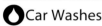Parking

- 50 E Harrison St
- 710 S Wabash Ave
- 640 S Wabash Ave
- 165 W Harrison St
- 633 S La Salle St
- 65 E Harrison St
- 511 S Plymouth Ct
- 705 S Clark St
- 75 W Harrison St
- 605 S Wabash Ave
- 524 S Wabash Ave
- 640 N La Salle St
- 740 S Clark St
- 919 S State St
- 711 S Plymouth Ct
- 610 S Wabash Ave
- 525 S Wabash Ave
- 609 S State St

Pharmacies

- **Osco Drug** · 1224 S Wabash St
- **Printers Row Pharmacy** · 719 S Dearborn St

⬤Pizza

- **Edwardo's Natural Pizza** · 521 S Dearborn St
- **Pat's Pizzeria** · 638 S Clark St
- **Trattoria Caterina** · 616 S Dearborn St

⬤Police

- **Chicago Police Dept** · 1121 S State St
- **Chicago Police Professional Standards** · 1130 S Wabash Ave

⬤Schools

- **Chicago Hope Academy** · 601 S La Salle St
- **Columbia College** · 33 E Congress Pkwy
- **Columbia College of Audio Tech** · 676 N La Salle St
- **Columbia College Theatre Music** · 72 E 11th St
- **Daystar Education Association** · 800 S Wells St
- **Jones Academic Magnetic College** · 600 S State St
- **MacCormac College** · 506 S Wabash Ave

⬤Supermarket

- **Jewel** · 1224 S Wabash Ave

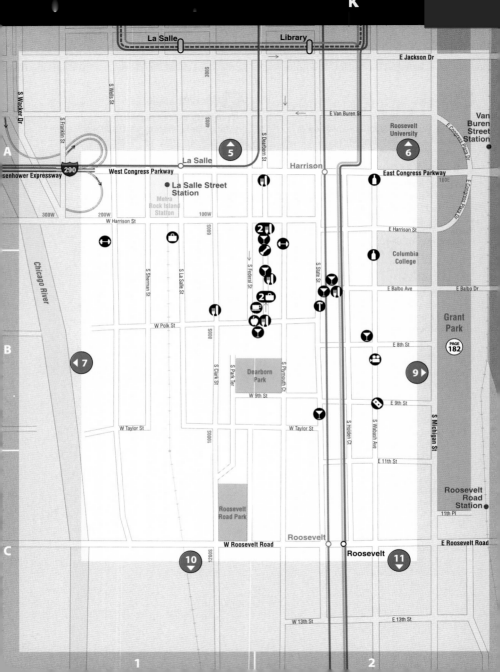

The eclectic bar scene makes the neighborhood lively after work. Casual watering holes include South Loop Club and cash-only Kasey's. Buddy Guy's Legends blasts great Blues and Buddy hangs out at his own place. Sandmeyers Book Store is stocked with good reads. Go to Kozy's Bike Shop for anything on two wheels, including purchases and repairs. Hothouse has avant-garde live performances nightly, which include poetry slams, jam sessions and drama.

Bars
- **Bar Louie** · 47 W Polk St
- **Buddy Guy's Legends** · 754 S Wabash Ave
- **Hothouse** · 31 E Balbo St
- **Kasey's** · 618 S Dearborn St
- **Kasey's Tavern** · 701 S Dearborn St
- **South Loop Club** · 701 S State St
- **Tantrum** · 1023 S State St

Coffee
- **Gourmand** · 728 S Dearborn St
- **Starbuck's** · 600 S Dearborn St

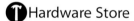Farmer's Market
- **Farmer's Market** · Polk St & Dearborn St

Gyms
- **Bally's** · 400 S Wells St
- **Chicago Training Club** · 641 S Plymouth Ct

Hardware Store
- **South Loop Ace Hardeware** · 725 S State St

Liquor Stores
- **George's Cocktail Lounge** · 646 S Wabash Ave
- **Warehouse Liquors** · 531 S Wabash Ave

Movie Theater
- **Cineplex Odeon** · 826 S Wabash Ave

Pet Shop
- **Animal House** · 630 S Dearborn St

Restaurants
- **Bar Louie** · 47 W Polk St
- **Blackies** · 755 S Clark St
- **Hackneys** · 733 S Dearborn St
- **Prairie** · 500 S Dearborn St
- **South Loop Club** · 1 E Balbo St
- **SRO** · 612 S Dearborn St
- **Trattoria Caterina** · 616 S Dearborn St

Shopping
- **Kozy's Bike Shop** · 600 S LaSalle St
- **Printers Row Fine and Rare Books** · 715 S Dearborn St
- **Sandmeyers Book Store** · 714 S Dearborn St

Video Rental
- **Movietime Home Video** · 900 S Wabash Ave

Map 9 · **South Loop / South Michigan Ave**

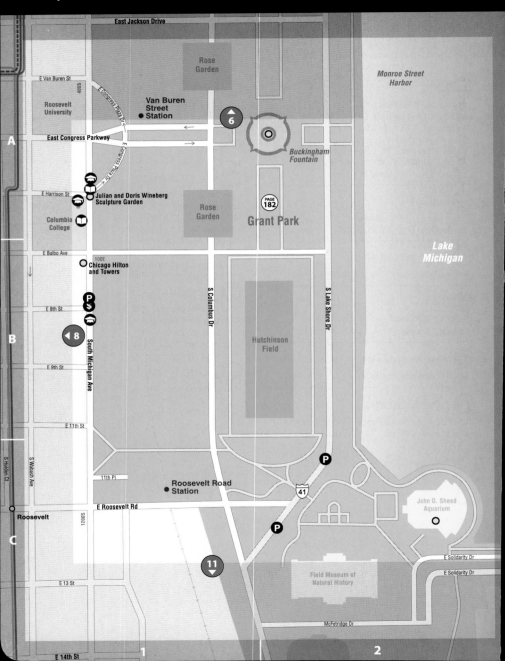

East Jackson Drive

Rose
Garden

Monroe Street
Harbor

E Van Buren St

Van Buren
Street
● Station

Roosevelt
University

6

A

East Congress Parkway

Buckingham
Fountain

E Harrison St

Julian and Doris Wineberg
Sculpture Garden

Rose
Garden

PAGE
182

Columbia
College

Grant Park

E Balbo Ave

100E
Chicago Hilton
and Towers

Lake
Michigan

P

E 8th St

$

8

South Michigan Ave

B

Hutchinson
Field

E 9th St

S Columbus Dr

S Lake Shore Dr

E 11th St

S Holden Ct

S Wabash Ave

P

11th Pl

Roosevelt Road
● Station

41

John G. Shedd
Aquarium

E Roosevelt Rd

Roosevelt

P

C

E Solidarity Dr

E Solidarity Dr

11

E 13 St

Field Museum of
Natural History

McFetridge Dr

E 14th St

1

2

Green could describe this part of the City, from the gardens of Grant Park to the ecologically sensitive Shedd Aquarium on the Museum Campus. Beginning at dusk, Buckingham Fountain's skyrocketing water display, accompanied by lights and music, occurs every hour on the hour for twenty minutes until 11 p.m. This routine occurs daily from April to October.

Bank

- **Albany Bank** · 800 S Michigan Ave

Landmarks

- **Buckingham Fountain** ·
  Columbus Dr & E Congress Pkwy
- **Chicago Hilton and Towers** · 720 S Michigan Ave
- **Julian and Doris Wineberg Sculpture Garden** ·
  681 S Michigan Ave
- **Shedd Aquarium** · 1200 S Lake Shore Dr

Libraries

- **Asher Library-Spertus Institute** ·
  618 S Michigan Ave
- **Library** · 600 S Michigan Ave

Parking

- 800 S Michigan Ave

Schools

- **Brandeis University** · 618 S Michigan Ave
- **Columbia College Chicago** · 600 S Michigan Ave
- **East-West University** · 816 S Michigan Ave
- **Roosevelt University** · 430 S Michigan Ave

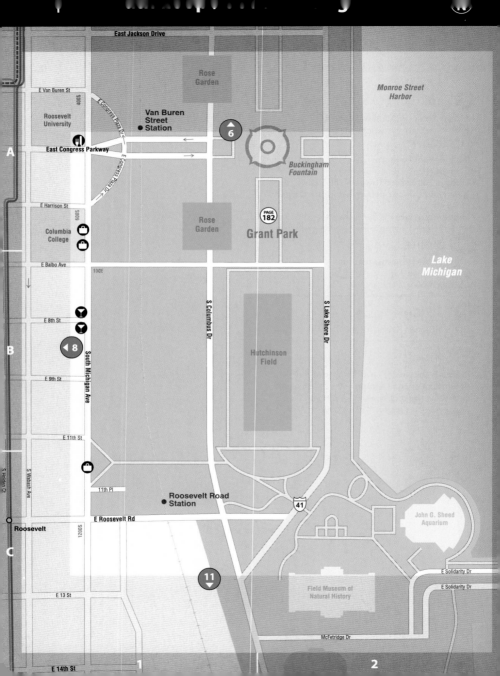

East Jackson Drive

Rose Garden

Monroe Street Harbor

E Van Buren St

Roosevelt University

400S

E CONGRESS PKWA DR

Van Buren Street
● Station

6

Buckingham Fountain

East Congress Parkway

E CONGRESS PLAZA PL

E

E Harrison St

600S

Columbia College

Rose Garden

PAGE 182

Grant Park

Lake Michigan

E Balbo Ave

100E

E 8th St

8

South Michigan Ave

S Columbus Dr

S Lake Shore Dr

Hutchinson Field

E 9th St

E 11th St

S Wabash Ave

11th Pl

Roosevelt Road
● Station

41

John G. Shedd Aquarium

S Holden Ct

1200S

E Roosevelt Rd

Roosevelt

E Solidarity Dr

C

E Solidarity Dr

11

Field Museum of Natural History

E 13 St

McFetridge Dr

E 14th St

1

2

A

B

The Chicago Hilton & Towers Hotel, the one at which the cops tossed Tom Hayden through a window during the 1968 Democratic Convention, anchors S. Michigan Ave.'s gentrification. After a few Killians at Kitty O'Shea's, sneak up to the spectacular 1927 Grand Ballroom for a twirl back in time. A flick at the Fine Arts Theater followed by a honking banana split is a fine way to spend a rainy day.

Map

Bars

- **Kitty O'Shea's** · 720 S Michigan Ave
- **Savoy Bar and Grill** · 800 S Michigan Ave

Restaurant

- **Artist's Cafe** · 412 S Michigan Ave

Shopping

- **Bariff Shop** · 618 S Michigan Ave
- **Clancy's Market** · 1130 S Michigan Ave
- **Rain Dogs Books & Cafe** · 408 S Michigan Ave

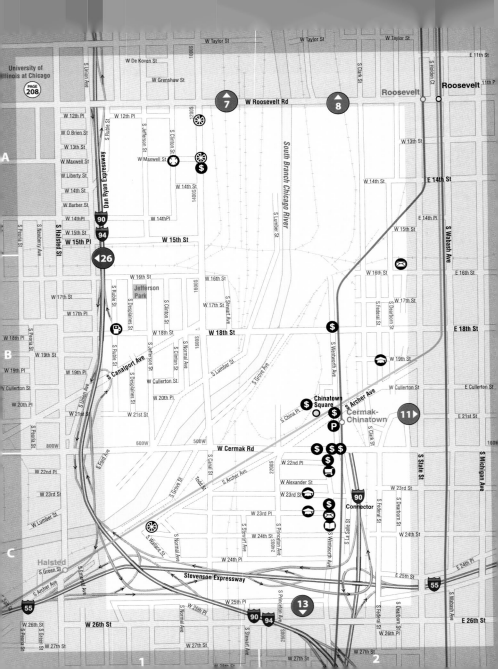

East Pilsen's bodegas mingle on the fringes of growing Chinatown's noodle shops. The intersection of Cermak and Archer around Wentworth Ave is the heart of Chinatown, one of the oldest and most influential communities in Chicago. Chinatown continues to grow and expand its borders as more immigrants move in. The Chinatown Branch Library doubles as a vibrant community center and epicenter of Chicago's Chinese culture.

Map

25	26	7	8	9	
			10		11
	12	13	14	

Banks

- **BankOne** · 1340 S Canal St
- **Charter One Bank** · 2131 S China Pl
- **International Bank Of Chicago** · 208 W Cermak Rd
- **Lakeside Bank** · 2115 S Wentworth Ave
- **MB Financial** · 200 W 18th St
- **New Asia Bank** · 222 W Cermak Rd
- **New Asia Bank** · 250 W Cermak Rd
- **South Central Bank** · 2335 S Wentworth Ave

Fire Department

- **Chicago Fire Dept-Paramedic** · 1338 S Clinton St

Gas Station

- **Irvin's Shell** · 1741 S Ruble St

Landmark

- **Chinatown Square** · S Archer Ave

Library

- **Chinatown Library** · 2353 S Wentworth Ave

Parking

- 2135 S Wentworth Ave

Pizza

- **Connie's Pizza Inc** · 2373 S Archer Ave
- **Dominick's Finer Foods** · 1340 S Canal St
- **Domino's** · 1234 S Canal St

Post Offices

- 2345 S Wentworth Ave
- 19 W 16th St

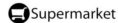Schools

- **John C Haines School** · 247 W 23rd Pl
- **South Loop Branch School** · 1915 S Federal St
- **St Therese School** · 247 W 23rd St

Supermarket

- **Tai Wah Grocery** · 2226 S Wentworth Ave

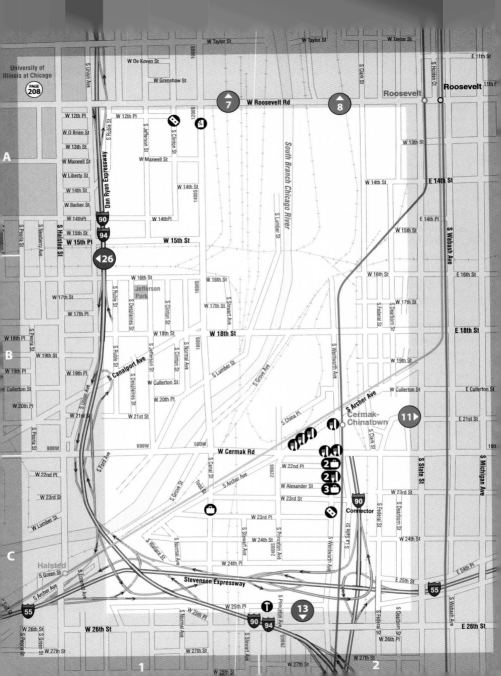

Skip Crate & Barrel and head to Chinatown for great cookware. Browse the shops along Wentworth Ave. for cooking utensils, Chinese furnishings and imported wares. Woks 'n' Things gets our vote for best cookery. Ten Ren Tea & Ginseng Co. wins for exotic teas and accoutrements. If you haven't done dim sum at the Happy Chef, you should. The Phoenix Café is where the locals go out to eat.

Copy Shop

- **Kinko's** · 1242 S Canal St

Hardware Store

- **Zweifel True Value Hardware** · 345 W 25th Pl

Restaurants

- **Emperor's Choice** · 2238 S Wentworth Ave
- **Hong Min** · 221 W Cermak Rd
- **Lao Sze Chuan** · 2172 S Archer Ave
- **Penang** · 2201 S Wentworth Ave
- **The Happy Chef Dim Sum House** · 2164 S Archer Ave
- **The Phoenix Cafe** · 2131 S Archer Ave
- **Three Happiness** · 2130 S Wentworth Ave
- **Won Kow** · 2237 S Wentworth Ave

Shopping

- **Chinatown Bazaar** · 2221 S Wentworth Ave
- **Chinatown Furniture** · 2326 S Canal St
- **Pacific Imports** · 2200 S Wentworth Ave
- **Sun Sun Tong** · 2260 S Wentworth Ave
- **Ten Ren Tea & Ginseng Co** · 2247 S Wentworth Ave
- **Woks 'n' Things** · 2234 S Wentworth Ave

Video Rental

- **88 Video & Gift Shop** · 2337 S Wentworth Ave
- **Video Update** · 1245 S Clinton St

Map 11 • South Loop / McCormick Place

The City's economic engine, McCormick Place, helps power the South Loop's steady gentrification. Construction has become a lifestyle here including the new Soldier Field, an abundance of new housing development and McCormick Place breaking ground in 2003 for yet another expansion. Museum Campus is the cultural anchor on the neighborhood's north end, while Burnham Park is its front yard.

 Bank
- **Lakeside Bank** · 2141 S Indiana Ave

 **Car Washes**
- **Strictly By Hand** · 2007 S Wabash Ave

 Gas Station
- **BP** · 1221 S Wabash Ave

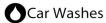 **Hospital**
- **Mercy Hospital & Medical Center** · 2525 S Michigan Ave

Landmarks
- **America's Courtyard** · 700 E Solidarity Dr
- **Clarke House** · 1827 S Indiana Ave
- **Hillary Rodham Clinton Women's Park and Gardens of Chicago** · Prairie Ave
- **Hyatt Regency McCormick Place** · 2233 South Martin Luther King Dr
- **McCormick Place** · 2301 South Lake Shore Dr
- **Merrill C Meigs Field Airport** · 1500 S Lake Shore Dr
- **Monument to the Great Northern Migration** · Martin Luther King Dr
- **National Vietnam Veterans Art Museum** · 1801 S Indiana Ave
- **Quinn Chapel, African Methodist Episcopal Church** · 2401 S Wabash Ave
- **Raymond Hilliard Homes** · 2030 South State St
- **Second Presbyterian Church** · 1936 S Michigan Ave
- **Soldier Field** · 425 E McFetridge Dr
- **The Chicago Daily Defender** · 2400 S Michigan Ave
- **The Wheeler Mansion** · 2020 S Calumet Ave
- **Willie Dixon's Blues Heaven Foundation** · 2120 S Michigan Ave
- **Women Made Gallery** · 1900 S Prairie Ave

 Parking
- 1356 S Michigan Ave
- 1220 S Michigan Ave
- 1400 S Michigan Ave
- Martin Luther King Dr
- 2300 S Prairie Ave
- 1241 S Michigan Ave
- 1330 S Michigan Ave
- 1245 S State St

 Police
- **Chicago Police Dept** · 1718 S State St

Post Office
- 2035 S State St

While the influx of businesses to service the pioneering residents is slow, the cultural scene is as diverse as the shows at McCormick Place. Take in the Prairie Avenue Historic District between 18th and E Cullerton Sts, where wealthy Chicagoans from the 1800s resided in swank, Victorian mansions. Go to the Firehouse for juicy steaks and fresh seafood. Famous 1940s juke joint, The Cotton Club, rocks with jazz and hip hop.

Bars

- **Bobby McGee's Sports Bar & Grill** ·
  1239 S State St
- **E-2** · 2347 S Michigan Ave
- **Strictly Business Cocktail Lounge** ·
  1355 S Michigan Ave
- **The Cotton Club** · 1710 South Michigan Ave

Coffee

- **Dunkin Donuts** · 1231 S Wabash Ave

Farmer's Market

- **South Loop Farmers Market** ·
  18th St & Wabash Ave

Gym

- **Phenomenal Fitness Inc** · 1468 S Michigan Ave

Restaurants

- **Chef Luciano** · 49 East Cermak Rd
- **Firehouse Resturant** · 1401 S Michigan Ave
- **Giocco** · 1312 S Wabash Ave
- **NetWorks (at Hyatt Regency McCormick Place)** ·
  2233 South Martin Luther King Dr
- **The Fine Print Restaurant** · McCormick Place,
  Grand Concourse, Level 2.5

Shopping

- **Blossoms of Hawaii** · 1631 S Michigan Ave
- **Blue Star Auto Stores** · 2001 S State St
- **Waterware** · 1829 S State St
- **Y'Ionn Salon** · 1802 S Wabash Ave

Map 12 • **Bridgeport (West)**

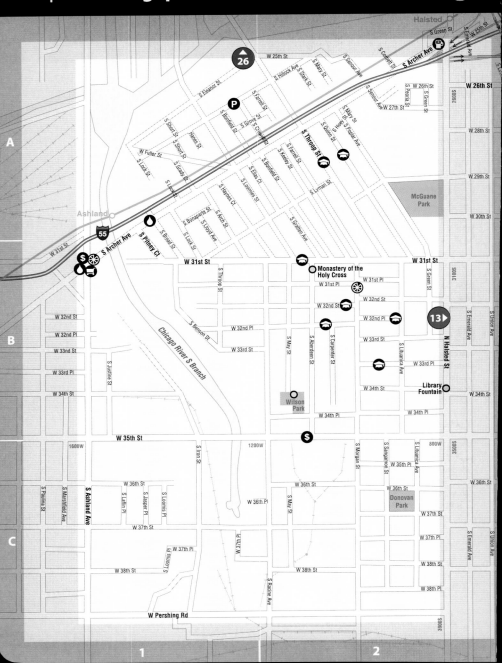

Old Style and Chicago fit cheek-to-jowl in Bridgeport. The Irish neighborhood's name is as working class in origin as the closely-knit residents. The neighborhood is home to the final port and bridge on the South Branch of the Chicago River, where boats unloaded cargo in the 1800s. Chinatown's and South Loop's building boom has initiated a Bridgeport revival. The City's largest new subdivision of single-family homes is being built east of the river and north of 35th St.

$ Banks
- **BankOne** · 3145 S Ashland Ave
- **Chicago Community Bank** · 1110 W 35th St

⬤ Car Washes
- **Windy City Car Wash & Detail** · 3117 S Archer Ave
- **Z Best Detailing Center** · 3033 S Archer Ave

ⓟ Gas Station
- **Citgo** · S Halsted St & S Archer Ave

Landmarks
- **Library Fountain** · W 34th St & Halsted St
- **Monastery of the Holy Cross** · 3111 S Aberdeen St
- **Wilson Park** · 3225 S Racine Ave

Ⓟ Parking
- · 2706 S Hillock Ave

⊛ Pizza
- **Dominick's Finer Foods** · 3145 S Ashland Ave
- **Lina's Pizza** · 3132 S Morgan St

⬤ Schools
- **Armour Elementary School** · 950 W 33rd Pl
- **Bridgeport Catholic Academy** · 1023 W 32nd St
- **Bridgeport Catholic Academy** · 1040 W 32nd Pl
- **Holden Elementary School** · 1104 W 31st St
- **Philip Armour School** · 911 W 32nd Pl
- **St Barbara Grammar School** · 2867 S Throop St
- **St Barbara High School** · 2800 S Quinn St

⬤ Supermarket
- **Dominick's** · 3145 S Ashland Ave

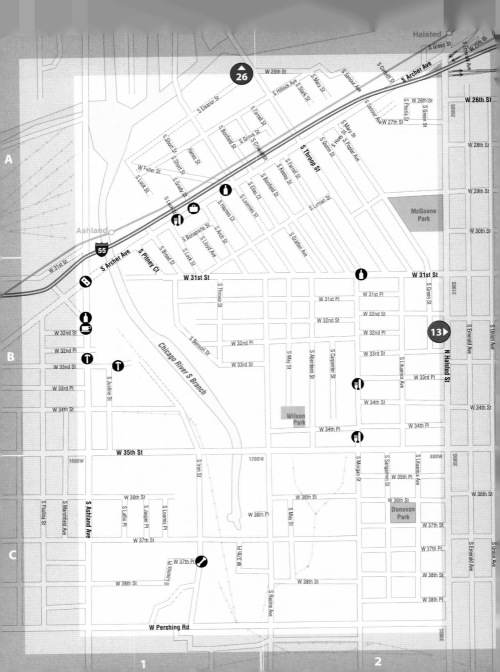

Hopefully Bridgeport's residential revival will eventually spur business and entertainment in the community. Right now, a big night out is watching a Sox game at a corner tavern or renting a video from Blockbuster.

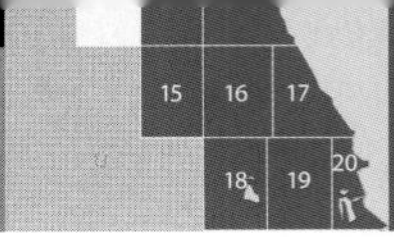

15 | 16 | 17
18 | 19 | 20

Map 1

Coffee
- **Dunkin Donuts** · 3170 S Ashland Ave

Hardware Stores
- **Ace Hardware** · 1514 W 33rd St
- **Ace Hardware** · 3240 S Ashland Ave

Liquor Stores
- **All Star Food & Liquors** · 2911 S Archer Ave
- **Ashland S Inc** · 3162 S Ashland Ave
- **J & Lee Co** · 960 W 31st St

Pet Shop
- **PDK Pet Supplies** · 1337 W 37th Pl

Restaurants
- **Johnny O's** · 3461 S Morgan St
- **Mexico Steak House** · 2983 S Archer Ave
- **Polo's Nut & Candy Cafe** · 3322 S Morgan St

Shopping
- **Bridgeport Antiques** · 2963 S Archer Ave

Video Rental
- **Blockbuster Video** · 3145 S Ashland Ave

S Green St
S Archer Ave
S 35th St
S Canal St
S Princeton Ave
S 24th St
55
S Wabash Ave
E 24th St

S Corbett St
W 26th St
S Peoria St S Green St
W 26th St
S Lowe Ave
S Normal Ave
26005
W 25th Pl
W 25th Pl
W 25th St
90 94
10
S Federal St
W 26th Pl
S Dearborn St
E 26th St

W 27th St
W 27th St
S Halsted St
W 27th St
S Stewart Ave
W 28th St
W 27th St
W 27th St
S State St
E 28th St

A
800W
500W
W 28th St
W 28th Pl
400W
W 28th Pl
Williams Park
E 29th St

McGuane Park
S Poplar Ave
W 29th St
S Shields Ave
S Princeton Ave
S Wells Ave
W 29th St
S Federal St
S 29th St
S State St

W 30th St
W 30th St
W 29th St
W 30th St
S Canal St
W 30th St
Old Neighborhood Italian American Club
W 30th St
S Wells St
W 30th St
S Federal St

W 31st St
Rx
S Green St
3100S
W 31st St
E 31st St
S Federal St
E 31st St

W 31st Pl
W 32nd St
S Lowe Ave
W 32nd St
14
E 32nd St

W 32nd Pl
W 33rd St
S Parnell Ave
S Federal St
Illinois Institute Of Tech
E 33rd

W 33rd St
12
B

S Lituanica Ave
W 33rd Pl
Armour Square Park
W 34th St
E 34th St

W 34th St
W 34th St
W 34th Pl
S Lowe Ave

800W
35th-Bronzeville-IIT
Illinois Ce Of Opto

W 35th St
3500S
35th-
Sox-35th
S Federal St
E 36

Richard J. Daley House
Comiskey Park
S Sangamon St
S Lituanica Ave
W 35th Pl
S Emerald Ave
S Union Ave
S Wallace St
S Normal Ave

W 36th St
W 36th St
E 36

Donovan Park
W 37th St
W 37th St
W 37th St
S Shields Ave
S Princeton Ave
90 94
Stateway Gardens Park
E Carv
E 37t

W 37th Pl
W 37th Pl
W 37th Pl
W De Saible St
S Wells St
C

W 38th St
W 38th St
W 38th St
Wentworth Gardens Park
W 38th St
S Dearborn St
E 38

W 38th Pl
W 38th Pl
W 38th Pl

W Pershing Rd
3900S
S Canal St
15
S Princeton Ave
S Wentworth Ave
S La Salle St
S Federal St

1
2
W 40th Pl
W 40th St

Bridgeport is the home turf of the Daley political dynasty and three other mayors. This part of Bridgeport is a gritty mix of urban styles and cultures: Irish, Italian, Chinese and African American. The Illinois Institute of Technology is in the throes of a multi-million-dollar rebuilding program to beautify its ugly campus, which will hopefully ignite more gentrification in these blocks that are presently filled with Chicago-style brick bungalows.

| 15 | 16 | 17 |
| 18 | 19 | 20 |

Map

$ Banks
- **Access Credit Union** • 600 W 26th St
- **Charter One Bank** • 600 W 37th St
- **Citibank** • 3430 S Halsted St
- **Marquette Bank** • 615 W 31st
- **South Central Bank** • 3032 S Halsted St

Car Wash
- **J & J Full Service Car Wash** • 349 W 31st St

Gas Stations
- **Accutech Inc** • 444 W 26th St
- **BP** • W 31st St & S Halsted St
- **Bridgeport Shell & Food Mart** • 215 W 31st St
- **Gas Express Inc** • 501 W 31st St
- **Marathon** • W 31st St & S Union Ave

Landmarks
- **McGuane Park** • W 29th St & S Halsted St
- **Richard J. Daley House** • 3536 S Lowe Ave
- **The Old Neighborhood Italian American Club** • 3031 S Shields Ave

Library
- **Daley Public Library** • 3400 S Halsted St

Pharmacy
- **Osco Drug** • 741 W 31st St

Pizza
- **Donnie's Pizza & Cafe** • 3258 S Wells St
- **Freddie's Pizza & Pasta Parlor** • 701 W 31st St
- **Little Caesar's Pizza** • 3010 S Halsted St
- **Nikko's Pizza** • 537 W 31st St
- **Paulie's Pizza & Italian Sandwiches** • 2600 S Wallace St
- **Phil's Pizza** • 3551 S Halsted St
- **Ricobene's Pizzeria** • 252 W 26th St

Police
- **Chicago Police Dept** • 3501 S Lowe Ave
- **Emergency Patrol-II Traffic** • 3501 S Normal Ave

Schools
- **Attucks Elementary School** • 3813 S Dearborn St
- **Bridgeport Catholic Academy** • 3700 S Lowe Ave
- **Bridgeport Catholic Academy** • 512 W 28th Pl
- **Bridgeport Child Development Center** • 3053 S Normal Ave
- **Daniel H Williams School** • 2710 S Dearborn St
- **Healy Elementary School** • 3010 S Parnell Ave
- **James Ward Elementary School** • 2701 S Shields Ave
- **M Sheridan Elementary School** • 533 W 27th St
- **Robert Abbott Elementary School** • 3630 S Wells St
- **Santa Lucia School** • 3017 S Wells St
- **St Jerome's Catholic School** • 2805 S Princeton Ave
- **Vandercook College Of Music** • 3140 S Federal St

Supermarkets
- **Chinese Fresh Food Market** • W 30th St & S Halsted St
- **Jewel** • 3033 S Halsted St
- **Russo's Deli** • 3160 S Wells St

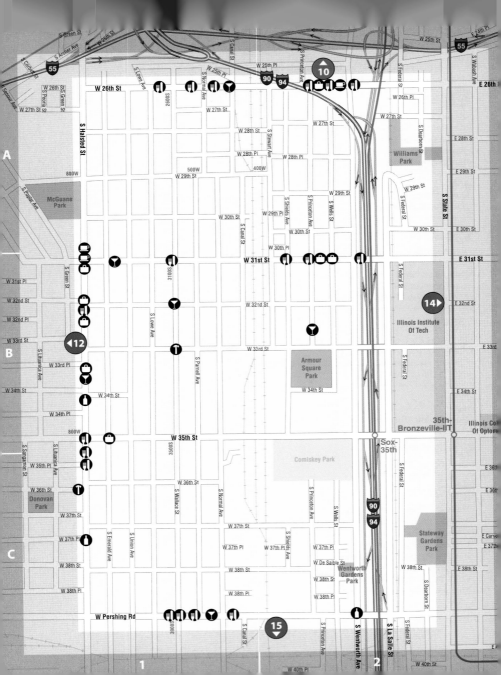

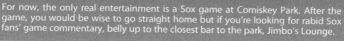

Map 13

For now, the only real entertainment is a Sox game at Comiskey Park. After the game, you would be wise to go straight home but if you're looking for rabid Sox fans' game commentary, belly up to the closest bar to the park, Jimbo's Lounge.

Bars

- **Black Orchid Sports Bar** · 718 W 31st St
- **Boston Tavern** · 451 W 26th St
- **Cobblestone's Bar and Grill** · 514 Pershing Rd
- **Jimbo's Lounge** · 3258 S Princeton Ave
- **Puffer's Bar** · 3356 S Halsted St
- **Redwood Lounge** · S Wallace St & W 32nd St

Coffee

- **Dunkin Donuts** · 3100 S Halsted St
- **Wired 4 Sound Cafe** · 244 W 26th St

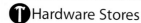Hardware Stores

- **Bridgeport Home Center** · 824 W 36th St
- **Joe Harris Paint & Hardware** · 3301 S Wallace St

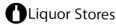Liquor Stores

- **Brennan's Liquor Store** · 3738 S Halsted St
- **Bridgeport Liquors** · 3411 S Halsted St
- **Express Food & Liquor** · 3904 S Wentworth Ave

Restaurants

- **August Moon Restaurant** · 225 W 26th St
- **Bridgeport Restaurant** · 3500 S Halsted St
- **Cugino's, The Original Cheesie Beef** · 300 W 26th St
- **Dox Grill** · 600 W Pershing Rd
- **Ferro's Homemade Italian Lemonade** · 200 W 31 St
- **Franco's Ristorante** · 300 W 31st St
- **Graziano's Ristorante** · 605 W 31st St
- **Healthy Food Lithuanian Restaurant** · 3236 S Halsted St
- **Kevin's Hamburger Heaven** · 554 W Pershing Rd
- **Offshore Steak House** · 480 W 26th St
- **Phil's Pizza** · 3551 S Halsted St
- **Ramova Grill** · 3518 S Halsted St
- **Red's Snack Shop** · 452 Pershing Rd
- **Scumaci's Italian Sandwiches** · 220 W 31 St
- **Sugar Shack** · 630 W 26th St
- **Wing Yip Chop Suey** · 537 W 26th St

Shopping

- **Accutek Printing & Graphics** · 260 W 26th St
- **Ace Bakery** · 3200 S Halsted St
- **Augustine's Spiritual Goods** · 3114 S Halsted St
- **Bridgeport News Travel & Tours** · 3252 S Halsted St
- **Chicago Technical Center** · 3500 S Emerald Ave
- **Health King Enterprises Chinese Medicinals** · 238 W 31st St
- **Let's Boogie Records & Tapes** · 3321 S Halsted St
- **Modern Bookstore** · 3118 S Halsted St
- **Petals From Heaven Flowers** · 244 W 31st St

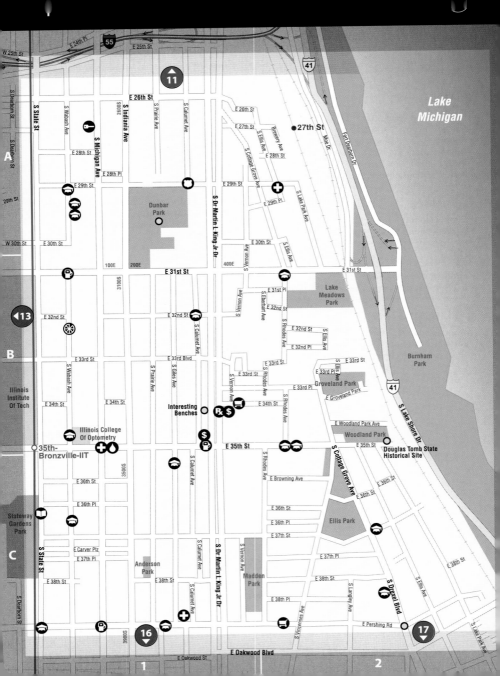

Prairie Shores and Lake Meadows compose a residential high-rise neighborhood along the lakefront. The former Chicago Bee newspaper building, a restored 1929 Art Deco gem, is now the community's public library that houses an impressive African American history collection. Although undergoing a resurgence, the neighborhood is still quite rough around the western edge on S State St. where the Robert Taylor Homes, a crime-riddled public housing complex, is located.

 ## Banks
- **BankOne** · 3500 S King Blvd
- **Shore Bank** · 3401 S King Dr

 ## Car Rental
- **Enterprise Car Rental/Rogers Auto Group** · 2700 S Michigan Ave

 ## Car Wash
- **Starvin' Marvin Hand Car Wash** · 114 E 35th St

 ## Gas Stations
- **31st Amoco** · 3101 S Wabash Ave
- **A & Y Amoco** · 94 E Pershing Rd
- **Burrell's Standard** · 342 E 35th St

 ## Hospitals
- **Bronzeville's Medical Center** · 300 E Pershing Rd
- **Chen's Medical Center** · 100 E 35th St
- **Michael Reese Hospital & Med Center** · 2929 S Ellis Ave

Landmarks
- **Benches** · S King Dr, between E 33rd St & E 35th St
- **Douglas Tomb State Historical Site** · E 35th St & Lake Park Ave
- **Dunbar Park** · S Indiana Ave & E 31st St

 ## Library
- **Chicago Bee Library** · 3647 S State St

Pharmacy
- **Walgreens** · 3405 S King Dr

 ## Pizza
- **Luigi's Pizza** · 3200 S Wabash Ave

 ## Police
- **Chicago Police Dept** · 300 E 29th St

Schools
- **Ada S McKinley Alternative School** · 2925 S Wabash Ave
- **Benjamin W Raymond Elementary** · 3663 S Wabash Ave
- **Chicago Military Academy** · 3533 S Giles Ave
- **Dawson Technical Institute** · 3901 S State St
- **De La Salle High School** · 3455 S Wabash Ave
- **Doolittle East Interm School** · 535 E 35th St
- **Douglas Community Academy** · 3200 S Calumet Ave
- **Einstein Elementary School** · 3830 S Cottage Grove Ave
- **George T Donoghue School** · 707 E 37th St
- **Henry Booth House Head Start** · 2929 S Wabash Ave
- **Holy Angels** · 545 E Oakbrook Ave
- **James R Doolittle Primary School** · 521 E 35th St
- **Pershing Elementary School** · 3113 S Rhodes Ave
- **Phillips Academy High School** · 244 E Pershing Rd
- **St James School** · 2920 S Wabash Ave

 ## Supermarkets
- **Jewel** · 443 E 34th St
- **Sunrise Supermarket** · 549 E Pershing Rd

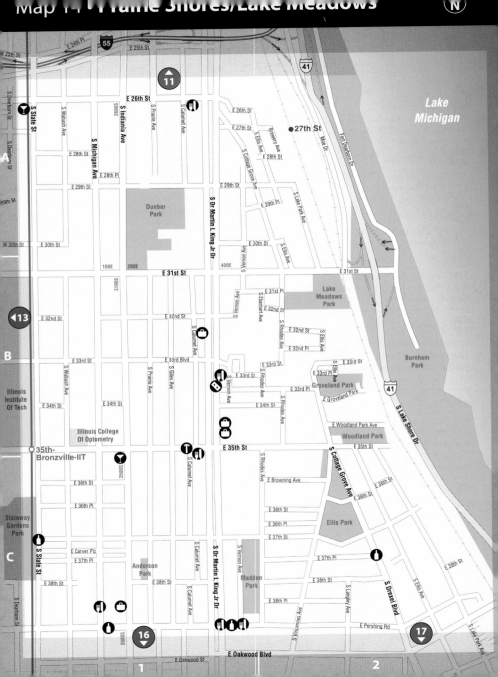

Map 14 Prairie Shores/Lake Meadows

N

Lake
Michigan

11

E 24th Pl
E 24th St
E 25th St
55
E 25th St

41

S Dearborn St
W 25th St

S State St
S Wabash Ave
S Dearborn St
S Michigan Ave
S Indiana Ave
S Prairie Ave
S Calumet Ave

E 26th St
E 26th St
E 27th St
27th St
Brewery Ave
Moe Dr

A
S Dearborn St
E 28th St
E 28th St
S Ellis Ave
S Cottage Grove Ave

E 28th Pl
S Lake Park Ave
E 29th St
E 29th St
E 29th St
Fort Dearborn Dr

Dunbar
Park
E 30th St
E 30th St
E 30th St
S Vernon Ave
S Ellis Ave

W 30th St
100E
200E
400E
S Dr Martin L King Jr Dr

E 31st St
E 31st St
Lake
Meadows
Park

13
E 32nd St
E 31st Pl
S Vernon Ave
S Eberhart Ave
S Rhodes Ave
E 32nd St
S Ellis Ave

3100S
E 32nd St
E 32nd St
E 32nd St
Burnham
Park

B
E 33rd Blvd
E 33rd St
E 33rd St
E 33rd St
S Ellis Ave
E 33rd St
S Lake Shore Dr

Illinois
Institute
Of Tech
S Wabash Ave
S Prairie Ave
S Giles Ave
E 34th St
Vernon Ave
E 33rd St
S Rhodes Ave
Groveland Park
E 33rd St
E Groveland Park
41

E 34th St
E 34th St
S Rhodes Ave
E Woodland Park Ave
S Cottage Grove Ave

Illinois College
Of Optometry
E 35th St
Woodland Park

35th-
Bronzville-IIT
E 35th St
E 35th St
35th St

E 36th St
S Calumet Ave
E Browning Ave
S Rhodes Ave
E 36th St

5000S
E 36th Pl
E 36th St
S Ellis Ave

C
Stateway
Gardens
Park
S State St
E Carver Plz
E 37th Pl
E 37th St
E 36th Pl
Ellis Park
E 37th Pl

Anderson
Park
S Calumet Ave
S Calumet Ave
S Dr Martin L King Jr Dr
S Vernon Ave
E 38th St
Madden
Park
E 37th Pl
S Langley Ave
S Drexel Blvd
S Ellis Ave

5000S
E 38th St
E 38th St
S Vincennes Ave
E 38th Pl
E Pershing Rd

16
17
S Dearborn St
E Oakwood St
E Oakwood Blvd

1
2

There are plenty of parks and several architecturally significant sites worth a visit. The Douglas Tomb State Historic Site at E 35th commemorates Illinois Senator Stephen A. Douglas who faced off against Abe Lincoln in the 1858 debates. Historic Bronzeville starts around Douglas's Tomb. Restored mansions on S. 31st St. and further south date from the glitzy 1920s.

Bars
- **Darryl's Den** · 2600 S State St
- **Mr. T's Lounge** · 3528 S Indiana Ave

Hardware Store
- **Meyers Ace Hardware** · 315 E 35th St

Liquor Stores
- **Grove Food & Liquors** ·
  3751 S Cottage Grove Ave
- **Midwest Food & Liquors Inc** · 3701 S State St
- **Nevada & Dallas Liquor Inc** · 419 E Pershing Rd
- **Rothchild Liquor Marts** · 124 E Pershing Rd

Restaurants
- **Blue Sea Drive Inn** · 427 E Pershing Rd
- **Bronzville Market & Deli** · 339 E 26th St
- **Fisher Fish & Chicken** · 3901 S King Dr
- **Hong Kong Delight** · 327 E 35th St
- **Mississippi Rick's** · 3351 S King Dr
- **The Rib Joint** · 3851 S Michigan Ave

Shopping
- **Ashley Stewart** · 3455 S King Dr
- **Avenue** · 3427 S King Dr
- **Living Word Book Store** · 3512 S King Dr
- **SMW Flea Market** · 3852 S Indiana Ave

Video Rental
- **Blockbuster Video** · 3349 S King Dr

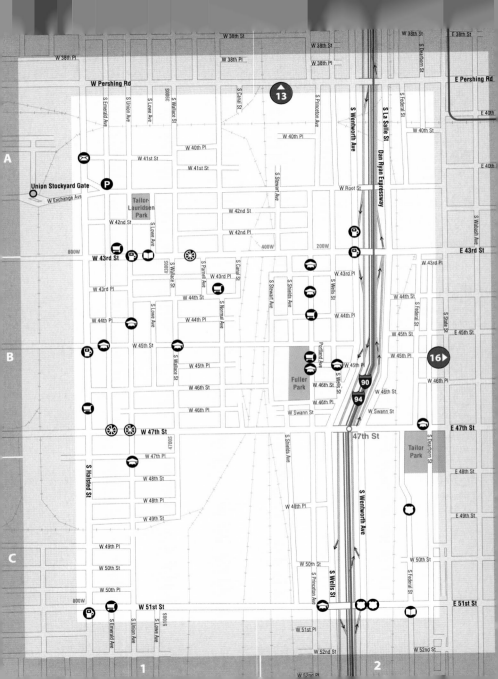

This is a rough neighborhood you should avoid unless jury duty demands you travel to the Cook County Criminal Court building on W 51st St. Public housing projects fraught with gang skirmishes dominate the streets. Here, the Union Stockyards that earned Chicago's reputation as "hog butcher to the world" once stood. All that's left is the limestone entrance gate to the stockyards. Pass on the sightseeing and keep heading south to upbeat Bronzeville.

Gas Stations

- **Citgo Gas** · 4300 S Wentworth Ave
- **James Amoco** · 4248 S Wentworth Ave
- **James Amoco** · 5101 S Halsted St
- **Stockyards Truck Stop** · 4512 S Halsted St
- **Tuxedo Junction** · 4300 S Union Ave

Landmark

- **Union Stockyard Gate** ·
  Exchange Ave & Peoria St

Libraries

- **Canaryville Library** · 642 W 43rd St
- **Chicago Robert Taylor Library** ·
  5120 S Federal St

Parking

- 4140 S Emerald Ave

Pizza

- **Italica** · 745 W 47th St
- **Paisans III** · 704 W 47th St
- **Tagliere's Restaurant** · 558 W 43rd St

Police

- **Chicago Police Dept** · 4947 S Federal St
- **Chicago Police Dept** · 5101 S Wentworth Ave
- **Cook County Criminal Court** · 155 W 51st St

Post Offices

- 4101 S Halsted St

Schools

- **Coleman Elementary School** ·
  4655 S Dearborn St
- **Garfield Alternative High School** · 220 W 45th Pl
- **Graham Elementary School** · 4436 S Union Ave
- **Graham Primary School** · 745 W 45th St
- **McKinley Fellowship Headstart** ·
  4543 S Princeton Ave
- **Milton Olive APC** · 5125 S Princeton Ave
- **Parkman Elementary School** · 245 W 51st St
- **St Gabriel's School** · 4500 S Wallace St
- **Thomas A Hendricks Community Academy** ·
  4316 S Princeton Ave
- **Tilden High School** · 4747 S Union Ave

Supermarkets

- **A&M Food Market** · 4425 S Princeton Ave
- **A&M Food Market** · 5122 S Princeton Ave
- **Canaryville Food Center** · 710 W 43rd St
- **Corner Store** · 501 W 44th St
- **Fairplay Finer Foods** · 4640 S Halsted St
- **Shamsan Food and Liquor** · 737 W 51st St

Map

15 16 17

18 19 20

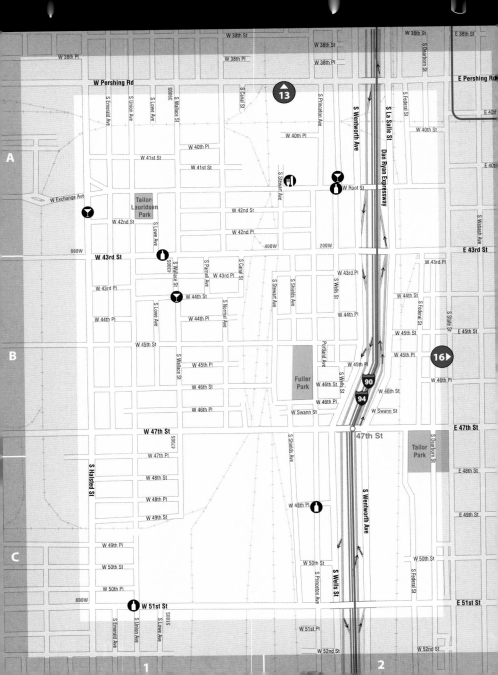

If Chicago ever hosts the Olympics, this will be the perfect neighborhood to host the shooting event.

Bars

- **Horn Palace** · 4189 S Halsted St
- **Kelley's Tavern** · 4403 S Wallace St
- **Root End Lounge** · 230 W Root St

Liquor Stores

- **Canaryville Liquors** · 619 W 43rd St
- **Lloyd's Food & Liquors** · 4845 S Princeton Ave
- **Root Inn** · 234 W Root St
- **Shamsan Food and Liquor** · 737 W 51st St

Restaurant

- **Chicago Ice Cream Cart Inc** · 356 W Root St

Map 16 · **Bronzeville**

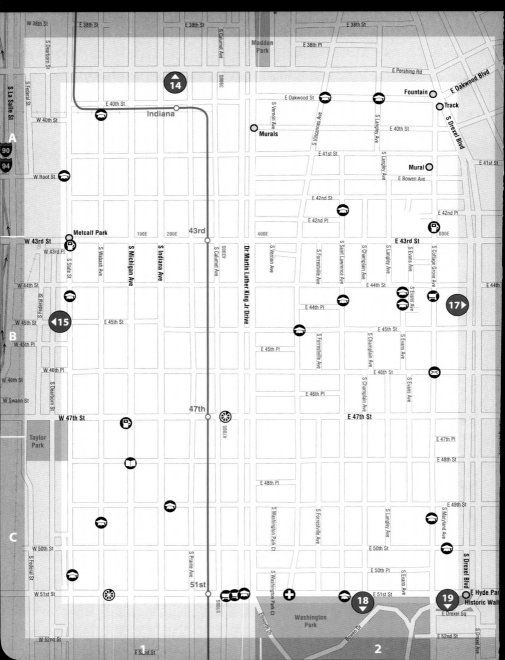

The once-thriving, African-American neighborhood of Bronzeville had the vibe of New York's Harlem and now it's coming back. Bronzeville is experiencing a resurgence, thanks to community efforts to preserve its architecturally significant buildings dating from the 1920s. Neighborhood notables recognized on the Bronzeville Walk of Fame include horn blower Louis Armstrong, crooner Nat King Cole, astronaut Mae Jemison, choreographer Katherine Dunham (a graduate of the University of Chicago) and architect Walter T. Bailey.

Gas Stations
- **Ken's Amoco** · 4300 S State St
- **Marathon** · E 47th St & S Michigan Ave
- **Stop & Go 24-Hr Towing** ·
  4257 S Cottage Grove Ave

Hospital
- **Provident Hospital** · 500 E 51st St

Landmarks
- **Fountain** · S Drexel Blvd & E Oakwood Blvd
- **Historic Walk** · S Drexel Blvd & E Hyde Park Blvd
- **Metcalf Park** · S State St & E 43rd St
- **Mural** · S Cottage Grove Ave & E 41st St
- **Murals** · S King Dr & E 40th St
- **Track** · S Cottage Grove Ave & E Oakwood Blvd

Library
- **Hall Public Library** · 4801 S Michigan Ave

Pizza
- **Famous Magic Crust Pizza** · 345 E 47th St
- **Wing King** · 51 E 51st St

Post Office
- · 4601 S Cottage Grove Ave

Schools
- **Beethoven Elementary School** · 25 W 47th St
- **Cains Barber College** · 365 E 51st St
- **Carter G Woodson School** · 4444 S Evans Ave
- **Center For Inner City Studies** ·
  700 E Oakwood Blvd
- **Colman Elementary School** · 4655 S Dearborn St
- **Diamond Academy** · 4501 S Vincennes Ave
- **Dyett Middle School** · 555 E 51st St
- **Forrestville Playground School** ·
  4419 S Saint Lawrence Ave
- **Fuller Elementary School** ·
  4214 S Saint Lawrence Ave
- **Hales Franciscan High School** ·
  4930 S Cottage Grove Ave
- **Hartigan Elementary School** · 8 W Root St
- **Helen J McCorkle Elementary** · 4421 S State St
- **Holy Angels School** · 545 E Oakwood Blvd
- **Jean Baptiste du Sable High** ·
  4934 S Wabash Ave
- **John Farren Elementary School** · 5055 S State St
- **Overton Elementary School** · 221 E 49th St
- **Reavis Elementary School** · 834 E 50th St
- **St Elizabeth's School** · 4052 S Wabash Ave
- **William Reavis Elementary School** ·
  834 E 50th St
- **Woodson North Elementary School** ·
  4414 S Evans Ave

Supermarkets
- **Red Apple Food** · 351 E 51st St
- **Royal Food Center** · 4425 S Cottage Grove Ave
- **Zaid Foods** · 343 E 51st St

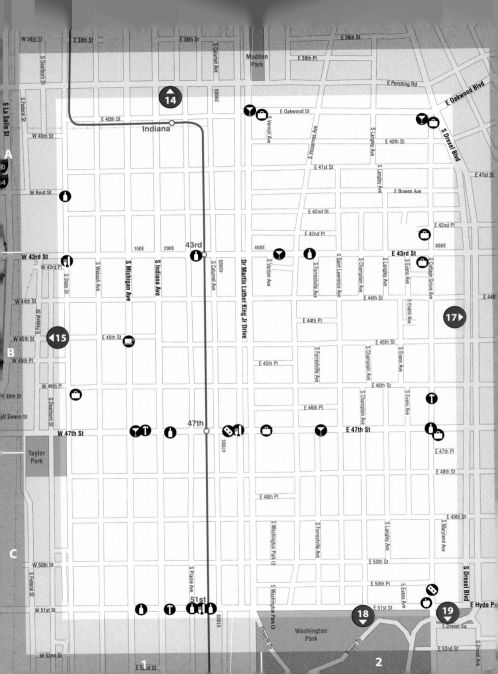

Harold's Chicken Shack on 47th and 51st dishes the best fried bird in town, for sure. The African Hair & Braiding Weaving Center is Bronzeville's best beauty shack. Blues kings Buddy Guy and Junior Wells perform live at the Checkerboard Lounge on 43rd.

Bars

- **Checkerboard Lounge** · 423 E 43rd St
- **Lake Shore Bar & Grill** · S Cottage Grove Ave & E Oakland St
- **New Bonanza Lounge** · 552 E 47th St
- **The New 113 Club** · 113 E 47th St

Coffee

- **Some Like It Black Coffee Club** · 4500 S Michigan Ave

Farmer's Market

- **Farmers Market** · Cottage Grove Ave & E 51st St

Hardware Stores

- **Brooks Hardware** · 110 E 47th St
- **Hyde Park Building Materials** · 4630 S Cottage Grove Ave
- **Tarson Mastercraft Hardware** · 221 E 51st St

Liquor Stores

- **300 Cut Rate Liquor Inc** · 300 E 51st St
- **47th Liquors Ltd** · 234 E 47th St
- **Calumet Food & Liquor Inc** · 315 E 43rd St
- **Joy Food & Liquors** · 526 E 43rd St
- **Lat's Food & Liquors** · 4121 S State St
- **Pappy's Liquors** · 4700 S Cottage Grove Ave
- **Petra Inc** · 128 E 51st St
- **Red Apple Food & Liquor Store** · 317 E 51st St

Restaurants

- **Crescent Subs** · 4307 S State St
- **Harold's Chicken Shack** · 307 E 51st St
- **Harold's Chicken Shack** · 364 E 47th St

Shopping

- **Alvin's Watch Repair** · 4317 S Cottage Grove Ave
- **Chicago Furniture Co** · 4238 S Cottage Grove Ave
- **Dollar Junction** · 4701 S Cottage Grove Ave
- **Issues Barber & Beauty Salon** · 3958 S Cottage Grove Ave
- **Moone's Goodie Shop** · 413 E Oakwood Blvd
- **Parker House Sausage Co.** · 4601 S State St
- **The African Hair & Braiding Weaving Center** · 428 E 47th St

Video Rental

- **Blockbuster Video** · 5052 S Cottage Grove Ave
- **Kat Video** · 360 E 47th St

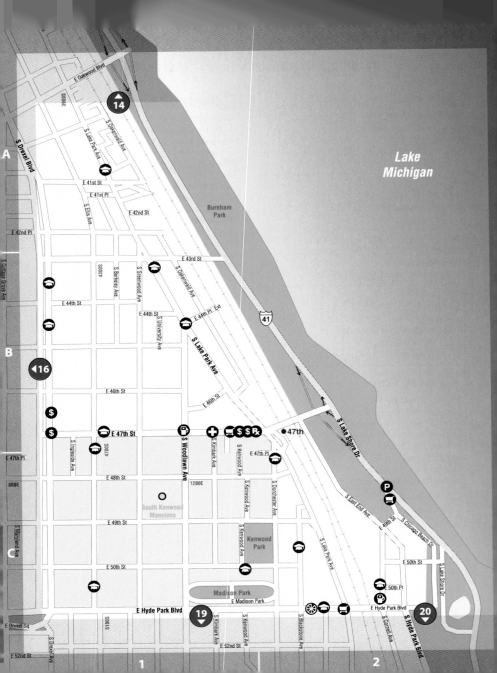

Largely residential, Kenwood is the address for astounding, renovated Victorian mansions. Muhammad Ali once lived in the grand dame at 4944 S Woodlawn Ave and an 1897 Frank Lloyd Wright house is at 5132 S. Woodlawn Ave. The graceful, tree-lined streets of South Kenwood are where the University of Chicago professors live, while students live on campus in neighboring Hyde Park just to the south.

Banks

- **Citibank** · 1320 E 47th St
- **Harris Trust & Savings Bank** · 901 E 47th St
- **Southshore Bank** · 4658 S Drexel Blvd
- **United Credit Union** · 1300 E 47th St 2nd Fl

Gas Stations

- **Cornell Amoco** · 5048 S Cornell Ave
- **Woodlawn Amoco** · 1158 E 47th St

Hospitals

- **University of Chicago Physicians Group** · 1301 E 47th St

Landmark

- **South Kenwood Mansions** · Between S Dorchester Ave, S Ellis Ave, S Hyde Park Blvd & E 47th St

Parking

- 4800 S Chicago Beach Dr

Pharmacy

- **Walgreens** · 1320 E 47th St

Pizza

- **Domino's** · 1453 E Hyde Park Blvd

Schools

- **Alcona Montessori School** · 4770 S Dorchester Ave
- **Ariel Community Academy** · 4434 S Lake Park Ave
- **Future Stomures High School** · 4071 S Lake Park Ave
- **Harvard School** · 4731 S Ellis Ave
- **Kenwood Academy** · 5015 S Blackstone Ave
- **Louis Wirth Experimental School** · 4959 S Blackstone Ave
- **Martin Luther King High School** · 4445 S Drexel Blvd
- **Price Elementary School** · 4351 S Drexel Ave
- **Roberts University Assoc** · 5045 S Ellis Ave
- **Robinson Elementary School** · 4225 S Lake Park Ave
- **Shoesmith Elementary School** · 1330 E 50th St
- **St Ambrose Catholic School** · 1014 E 47th St
- **University of Chicago Printing** · 5020 S Cornell Ave

Supermarkets

- **Co-op Market** · 1300 E 47th St
- **The Newport Mart** · 4800 S Chicago Beach Dr
- **Village Foods** · 1521 E Hyde Park Blvd

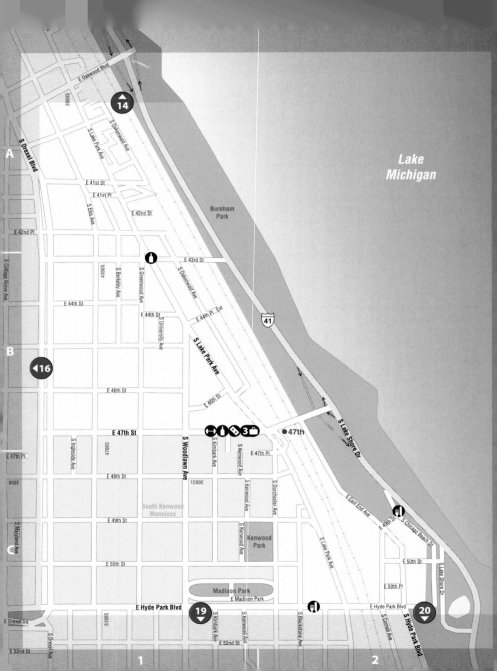

When there are students nearby, count on good, cheap eats. Kenny's on E Hyde Park Blvd is the go-to place for cheap, finger-lickin'-good ribs. Get your music at Coop's Records and movies at Top Dollar Video and DVD, both on E 47th St.

Gym

- **Bally's** · 1301 E 47th St

Liquor Stores

- **Co-op Market** · 1300 E 47th St
- **One Stop Food & Liquors** · 4301 S Lake Park Ave

Restaurants

- **Kenny's Ribs & Chicken** · 1461 E Hyde Park Blvd
- **Lake Shore Cafe** · 4900 S Lake Shore Dr

Shopping

- **Coop's Records** · 1350 E 47th St
- **Footlocker** · 1340 E 47th St
- **South Shore Decor** · 1328 E 47th St

Video Rental

- **Top Dollar Video and DVD** · 1300 E 47th St

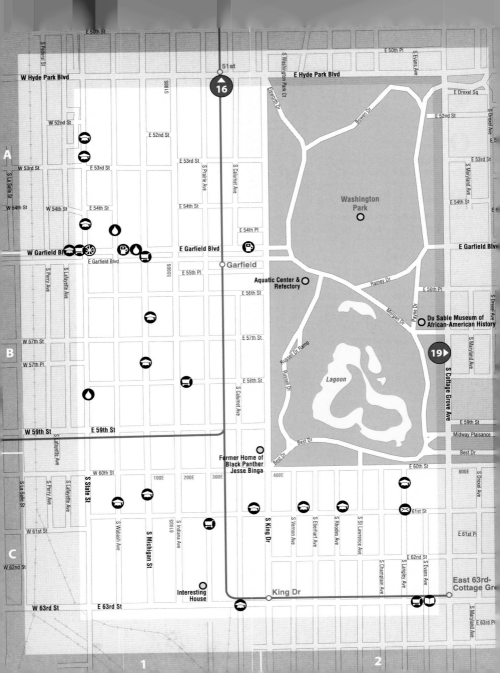

Designed in 1871 and one of the sites for the 1893 World Columbian Exposition, Washington Park dominates the neighborhood. Lorado Taft's depressing but impressive Fountain of Time stone sculpture portrays how life goes on while the clock tick-tocks. Within the 367-acre park's confines is the often overlooked DuSable Museum of African American History. The museum's collections preserve and interpret the African-American experience.

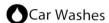Car Washes
- **Adam's Car Wash** · 48 E Garfield Blvd
- **Hand-Off Professional Car Wash** · 5812 S State St
- **Ricco's Car Wash** · 5437 S Wabash Ave

Gas Stations
- **2001** · 368 E Garfield Blvd
- **Adams Station** · 48 E Garfield Blvd

Landmarks
- **Du Sable Museum of African-American History** · 740 E 56th Pl
- **Former Home of Black Panther Jesse Binga** · 5922 S King Dr
- **Interesting House** · 6215 S Prairie Ave
- **Washington Park** · Between S King Blvd, S Cottage Grove Ave, E 60th St & E Hyde Park Blvd
- **Washington Park Aquatic Center & Refectory** · 5531 S Russell Dr

Library
- **Bessie Coleman Library** · 731 E 63rd St

Pizza
- **B & B Pizza King** · 4 W Garfield Blvd

Post Office
- 700 E 61st St

Schools
- **AO Sexton School** · 6020 S Langley Ave
- **Beasley Academic Center** · 5255 S State St
- **Betsy Ross School** · 6059 S Wabash Ave
- **Bright ID Daycare** · 454 E 61st St
- **Garfield Head State Center** · 30 W Garfield Blvd
- **John Farren Child Parent Center** · 5165 S State St
- **John Foster Dulles School** · 6311 S Calumet Ave
- **Little Angels Family II** · 550 E 61st St
- **Love Learning Center Daycare** · 362 E 61st St
- **Mary C Terrell School** · 5410 S State St
- **Saint Anselm School** · 6045 S Michigan Ave
- **The Bishop SS Morris Center Head Start** · 5627 S Michigan Ave
- **William W Carter School** · 5740 S Michigan Ave

Supermarkets
- **Bakery Thrift Shop** · 10 E Garfield Blvd
- **Brothers Food Market** · 723 E 63rd St
- **Frank's Meat Market** · 230 E 58th St
- **Johns Dairy Products** · 6115 S Prairie Ave
- **Twenty-One Grocery** · 5539 S Michigan Ave

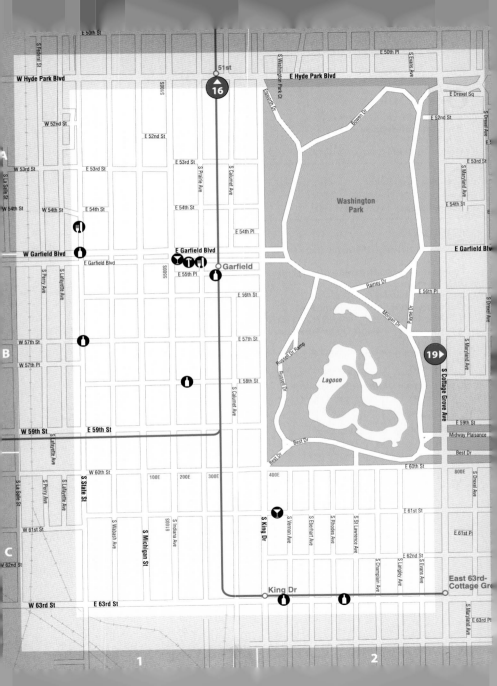

Washington Park exudes a relaxed attitude. Lots of great fried chicken joints can be found in this neighborhood, making it perfect for picnics. Look to the park for things to do. Its outdoor swimming pool, playing fields, fishing lagoons and peaceful nature areas keep residents outdoors and active. The food at Rose's BBQ on S. State St. satisfies a hearty appetite.

| 15 | 16 | 17 |
| 18 | 19 | 20 |

Map

Bars

· **Hanks Lounge** · 415 E 61st St
· **The Odyssey Cocktail Lounge** ·
  211 E Garfield Blvd

Hardware Store

· **Boulevard Ace Hardware** · 227 E Garfield Blvd

Liquor Stores

· **Garden State Liquors** · 5701 S State St
· **Jordan Food & Liquor** · 315 E 55th St
· **Midway Food & Liquor** · 5500 S State St
· **Rothschild Liquor Marts** · 425 E 63rd St
· **S & J Food & Liquors Inc** · 241 E 58th St
· **Steve's Liquors** · 558 E 63rd St

Restaurants

· **Ms. Lee's Good Food** · 203 E Garfield Blvd
· **Rose's BBQ Chicken** · 5426 S State St

The brainy University of Chicago breeds culture like its scientists rack up Nobel Prizes. With concerts in the soaring Rockefeller Memorial Chapel, archeological wonders at the free Oriental Institute, the professional Court Theatre, Frank Lloyd Wright-designed Robie House and the Smart Museum's moving contemporary artworks, U of C should be drawing more culturally-inclined Chicagoans south of the Stevenson Expressway.

💲Banks
- **Citibank** · 5812 S Ellis Ave
- **Cole Taylor Bank** · 824 E 63rd St
- **Hyde Park Bank** · 1525 E 53rd St
- **United Credit Union** · 1526 E 55th St
- **University National Bank** · 1354 E 55th St
- **University National Bank** · 5500 S Lake Park Ave

⭕Car Washes
- **Hyde Park Amoco** · 5130 S Lake Park Ave
- **Hyde Park Car Wash Inc** · 1330 E 53rd St

🅿Gas Stations
- **Amoco** · 6110 S Cottage Grove Ave
- **Hyde Park Community Shell** · 5200 S Lake Pk Ave
- **Hyde Park Mobil** · 1330 E 53rd St
- **Lang's Standard Service Station** · 6011 S Cottage Grove Ave

➕Hospitals
- **Bernard Mitchell Hospital** · 5815 S Maryland Ave
- **Duchossois Center for Advanced Medicine (DCAM)** · 5758 S Maryland Ave
- **University of Chicago Children's Hospital** · 5839 S Maryland Ave
- **University of Chicago Hospital** · 5841 S Maryland Ave
- **University of Chicago Hospital** · 901 E 58th St
- **University of Chicago Hospital** · 800 E 55th St

Landmarks
- **Frederick C Robie House** · 5757 S Woodlawn Ave
- **Midway Plaisance Park & Skating Rink** · S Ellis Ave & S University Ave-Between E 59th St & E 60th St
- **Rockefeller Memorial Chapel** · 1156 E 59th Ave

📖Library
- **Harper Memorial Library** · 1116 E 59th St

🅿Parking
- S Lake Park Ave between E 52nd St & E 53rd St
- 5840 S Maryland Ave
- 5525 S Ellis Ave
- S Maryland Ave between E 58th St & E 59th St

℞Pharmacies
- **Katsaros Pharmacy** · 1521 E 53rd St
- **Osco Drug** · 1420 E 53rd St
- **Walgreens** · 1554 E 55th St

🍕Pizza
- **Caffe Florian** · 1450 E 57th St
- **Edwardo's Natural Pizza** · 1321 E 57th St
- **Giordano's** · 5311 S Blackstone Ave
- **Medici on 57th** · 1327 E 57th St
- **Nicky's Chinese Food** · 5231 S Woodlawn Ave
- **Pizza Capri** · 1501 E 53rd St
- **Pizza Hut** · 1406 E 53rd St

✉Post Offices
- 1526 E 55th St
- 956 E 58th St

🎓Schools
- **Andrew Carnegie School** · 1414 E 61st Pl
- **Charles Kozminski School** · 936 E 54th St
- **Chicago Theological Seminary** · 1220 E 58th St
- **Chicago Theological Seminary** · 5757 S University Ave
- **Graduate School of Business** · 1101 E 58th St
- **Graduate School of Business** · 6030 S Ellis Ave
- **Graham School of General Studies** · 5835 S Kimbark Ave
- **Health Administration Studies** · 969 E 60th St
- **Hyde Park Day School** · 1375 E 60th St
- **John Crear Library** · 5730 S Ellis Ave
- **John Fiske School** · 6145 S Ingleside Ave
- **Laboratory Schools** · 1362 E 59th St
- **Latin American Studies Center** · 5848 S University Ave
- **Liberty School Bible Pathway** · 6207 S University Ave
- **McCormick Seminary** · 5555 S Woodlawn Ave
- **Phillip Murray School** · 5335 S Kenwood Ave
- **Pritzker School of Medicine** · 924 E 57th St
- **St Thomas Elementary School** · 5467 S Woodlawn Ave
- **University of Chicago** · 5801 S Ellis Ave
- **William H Ray School** · 5631 S Kimbark Ave

🛒Supermarkets
- **Bonne Sante Health Food** · 1512 E 53rd St
- **Co-op Market** · 1526 E 55th St
- **Co-op Market Express** · 1226 E 53rd St
- **Hyde Park Produce** · 1312 E 53rd St
- **Jimmy's Food Center** · 5131 S Cottage Grove Ave
- **Sunflower Seed Health Food** · 5210 S Harper Ave

Map 19 · **Hyde Park**

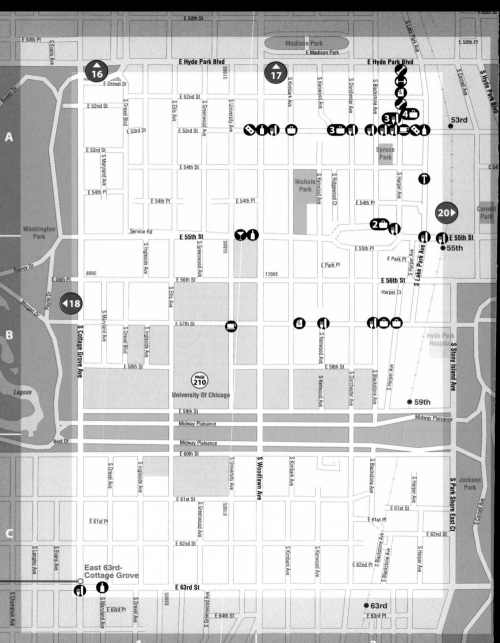

Synonymous with the University of Chicago, Hyde Park is full of things to discover. Odds are good that you could be standing in line for coffee next to a Nobel laureate at the C-Shop on S. University Ave. The leafy, limestone campus oozes old money and intellectual achievements. Powell's Bookstore on 57th is a favorite haunt for serious page-turners.

Bar
- **Woodlawn Tap** · 1172 E 55th St

Coffee
- **C-Shop** · 5706 S University Ave
- **Starbucks** · 1508 E 53rd St

Copy Shops
- **Copy Works Ltd** · 5210 S Harper Ave
- **Kinko's** · 1315 E 57th St

Gym
- **Women's Workout World** · 5201 S Harper Ave

Hardware Store
- **Anderson's Ace Hardware** · 5422 S Lake Park Ave

Liquor Stores
- **Chalet Wine & Cheese Shop** · 1531 E 53rd St
- **Fair Discount** · 801 E 63rd St
- **Kimbark Liquors & Wine Shop** · 1214 E 53rd St
- **Woodlawn Tap & Liquor Store** · 1172 E 55th St

Pet Shops
- **Hyde Park Pet Inc.** · 5201 S Harper Ave
- **Hyde Park Pet Spa** · 5226 S Harper Ave

Restaurants
- **Calypso** · 5211 S Harper Ave
- **Daley's Restaurant** · 805 E 63rd St
- **Dixie Kitchen and Bait Shop** · 5225 S Harper Ave
- **Jarunee Thai 55 Restaurant** · 1607 E 55th St
- **Kikuya Japanese Restaurant** · 1601 E 55th St
- **La Petite Folie** · 1504 E 55th St
- **Leona's** · 1228 E 53rd St
- **Maravilla's Mexican Restaurant** · 5211 S Harper Ave
- **Medici on 57th** · 1327 E 57th St
- **Mellow Yellow** · 1508 E 53rd St
- **Noodles Etc** · 1460 E 53rd St
- **Rajun Cajun** · 1459 E 53rd St
- **Ribs N Bibs** · 5300 S Dorchester Ave
- **Salonica Restaurant** · 1440 E 57th St

Shopping
- **Artisans 21** · 5225 S Harper Ave
- **Brush Strokes** · 1369 E 53rd St
- **Calla Lily Gift Shop** · 5225 S Harper Ave
- **Cohn & Stern For Men** · 1500 E 55th St
- **Dr. Wax Records and Tapes** · 5225 S Harper Ave
- **Freehling Pot & Pan Co** · 1365 E 53rd St
- **Futons N More** · 1370 E 53rd St
- **O'Gara and Wilson, Ltd** · 1448 E 57th St
- **Powell's Bookstore** · 1501 E 57th St
- **Tony's Sports** · 1308 E 53rd St
- **Wesley's Shoe Corral** · 1506 E 55th St
- **Wheels and Things** · 5210 S Harper Ave

Video Rental
- **Hollywood Video** · 1530 E 53rd St
- **Video Connection** · 1204 E 53rd St

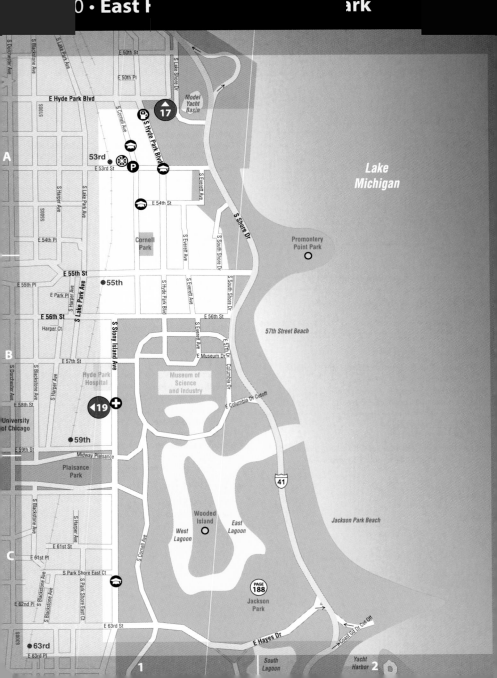

Lake
Michigan

E 50th St

E 50th Pl

E Hyde Park Blvd

S Dorchester Ave
S Blackstone Ave
S Lake Park Ave
S Cornell Ave
S Hyde Park Blvd
S Lake Shore Dr

Model
Yacht
Basin

17

53rd

E 53rd St

A

S 51S
S 52S

S Harper Ave
S Lake Park Ave

P

E 54th St

S Everett Ave
S Hyde Park Blvd
S Everett Ave
S South Shore Dr
S Shore Dr

Cornell
Park

E 54th Pl

E 55th St

E Park Pl

E 55th Pl

Promontery
Point Park

55th

S Lake Park Ave
S Harper Ave

E 56th St

Harper Ct

57th Street Beach

B

E 57th St

E 56th St

S Dorchester Ave
S Blackstone Ave
S Stony Island Ave

Hyde Park
Hospital

E Museum Dr

Museum of
Science
and Industry

E 57th Dr
E Columbia Dr

119 ✚

E 58th St

University
of Chicago

59th

E 59th St

E Columbia Dr Cutoff

Midway Plaisance

Plaisance
Park

S Blackstone Ave

41

Jackson Park Beach

C

E 61st Pl

E 61st St

S Blackstone Ave
S Harper Ave
S Park Shore East Ct

S Park Shore East Ct
S Park Shore East Ave

Wooded
Island

West
Lagoon

East
Lagoon

S Cornell Ave

E 62nd Pl

S 63S

PAGE 188
Jackson
Park

63rd

E 63rd St

E 63rd Pl

E Hayes Dr

South
Lagoon

Yacht
Harbor

Coast Gd Dr Dr Cut Off

1

2

This is a great neighborhood in which to relax. Recently, the Chicago Park District dumped money into upgrading the neighborhood's lakefront. The 57th St. and 63rd St. beaches are less crowded than those on the North Side. The Museum of Science and Industry deserves multiple visits but beware, brain freeze sets in fast from all the information the institute presents. Osaka Garden on Wood Island and Promontory Point Park are prime places to chill out.

Gas Station

- **Amoco** · 5048 E Hyde Park Blvd

Hospital

- **Doctors Hospital of Hyde Park** ·
  5800 S Stony Island Ave

Landmarks

- **Osaka Garden/Wooded Island** · Between the
  West Lagoon & East Lagoon
- **Promontory Point Park** · 5491 S Shore Dr

Parking

- 1608 E 53rd St

Pizza

- **Cholie's Pizza** · 1601 E 53rd St

Schools

- **Akiba-Schechter Jewish Day School** ·
  5235 S Cornell Ave
- **Catholic Theological Union** · 5401 S Cornell Ave
- **Hyde Park Art Center & School** ·
  5307 S Hyde Park Blvd
- **Hyde Park Career Academy** ·
  6220 S Stony Island Ave

E 50th St

E 50th Pl

S Lake Shore Dr

Model Yacht Basin

E Hyde Park Blvd

S Cornell Ave

S 51st St

17

A

53rd

E 53rd St

S Hyde Park Blvd

S Everett Ave

Lake Michigan

E 54th St

S Harper Ave

S Lake Park Ave

S 55th St

E 54th Pl

S Everett Ave

S Shore Dr

Cornell Park

Promontery Point Park

S Everett Ave

S South Shore Dr

E 55th St

S Hyde Park Blvd

55th

S Lake Park Ave

E Park Ave

S Harper Ave

S Everett Ave

S South Shore Dr

B

E 55th Pl

E 56th St

E 56th St

Harper Ct

S Stony Island Ave

57th Street Beach

E 57th St

Hyde Park Hospital

S Everett Ave

E Museum Dr

19

S Dorchester Ave

S Blackstone Ave

S Harper Ave

Museum of Science and Industry

E 57th Dr

E Columbia Dr

E 58th St

University of Chicago

E Columbia Dr Cutoff

59th

E 59th St

Midway Plaisance

Plaisance Park

41

C

S Cornell Ave

Wooded Island

West Lagoon

East Lagoon

Jackson Park Beach

E 61st Ave

S Dorchester Ave

S Blackstone Ave

S Harper Ave

E 61st Pl

S Park Shore East Ct

S Park Shore East Ct

E 62nd Pl

S Blackstone Ave

S Park Shore East Ct

S 63rd

PAGE 188

Jackson Park

63rd

E 63rd St

Coast Gd Dr Cut Off

E 63rd Pl

E Hayes Dr

1

South Lagoon

Yacht Harbor

2

Map 2

The bike path hugs the lake in these parts and riding early in the peaceful morning will leave you in a Zen-like state. Rely on Art's Cycle on E 55th for your wheels. For good and cheap Middle Eastern eats, try Cedars of Lebanon on 53rd St. Boaters sway to live, smooth jazz Friday nights and Sundays at Jackson Harbor Grill by the yacht club where lake views are amazing.

Bar

- **The Cove Cocktail Lounge** · 1750 E 55th St

Coffee

- **Cafe Sienna** · 1617 E 55th St
- **Future World** · 1744 E 55th St

Restaurants

- **Cedars of Lebanon** · 1618 E 53rd St
- **Jackson Harbor Grill** · 6401 S Coast Guard Dr
- **Morry's Deli** · 5500 S Cornell Ave
- **Orly's Cafe** · 1660 E 55th St
- **Piccolo Mondo** · 1642 E 56th St
- **Post Link** · 1634 E 53rd St
- **The Nile Restaurant** · 5500 S Hyde Park Blvd

Shopping

- **Art's Cycle Sales & Service** · 1646-48 E 55th St

Video Rental

- **Blockbuster Video** · 1644 E 53rd St

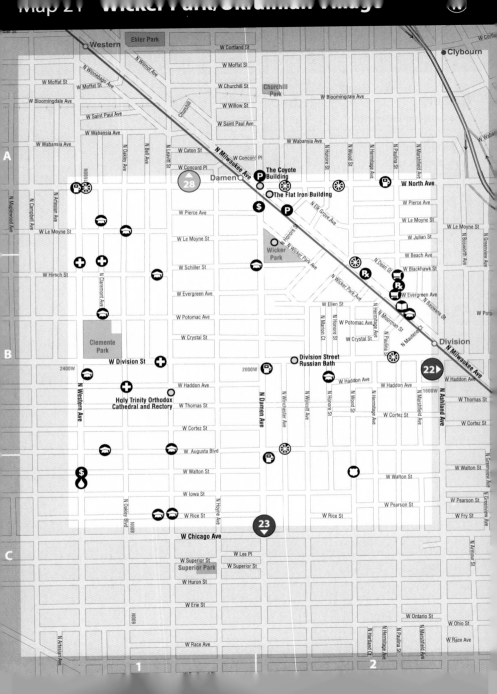

Historically an ethnic enclave first settled by Germans, then home to Polish immigrants and most recently Latinos, this neighborhood was tenuous until recently. Once again, the starving artists, pioneering barkeeps and restaurateurs paved the way for gentrification. Young hipsters are renovating the Victorians and brownstones. Built-up traffic at the three-way intersection at Milwaukee, North and Damen Aves is maddening.

Banks

- **First Security Federal Savings** ·
  936 N Western Ave
- **North Community Bank** · 1555 N Damen Ave

Car Wash

- **Elite Car Wash** · 823 N Western Ave

Gas Stations

- **Amoco** · 1600 N Western Ave
- **Clark Retail Enterprises** · 1949 W Augusta Blvd
- **Fire King Citgo** · 1720 W North Ave
- **Gomez Shell** · 1950 W Division St

Hospitals

- **Nazareth Family Center** · 1127 N Oakley Blvd
- **St Elizabeth's Hospital** · 1431 N Claremont Ave
- **St Elizabeth's Hospital Family** ·
  1431 N Western Ave
- **St Mary of Nazareth Hospital** ·
  2233 W Division St

Landmarks

- **Division Street Russian Bath** ·
  1916 W Division St
- **Holy Trinity Orthodox Cathedral and Rectory** ·
  1121 N Leavitt St
- **The Coyote Building** · 1600 N Milwaukee Ave
- **The Flat Iron Building** · 1579 N Milwaukee Ave
- **Wicker Park District** · Pierce & Hoyne St

Library

- **West Town Public Library** ·
  1271 N Milwaukee Ave

Parking

- 1532 N Milwaukee Ave
- 1605 N Damen Ave

Pharmacies

- **Osco Drug** · 1343 N Paulina St
- **Walgreens** · 1372 N Milwaukee Ave

Pizza

- **Big Tony's Pizza** · 1393 N Milwaukee Ave
- **Leona's** · 1936 W Augusta Blvd
- **Piece** · 1927 W North Ave
- **Pizza Hut** · 1601 N Western Ave
- **Pizza Metro** · 1707 W Division St
- **Zio Pino's Place** · 1814 W North Ave

Police

- **Chicago Police Dept** · 937 N Wood St

Schools

- **AN Pritzker School** · 2009 W Schiller St
- **Christopher Columbus School** · 1003 N Leavitt St
- **Clemente High School** · 1147 N Western Ave
- **De Diego** · 1313 N Claremont Ave
- **Hans Christian Andersen School** ·
  1148 N Honore St
- **Josephinum High School** · 1501 N Oakley Blvd
- **Richard Milburn High School** ·
  1279 N Milwaukee Ave
- **Sabin Magnet School** · 2216 W Hirsch St
- **Simpson Alternative School** · 1321 S Paulina St
- **St Aloysius School** · 1526 N Claremont Ave
- **St Helen's School** · 2347 W Augusta Blvd
- **St Nicholas School** · 2224 W Rice St

Supermarket

- **Jewel Osco** · 1341 N Paulina St

The vibe is constant. Dance club Red Dog howls all night long. The Double Door on Milwaukee is a rock'n'roll place of worship where the Stones performed. All the neighborhood's ornate Ukrainian Orthodox churches provide the perfect venue for atonement after a guaranteed raucous night out. On weekends, get to the Bongo Room for breakfast early and take a paper because you'll wait in line.

Bars

- **Bar Thirteen** · 1944 W Division St
- **Borderline** · 1958 W North Ave
- **Double Door** · 1572 N Milwaukee Ave
- **Empty Bottle** · 1035 N Western Ave
- **Estelle's Cafe & Lounge** · 2013 W North
- **Ezuli** · 1415 N Milwaukee Ave
- **Gold Star Bar** · 1755 W Division St
- **Holiday Club** · 1471 N Milwaukee Ave
- **Lava Lounge** · 859 N Damen Ave
- **Red Dog** · 1958 W North Ave
- **Sinibar** · 1540 N Milwaukee Ave
- **Subterranean Café** · 2011 W North Ave
- **The Note** · 1565 N Milwaukee Ave

☕Coffee

- **Alliance Bakery** · 1736 W Division St
- **Earwax Cafe** · 1564 N Milwaukee Ave
- **Gallery Cafe** · 1760 W North Ave
- **Jinx** · 1928 W Division St
- **Letizia's Natural Bakery** · 2144 W Division St
- **Off the Wall Wireless Cafe** · 1904 W North Ave
- **Sweet Thang** · 1921 W North Ave
- **The Grasshopper** · 937 N Damen Ave

🖨Copy Shops

- **Copy Max** · 1573 N Milwaukee Ave
- **Kinko's** · 1800 W North Ave

☘Farmer's Market

- **Wicker Park/Bucktown** ·
  Wicker Park Ave & Damen Ave

➕Gyms

- **Bikram Yoga College of India** ·
  1344 N Milwaukee Ave
- **Bucktown Fitness Club** · 2100 W North Ave
- **Chang's Martial Arts** · 1534 N Milwaukee Ave
- **Cheetah's Gym** · 1934 W North Ave
- **Global Yoga** · 1823 W North Ave

Liquor Stores

- **Double Door Nightclub** · 1572 N Milwaukee Ave
- **Ola's Liquor** · 947 N Damen Ave
- **Universal Food & Liquor** · 1803 W North Ave
- **Wicker Park Liquor Co** · 2006 W Division St

🐾Pet Shops

- **For Dog's Sake** · 2257 W North Ave
- **Wicker Pet** · 2029 W North Ave

🍴Restaurants

- **Blue Fin** · 1952 W North Ave
- **Bongo Room** · 1470 N Milwaukee Ave
- **Cafe Absinthe** · 1958 W North Ave
- **Cold Comfort Cafe & Deli** · 2211 W North Ave
- **D'Vine** · 1950 W North Ave
- **Feast** · 1616 N Damen Ave
- **Hi Ricky Noodle Shop** · 1825 W North Ave
- **Las Palmas** · 1835 W North Ave
- **Lulu's Hot Dogs** · 1000 S Leavitt St
- **Mas** · 1670 W Division St
- **Mirai Sushi** · 2020 W Division St
- **MOD** · 1520 N Damen Ave
- **Pacific Cafe** · 1619 N Damen Ave
- **Piece** · 1927 W North Ave
- **Pontiac Cafe** · 1531 N Damen Ave
- **Smoke Daddy** · 1804 W Division St
- **Soju** · 1745 W North Ave
- **Souk** · 1552 N Milwaukee Ave
- **Soul Kitchen** · 1576 N Milwaukee Ave
- **Spring** · 2039 W North Ave
- **Sultan's Market** · 2057 W North Ave
- **Thai Lagoon** · 2322 W North Ave
- **The Blue Penguin** · 1924 W Division St

🛍Shopping

- **Asian Essence** · 2025.5 W North Ave
- **Asrai Garden** · 1935 W North Ave
- **Brooke James, Ltd** · 1460 N Milwaukee Ave
- **City Soles/Niche** · 2001 W North Ave
- **Fly Boutique** · 1472 N Milwaukee Ave
- **Lille** · 1923 W North Ave
- **Noir** · 1746 W Division St
- **Paper Doll** · 1747 W Division St
- **Quimby's Bookstore** · 1854 W North Ave
- **Reckless Records** · 1532 N Milwaukee Ave
- **Sasabee** · 1849 W North Ave
- **The Silver Room** · 1410 N Milwaukee Ave

📀Video Rental

- **Coconuts Music & Video** · 1520 N Damen Ave
- **North Coast Video** · 2014-16 W Division St
- **Star Video** · 2334 W North Ave

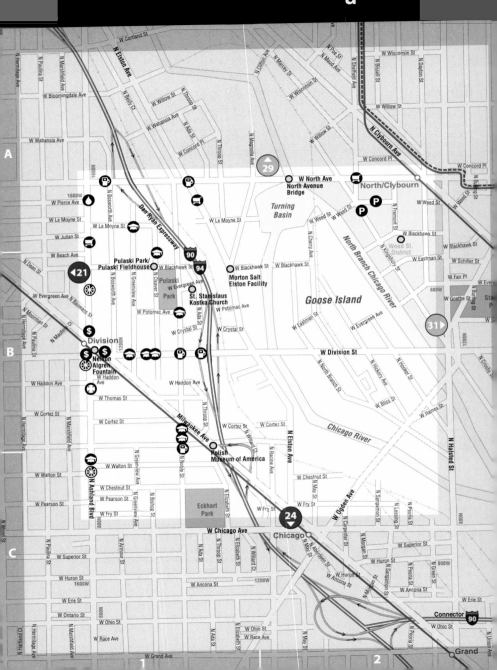

Gritty industry, healthy retail and alternative culture swirl together throughout this spicy neighborhood, which thrives on artistic ingenuity and Latin spirit. On Saturdays, it seems like the whole city drives here to fill up and go to Home Depot. Traffic on North Avenue Bridge is wretched.

Banks

- **Fifth Third Bank** · 1209 N Milwaukee Ave
- **Harris Bank** · 1242 N Ashland Blvd
- **Manufacturers Bank** · 1200 N Ashland Blvd

Car Wash

- **B & B Car Wash** · 1550 N Ashland Blvd

Fire Department

- **Engine Co 30** · 1125 N Ashland Blvd

Gas Stations

- **Augusta Noble Power King** ·
  1401 W Augusta Blvd
- **Division Amoco** · 1334 W Division St
- **Division-Noble Shell** · 1400 W Division St
- **North & Ashland Amoco** · 1551 W North Ave
- **North & Elston Amoco** · 1600 N Elston Ave

Landmarks

- **Morton Salt Elston Facility** ·
  Elston Ave & Blackhawk St
- **Nelson Algren Fountain** ·
  Division St & Ashland Blvd
- **North Avenue Bridge**
- **Polish Museum of America** ·
  984 N Milwaukee Ave
- **Pulaski Park/Pulaski Fieldhouse** ·
  Blackhawk St & Cleaver St
- **St Stanislaus Kostka Church** ·
  1351 W Evergreen Ave
- **Weed St District** ·
  Between Chicago River & Halsted St

Parking

- 1551 N Kingsbury St
- 955 W Weed St

Pizza

- **Adorno's Restaurant** · 925 N Ashland Ave
- **Little Caesar's Pizza** · 1360 N Ashland Ave
- **Pizza Hut** · 1601 W Division St

Post Offices

- 1635 W Division St

Schools

- **Elizabeth P Peabody School** ·
  1444 W Augusta Blvd
- **Holy Trinity High** · 1443 W Division St
- **Montessori School-Near North** ·
  1434 W Division St
- **Noble Street Charter School** · 1010 N Noble St
- **Rudy Lozano Elementary School** ·
  1424 N Cleaver St
- **Rudy Lozano Elementary School** ·
  1501 N Greenview Ave
- **St Stanislaus Kostka Grade** · 1255 N Noble St
- **The College of Office Technology** ·
  1520 W Division St
- **William H Wells Community High School** ·
  936 N Ashland Ave

Supermarkets

- **Guanajuato Grocery** · 1438 N Ashland Blvd
- **Stanley's Fresh Fruit & Vegetables** ·
  1558 N Elston Ave
- **Whole Foods Market** · 1000 W North Ave

Mainstream and alternative co-exist in this 'hood. Old Navy by day, leather by night and Restoration Hardware at home. Try the jerked shark at Watusi. The dance club Circus on Weed St. attracts celebrities David Schwimmer and Michael Jordan. Puppets taller than His Airness deliver messages to patrons. Caged babes gyrate at Crobar on Lunacy Night (Wednesdays). Exit is Chicago's renowned punk bar.

25	26	7	8	9
10	11
12	13	14

Bars

- **Biology Bar** · 1520 N Fremont St
- **Borderline Tap** · 958 W North Ave
- **Circus** · 901 W Weed St
- **Crazy Horse Too** · 1531 N Kingsbury St
- **Crobar** · 1543 N Kingsbury St
- **Exit** · 1315 W North Ave
- **Glow** · 1615 N Claybourn Ave
- **Joe's** · 940 W Weed St
- **Mudbug/Trackside** · 901 W Weed St
- **Slow Down, Life's Too Short** · 1177 N Elston Ave

Gyms

- **Lake Shore Academy Of Artistic Gymnastics** · 937 W Chestnut St
- **North Beach** · 1551 N Sheffield St

 Hardware Stores

- **Ace Hardware** · 1013 N Ashland Ave
- **Paragon Hardware & Mill Supply** · 1512 N Ashland Ave

Liquor Stores

- **Crater Food & Beer** · 1144 N Milwaukee Ave
- **D & D Liquors** · 1625 W North Ave
- **Rodriguez Grocery & Liquor** · 1415 N Ashland Blvd

Restaurants

- **Corosh** · 1072 N Milwaukee Ave
- **El Barco Mariscos Seafood** · 1035 N Ashland Blvd
- **Hilary's Urban Eatery** · 1500 W Division St
- **Hollywood Grill** · 1601 W North Ave
- **Luc Thang** · 1524 N Ashland Blvd
- **Watusi** · 1540 W North Ave

 Shopping

- **Balloonz Special Event Decor** · 1121 N Ashland Blvd
- **Casa Loca Furniture** · 1130 N Milwaukee Ave
- **Dusty Groove Records** · 1120 N Ashland Blvd
- **Eastern Mountain Sports (EMS)** · 1000 W North Ave
- **Home Depot** · 1232 W North Ave
- **Old Navy** · 1569 N Kingsbury St
- **Olga's Flower Shop** · 1041 N Ashland Blvd
- **Restoration Hardware** · 938 W North Ave
- **Right-on Futon** · 1184 N Milwaukee Ave

Video Rental

- **Blockbuster Video** · 1500 W North Ave
- **Hi-Fi Video** · 957 N Ashland Ave

Map 23

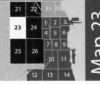
United Center draws the faithful to Bulls and Blackhawks games. Hip Ukrainian Village seeps down into West Town's north end making this area a mix of young professionals, working-class folk and students from nearby University of Illinois at Chicago. Along Grand and Western are the City's best hand car washes and detailing outfits.

Banks

- **First Security Federal Savings** ·
820 N Western Ave
- **Self Reliance Ukrainian Credit Union** ·
2332 W Chicago Ave

Car Washes

- **Boss Hand Car Wash** · 23 S Western Ave
- **G & L Car Wash & Detail** · 2215 W Grand Ave
- **Grand & Oakley Car Wash** · 2306 W Grand Ave
- **Quiroga's Detail & Hand Car** · 2036 W Grand Ave

Gas Stations

- **BP Amoco BP Connect** · 101 N Western Ave
- **Western Marathon** · 225 N Western Ave
- **Western & Warren Shell** · 45 N Western Ave

Landmarks

- **First Baptist Congregational Church** ·
60 N Ashland Ave
- **Metropolitan Missionary Baptist Church** ·
2151 W Washington Blvd
- **Ukrainian Cultural Center** · 2247 W Chicago Ave
- **Ukrainian National Museum** · 721 N Oakley Blvd
- **United Center** · 1901 W Madison St

Libraries

- **Mabel Manning Public Library** · 6 S Hoyne Ave
- **Midwest Public Library** · 2335 W Chicago Ave

Parking

- 36 N Paulina St
- 15 N Paulina St
- 2135 W Madison St

Pizza

- **Angie's Restaurant** · 1715 W Chicago Ave
- **Bacci Pizzeria Inc** · 2356 W Chicago Ave
- **Bella's Pizza & Restaurant** · 1952 W Chicago Ave
- **Naty's Pizza 2** · 1757 W Chicago Ave

Post Office

- 2419 W Monroe St

Schools

- **Crane Technical Prep Common School** ·
2245 W Jackson Blvd
- **Ellen Mitchell Branch School** · 2315 W Erie St
- **Ellen Mitchell School** · 2233 W Ohio St
- **Foundations School** · 2040 W Adams St
- **Henry Suder School** · 2022 W Washington Blvd
- **Malcolm X College** · 1900 W Van Buren St
- **Mancel Talcott School** · 1840 W Ohio St
- **Maryville Academy St Malachy** ·
2248 W Washington Blvd
- **R Nathaniel Dett Elem School** ·
2306 W Maypole Ave
- **Ukrainian Catholic University** ·
2247 W Chicago Ave
- **Victor Herbert Elementary School** ·
2131 W Monroe St
- **William H Brown School** · 54 N Hermitage Ave

Supermarkets

- **Edmar Foods** · 2019 W Chicago Ave
- **Ukrainian Village Grocery** · 2105 W Chicago Ave

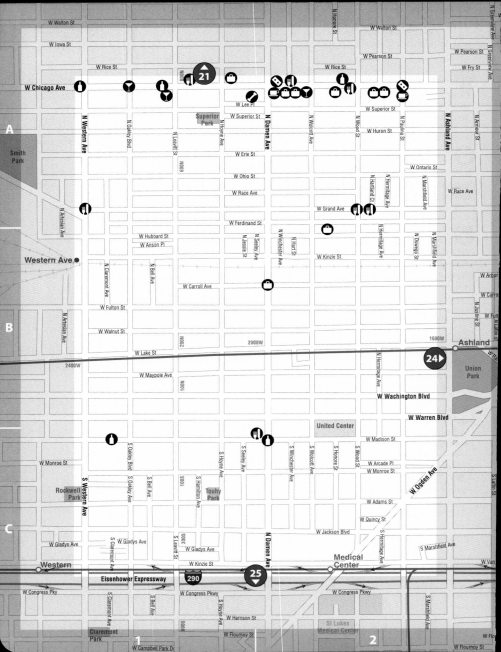

Map 23 • **West Town/Near West Side**

Map 23

The warehouse commercial district around Damen Ave and Kinzie St is a burgeoning shopping district. If you're in the market for gargoyles or vintage marble fireplace mantles, go to Salvage One on Hubbard. For Cuban cigars, head to Donofrio's on Chicago. Ethnic eateries reflect the area's mish-mash of influences. Tiny, tasty, artsy Munch serves solid breakfasts.

 Bars

- **Cleo's** · 1935 W Chicago Ave
- **Sak's Ukrainian Village Restaurant** · 2301 W Chicago Ave
- **Tuman's Tavern and Alcohol Abuse Center** · 2201 W Chicago Ave

 Coffee

- **Atomix** · 1957 W Chicago Ave
- **DeMar's** · 1701 W Chicago Ave

 Liquor Stores

- **Castlewood Wine & Liquor** · 2225 W Chicago Ave
- **DiCarlo's Armanetti Liquors** · 515 N Western Ave
- **J & L** · 1801 W Chicago Ave
- **Main Street Liquors** · 2000 W Madison St
- **Prestige Liquors Inc** · 2341 W Madison St
- **Trier's Liquors** · 2407 W Chicago Ave

Pet Shops

- **Liz's Bird Shop** · 2052 W Chicago Ave

Restaurants

- **China Dragon Restaurant** · 2008 W Madison St
- **Darkroom** · 2210 W Chicago Ave
- **Dionises Restaurant & Café** · 510 N Western Ave
- **Il Jack's Italian Restaurant** · 1754 W Grand Ave
- **Munch** · 1800 W Grand Ave
- **Old Lviv** · 2228 W Chicago Ave
- **Privata Café** · 1936 W Chicago Ave
- **Tecalitlan Restaurant** · 1814 W Chicago Ave

 Shopping

- **Alcala's** · 1733 W Chicago Ave
- **Decoro Studio** · 2000 W Carroll Ave
- **Donofrio's Double Corona Cigars** · 2058 W Chicago Ave
- **Edie's** · 1937 W Chicago Ave
- **H & R Sports** · 1741 W Chicago Ave
- **Salvage One Architectural Artifacts** · 1840 W Hubbard St
- **Through Maria's Eyes** · 1953 W Chicago Ave
- **Tomato Tattoo** · 1855 W Chicago Ave

Video Rental

- **Fredie's Video** · 1706 W Chicago Ave
- **Latin Video** · 1950 W Chicago Ave

Map 24 • **River West / West Town**

This neighborhood was once the heart of the City's produce and meat markets and a few food supplier warehouses still exist, mixing in with loft conversions. Randolph St is Chicago's hottest restaurant row and a growing gallery district. The high priestess of talk, Oprah Winfrey, reigns over West Town from her broadcasting palace, Harpo Studios on Washington. D'Amato's Bakery supplies eateries all over the city with its crusty loaves.

Banks

- **Banco Popular** · 1445 W Chicago Ave
- **First Bank West Town** · 745 N Milwaukee Ave

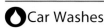 Car Washes

- **Berts Car Wash Inc** · 1231 W Grand Ave
- **Jackson & Morgan Shell** · 1001 W Jackson Blvd
- **Red Carpet Car Wash** · 915 W Washington Blvd
- **Ultimate Detail Inc** · 1352 W Lake St

 Fire Department

- **Engine Co 14** · 1129 W Chicago Ave

Gas Stations

- **Circle Campus Shell** · 1160 W Van Buren St
- **Gas-4-Less** · 649 N Ashland Ave
- **Grand & Aberdeen Service Inc** ·
  1100 W Grand Ave
- **Jackson & Morgan Shell** · 1001 W Jackson Blvd
- **Shell Food Mart** · 505 N Ashland Ave
- **Van Buren & Ashland Amoco** ·
  1600 W Van Buren St

Landmarks

- **Eckhart Park/Ida Crown Natatorium** ·
  Noble St & Chicago Ave
- **Goldblatt Bros Department Store** ·
  1613-35 W Chicago Ave
- **Harpo Studios** · 1058 W Washington Blvd

Library

- **Chicago Public Library, Eckhart Park Branch** ·
  1371 W Chicago Ave

Parking

- 1640 W Jackson Blvd
- 933 W Van Buren St

Pharmacy

- **Osco Drug** · 771 N Ogden Ave

Pizza

- **D'Amato's Bakery** · 1124 W Grand Ave
- **Davinci Gourmet Catering** · 1407 W Grand Ave
- **Di's Best** · 1521 W Grand Ave
- **Moretti's** · 1645 W Jackson Blvd
- **Penny's Pizza** · 234 S Ashland Ave
- **Salerno's Restaurant** · 1201 W Grand Ave
- **Via Bella Restaurant** · 1061 W Madison St

Police

- **Chicago Police Deptartment 12** ·
  100 S Racine Ave
- **Chicago Police Training Division** ·
  1300 W Jackson Blvd

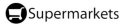 Schools

- **Chicago Academy for the Arts** ·
  1010 W Chicago Ave
- **Holy Innocents School** · 1448 W Superior St
- **James Otis School** · 525 N Armour St
- **Jesse Spaulding School** ·
  1628 W Washington Blvd
- **Mark Skinner School** · 111 S Throop St
- **Midwest Apostolic Bible College** ·
  14 S Ashland Ave
- **Philo Carpenter School** · 1250 W Erie St
- **Santa Maria Addolorata School** · 1337 W Ohio St
- **St Gregory Episcopal School** · 201 S Ashland Ave
- **Whitney Young High School** · 211 S Laflin St

Supermarkets

- **Bari Italian Grocery** · 1120 W Grand
- **Cyd & D'Pano** · 1325 W Randolph St

Map 24 • **River West / West Town**

Map 24

West Town has some great dining. We recommend breakfast at Wishbone, seafood at Crab Street Saloon and Marché for theatrical French. Matchbox is as trendy as the Jack's Tap bar is basic. Construction booms on plenty of corners, but services have been slow to follow. Residents badly need a Dominicks.

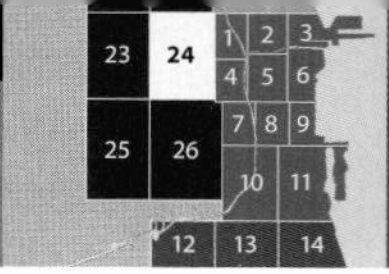

Bars

- **Bone Daddy** · 551 N Ogden Ave
- **Café Fresco** · 1202 W Grand Ave
- **Jaks Tap** · 901 W Jackson Blvd
- **Matchbox** · 770 N Milwaukee Ave
- **The Tasting Room** · 1415 W Randolph St

Coffee

- **Dulce Vida Cafe** · 1338 W Madison St
- **House of Coffee** · W Grand Ave & N Morgan St
- **Sip Coffee House** · 1223 W Grand Ave

Gyms

- **Cutting Edge Fitness** · Randolph St & Morgan St
- **Eye Catchers Physique** · 14 N Peoria St
- **Naturally Fit** · 310 S Racine Ave

Hardware Stores

- **Tru Value Hardware** · 1208 W Grand Ave

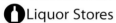Liquor Stores

- **Loop Tavern** · 1610 W Chicago Ave
- **Randolph Wine Cellars** ·
  Randolph St & Ogden Ave
- **Rothchild Liquor Marts** · 1532 W Chicago Ave

Movie Theater

- **Uffish Theater Co** · 312 N Laflin St

Pet Shops

- **Downtown Kennel & Supply Inc** · 25 N May St
- **Pet Groom Products** · 1217 W Washington Blvd
- **Petcare Plus** · Grand Ave and Racine Ave

Restaurants

- **160 Blue** · 160 N Loomis St
- **Breakfast Club** · 1381 W Hubbard St
- **Crab Street Saloon** · 1061 W Madison Ave
- **Flo** · 1434 W Chicago Ave
- **Hacienda Tecalitlan** · 820 N Ashland Blvd
- **Jerry's Sandwiches** · 1045 W Madison Ave
- **La Borsa** · 375 N Morgan St
- **Marche**· 833 W Randolph St
- **Moretti's** · 1645 W Jackson Blvd
- **Wishbone** · 1001 W Washington

Shopping

- **Arrow Vintage** · 1452 W Chicago Ave
- **Hollis Funk** · 949 W Fulton Market
- **Upgrade Cycle Works** · 1128-1130 W Chicago Ave

Video Rental

- **Grand Slam Video** · 1369 W Grand Ave

Health is at the heart of this neighborhood. Several hospitals and UIC's medical school are centered here, including publicly funded Cook County Hospital built in 1913. Doc-shock TV show ER was inspired by Cook's hectic emergency room treating some of Chicago's gang crime victims. If you get shot, this is where you want to go.

Banks

- **BankOne** · 2000 W Cermak Rd
- **Metropolitan Bank & Trust** · 2201 W Cermak Rd

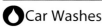 Car Washes

- **BP Touch Free Car Wash** · 1602 E Cermak Rd
- **G Express Hand Car Wash** · 2323 W 18th St
- **Roosevelt & Western Shell** · 2401 W Roosevelt Rd

Gas Stations

- **BP Connect** · 1602 W Cermak Rd
- **Cer Dam Amoco** · 1955 W Cermak Rd
- **Clark Oil and Refining** · 1721 S Paulina St
- **Roosevelt & Western Shell** · 2401 W Roosevelt Rd
- **Southwestern Citgo** · 2107 S Western Ave

Hospitals

- **Cook County Hospital** · 1835 W Harrison St
- **Johnston R Bowman Health Center** · 710 S Paulina St
- **Rush-Presbyterian St Luke's** · 1725 W Harrison St
- **University Of Illinois at Chicago Hospital** · 1740 W Taylor St
- **US Veterans Medical Center** · 820 S Damen Ave

Parking

- 1101 S Hamilton Ave

Pizza

- **Damenzo's Pizza** · 2324 W Taylor St
- **Pisa Pizza** · 2057 W Cermak Rd
- **Pizza Nova** · 1842 W 18th St

Schools

- **Children of Peace School** · 2187 W Bowler St
- **Cooper Branch School** · 1641 W 16th St
- **Cristo Rey High School** · 1852 W 22nd Pl
- **Holy Trinity School** · 1900 W Taylor St
- **Illinois College of Medicine** · 1853 W Polk St
- **Montefiore Boys School** · 1300 S Ashland Ave
- **Nancy Jefferson Schools** · 1100 S Hamilton Ave
- **Octavio Paz Charter School** · 2401 W Congress Pkwy
- **Orozco Community Academy** · 1940 W 18th St
- **Pickard Elementary School** · 2301 W 21st Pl
- **St Ann Grade School** · 2211 W 18th Pl
- **UIC University of Illinois** · 818 S Wolcott Ave
- **University of Illinois Health** · 901 S Wolcott Ave
- **Washington Irving Schools** · 749 S Oakley Blvd
- **William E Gladstone School** · 1231 S Damen Ave

Supermarkets

- **Aldi Supermarket** · 1703 W Cermak Rd
- **DelRay Farms** · 1701 W Cermak Rd
- **Supermercado Guzman** · 1758 W 18th St
- **Supermercados Guero** · 2101 W Cermak Rd

Map 25 · **Illinois Medical District**

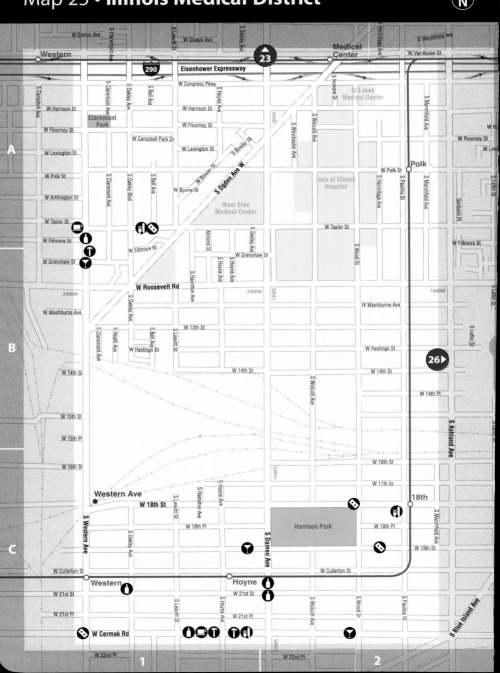

It's a Blockbuster night.

Bars
· **Cerwood Inn** · 1759 W Cermak Road
· **Simpson's** · Grenshaw St & Western Ave
· **White Horse Lounge·** · 2059 W 19th St

Coffee
· **Taylor Made Deli** · Western Ave & Taylor St
· **Wagner's Bakery** · 2148 W Cermak Rd

Hardware Stores
· **City Hardware** · 921 S Western Ave
· **Duran Hardware** · 2047 W Cermak Rd
· **Mitchell Hardware & Paints** · 2141 W Cermak Rd

Liquor Stores
· **El Valle Food & Liquors** · 2200 W 21st St
· **Helen's Grocery & Liquors** ·
  W 21st St & S Oakley Ave
· **Three Star Liquor** · 2015 S Damen Ave
· **Topless Liquor** · 916 S Western Ave
· **Yo Yo's Liquor** · 2155 W Cermak Rd·

Restaurants
· **Carnitas Uruapan Restaurant** · 1725 W 18th St
· **El Charco Verde** · 2253 W Taylor St
· **TJ's Family Restaurant** · 1928 E Cermak Rd

Video Rental
· **Blockbuster Video** · 2425 W Cermak Rd
· **Junior's Video** · 1810 W 18th St
· **Pedraza Video** · 1758 W 19th St
· **Taylor Video & VCR Repair** · 2234 W Taylor St

Map 28 • University Village/Little Italy/Pilsen

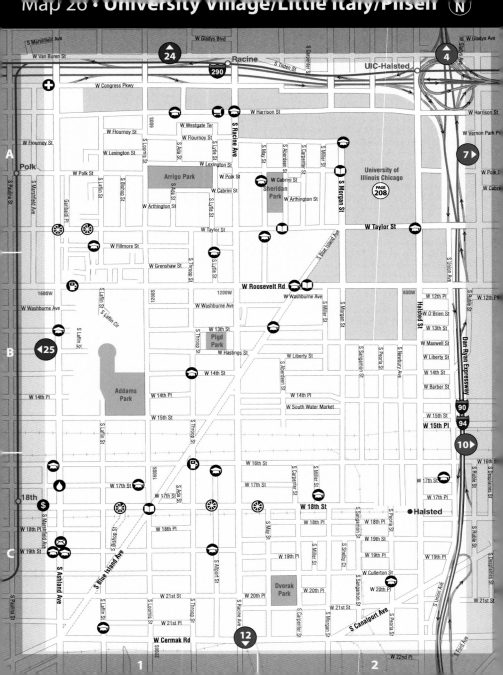

University of Illinois at Chicago is consuming blocks like the Great Chicago Fire of 1871 that started nearby. The campus expansion stretches south of Roosevelt Rd. What's left of Little Italy from the last UIC expansion centers around Taylor St. where Tuscan and Sicilian are spoken. Any pizza parlor is a good pick, but Pompeii's pies rule. The vibrant Latino Pilsen neighborhood starts here and spreads south.

Map

Bank
- **Mid-City National Bank** · 1618 W 18th St

Car Wash
- **Speed Hand Car Wash** · 1700 S Ashland Ave

Gas Stations
- **Louis Auto Service** · 1301 W 16th St
- **Shell** · 1549 W Roosevelt Rd

Hospital
- **Rush Presbyterian Hospital** · 1653 W Congress Pkwy

Libraries
- **Illinois Regional Library** · 1055 W Roosevelt Rd
- **Lozano Library** · 1805 S Loomis St
- **Roosevelt Branch Library** · 1101 W Taylor St
- **University Of Chicago Illinois** · 801 S Morgan St

Pizza
- **Alfred** · 1447 W 18th St
- **Benny's Pizza Inc II** · 1236 W 18th St
- **Caire's Pizza** · 1165 W 18th St
- **Pompei Bakery** · 1531 W Taylor St
- **Pompei Taylor St** · Taylor St & Ashland Ave

Post Office
- 1859 S Ashland Ave

Schools
- **Andrew Jackson Language Academy** · 1340 W Harrison St
- **Benito Juarez High School** · 2150 S Laflin St
- **El Centro De La Causa School** · 731 W 17th St
- **Galileo School** · 820 S Carpenter St
- **Holy Family School** · 1029 S May St
- **Jacob A Riis Elementary School** · 1018 S Lytle St
- **John A Walsh School** · 2031 S Peoria St
- **John M Smyth School** · 1059 W 13th St
- **Joseph Jungman School** · 1746 S Miller St
- **Joseph Medill Primary School** · 1301 W 14th St
- **Montefiore Boys School** · 1300 S Ashland Ave
- **Perez School** · 1241 W 19th St
- **Peter Cooper School** · 1624 W 19th St
- **Pilsen Academy** · 1420 W 17th St
- **Ruben Salazar Bilingual Branch** · 1641 W 16th St
- **Simpson Alternative School** · 1321 S Paulina St
- **St Ignatius College Prep** · 1076 W Roosevelt Rd
- **St Pius School** · 1919 S Ashland Ave
- **St Procopius School** · 1625 S Allport St
- **Thomas Jefferson School** · 1522 W Fillmore St
- **University Of Illinois** · 1200 W Harrison St
- **University Of Illinois Library** · 801 S Morgan St
- **University Of Illinois Library** · 805 W Taylor St

Supermarket
- **Jewel** · 1240 W Harrison St

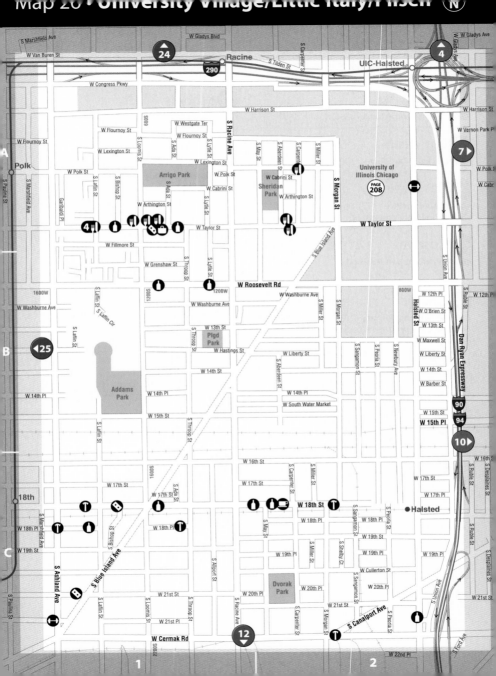

Map 20 ▸ **University Village/Little Italy/Pilsen** Ⓝ

Map 2

Try Taylor St. for authentic Italian. Sports fans chow down here before games at the United Center. Just like mama, Gennaro's dishes up generous portions. Where's the beef? At Al's. Buy Scafuri Bakery's cannoli by the dozen. The murals in Pilsen, especially at the 18th St. El station, are outstanding. Come here for authentic Mexican tacos as restaurants and bodegas line the streets.

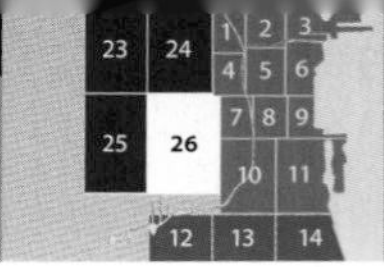

Coffee
- **Cafe Sol.net** · 1134 W 18th St

Gyms
- **University of Illinois Chicago** · 750 S Halsted St
- **YMCA** · 1608 W 21st Pl

Hardware Stores
- **A K Auto Supply Co** · 1535 W 18th St
- **Alvarez Hardware** · 1323 W 18th Pl
- **La Brocha Gorda** · 974 W 18th St
- **Seigle's Lumber** · 977 W Cermak Rd
- **Torres Hardware** · 1836 S Ashland Ave

Liquor Stores
- **5th City Food & Liquor** · 1257 W Roosevelt Rd
- **Amador Liquors** · 1167 W 18th St
- **Conte Di Savoia European Specialty** · 1438 W Taylor St
- **El Trebol Liquors** · 1135 W 18th St
- **F & R Liquor Inc** · 2129 S Halsted St
- **Guadalajara Food & Liquors Inc** · 1527 W 18th Pl
- **Harbee Liquor** · 1345 W 18th St
- **Mike & Sons Food & Liquor** · 1359 W Roosevelt Rd
- **Three Sons Food & Liquor Inc** · 1311 W Taylor St

Restaurants
- **Al's Number 1 Italian Beef** · 1079 W Taylor St
- **Café Viaggio** · 1435 W Taylor St
- **Carm's Beef and Snack Shop** · 1057 W Polk St
- **Chez Joel** · 1119 W Taylor St
- **Falbo's** · 1335 W Taylor St
- **Francesca's** · 1400 W Taylor St
- **Genarro's** · 1352 W Taylor St
- **New Rosebud Café** · 1500 W Taylor St
- **Siam Pot** · 1509 Taylor St
- **Taj Mahal** · 1512 Taylor St

Shopping
- **Scafuri Bakery** · 1337 W Taylor St

Video Rental
- **Central Video Mart** · 1354 W Taylor St
- **Manny's Video** · 1546 W 21st St
- **Manny's Video II** · 1943 S May St
- **Roly's Video** · 1448 W 18th St

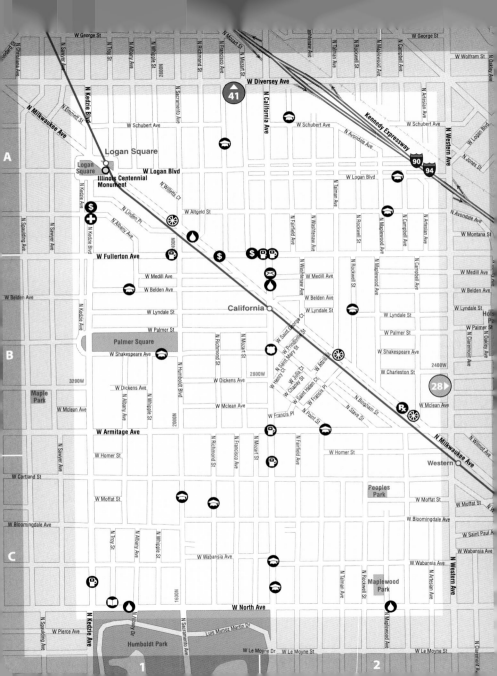

Banks

- **Banco Popular** · 2525 N Kedzie Blvd
- **Liberty Bank For Savings** ·
  2392 N Milwaukee Ave
- **Northern Trust Bank** · 2814 W Fullerton Ave

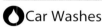 Car Washes

- **California Car Wash** · 2340 N California Ave
- **Edgar's Hand Car Wash** · 2524 W North Ave
- **Logan Square Car Wash II** ·
  2436 N Milwaukee Ave
- **Puerto Rico Car Wash** · 3110 W North Ave

Gas Stations

- **Amoco Food Shop** · 2800 W Fullerton Ave
- **Citgo** · 3000 W Fullerton Ave
- **Frank's Service Center** · 2801 W Armitage Ave
- **Fullerton & California Shell** ·
  2811 W Fullerton Ave
- **Olvin Service Station** · 1654 N Kedzie Ave
- **Valencia Super Service** · 1935 N California Ave

Hospital

- **Advocate Health Centers-Logan Square** ·
  2511 N Kedzie Blvd

Landmark

- **Illinois Centennial Monument** ·
  3100 W Logan Blvd

Library

- **Chicago Public Library** · 1605 N Troy St

Pharmacy

- **Osco Drug** · 2053 N Milwaukee Ave

Pizza

- **Congress Pizzeria** · 2033 N Milwaukee Ave
- **Father & Son Pizza** · 2475 N Milwaukee Ave
- **Lucky Vito's Pizzeria** · 2171 N Milwaukee Ave

 Police

- **Chicago Police Dept** · 2150 N California Ave

Post Offices

- 2339 N California Ave

 Schools

- **Charles R Darwin School** · 3116 W Belden Ave
- **City Colleges Of Chicago** · 1645 N California Ave
- **Humboldt Community Christian** ·
  1847 N Humboldt Blvd
- **J W Von Goethe School** · 2236 N Rockwell St
- **Lorenz Brentano School** · 2723 N Fairfield Ave
- **Moos Elementary School** · 1711 N California Ave
- **Prince Of Peace Luthern School** ·
  2649 N Francisco Ave
- **Richard Yates School** · 1839 N Richmond St
- **Salomon P Chase School** · 2021 N Point St
- **St John Berchmans School** · 2511 W Logan Blvd
- **St John Berchmans School** · 2524 W Altgeld St
- **St Sylvesters School** · 3027 W Palmer Blvd

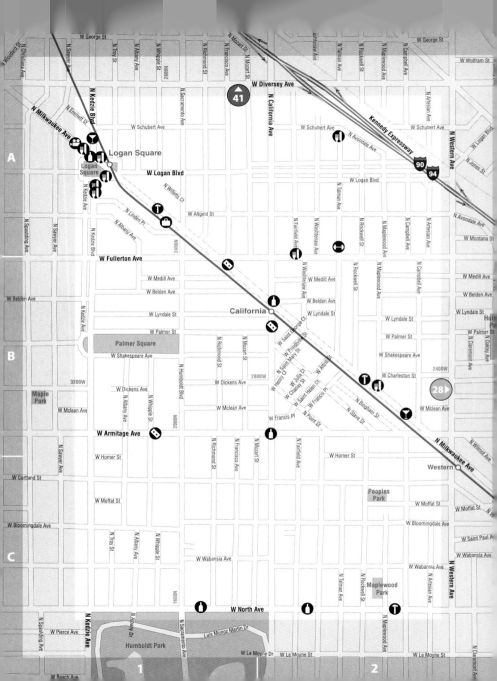

Come to Logan Square for the Latino food. El Nandu on Fullerton has live classical guitar music, Argentinean wine and tasty empanadas for little cash. We like Abril's big burrito and mole enchiladas. Because lots of other people like Abril too, get there early or at off-peak hours. Ask for a booth near the window to watch this lively neighborhood's colorful street scene.

Bars
- **Palladium** · 2047 N Milwaukee Ave
- **The Winds Café** · 2657 N Kedzie Blvd

Gym
- **TLC Fitness Consulting** · 2419 N Talman Ave

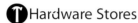Hardware Stores
- **Gillman's Hardware Co** · 2129 N Milwaukee Ave
- **Monroy's Hardware Store** · 2511 W North Ave
- **Tony's Tools** · 2500 N Milwaukee Ave

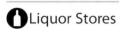Liquor Stores
- **D & D Liquors** · 2958 W North Ave
- **Foremost Liquor Stores** · 2300 N Milwaukee Ave
- **International Liquor Store** ·
  2001 N California Ave
- **Logan Liquors** · 2639 N Kedzie Ave
- **Yafa Corp** · 2700 W North Ave

Movie Theater
- **Logan Theater** · 2646 N Milwaukee Ave

Restaurants
- **Abril Mexican Restaurant** ·
  2607 N Milwaukee Ave
- **Boulevard Café** · 3137 W Logan Blvd
- **Café Bolero** · 2252 N Western Ave
- **Choi's Chinese Restaurant** ·
  2638 N Milwaukee Ave
- **El Cid** · 2115 N Milwaukee Ave
- **El Nandu** · 2731 N Fullerton Ave
- **Johnny's Grill** · 2545 N Kedzie Blvd
- **Lula** · 2537 N Kedzie Blvd

Shopping
- **MegaMall** · 2502 N Milwaukee Ave

Video Rental
- **California Video Inc** · 2208 N California Ave
- **Hi-Fi Video** · 3026 W Armitage Ave
- **Morelia Video** · 2381 N Milwaukee Ave

Map 28 · Bucktown

Although still known as Chicago's struggling artist center, Bucktown's creative scene has fallen victim to real estate greed. Soaring rents are sending artists packing further west. The few remaining galleries fight to keep their spaces from becoming Starbucks, valet parking, restaurants, antique shops and chic loft residences. Even the flagship "Around the Coyote Festival" (in September) increasingly feels like a fabricated cash cow rather than a celebration of the neighborhood's creative spirit.

Banks

- **Cole Taylor Bank** • 1965 N Milwaukee Ave
- **Mid America Bank** • 2300 N Western Ave
- **Mid Town Bank** • 1830 W Fullerton Ave
- **Mid Town Bank** • 1955 N Damen Ave
- **TCF National Bank** • 2627 N Elston Ave

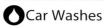Car Washes

- **Celina's Hand Car Wash** • 1815 N Western Ave
- **Clybourn Express & Car Wash** •
  2452 N Clybourn Ave
- **Express Car Wash** • 2111 W Fullerton Ave
- **Fast Eddie's Hand Car Wash** •
  1828 W Webster Ave
- **Wash Express** • 1657 N Milwaukee Ave

Gas Stations

- **Amoco Food Shop** • 1768 W Armitage Ave
- **Anderson's Service Station** •
  1700 N Milwaukee Ave
- **J & J Amoco** • 2357 W Fullerton Ave
- **Larry's Service Center** • 1834 N Damen Ave
- **Marathon** • 2346 N Western Ave
- **N Western Avenue Citgo** • 1750 N Western Ave

Landmarks

- **Crumbling Bucktown** • 579 N Milwaukee Ave
- **Margie's Candies** • 1960 N Western Ave

Library

- **Damen Avenue Library** • 2056 N Damen Ave

Pizza

- **Barcello's Pizzeria** • 1647 N Milwaukee Ave
- **Chuck E Cheese's** • 1730 W Fullerton Ave
- **Domino's** • 2455 W Fullerton Ave
- **John's Restaurant & Lounge** •
  2104 N Western Ave
- **Plazzio's Pizza** • 1901 N Western Ave
- **Sonny's Pizza** • 2431 N Western Ave

Schools

- **Casimir Pulaski Academy** • 2230 W Mclean Ave
- **Pedro Albizu Campos High School** •
  1671 N Claremont Ave
- **St Mary of the Angels School** •
  1810 N Hermitage Ave
- **Thomas Drummond School** • 1845 W Cortland St
- **William H Prescott School** •
  1632 W Wrightwood Ave

Supermarkets

- **Aldi** • 1767 N Milwaukee Ave
- **Always Open** • 1704 N Milwaukee Ave
- **Costco** • 2746 N Clybourn Ave
- **Cub Foods** • 2627 N Elston Ave
- **Dominick's** • 2550 W Clybourn Ave

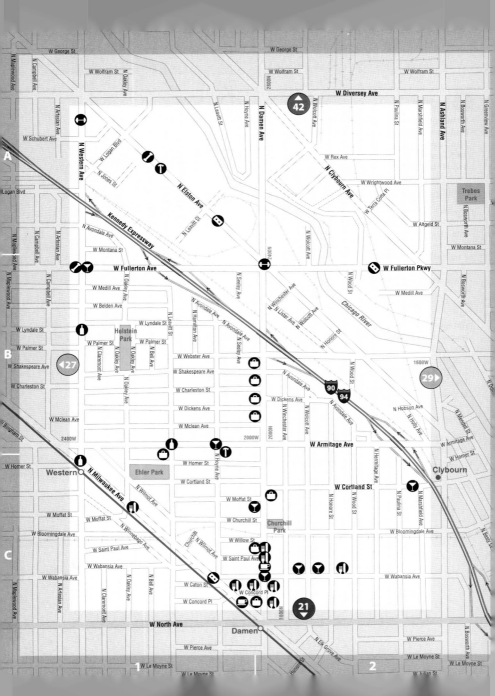

Not too long ago, Bucktown was a seedy mix of Bohemian cafés, ethnic street stalls and greasy-spoon diners. Experience what's left of that funky aura at Northside Tavern & Grill, a Bucktown institution with basic food, cold beer and good company. Club Lucky has been forever dishing pasta and serving suds. Roong Thai is good for tasty takeout.

Bars
- **Artful Dodger Pub** · 1734 W Wabansia Ave
- **Bar Louie** · 1704 N Damen Ave
- **Charleston Tavern** · 1643 W Cortland St
- **Lemings** · 1850 N Damen Ave
- **Lincoln Tavern** · 1858 W Wabansia Ave
- **Quencher Saloon** · 2401 N Western Ave
- **The Map Room** · 2100 W Armitage Ave

Coffee
- **Caffe De Luca** · 1721 N Damen Ave
- **Red Hen Bread** · 1623 N Milwaukee Ave

Gyms
- **Hapkido & Karate School** · 2743 N Western Ave
- **Mid-Town Tennis Club** · 2428 N Elston Ave

Hardware Stores
- **Great Ace Hardware** · 2639 N Elston Ave
- **Novak's Paint & Hardware Co** · 2000 N Hoyne Ave

Liquor Stores
- **Bon Song Liquors** · 2000 N Leavitt St
- **Danny's Buy-Low Liquors** · 2220 N Western Ave
- **M W Food & Liquor** · 1950 N Milwaukee Ave

Pet Shops
- **And Feathers Bird Studio** · 2406 W Fullerton Ave
- **Petsmart** · 2665 N Elston Ave

Restaurants
- **Café Bolero** · 2252 N Western Ave
- **Café Matou** · 1848 N Milwaukee Ave
- **Cafe De Luca** · 1721 N Damen Ave
- **Club Lucky** · 1824 W Wabansia Ave
- **Northside Tavern & Grill** · 1635 N Damen Ave
- **Roong Thai Restaurant** · 1633 N Milwaukee Ave
- **Silver Cloud Supper Club** · 1700 N Damen Ave
- **Zoom Kitchen** · 1646 N Damen Ave

Shopping
- **Bleeker Street Antiques** · 1946 N Leavitt
- **Eclectic Junction** · 1630 N Damen Ave
- **Gypsy** · 2131 N Damen Ave
- **Jean Alan** · 2134 Damen Ave
- **Pagoda Red** · 1714 N Damen Ave
- **Pavilion Antiques** · 2055 N Damen Ave
- **Red Balloon Company** · 2060 N Damen Ave
- **Yardifacts** · 1864 N Damen Ave

Video Rental
- **Blockbuster Video** · 1704 N Milwaukee Ave
- **Blockbuster Video** · 1730 W Fullerton Ave
- **Video Corp of America** · 2525 N Elston Ave

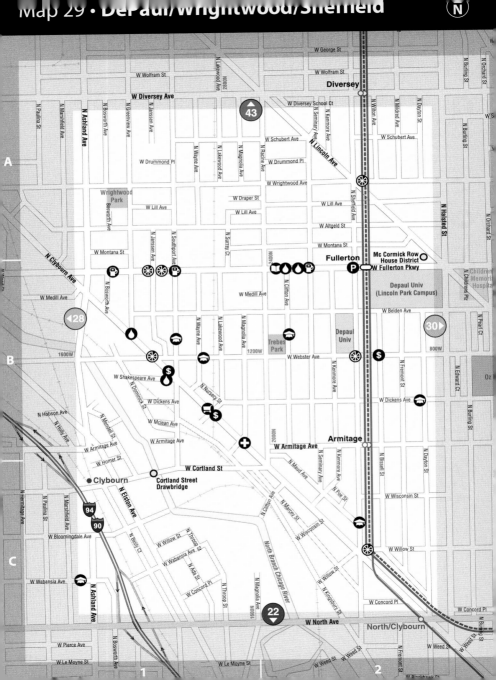

Map 29 • DePaul/Wrightwood/Sheffield

Abodes on the quiet, shady streets around DePaul University and west of the El tracks command big mortgages and high rents. Always super-size when ordering Stefani's pizza because you'll want some for breakfast. The Clybourn Corridor's heavy traffic can be infuriating and narrow side streets crowded with parked cars and SUVs don't offer much relief. Around the area's eastern half, it's wiser to take the El and hoof it.

Banks

- **BankOne** · 2170 N Clybourn Ave
- **La Salle Bank** · 2112 N Clybourn Ave
- **North Community Bank** · 941 W Webster Ave

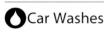Car Washes

- **Big Bear's Hand Car Wash** · 2261 N Clybourn Ave
- **Milito's Car Wash** · 1112 W Fullerton Ave
- **R & S Car Wash Inc** · 1142 W Fullerton Ave
- **White Glove Car Wash Inc** ·
  1415 W Shakespeare Ave

Gas Stations

- **Fullerton & Southport Shell** ·
  1400 W Fullerton Ave
- **Fullerton-Seminary Standard** ·
  1106 W Fullerton Ave
- **Lube N Oil Exchange** · 1540 W Fullerton Ave

Hospital

- **Schwab** · 2020 N Clybourn Ave

Landmarks

- **Courtland Street Drawbridge** · 1440 W Cortland
- **McCormick Row House District** ·
  833-927 Fullerton Ave

Library

- **Lincoln Park Public Library** ·
  1150 W Fullerton Ave

Parking

- 2400 N Sheffield Ave

Pizza

- **Lou Malnati's Pizzeria** · 958 W Wrightwood Ave
- **Pequod's Pizzeria** · 2207 N Clybourn Ave
- **Rizzatas Pizza** · 953 W Willow St
- **Stefani's** · 1418 W Fullerton Ave
- **Tomato Head Pizza Kitchen** ·
  1001 W Webster Ave
- **Via-Carducci's Italian Eatery** ·
  1419 W Fullerton Ave

Schools

- **Arts Of Living School** · 1855 N Sheffield Ave
- **Jonathan Burr School** · 1621 W Wabansia Ave
- **Oscar F Mayer School** · 2250 N Clifton Ave
- **St James Lutheran School** · 850 W Dickens Ave
- **St Josephat School** · 2245 N Southport Ave
- **The Chopping Block** · 1324 W Webster Ave

Supermarket

- **Treasure Island** · 2121 N Clybourn Ave

Map

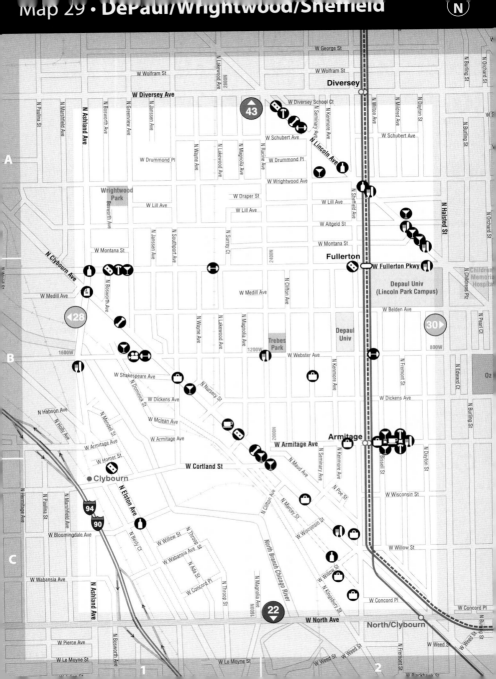

Map 29 · DePaul/Wrightwood/Sheffield

An afternoon is well spent swigging suds at one of the neighborhoods' local taverns. Wrightwood Tap and Kincades are our favorites. If you haven't had the fish 'n' chips at the Red Lion, you should - it's across from the Biograph Theater on Lincoln where notorious bank robber John Dillinger was gunned down by G-men. Be wary if your date wears red. Wine Discount Center on Elston is the ultimate bottle shop for wine enthusiasts.

Bars

- **Gin Mill** · 2462 N Lincoln Ave
- **Hog Head McDunna's** · 1505 W Fullerton Ave
- **Irish Eyes** · 2519 N Lincoln Ave
- **Jack Sullivan's** · 2142 N Clybourn Ave
- **Kincade's** · 950 W Armitage Ave
- **Kustom** · 1997 N Clybourn Ave
- **Lush** · 948 W Armitage Ave
- **Red Lion Pub** · 2446 N Lincoln Ave
- **Webster Wine Bar** · Dominick St & Webster Ave
- **Wrightwood Tap** · 1059 W Wrightwood Ave
- **Zella** · 1983 N Clybourn Ave

Coffee

- **Caribou Coffee Co** · 2070 N Clybourn Ave
- **Urban Blend** · 917 W Armitage Ave

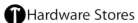Copy Shop

- **Kinko's** · 2300 N Clybourn Ave

Gyms

- **Bally's** · 1455 W Webster Ave
- **Gorilla Sports** · 2727 N Lincoln Ave
- **Lakeshore Athletic Club** · 1320 W Fullerton Ave
- **Webster Fitness Club** · 957 W Webster Ave

Hardware Stores

- **Ace Hardware** · 915 W Armitage Ave
- **Armitage Hardware & Building Supply** · 925 W Armitage Ave
- **Elston Ace Hardware** · 2767 N Lincoln Ave
- **Hollywood Industrial Supply** · 1524 W Fullerton Ave

Liquor Stores

- **Ala Carte Entertainment** · 2624 N Lincoln Ave
- **J & R Liquor & Foods** · 2401 N Ashland Ave
- **Kegs To Go** · 2581 N Lincoln Ave
- **Sam's Wines & Spirits** · 1720 N Marcey St
- **Wine Discount Center** · 1826 1/2 N Elston Ave

Movie Theater

- **Sony Theatre** · 1471 W Webster Ave

Pet Shops

- **Animal Lovers Pet Salon** · 2277 N Clybourn Ave
- **Galloping Gourmutts** · 2736 N Lincoln Ave
- **Petco** · 2000 N Clybourn Ave

Restaurants

- **BW3** · 2464 N Lincoln Ave
- **Clarke's Pancake House & Restaurant** · 2441 N Lincoln Ave
- **Demon Dogs** · 844 W Fullerton Ave
- **Goose Island Brewing Co** · 1800 N Clybourn Ave
- **Green Dolphin Street** · 2200 N Ashland Ave
- **John's Place** · 1202 W Webster Ave
- **Salt & Pepper Diner** · 2575 N Lincoln Ave
- **Shine/Morida** · 901 W Armitage Ave

Shopping

- **Active Endeavors** · 935 W Armitage Ave
- **Bed Bath & Beyond** · 1800 N Clybourn Ave
- **Best Buy** · 1700 N Marcey St
- **Gap** · 1740 N Sheffield Ave
- **Isabella Fine Lingerie** · 2150 N Seminary
- **Jayson Home & Garden** · 1885 & 1911 N Clybourn Ave
- **Jolie Joli** · 2131 N Southport Ave
- **Tabula Tua** · 1015 W Armitage Ave

Video Rental

- **Blockbuster Video** · 2037 N Clybourn Ave
- **Blockbuster Video** · 2400 N Sheffield Ave
- **Facets Multimedia** · 1517 W Fullerton Ave
- **Hollywood Video** · 1940 N Elston Ave
- **Star Video** · 2781 N Lincoln Ave

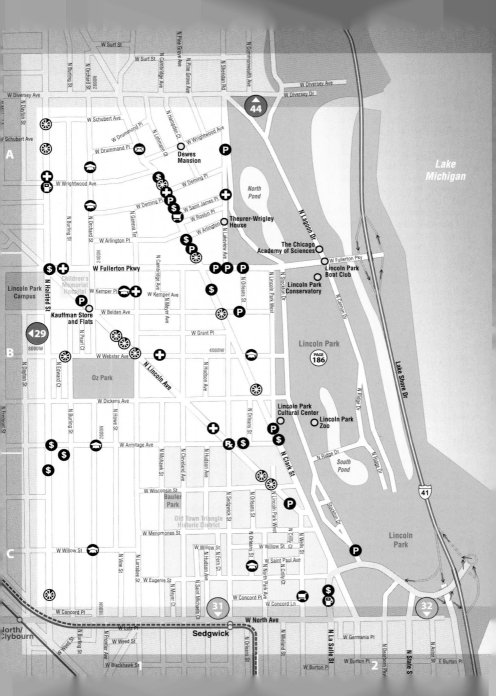

Lincoln Park is one of Chicago's most desirable neighborhoods. Let's face it, who wouldn't want to live on a leafy street in a renovated brownstone, overlooking the park, steps from the beach, around the corner from museums and a stone's throw from tons of restaurants and bars? For the many singles living here, all this makes Lincoln Park a happy hunting ground for love and lust.

Banks

- **Bridgeview Bank** · 1970 N Halsted St
- **Builder's Bank** · 1660 N La Salle St
- **Citibank** · 2001 N Halsted St
- **Citibank** · 2555 N Clark St
- **Corus Bank** · 2401 N Halsted St
- **First American Bank** · 356 W Armitage Ave
- **Mid Town Bank** · 2021 N Clark St
- **North Community Bank** · 2000 N Halsted St
- **North Community Bank** · 2335 N Clark St
- **North Community Bank** · 2500 N Clark St
- **Success National Bank** · 2424 N Clark St

Gas Stations

- **Archway Standard** · 1647 N La Salle Dr
- **Halsted & Wrightwood Shell** · 2600 N Halsted St

Hospitals

- **Advocate Health Care Center** · 2400 N Lincoln Ave
- **Augustana Hospital & Health** · 2035 N Lincoln Ave
- **Chicago Institute-Neurosurgery** · 2515 N Clark St
- **Children's Memorial Dialysis** · 2611 N Halsted St
- **Columbia Grant Hospital** · 550 W Webster Ave
- **Columbus Hospital** · 2520 N Lakeview Ave

Landmarks

- **Dewes Mansion** · 503 N Wrightwood Ave
- **Kauffman Store and Flats** · 2312-14 N Lincoln Ave
- **Lincoln Park Boat Club** · Cannon Dr & Fullerton Ave
- **Lincoln Park Conservatory** · 2400 N Stockton Dr
- **Lincoln Park Cultural Center** · 2045 N Lincoln Park West
- **Lincoln Park Zoo** · Cannon Dr & Fullerton Pkwy
- **The Chicago Academy Of Sciences** · 2430 N Cannon Dr
- **Theurer-Wrigley House** · 2466 N Lakeview Ave

Parking

- 2400 N Lakeview Ave
- 2650 N Lakeview Ave
- 1730 N Stockton Dr
- 2330 N Lincoln Ave
- 1850 N Lincoln Ave
- 2431 N Clark St
- 2515 N Clark St
- 350 W Belden Ave
- 345 W Fullerton Pkwy
- 444 W Fullerton Pkwy
- 2036 N Clark St

Pharmacy

- **CVS Pharmacy** · 401 W Armitage Ave

Pizza

- **Bacino's Pizza** · 2204 N Lincoln Ave
- **Bricks** · 1909 N Lincoln Ave
- **Cafe Luigi** · 2548 N Clark St
- **Chicago's Pizza & Oven Grinder Co** · 2121 N Clark St
- **Domino's** · 2231 N Lincoln Ave
- **Edwardo's Natural Pizza** · 2662 N Halsted St
- **Lincoln Avenue Pizza** · 2245 N Lincoln Ave
- **My Pie Pizzeria** · 2417 N Clark St
- **O'Fame** · 750 W Webster Ave
- **Pane Pomodoro Restaurant** · 2703 N Halsted St
- **Pizza Capri** · 1733 N Halsted St
- **Ranalli's** · 2301 N Clark St
- **Ranalli's On** · 1925 N Lincoln Ave

 Post Office

- 2643 N Clark St

Schools

- **Abraham Lincoln School** · 615 W Kemper Pl
- **Francis W Parker School** · 330 W Webster Ave
- **La Salle Language Academy** · 1734 N Orleans St
- **Lincoln Park High School** · 2001 N Orchard St
- **Louisa May Alcott School** · 2625 N Orchard St
- **Newberry Magnet School** · 700 W Willow St
- **St Clement School** · 2524 N Orchard St

Supermarkets

- **Lincoln Park Super Market** · 2500 N Clark St
- **Treasure Island** · 1639 N Wells St

Map 30 · **Lincoln Park**

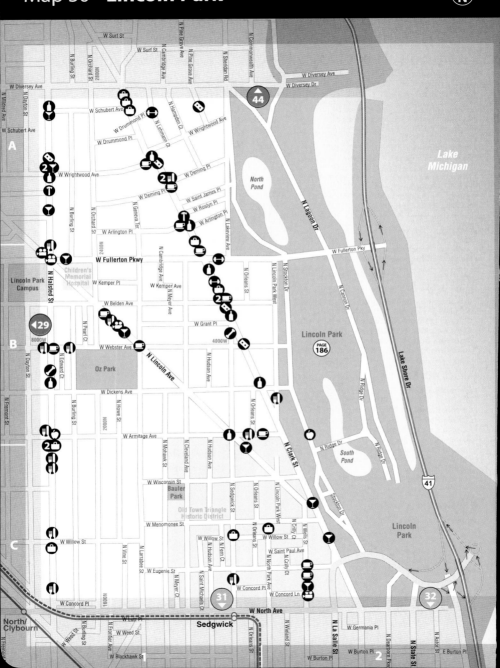

Lincoln Park provides the best outdoor entertainment in this high-rent district. Lincoln Park Zoo is the nation's oldest free zoo. Catch a live act at Park West. Post-show, settle in at Hidden Shamrock with a pint of Guinness. Lori's Designer Shoes is an institution among footwear fanatics. The French toast stuffed with mascarpone cheese and strawberry puree at Toast is worth the wait.

Bars

- **Bar Louie on the Park** · 1800 N Lincoln Ave
- **Blu** · 2247 N Lincoln Ave
- **Corner Pocket** · 2610 N Halsted St
- **Game Keepers** · 1971 N LincolnAve
- **Girlbar** · 2625 N Halsted St
- **GoodBar** · 2512 N Halsted St
- **Hidden Shamrock** · 2723 N Halsted St
- **Parkway Tavern** · 746 W Fullerton Ave
- **Sauce** · 1750 N Clark St
- **Tequila Roadhouse** · 1653 N Wells St

Coffee

- **Caribou Coffee Co** · 2453 N Clark St
- **Classic Cafe** · 341 W Armitage Ave
- **Crescent City Beignets** · 2200 N Lincoln Ave
- **Crescent City Beignets** · 2314 N Clark St
- **Monterotondo** · 612 W Wrightwood Ave
- **Savories** · 1651 N Wells St
- **Screenz Digital Universe** · 2717 N Clark St
- **Seattle's Best** · 1700 N Wells St
- **Siena Coffee** · 2308 N Clark St
- **Starbucks** · 2273 N Lincoln Ave
- **Starbucks** · 2529 N Clark St
- **Starbucks** · Webster Ave & Halsted St

Farmer's Markets

- **Lincoln Park** · Armitage Ave & Halsted St
- **Lincoln Park Zoo** · 2001 N Stockton Dr

Gyms

- **Holistic Fitness Dahnm Center/Yoga** · 2732 N Clark St
- **Lehmann Sports Club** · 2700 N Lehmann Ct
- **Lincoln Park Barbell** · 444 W Fullerton Pkwy
- **Lincoln Park Fitness Center** · 2342 N Clark St

Hardware Stores

- **Arlington Hardware** · 2465 N Clark St
- **Wahler Brothers True Value** · 2551 N Halsted St

Liquor Stores

- **Chalet Wine & Cheese Shop** · 405 W Armitage Ave
- **Clark Bar** · 2116 N Clark St
- **Country Fresh Finer Foods** · 2583 N Clark St
- **Dynamic Liquors Inc** · 2132 N Halsted St
- **Field House** · 2455 N Clark St
- **Miska's Wine Beer & Liquors** · 2353 N Clark St
- **Park West Food & Liquor** · 2733 N Halsted St
- **Park West Foods & Liquors** · 2427 N Lincoln Ave
- **R & A Grocery** · Halsted St & Wrightwood Ave
- **Seven Eleven** · 2264 N Clark St

Movie Theaters

- **Biograph Theatre** · 2433 N Lincoln Ave
- **Sony Theatre** · 1616 N Wells St
- **Three Penny Theatre** · 2424 N Lincoln Ave
- **Victory Gardens Theatre** · 2257 N Lincoln Ave

Pet Shops

- **Park View Pet Shop** · 2222 N Clark St
- **Three Dog Bakery** · 2142 N Halsted St

Restaurants

- **Alladin Cafe** · 2269 N Lincoln Ave
- **Asiana** · 2546 N Clark St
- **Athenian Room** · 807 W Webster Ave
- **Aubriot** · 1962 N Halsted St
- **Charlie Trotter's** · 816 W Armitage Ave
- **Frances** · 2552 N Clark St
- **Hi.Ma.Wa.Ri** · 346 W Armitage Ave
- **King Crab** · 1816 N Halsted St
- **L'Olive** · 1629 N Halsted St
- **RJ Grunts** · 2056 Lincoln Park West
- **Taco Burrito Palace #2** · 2441 N Halsted St
- **Tilli's** · 1952 N Halsted St
- **Toast** · 746 W Webster Ave
- **Twin Anchors** · 1655 N Sedgwick St

Shopping

- **Art & Science** · 1971 N Halsted St
- **Coconuts Music & Movies** · 2747 N Clark St
- **Cynthia Rowley** · 808 W Armitage Ave
- **Ethan Allen** · 1700 N Halsted St
- **Gallery 1756** · 1756 N Sedgwick St
- **GNC** · 2740 N Clark St
- **Kwik Mart** · 2427 N Clark St
- **Lori's Designer Shoes** · 824 W Armitage Ave
- **Sally Beauty Supply** · 2723 N Clark St
- **Triangle Gallery of Old Town** · 1763 N North Park Ave
- **Walgreens** · 2317 N Clark St

Video Rental

- **Blockbuster Video** · 2200 N Clark St
- **Blockbuster Video** · 2577 N Clark St
- **Emmy's & Oscar's** · 2619 N Halsted St
- **Tokyo Video of Chicago** · 2755 N Pine Grove Ave
- **Tower Records** · 2301 N Clark St

Close to all the action on Mag Mile and the lake front, this area is packed with people, history and significant architecture. Old Town Triangle District is on the National Registry of Historic Places. The neighborhood's sophisticated, artsy flair is showcased during the annual Old Town Art Fair (June). The well-heeled live along State St. near the park in exquisite single-family homes.

$ Banks
- **BankOne** · 424 W Division St
- **La Salle Bank** · 758 W North Ave
- **North Community Bank** · 1561 N Wells St

Car Washes
- **Gold Coast Car Wash** · 875 N Orleans St
- **We'll Clean** · 1520 N Halsted St

Fire Department
- **Chicago Breathing Apparatus** · 1044 N Orleans St

Gas Station
- **North Halsted Amoco** · 1560 N Halsted St

Library
- **Near North Branch Library** · 310 W Division St

P Parking
- 1350 N Wells St
- 222 W North Ave

Rx Pharmacy
- **Walgreens** · 1601 N Wells St

Pizza
- **Domino's** · 143 W Division St
- **Marcello's** · 645 W North Ave

Police
- **Chicago Police-Public Housing** · 365 W Oak St
- **Near North Police Station** · 1160 N Larrabee St

Schools
- **Catherine Cook School** · 226 W Schiller St
- **Edward Jenner School** · 1009 N Cleveland Ave
- **Franklin Fine Art Center** · 225 W Evergreen Ave
- **Manierre Elementary School** · 1420 N Hudson Ave
- **Motorcycle Riding School** · 1400 N Halsted St
- **Near North Career Magnet High** · 1450 N Larrabee St
- **Richard E Byrd School** · 363 W Hill St
- **Ruben Salazar Bilingual Education** · 160 W Wendell St
- **Schiller Elementary School** · 640 W Scott St
- **Sojourner Truth School** · 1443 N Ogden Ave
- **St Joseph's School** · 1065 N Orleans St
- **Walter Payton College Prep High School** · 1034 N Wells St

Supermarket
- **Dominicks** · 424 W Division St

Map 31 · **Old Town/Near North**

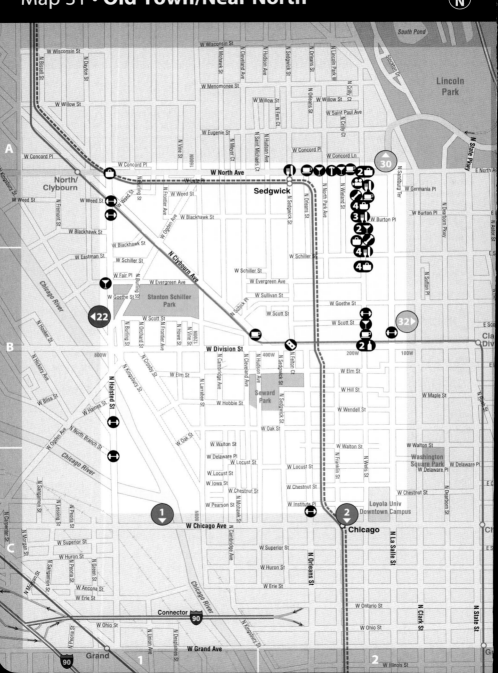

You could be laughing with a rising star at Second City, Chicago's famed improv club where John Belushi, Bill Murray, Gilda Radner, Rick Moranis and Mike Myers got their starts. When in town, Minnie Driver and Gary Sinise browse for books at Barbara's. Topo Gigio's grilled calamari is never rubbery and for sushi as fresh as fish can get out of water, go to Kamehachi.

Bars

- **Burton Place** · 1447 N Wells St
- **Dragon Room** · 809 W Evergreen St
- **Hobo's** · 1446 N Wells St
- **North Park Tap** · 313 W North Ave
- **Old Town Ale House** · 219 W North Ave
- **Spoon** · 1240 N Wells St
- **Weeds** · 1555 N Dayton St

Coffee

- **Chocolateer Confections** · 1212 N Wells St
- **Dunkin Donuts** · 333 W North Ave
- **Einstein Bagels** · 1549 N Wells St
- **Starbucks** · 1229 N Clybourn Ave
- **Starbucks** · 210 W North Ave

Gyms

- **Bally's** · 820 N Orleans St
- **Body Endeavors** · 1528 N Halsted St
- **Energy Training Center** · 900 N North Branch St
- **Fitplex** · 1235 N La Salle Dr
- **Nautilus: A Women's Gym** · 1248 N Wells St
- **New City YMCA** · 1515 N Halsted St
- **The American Fighting Academy** ·
  1030 N Halsted St

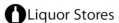

Hardware Store

- **Tipre Hardware** · 227 W North Ave

Liquor Stores

- **House of Glunz** · 1206 N Wells St
- **Old Town Liquors** · 1200 N Wells St

Movie Theater

- **Piper's Alley** · 1608 N Wells St

Pet Shops

- **Collar & Leash** · 1435 N Wells St
- **Old Town Aquarium** · 1538 N Wells St

Restaurants

- **Bistrot Margot** · 1437 N Wells St
- **Cucina Bella Osteria** · 1612 N Sedgwick Ave
- **Fireplace Inn** · 1448 N Wells St
- **Fresh Choice** · 1534 N Wells St
- **Kamehachi** · 1400 N Wells St
- **Las Pinatas** · 1552 N Wells St
- **O'Briens** · 1528 N Wells St
- **Old Jerusalem** · 1411 N Wells St
- **Topo Gigio** · 1516 N Wells St

Shopping

- **Atom Antiques** · 1219 N Wells St
- **Barbara's Bookstore** · 1350 N Wells St
- **Crate & Barrel Outlet Store** · 800 W North Ave
- **Etre** · 1361 N Wells St
- **Fleet Feet Sports** · 210 W North Ave
- **Fudge Pot** · 1532 N Wells St
- **Jumbalia** · 1427 N Wells St
- **Old Town Gardens** · 1555 N Wells St
- **See Hear Music** · 217 W North Ave
- **Sofie** · 1343 N Wells St
- **The Spice House** · 1512 N Wells St
- **Vagabonds Boutique** · 1357 N Wells St

Video Rental

- **Blockbuster Video** · 400 W Division St

Map 32 • **Gold Coast/Mag Mile**

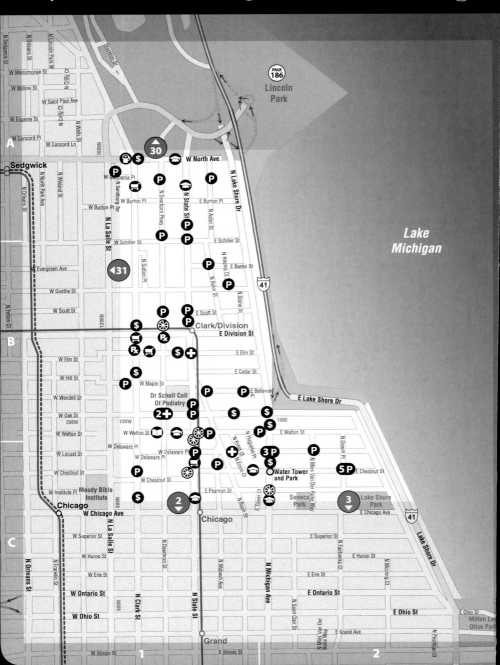

Money, money, money equals location, location, location. The butter-yellow stone Water Tower that survived the Great Chicago Fire of 1871 anchors the City's most expensive and exclusive place to live and play. You'll drop about $400 bucks for a bed at The Ritz, Park Hyatt, Peninsula or Four Seasons. A high school education at private, pricey Latin School of Chicago could buy a fleet of Mercedes.

Banks

- **BankOne** · 1122 N Clark St
- **BankOne** · 875 N Michigan Ave
- **Citibank** · 68 E Oak St
- **Cosmopolitan Bank and Trust** ·
  Clark St & Chicago Ave
- **La Salle Bank** · 940 N Michigan Ave
- **North Community Bank** · 10 W Elm St
- **North Federal Savings Bank** · 100 W North Ave
- **Northern Trust Bank** · 120 E Oak St
- **St Paul Federal Bank-Savings** · 1201 N Clark St

Gas Stations

- **North & La Salle Shell** · 130 W North Ave

Hospitals

- **Columbia Michael Reese North** · 60 E Delaware Pl
- **Foot Ankle Clinics of America** · 1001 N Dearborn St
- **Herron Medical Center Ltd** · 1150 N State St
- **Northwestern Hospital** · Oak St & Dearborn St

Landmark

- **Water Tower and Park** ·
  Michigan Ave between Chicago Ave & Chestnut St

Library

- **Newberry Library** · 60 W Walton St

Parking

- 856 N Clark St
- 1410 N State Pkwy
- 1555 N Astor St
- 33 E Cedar St
- 260 E Chestnut St
- 1005 N State St
- 1258 N State Pkwy
- 100 E Bellevue Pl
- 1221 N State Pkwy
- 200 E Delaware Pl
- 221 E Chestnut St
- 1325 N State St
- 868 N Wabash Ave
- 1445 N State Pkwy
- 201 E Chestnut St
- 25 E Walton St
- 14 E Cedar St

- 1030 N State St
- 1415 N Dearborn St
- 1340 N Astor St
- 875 N Michigan Ave
- 1 E Delaware Pl
- 111 E Chestnut St
- 120 E Walton St N
- 1250 N Dearborn St
- 247 E Chestnut St
- 900 N Michigan Ave
- 1025 N Clark St
- 111 W Maple St
- 1560 N Sandburg Ter
- 275 E Chestnut St
- 79 W Elm St
- 1555 N Dearborn Pkwy
- 1310 N Ritchie Ct
- 50 E Bellevue Pl

Pharmacies

- **Osco Drug** · 1165 N Clark St
- **Walgreens** · 1200 N Dearborn St

Pizza

- **California Pizza Kitchen** · 835 N Michigan Ave
- **Casa Del Pacci** · 941 N State St
- **Edwardo's Natural Pizza** · 1212 N Dearborn St
- **Gino's Pizzeria** · 930 N Rush St
- **Mama's Pizzeria** · 11 W Division St
- **Pizano's Pizza & Pasta** · 864 N State St

Schools

- **Illinois Wesleyan University** · 1540 N State Pkwy
- **Latin School Of Chicago** · 59 W North Ave
- **Loyola School of Law** · Pearson St & State St
- **Loyola University Of Chicago** · 820 N Michigan Ave
- **Quigley Preparatory Seminary** · 103 E Chestnut St
- **William B Ogden School** · 24 W Walton St

Supermarkets

- **Jewel** · 1210 N Clark St
- **Potash Brothers** · 1525 N Clark St
- **Potash Brothers** · 875 N State St
- **Treasure Island** · 75 W Elm St

Map 32 · **Gold Coast/Mag Mile**

Shopping, shopping, shopping. Oak Street is Chicago's answer to L.A.'s Rodeo Dr —overpriced and unpractical fashion. For multiple pairs of cheap, stylish shades shop at Urban Outfitters. Elements has cool home accessories and creative jewelry. The Downtown strip is sagging but the Rush and Division Street bars still pack 'em in. Bono hangs at Le Passage after U2's sell-out concerts at United Center.

Map 32

Bars
- **Bar Chicago** · 9 W Division St
- **Cactus** · 1112 N State St
- **Cru Wine Bar** · 888 N Wabash Ave
- **Dublin's** · 1030 N State St
- **Le Passage** · 1 E Oak St
- **Leg Room** · 7 W Division St
- **Mothers** · 26 W Division St
- **The Hunt Club** · 1100 N State St
- **The Whisky** · 1015 N Rush St
- **Zebra Lounge** · 1220 N State St

Coffee
- **Coffee Expressions** · 100 W Oak St
- **Starbucks** · 932 Rush St
- **Starbucks** · 39 W Division St
- **Starbucks** · 108 W Germania Pl

Copy Shop
- **Kinko's** · 1201 N Dearborn St

Farmer's Markets
- **Chicago's Green City Market** · 1601 N Clark St
- **Near North** · Dearborn St & Division St

Gyms
- **Body Balance** · 1011 N Rush St
- **Gold Coast Multiplex** · 1030 N Clark St
- **Women's Workout World** · 1031 N Clark St

Hardware Stores
- **Gordon's Ace Hardware** · 24 W Maple St
- **Sandberg Ace Hardware** · 110 W Germania Pl
- **State Street True Value** · 845 N State St

Liquor Stores
- **Bragno World Wines** · 919 N Michigan Ave
- **Chalet Wine & Cheese Shop** · 40 E Delaware Pl

Movie Theaters
- **900 North Michigan Cinemas** · 900 N Michigan Ave
- **Esquire Theater** · 58 E Oak St
- **Village Theater** · 1548 N Clark St
- **Water Tower Theater** · 175 E Chestnut St
- **Water Tower Theater** · 845 N Michigan Ave

Pet Shop
- **Paws-a-Tively** · 109 W North Ave

Restaurants
- **Ashkenaz** · 12 E Cedar St
- **Bistro 110** · 110 E Pearson St
- **Gibson's** · 1028 N Rush St
- **Jilly's** · 1009 N Rush St
- **Johnny Rockets** · 901 N Rush St
- **Le Colonial** · 937 N Rush St
- **McCormick & Schmick** · 41 E Chestnut St
- **Mike Ditka's** · 100 E Chestnut St
- **Pane Caldo** · 72 E Walton St
- **Spiaggia** · 940 N Michigan Ave
- **Tavern on Rush** · 1031 N Rush St
- **Tempo** · 6 E Chestnut St
- **The Cheesecake Factory** · 875 N Michigan Ave
- **The Original Pancake House** · 22 E Bellevue Pl
- **The Pump Room** · 1301 N State Pkwy
- **Tsunami** · 1160 N Dearborn St
- **Whiskey Bar and Grill** · 1015 N Rush St

Shopping
- **Anthropologie** · 1120 N State St
- **Barney's** · 25 E Oak St
- **BCBG** · 103 E Oak St
- **Blomingdales** · 900 N Michigan Ave
- **Bravco** · 43 E Oak St
- **Chanel at the Drake Hotel** · 140 E Walton St
- **Diesel** · 923 N Rush St
- **Elements** · 102 E Oak St
- **Europa Books** · 832 N State St
- **Frette** · 41 E Oak St
- **G'bani** · 949 N State St
- **Gucci** · 900 N Michigan Ave
- **MAC** · 40 E Oak St
- **Nicole Miller** · 63 E Oak St
- **Portico** · N Rush St & Pearson St
- **Prada** · 30 E Oak St
- **Pratesi** · 67 E Oak St
- **Tod's** · 121 E Oak St
- **Ultimate Bride** · 106 E Oak St, 2nd Fl
- **Ultimo** · 114 E Oak St
- **Urban Outfitters** · 935 N Rush St
- **Water Tower** · 845 N Michigan Ave

Video Rental
- **Blockbuster Video** · 1201 N Clark St

Map 33 · **West Rogers Park**

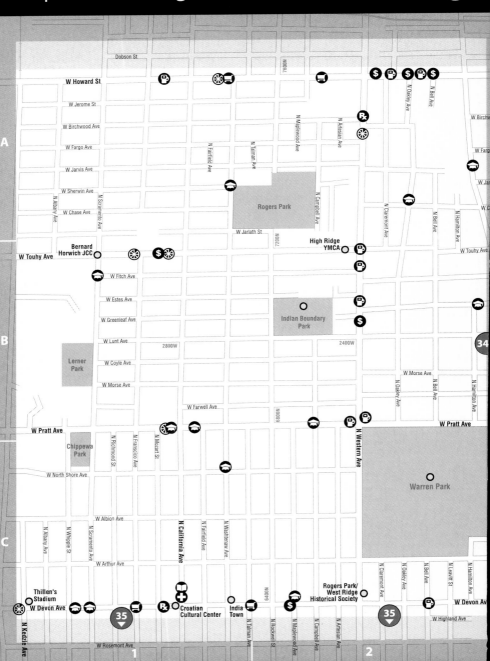

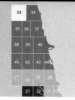

Map 33

Turbans, tandoori chicken, fedoras, kosher pizza, saris, live chickens and chop suey. Devon Ave is a chaotic global marketplace where shopkeepers know how to make a buck in any language. Devon is a parking lot on weekends. Walking is the only way to negotiate this tempting and tasty international stretch. Side streets off Pratt and Touhy look like Skokie with modest single-family homes on compact lots lining the surprisingly bucolic streets.

Banks

- **BankOne** · 7015 N Western Ave
- **Charter One Bank** · 1325 Howard St
- **Charter One Bank** · 1355 Howard St
- **First Commercial Bank** · 2201 W Howard St
- **La Salle Bank** · 2545 W Devon Ave
- **La Salle Bank** · 2855 W Touhy Ave

Gas Stations

- **Amoco** · 7130 N Western Ave
- **Bee-Zee Service Station** · 1701 Howard St
- **Citgo Service Station** · Pratt Ave & Western Ave
- **Clark Oil & Refining** · 7050 N Western Ave
- **Dankha's Service Station** · 2225 W Devon Ave
- **Howard Auto Service** · 2857 W Howard St
- **M & M Power King** · 1201 Howard St
- **Marathon Service Station** ·
  Touhy Ave & Western Ave
- **Patio Gas 76** · 6801 N Western Ave

Hospital

- **California Devon Medical Center** ·
  6420 N California Ave

Landmarks

- **Bernard Horwich JCC** · 3003 W Touhy Ave
- **Croatian Cultural Center** · 2845 W Devon Ave
- **High Ridge YMCA** · 2430 W Touhy Ave
- **India Town** · W Devon Ave
- **Indian Boundary Park** · 2500 W Lunt Ave
- **Rogers Park / West Ridge Historical Society** ·
  6424 N Western Ave
- **Thillen's Stadium** · Devon Ave & Kedzie St
- **Warren Park** · 6601 N Western Ave

Library

- **Chicago Public Library** · 6435 N California Ave

Pharmacies

- **Osco Drug** · 2825 W Devon St
- **Walgreens** · 7510 N Western St

Pizza

- **Avraham's Ohel Pizza** · 2828 W Pratt Ave
- **Barnaby's** · 2832 W Touhy Ave
- **Candlelite Restaurant** · 7452 N Western Ave
- **Domino's** · 3144 W Devon Ave
- **Eastern Style Pizza** · 2911 W Touhy Ave
- **Gullivers Pizzeria** · 2727 W Howard St

Schools

- **Bethesda Lutheran School** ·
  6803 N Campbell Ave
- **Boone Elementary School** ·
  6710 N Washtenaw Ave
- **Brisk Rabbinical College Inc** · 3000 W Devon Ave
- **Consolidated Hebrew High School** ·
  2828 W Pratt Ave
- **Decatur Classical School** ·
  7030 N Sacramento Ave
- **George Armstrong Elementary School** ·
  2110 W Greenleaf Ave
- **Hanna Sacks Girls High School** ·
  3021 W Devon Ave
- **Keshet Day School** · 2755 W Pratt Ave
- **Little Angels** · 6407 N Maplewood Ave
- **Rogers Elementary School** ·
  7345 N Washtenaw Ave
- **St Margaret Mary School** · 7318 N Oakley Ave
- **St Scholastica High School** · 7416 N Ridge Blvd

Supermarkets

- **Dominick's** · 1763 W Howard St
- **Fresh Farms International Market** ·
  2626 W Devon Ave
- **Jewel Food Stores** · 2485 W Howard St
- **New York Kosher** · 2900 W Devon Ave

Map 33 · **West Rogers Park**

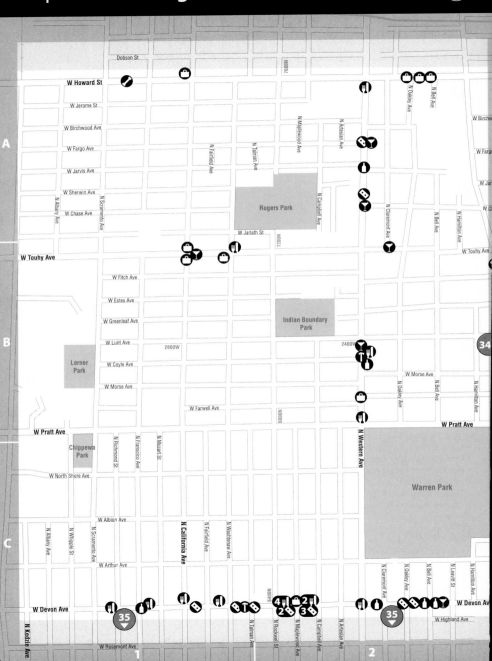

Map 3

Just stand on a street corner and watch the world walk by. If you're feeling active, we recommend the batting cages at Indian Boundary Park. Warren Park's sledding hill makes for a great dog run. The fabrics at Taj Sari Palace on Devon are frameable art. See what's playing in India's theaters at Bombay Video. Inexpensive kebabs and tandoori are the fare of this 'hood.

Bars

- **Cary's Lounge** · 2251 W Devon Ave
- **Mark II Chicago** · 7436 N Western Ave
- **McKellin's** · 2800 W Touhy Ave
- **Mullen's Sports Bar and Grill** · 7301 N Western Ave
- **Pinewood Inn** · 2310 W Touhy Ave

Hardware Stores

- **Basco Plumbing & True Value** · 2650 W Devon Ave
- **Coast To Coast Store** · 6942 N Western Ave

Liquor Stores

- **Adelphi Liquors** · 2351 W Devon Ave
- **Beatrice Liquor** · 2901 W Devon Ave
- **Extra Value Wine & Liquor** · 7300 N Western Ave
- **M & Y Liquor & Grocery Store** · 2252 W Devon Ave
- **Old City** · 2222 W Devon Ave
- **Western Liquor Store** · 6963 N Western Ave

Pet Shop

- **Animal Affinity** · 2125 W Howard St

Restaurants

- **Angus** · 7555 N Western Ave
- **Café Montenegro** · 6954 N Western Ave
- **Delhi Darbar Kabab House** · 6403 N California Ave
- **Desi Island** · 2401 W Devon Ave
- **Fluky's** · 6821 N Western Ave
- **Ghandi India Restaurant** · 2601 W Devon Ave
- **Gitel's Kosher Bakery** · 2745 W Devon Ave
- **Good Morgan Kosher Fish Market** · 2948 W Devon Ave
- **HaShalom** · 2905 W Devon Ave
- **Sala Thai** · 2739 W Touhy Ave
- **Tiffin, The Indian Kitchen** · 2536 W Devon Ave
- **Udupi Palace** · 2543 W Devon Ave
- **Viceroy of India** · 2518 W Devon Ave

Shopping

- **Best Buy** · 2301 W Howard St
- **Cheesecakes by JR** · 2841 W Howard St
- **Chicago Harley Davidson** · 6868 N Western Ave
- **Office Mart** · 2801 W Touhy Ave
- **Office Max** · 2255 W Howard St
- **Snoop Shop Too** · 2742 W Touhy Ave
- **Taj Sari Palace** · 2553 W Devon Ave
- **Target** · 2209 W Howard St
- **Z'Afrique Ltd** · 7156 N California Ave

Video Rental

- **Atlantic Video Rentals** · 2541 W Devon Ave
- **Big Video** · 2256 W Devon Ave
- **Blockbuster Video** · 7300 N Western Ave
- **Bombay Video** · 2634 W Devon Ave
- **Davika 5 Star Pan House** · 2502 W Devon Ave
- **Golden Video** · 2761 W Devon Ave
- **Jai Hind Plaza** · 2658 W Devon Ave
- **New Devon Video** · 2304 W Devon Ave
- **New Jhankar Video** · 2521 W Devon Ave
- **Super Star Video** · 2538 W Devon Ave
- **Video Sonido** · 7117 N Ridge Blvd
- **Video Vision** · 2524 W Devon Ave
- **Western Video** · 7439 N Western Ave

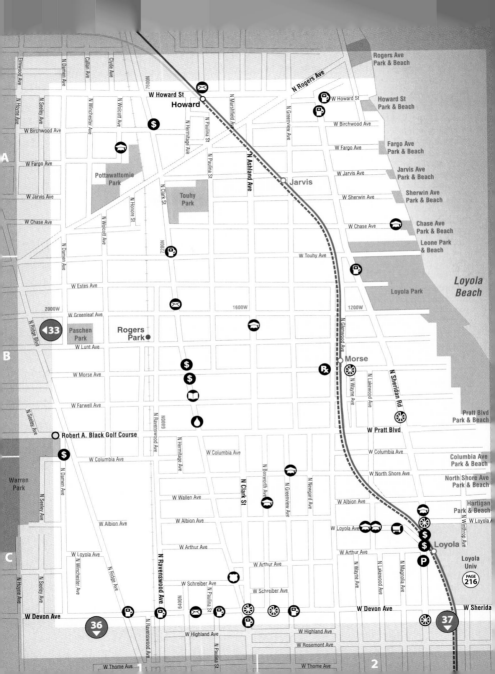

Students, seniors, liberals and every day urbanites mix in East Rogers Park. Loyola University anchors the southwest corner of the neighborhood. Renovated three-flats flank the tree-lined streets west of campus. A wall of ugly high-rises line the lake. Sheridan Rd. traffic heading into suburban Evanston is hellish during rush hours and on weekends.

Banks

- **First Commercial Bank** · 6930 N Clark St
- **First Commercial Bank** · 6945 N Clark St
- **First National Bank** · 6623 N Damen Ave
- **Harris Bank** · 6538 N Sheridan Rd
- **La Salle Banks** · 7516 N Clark St
- **Manufacturers Bank** · 6443 N Sheridan Rd

Car Wash

- **Roger's Park Hand Car Wash** · 6828 N Clark St

Gas Stations

- **Amoco** · 1841 W Devon Ave
- **Amoco** · 7550 N Sheridan Rd
- **Clark & Devon Shell** · 6346 N Clark St
- **Couret's Gas Station** · 1701 W Devon Ave
- **Frank's Auto Repair** · 1500 W Devon Ave
- **Norm's Auto Service** · 1419 W Howard St
- **Ridge & Devon Shell** · 6401 N Ridge Blvd
- **Rogers Park Citgo** · 7138 N Sheridan Rd
- **Sak's Service** · 7201 N Clark St

Landmark

- **Robert A. Black Golf Course** · 2045 W Pratt Blvd

Library

- **Rogers Park Public Library** · 6907 N Clark St

Parking

- 6455 N Sheridan Rd

Pharmacy

- **Osco Drug** · 1425 W Morse St

Pizza

- **Alberto's Pizza** · 1324 W Morse Ave
- **Carmen's Of Loyola Pizzeria** ·
  6568 N Sheridan Rd
- **Giordano's** · 6836 N Sheridan Rd
- **Hamilton's Pizza & Pub** · 6341 N Broadway St
- **Riccardo's Pizza** · 6349 N Clark St
- **Vince's Pizzeria** · 1527 W Devon Ave

Police

- **Chicago Police Dept** · 6464 N Clark St

Post Offices

- 1723 W Devon Ave
- 7056 N Clark St
- 7617 N Paulina St

Schools

- **Field Elementary School** · 7019 N Ashland Blvd
- **Jordan Community School** · 7414 N Wolcott Ave
- **Joyce Kilmer School** · 6700 N Greenview Ave
- **Loyola University** · 6525 N Sheridan Rd
- **Mundelein College** · 6525 N Sheridan Rd
- **Nancy Trueblood School** · 1301 W Loyola Ave
- **North Shore School** · 1217 W Chase Ave
- **Sullivan High School** · 6631 N Bosworth Ave
- **Waldorf School Of Chicago** · 1300 W Loyola Ave

Supermarket

- **Greenleaf Natural Grocery Company** ·
  1261 W Loyola Ave

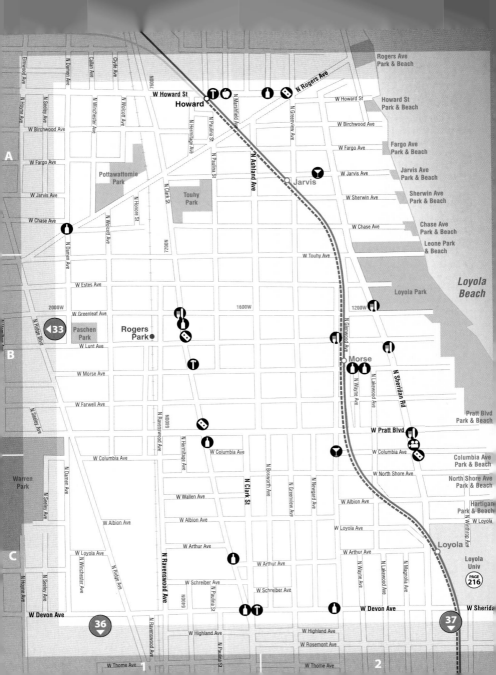

A

W Birchwood Ave
W Fargo Ave
W Jarvis Ave
W Chase Ave

N Elmwood Ave
N Damen Ave
Callan Ave
Clyde Ave
N Seeley Ave
N Winchester Ave
N Wolcott Ave

Pottawattomie
Park

N Clark St
Touhy
Park

N Honore St
W 2072N

N Hermitage Ave
N Paulina St

W Howard St
Howard

N Marshfield Ave
N Ashland Ave
N Greenview Ave
N Rogers Ave

Rogers Ave
Park & Beach

W Howard St
Howard St
Park & Beach

W Birchwood Ave
W Fargo Ave
Fargo Ave
Park & Beach

W Jarvis Ave
Jarvis Ave
Park & Beach
Jarvis

W Sherwin Ave
Sherwin Ave
Park & Beach

W Chase Ave
Chase Ave
Park & Beach

W Touhy Ave
Leone Park
& Beach

Loyola Park

Loyola
Beach

2000W
W Estes Ave
W Greenleaf Ave
1600W
1200W
133
N Ridge Blvd
Paschen
Park
Rogers
Park

B
W Lunt Ave
W Morse Ave
W Farwell Ave

N Damen Ave
N Wolcott Ave
N Seeley Ave
N Ravenswood Ave
N Hermitage Ave
W 2000N

N Glenwood Ave
Morse
N Wayne Ave
N Lakewood Ave
N Sheridan Rd

Pratt Blvd
Park & Beach

W Pratt Blvd
W Columbia Ave
Columbia Ave
Park & Beach

N Clark St
W Columbia Ave
W Wallen Ave
W Albion Ave

N Ravenswood Ave
N Hermitage Ave
W 2000N
N Bosworth Ave
N Greenview Ave
N Newgard Ave

North Shore Ave
Park & Beach

Warren
Park

W Albion Ave
W Arthur Ave
W Schreiber Ave

N Damen Ave
N Seeley Ave
N Winchester Ave
N Ridge Blvd
N Ravenswood Ave

W Loyola Ave
W Arthur Ave

N Wayne Ave
N Lakewood Ave
N Magnolia Ave
N Winthrop Ave

W Albion Ave
W Loyola Ave
Loyola
Univ
216

C
W Loyola Ave

W Devon Ave
36
N Horne Ave
N Seeley Ave
N Winchester Ave

W Schreiber Ave
W Highland Ave
N Paulina St
W 1600N

W Arthur Ave
W Schreiber Ave
W Devon Ave
W Highland Ave
W Rosemont Ave

Loyola
Loyola Univ
W Sheridan
37
W Sheridan

W Thome Ave
1
W Thome Ave
2

For a university neighborhood, the bar scene is barren. Lots of liquor stores supply the campus parties. Funky Heartland Café on Glenwood keeps flower power alive. Granola crunchers dig the vegetarian menu and health food store. Groove to live music including excellent folk and reggae. In summer, we recommend hanging out on the patio in your tie-dye T-shirt.

Bars

- **Don's Coffee Club** · 1439 W Jarvis Ave
- **No Exit** · 6730 N Glenwood Ave

Farmer's Market

- **Rogers Park** · Howard St & Marshfield Ave

Hardware Stores

- **Ace Hardware** · 6955 N Clark St
- **Clark-Devon Hardware** · 6401 N Clark St
- **Northside Hardware Co** · 1640 W Howard St

Liquor Stores

- **Dino's Liquors** · 6400 N Clark St
- **Golden Valley Liquors** · 1339 W Morse Ave
- **Hahn Liquors** · 1410 W Devon Ave
- **Lian's Liquor & Grocery** · 6507 N Clark St
- **Lunt-Liquors** · 7016 N Clark St
- **Morse Liquors** · 1400 W Morse Ave
- **Pelican Liquors** · 6761 N Clark St
- **Sandy's Food** · 1534 W Howard St
- **Summit Grocery** · 7300 N Rogers Ave

Movie Theater

- **Village North Theaters** · 6746 N Sheridan Rd

Restaurants

- **El Famous Burrito** · 7047 N Sheridan Rd
- **Ennui Café** · 6981 N Sheridan Rd
- **Heartland Café** · 7000 N Glenwood Ave
- **Panini Panini** · 6764 N Sheridan Rd
- **Tien Tsin** · 7018 N Clark St

Video Rental

- **Blockbuster Video** · 7007 N Clark St
- **Lakeside Mini Mart** · 6755 N Sheridan Rd
- **Syed Video** · 6808 N Clark St
- **United Video** · 1508 W Howard St

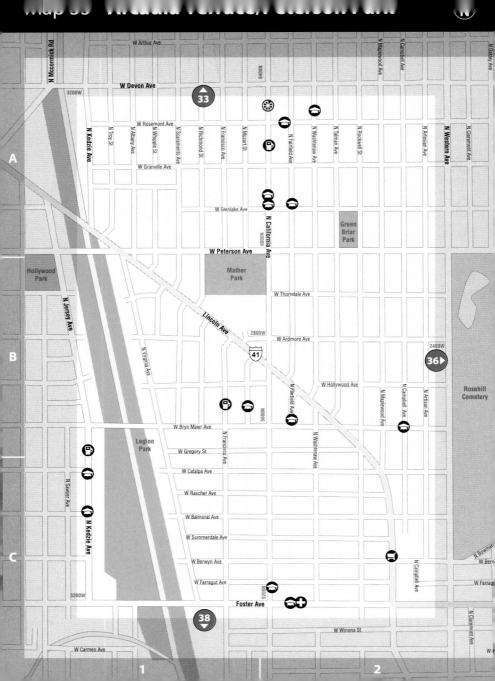

Map

Gas Stations
- **Kedzie Bryn Mawr Amoco** · 5547 N Kedzie Ave
- **Nortown Service** · 6251 N California Ave
- **Poovathur Amoco** · 5650 N Francisco Ave

Hospital
- **Swedish Covenant Prepaid Medical** ·
  2740 W Foster Ave

Pizza
- **Tel Aviv Kosher Pizza** · 6349 N California Ave

Schools
- **Bais Yaakov School** · 6122 N California Ave
- **Budlong Elementary School** · 2701 W Foster Ave
- **Cheder Lubavitch Girls' High School** ·
  2754 W Rosemont Ave
- **Clinton Elementary School** · 6110 N Fairfield Ave
- **CMS Learning Center** · 5400 N Kedzie Ave
- **Jamieson Elementary School** · 5650 N Mozart St
- **Northside College Prepatory** ·
  5501 N Kedzie Ave
- **Seventh-Day Adventist School** ·
  5220 N California Ave
- **St Hillary's School** · 5614 N Fairfield Ave
- **St Philip Evangelical Lutheran** ·
  2500 W Bryn Mawr Ave
- **St Timothys School** · 6330 N Washtenaw Ave

Supermarket
- **Super Buy Farmer's Market and Deli** ·
  5300 N Lincoln Ave

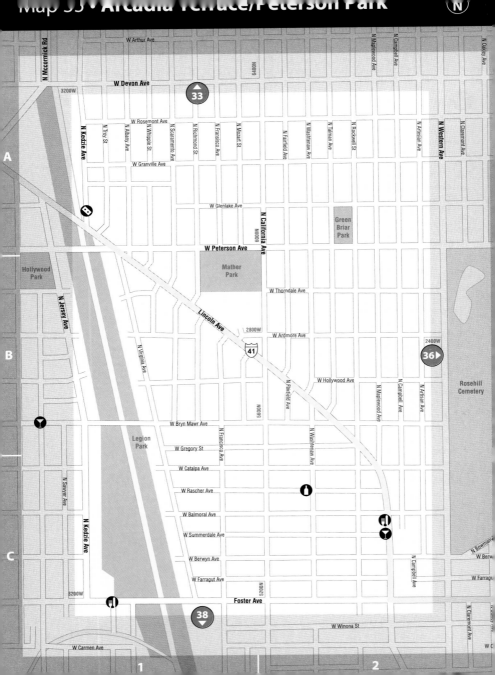

Bars
- **Hidden Cove** · 5336 N Lincoln Ave
- **Hollywood Lounge** · 3301 W Bryn Mawr Ave

Liquor Store
- **Kum's Liquors** · 2715 W Rascher Ave

Restaurants
- **Charcoal Delights** · 3139 W Foster Ave
- **Garden Buffet** · 5347 N Lincoln Ave

Video Rental
- **Lincoln Square Video II** · 6035 N Kedzie Ave

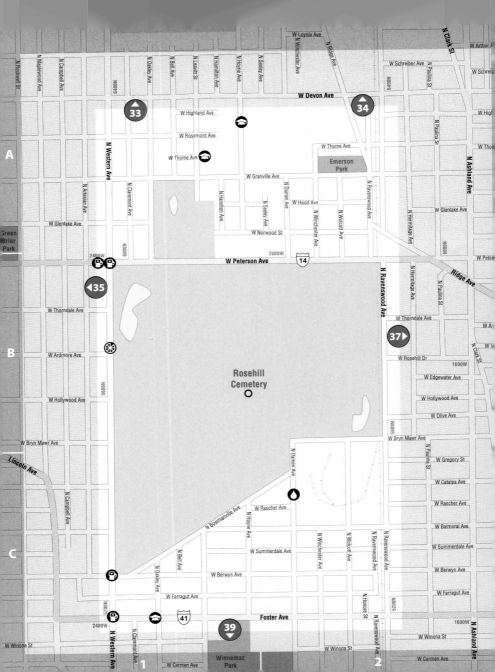

Bryn Mawr is residential - living and dead. Rosehill Cemetery takes up much of the neighborhood's real estate. The magnificent mausoleum houses mail-order magnates Montgomery Ward and Richard Warren Sears. Bryn Mawr has affordable homes, turn-of-the-century apartment buildings and a burgeoning art scene.

Car Wash

- **Superior Super Car Wash** · 5450 N Damen Ave

Gas Stations

- **Citgo** · 5300 N Western Ave
- **Peterson Citgo** · 1840 W Peterson
- **Peterson Western Shell** · 6000 N Western Ave
- **Western Foster Shell** · 5201 N Western Ave

Landmark

- **Rosehill Cemetery and Mausoleum** ·
  5800 N Ravenswood Avenue

Pizza

- **Delisi's Pizzeria** · 5806 N Western Ave

Schools

- **Luv 'n' Care Day School** · 2300 W Foster Ave
- **Northside Catholic Academy** ·
  6325 N Hoyne Ave
- **Stone Scholastic Academy** · 6239 N Leavitt St

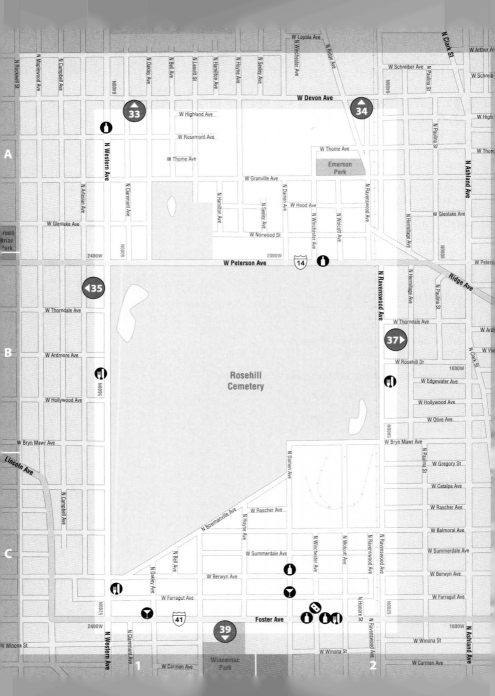

Bryn Mawr residents say that Rosehill Cemetery's mausoleum is haunted. Stop by local taverns where ghost stories might come up in the bar talk.

Bars
- **Claddagh Ring** · 2306 W Foster Ave
- **Leadway Bar, Café and Gallery** · 5233 N Damen Ave

Liquor Stores
- **A & B Grocery & Liquors** · 6320 N Western Ave
- **Aces & Eights** · 5306 N Damen Ave
- **Diala Grocery & Liquor** · 1935 W Foster Ave
- **Foster Food & Liquor** · 1900 W Foster Ave
- **L & M Food & Liquor** · 1958 W Peterson Ave

Restaurants
- **El Tipico** · 1836 W Foster Ave
- **Fireside Restaurant & Lounge** · 5739 N Ravenswood Ave
- **Max's Italian Beef** · 5754 N Western Avenue
- **San Goo Gab San Korean Restaurant and Sushi House** · 5247 N Western Ave

Video Rental
- **Foster Video** · 1931 W Foster Ave

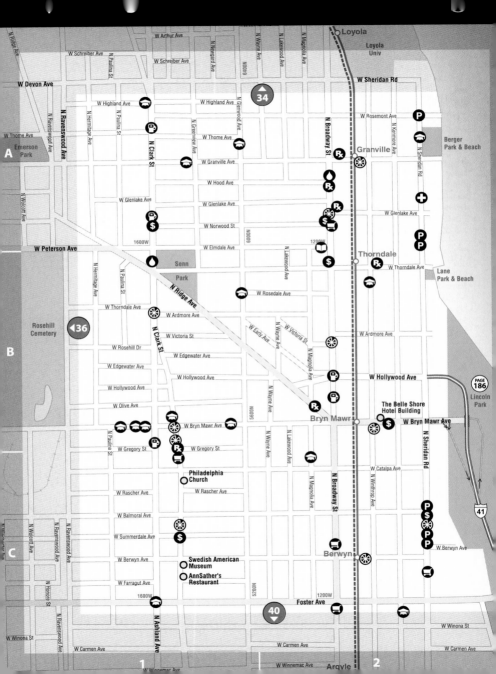

A former Swedish immigrant farming community, Andersonville now cultivates socially-conscious, seasoned yet still edgy adults. Charming brownstones surround Clark St, the neighborhood's main thoroughfare. Edgewater, predominantly a senior citizens community, is to the east on the lake. Daily, Social Security checks are delivered by the hundreds to Sheridan Road's sad, deteriorating high-rises. Brake for seniors crossing Sheridan Rd.

Banks

- **Broadway Bank** • 5960 N Broadway St
- **First National Bank** • 6009 N Broadway St
- **Uptown National Bank** • 1058 W Bryn Mawr Ave
- **Uptown National Bank** • 5345 N Sheridan Rd
- **Uptown National Bank** • 6041 N Clark St
- **US Bank** • 5340 N Clark St

Car Washes

- **Super Spray Car Wash** • 5970 N Clark St
- **Superior Hand Car Wash** • 6147 N Broadway St

Gas Stations

- **A-B Marathon** • 5550 N Ashland Ave
- **Broadway Hollywood Amoco** • 5657 N Broadway St
- **Hollywood Broadway Shell** • 5701 N Broadway St
- **Marathon** • 6262 N Clark St
- **Nicky's Auto Service** • 6059 N Clark St

Hospital

- **Kindred Chicago Lakeshore** • 6130 N Sheridan Rd

Landmarks

- **Ann Sather's Restaurant** • 5207 N Clark St
- **Philadelphia Church** • 5437 N Clark St
- **Swedish American Museum** • 5211 N Clark St
- **The Belle Shore Hotel building** •
  1062 W Bryn Mawr Ave

Library

- **Edgewater Branch** • 1210 W Elmdale St

Parking

- 6301 N Sheridan Rd
- 5415 N Sheridan Rd
- 6033 N Sheridan Rd
- 6007 N Sheridan Rd
- 5333 N Sheridan Rd
- 5301 N Sheridan Rd

Pharmacies

- **Granville Medical Pharmacy** • 1148 W Granville Ave
- **Osco Drug** • 5532 N Clark St
- **Osco Drug** • 6150 N Broadway St
- **Osco Drug** • 5345 N Broadway St
- **Thorndale Pharmacy** • 1104 W Thorndale Ave
- **Walgreens** • 6125 N Broadway St
- **Walgreens** • 5625 N Ridge Ave

Pizza

- **Barry's Spot Pizza** • 5759 N Broadway St
- **Calo Pizzeria Restaurant** • 5343 N Clark St
- **Dominick's Finer Foods** • 6009 N Broadway St
- **Domino's** • 5912 N Clark St
- **Franko's Pizza & Ice Cream** • 1109 W Bryn Mawr
- **Gino's North Pizzeria** • 1111 W Granville Ave
- **Monticello Pizzeria** • 5539 N Clark St
- **Pizzeria Aroma** • 1125 W Berwyn Ave
- **Primo Pizza** • 5600 N Clark St
- **Tedino's** • 5335 N Sheridan Rd

Schools

- **Hayt Elementary School** • 1518 W Granville Ave
- **Jose Marti Bilingual Education** •
  5126 N Kenmore Ave
- **Lake Shore Schools** • 5611 N Clark St
- **N Side Catholic Academy** • 5525 N Magnolia Ave
- **Northside Catholic Academy** •
  1643 W Bryn Mawr Ave
- **Northside Catholic Academy** •
  6216 N Glenwood Ave
- **Peirce Elementary School** • 1423 W Bryn Mawr Ave
- **Sacred Heart Schools Hardy** • 6250 N Sheridan Rd
- **Senn High School** • 5900 N Glenwood Ave
- **St Gregory's Grade School** • 1643 W Bryn Mawr Ave
- **St Gregory's High School** • 1677 W Bryn Mawr Ave
- **Swift Elementary School** • 5900 N Winthrop Ave
- **Trumbull Elementary School** • 5200 N Ashland Ave
- **Westbridge Academy** • 1610 W Highland Ave

Supermarkets

- **Delray Farms** • 5205 N Broadway St
- **Dominick's Fresh Store** • 5235 N Sheridan Rd
- **Dominick's Fresh Store** • 6009 N Broadway St
- **Jewel - Osco** • 5516 N Clark St
- **Jewel - Osco** • 5345 N Broadway St

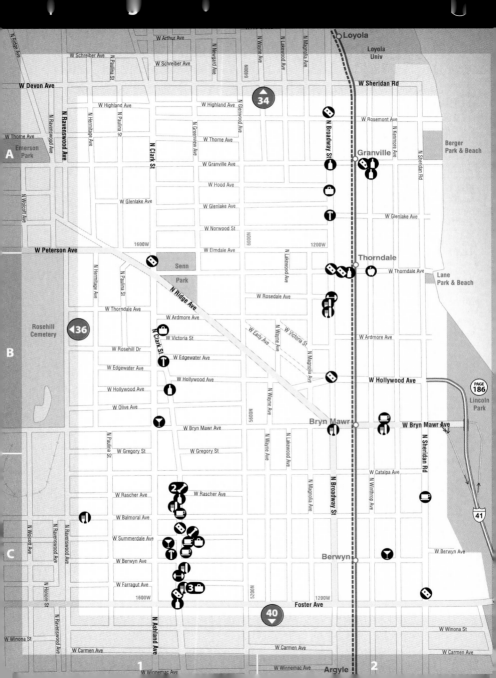

While there's Boystown with its bars and flamboyant parades, Andersonville is the real center of gay and lesbian life in Chicago. The liberal community around Clark and Foster has great depth. Pick up a read at Women & Children First bookstore and devour it at global Kopi Cafe. Edgewater entertainment consists of bingo and beach snoozing.

Bars

- **Edgewater Lounge** · 5600 N Ashland Ave
- **Madrigals** · 5316 N Clark St
- **Ollie's** · 1064 W Berwyn Ave

Coffee

- **Café Boost** · 5400 N Clark St
- **Chava Mocha Cafe** · 5440 N Sheridan Rd
- **Kopi, A Traveler's Café** · 5317 N Clark St
- **Starbucks** · 1070 W Bryn Mawr Ave
- **Starbucks** · 5300 N Clark St

Farmer's Market

- **Edgewater** · Broadway St & Thorndale Ave

Gyms

- **Cheetah Gym** · Broadway St & Rosedale Ave
- **Wild Kingdom Fitness** · 5248 N Clark St

Hardware Stores

- **Ace Hardware** · 5820 N Clark St
- **Cas Hardware Store** · 5305 N Clark St
- **Clarendon Electric & Hardware** · 6050 N Broadway St

Liquor Stores

- **Buy Low Liquors** · 5201 N Clark St
- **Castle Wines & Spirits** · 1128 W Thorndale Ave
- **Granville Liquors** · 1100 W Granville Ave
- **M & D Food Liquors** · 5652 N Clark St
- **Sovereign Liquors** · 6202 N Broadway St
- **Star Gaze Restaurant & Bar** · 5419 N Clark St
- **Sun Liquors Inc** · 1101 W Granville Ave

Pet Shops

- **Fido Food Fair** · 5416 N Clark St
- **Ruff 'n' Stuff Dog Obedience** · 5430 N Clark St
- **Scrub-a-Dub Dub** · 1478 W Summerdale Ave

Restaurants

- **Francesca's Bryn Mawr** · 1039 W Bryn Mawr Ave
- **Jin Ju** · 5203 N Clark St
- **Moody's Pub** · 5910 N Broadway
- **Pasteur** · 5525 N Broadway
- **Pauline's** · 1754 W Balmoral Ave
- **Reza's** · 5255 N Clark St
- **The Room** · 5900 N Broadway St
- **Tomboy** · 5402 N Clark St

Shopping

- **Broadway Antique Mart** · 6130 N Broadway St
- **Gethsemane Garden Center** · 5739 N Clark St
- **Paper Trail** · 5309 N Clark St
- **Surrender** · 5225 N Clark St
- **The Acorn Antiques & Uniques** · 5241 N Clark St
- **Women & Children First** · 5233 N Clark St

Video Rental

- **Broadway Grocery & Video** · 6322 N Broadway St
- **G-S Video Rental** · 5940 N Broadway St
- **Lion Video** · 5218 N Sheridan Rd
- **Magic Video** · 5725 N Broadway St
- **National Video** · 1108 W Granville Ave
- **Select Video** · 5358 N Clark St
- **Specialty Video Films Inc** · 5307 N Clark St
- **Video Town** · 1127 W Thorndale Ave
- **Yogi Video** · 5977 N Clark St

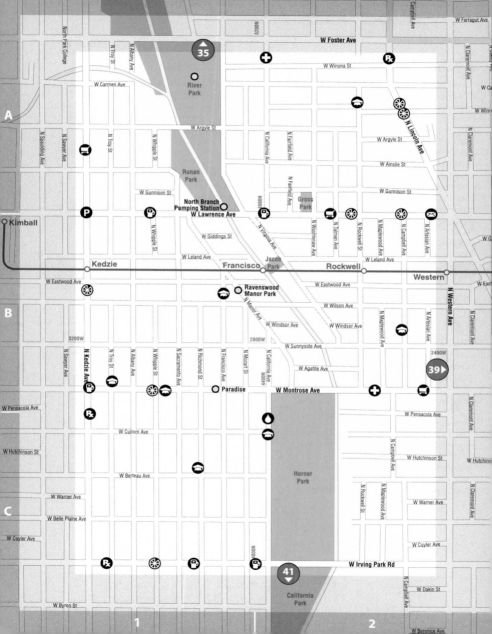

Within the Ravenswood neighborhood is The Manor, a small area of about a quarter of a mile that packs a lot of power and wealth. Generations of Chicago's elite live in this haven next to the river, where owls nest in trees and boat owners have private docks. Neighboring Albany Park residents are ethnic, working-class people living in tired flats and homes destined for gentrification. The mix of Persian, German, Latino and Thai cultures make Albany Park worth a visit.

Car Wash
- **Ruby Hand Carwash** · 4334 N California Ave

 Gas Stations
- **Bams** · 2816 W Irving Park Rd
- **Clark Oil & Refining** · 2954 W Irving Park Rd
- **International Auto Service** ·
  3056 W Lawrence Ave
- **Lawrence & California Shell** ·
  2800 W Lawrence Ave
- **Montrose-Kedzie Amoco** · 3201 W Montrose Ave

Hospitals
- **Kindred Hospital** · 2544 W Montrose Ave
- **Swedish Covenant Hospital** ·
  5145 N California Ave

Landmarks
- **North Branch Pumping Station** ·
  Lawrence Ave & the River
- **Paradise** · 2910 W Montrose Ave
- **Ravenswood Manor Park** · 4626 N Manor Ave
- **River Park** · 5100 N Francisco Ave

Parking
- N Kedzie Ave & W Lawrence Ave

 Pharmacies
- **Osco Drug** · 5158 Lincoln Ave
- **Walgreens** · 3153 W Irving Park Rd
- **Walgreens** · 4343 N Kedzie Ave

Pizza
- **Angelo's Pizza & Restaurant** ·
  3026 W Montrose Ave
- **Boomer's** · 5035 N Lincoln Ave
- **Golden Crust Pizzeria** · 4620 N Kedzie Ave
- **Little Caesar's Pizza** · 2501 W Lawrence Ave
- **Martini's Pizza** · 3038 W Irving Park Rd
- **Paisano's Pizza** · 5047 N Lincoln Ave
- **Papa Giorgio's Pizzeria** · 2604 W Lawrence Ave

Post Office
- 2522 W Lawrence Ave

Schools
- **Early Learning Center** · 3021 W Montrose Ave
- **Gospel Outreach Christian School** ·
  2800 W Cullom Ave
- **Le Ballet Petit School** · 4630 N Francisco Ave
- **Newton Bateman School** · 4220 N Richmond St
- **Our Lady Of Mercy** · 4416 N Troy St
- **Transfiguration School** · 5044 N Rockwell St
- **Waters Elementary School** ·
  4540 N Campbell Ave

Supermarkets
- **ALDI Foods** · 2431 W Montrose Ave
- **Harvestime Foods** · 2632 W Lawrence Ave
- **John's Food Mart** · 4947 N Kedzie Ave

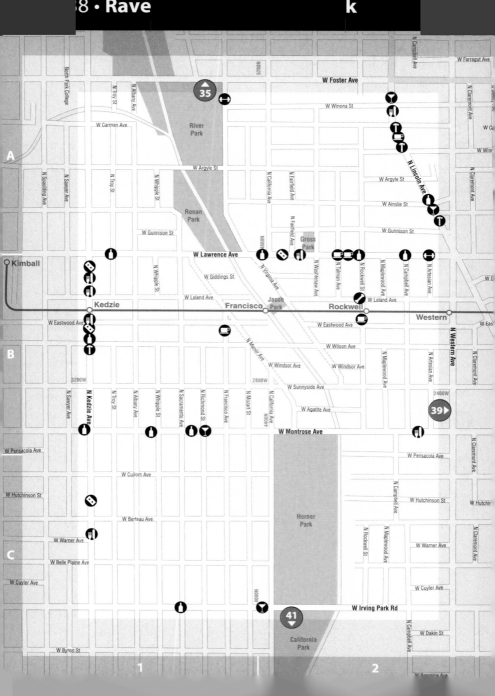

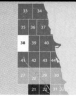
Here you'll find dollar stores for shopping and the world for dining. Go for bowling and brews at Lincoln Square Lanes. You won't hear a cell phone ring in Montrose Saloon. If your grandma was German, she served the same pastries as those made at Lutz Continental Café on Montrose. Eat cake in the old world tea room and on the green Astro Turf patio in summer.

Bars

- **Hot Shots** · 5151 N Lincoln Ave
- **Lincoln Square Lanes** · 4874 N Lincoln Ave
- **Montrose Saloon** · 2933 W Montrose Ave
- **Peek Inn** · 2825 W Irving Park Rd

Coffee

- **Art Café and Restaurant** · 4658 N Rockwell Ave
- **Bmsm Coffee Shop** · 5074 N Lincoln Ave
- **Go! Café** · 4642 N Francisco Ave
- **Sparti** · 2619 W Lawrence Ave
- **Tom's Bakery** · 2612 W Lawrence Ave

Gyms

- **Galter Lifecenter** · 5157 N Francisco Ave
- **Women's Workout World** · 2540 W Lawrence Ave

 Hardware Stores

- **Jay Hardware** · 4608 N Kedzie Ave
- **Just Ask Rental** · 5067 N Lincoln Ave
- **Lincoln Square Ace Hardware** ·
  4874 N Lincoln Ave
- **Singer's True Value Hardware** ·
  5075 N Lincoln Ave

Liquor Stores

- **AB Liquor** · 2807 W Lawrence Ave
- **Alpha Liquors** · 2600 W Lawrence Ave
- **C & K Food & Liquor** · 2941 W Montrose Ave
- **Cardinal Wine & Spirits** · 4905 N Lincoln Ave
- **Foremost Liquor Stores** · 4616 N Kedzie Ave
- **Jerusalem Liquors** · 3135 W Lawrence Ave
- **Leader Liquors** · 3000 W Irving Park Rd
- **P & B Liquor & Food** · 2501 W Lawrence Ave
- **Peacock Liquors** · 3056 W Montrose Ave
- **Prestige Liquors** · 3210 W Montrose Ave

Pet Shop

- **Ruff Haus Pets** · 4652 N Rockwell Ave

Restaurants

- **Arun's** · 4156 N Kedzie Ave
- **Lutz Continental Café** · 2458 W Montrose Ave
- **Noon O Kabab** · 4661 N Kedzie Ave
- **Osito Cheez** · 4714 N Kedzie Ave
- **Shelly's Freez** · 5119 N Lincoln Ave
- **Thai Little Home Café** · 4747 N Kedzie Ave
- **The Penguin** · 2723 W Lawrence Ave

Video Rental

- **Blanz Video** · 4634 N Kedzie Ave
- **Hollywood Video** · 4246 N Kedzie Ave
- **V & K Video** · 4750 N Kedzie Ave
- **Video Hall Sales & Rental** · 2752 W Lawrence Ave

Map 39 • **Ravenswood/North Center**

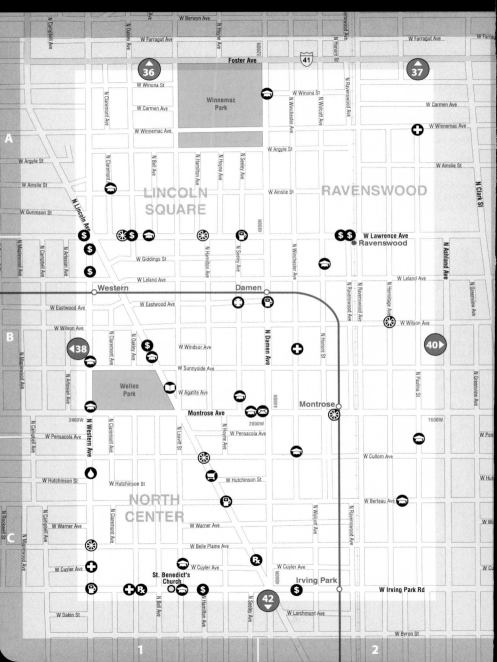

Germans, Eastern Europeans, Latinos and now yuppies who have discovered the comfortable housing, share these increasingly popular neighborhoods. The heart of ethnically diverse Ravenswood is Lincoln Square, the locus of German life in Chicago. The closest you'll get to Munich for Octoberfest without boarding a plane is here. The blocks around St Benedict's Church have spawned a growing, family-friendly neighborhood that goes by "St Ben's".

Banks

- **BankOne** · 1825 W Lawrence Ave
- **Community Bank of Ravenswood** · 2300 W Lawrence Ave
- **Corus Bank** · 2420 W Lawrence Ave
- **Corus Bank** · 4800 N Western Ave
- **First National Bank** · 1825 W Lawrence Ave
- **Great Bank of Lincoln Square** · 4725 N Western Ave
- **Lincoln Park Savings Bank** · 1946 W Irving Park Rd
- **Lincoln Park Savings Bank** · 2139 W Irving Park Rd
- **Uptown National Bank-Chicago** · 4553 N Lincoln Ave

Car Wash

- **Ravenswood Hand Car Wash** · 4250 N Western Ave

Fire Department

- **Chicago Fire Prevention** · 2100 W Eastwood Ave

Gas Stations

- **J & L Oil** · 4638 N Damen Ave
- **Mobil** · 4000 N Western Ave
- **Phil & Sons Gas For Less** · 4201 N Lincoln Ave
- **William Villegas** · 2034 W Lawrence Ave

Hospitals

- **Advocate Ravenswood Med Center** · 4550 N Winchester Ave
- **Methodist Hospital Of Chicago** · 5025 N Paulina St
- **Ravenswood Hospital Medical** · 2312 W Irving Park Rd
- **Ravenswood Hospital Medical** · 4055 N Western Ave

Landmark

- **St Benedict's Church** · 2215 W Irving Park Rd

Library

- **Conrad Sulzer Regional Library** · 4455 N Lincoln Ave

Pharmacies

- **Osco Drug** · 4051 N Lincoln Ave
- **Walgreens** · 2301 W Irving Park Rd

 Pizza

- **Chicago's Pizza** · 1742 W Wilson Ave
- **Giordano's** · 2124 W Lawrence Ave
- **Jako's Pizza** · 4300 N Lincoln Ave
- **Pizza Hut** · 2309 W Lawrence Ave
- **Riggio's Caffe Pranzo** · 4100 N Western Ave
- **Villa May Pizza** · 1834 W Montrose Ave

Post Office

- 2011 W Montrose Ave

Schools

- **Adler Schools** · 2239 W Lawrence Ave
- **Amundsen High School** · 5110 N Damen Ave
- **Coonley Elementary School** · 4046 N Leavitt St
- **Ethel Mary Courtenay School** · 1726 W Berteau Ave
- **McPherson Elementary School** · 4728 N Wolcott Ave
- **North Park Elementary School** · 2017 W Montrose Ave
- **Old Town School Of Folk Music** · 4544 N Lincoln Ave
- **Pilgrim Lutheran School** · 4300 N Winchester Ave
- **Queen of Angels** · 4520 N Western Ave
- **Queen of Angels School** · 4412 N Western Ave
- **Ravenswood Baptist Christian** · 4437 N Seeley Ave
- **Ravenswood School** · 4332 N Paulina St
- **St Benedict's Schools** · 2215 W Irving Park Rd
- **St Matthias School** · 4910 N Claremont Ave

 Supermarket

- **Jewel-Osco** · 4250 N Lincoln Ave

Map 39 • **Ravenswood/North Center**

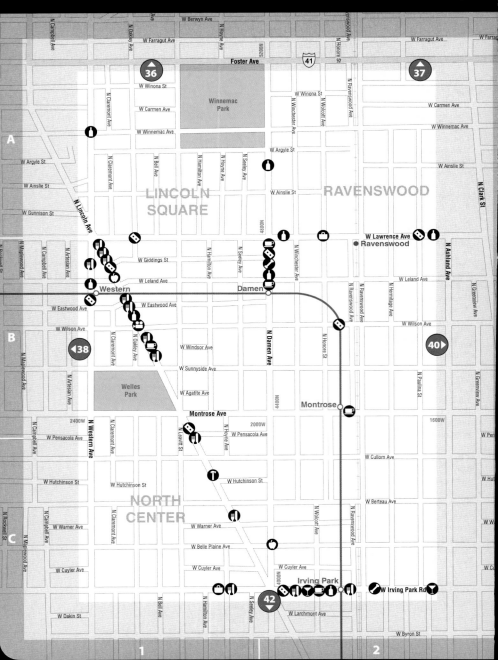

This area has new restaurants opening as fast as the cost for housing is rising. On Lincoln, She She across from the Old Town School of Folk Music's state-of-the-art performance venue is getting good lip service from foodies. Chicago Brauhaus is where you go for pints.

Bars
- **Lyon's Den** · 1934 W Irving Park Rd
- **The Long Room** · 1612 W Irving Park Rd

Coffee
- **Beans & Bagels** · 1812 W Montrose Ave
- **Bit Bytes & Beverages** · 4747 N Damen Ave
- **Katerina's** · 1920 W Irving Park Rd
- **Perfect Cup** · 4700 N Damen Ave
- **Starbucks** · 4553 N Lincoln Ave

Farmer's Markets
- **Lincoln Square** · W Leland Ave & N Lincoln Ave
- **North Center** · W Belle Plaine Ave & N Damen Ave

Hardware Store
- **Lincoln Square Ace Hardware** ·
  4250 N Lincoln Ave

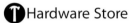Liquor Stores
- **Bozic's Imports & Wholesale** ·
  1964 W Lawrence Ave
- **Bright Corp** · 1628 W Lawrence Ave
- **Cotler's Liquors** · 4959 N Damen Ave
- **Fine Wine Brokers** · 4621 N Lincoln Ave
- **Fox Liquors** · 4707 N Damen Ave
- **Hank's Party Store** · 5029 N Western Ave
- **Houston Liquor & Foods Corp** ·
  1829 W Irving Park Rd
- **Leland Inn** · 4662 N Western Ave

Movie Theater
- **Davis Theatre** · 4614 N Lincoln Ave

Pet Shops
- **Paws For Thought** · 1821 W Irving Park Rd
- **Vahle's Bird & Pet Shop** · 4710 N Damen Ave

Restaurants
- **Café 28** · 1800 W Irving Park Rd
- **Café Selmarie** · 4729 N Lincoln Ave
- **Chicago Brauhaus** · 4732 N Lincoln Ave
- **Daily Bar & Grill** · 4560 N Lincoln Ave
- **Garcia's** · 4749 N Western Ave
- **Grecian Taverna** · 4761 N Lincoln Ave
- **Jury's Food & Drink** · 4337 N Lincoln Ave
- **La Boca della Verita** · 4618 N Lincoln Ave
- **O'Donovan's** · 2100 W Irving Park Rd
- **Pangea** · 1935 W Irving Park Rd
- **She She** · 4539 N Lincoln Ave
- **Tartufo Restaurante** · 4601 Lincoln Ave
- **Woody's** · 4160 N Lincoln Ave

Shopping
- **Play It Again Sports** · 2102 W Irving Park Rd
- **Sears** · 1900 W Lawrence Ave

Video Rental
- **21st Video** · 4737 N Damen Ave
- **B P Video** · 4652 N Western Ave
- **Blockbuster Video** · 1958 W Irving Park Rd
- **Blockbuster Video** · 2301 W Lawrence Ave
- **Darkstar Video** · 4353 N Lincoln Ave
- **Lincoln Square Video** · 4725 N Lincoln Ave
- **Supermagic Video** · 1700 W Lawrence Ave
- **Tom's Video** · 1830 W Wilson Ave

Map 40 · **Uptown**

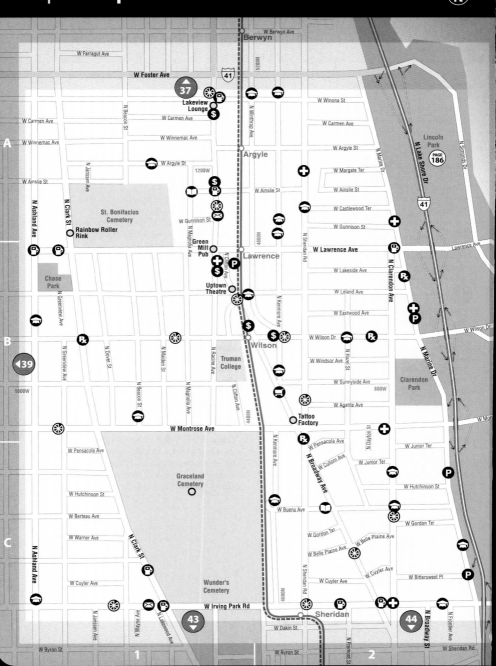

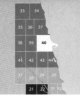
Uptown is haunted by its past. This edgy neighborhood's glitzy history shows through the grit in the ornate architecture of the Aragon Ballroom and Uptown Theater where Chicago's wise guys enjoyed the good life. A 120-acre necropolis filled with palatial mausoleums and haunting headstones, Graceland Cemetery is the final resting place of Chicago's rich, great and good. Rainbow Roller Rink is an adult midnight rumble on wheels.

Banks

- **Harris Trust & Savings Bank** · 4531 N Broadway Ave
- **International Bank** · 5067 N Broadway Ave
- **New Asia Bank** · 4926 N Broadway Ave
- **TCF National Bank** · 1050 W Wilson Ave
- **Uptown National Bank** · 4753 N Broadway Ave

Gas Stations

- **Citgo** · 1530 W Lawrence Ave
- **D'Agostino's Amoco** · 841 W Irving Park Rd
- **Foster Broadway Amoco** · 5156 N Broadway Ave
- **Gas City** · 4070 N Clark St
- **Irving & Clark Amoco** · 4000 N Clark St
- **Irving & Sheridan Shell** · 953 W Irving Park Rd
- **Lawrence Ashland Shell** · 4800 N Ashland Ave
- **Marine Drive Standard** · 755 W Lawrence Ave
- **Uptown Service Station** · 4900 N Broadway Ave

Hospitals

- **Columbia Chicago Lakeshore** · 4840 N Marine Dr
- **Columbus Maryville Clinic** · 810 W Montrose Ave
- **Louis A Weiss Memorial Hosp** · 4646 N Marine Dr
- **Ravenswood Hospital Medical** ·
  4753 N Broadway Ave
- **Thorek Hospital & Medical Center** ·
  850 W Irving Park Rd
- **Thorek Hospital Medical Office** ·
  4945 N Sheridan Rd

Landmarks

- **Graceland Cemetary** · 4001 N Clark St
- **Green Mill Pub** · 4802 N Broadway Ave
- **Lakeview Lounge** · 5110 N Broadway
- **Rainbow Roller Rink** · 4826 N Clark St
- **Tattoo Factory** · 4408 N Broadway Ave
- **Uptown Theatre** · 4707 N Broadway Ave

Libraries

- **Chicago Bezazian Library** · 1226 W Ainslie St
- **Uptown Library** · 929 W Buena Ave

Parking

- 4250 N Marine Dr
- 4646 N Marine Dr
- 4759 N Clifton Ave
- 4100 N Marine Dr

Pharmacies

- **Osco Drug** · 4355 N Sheridan Rd
- **Osco Drug** · 845 W Wilson Dr
- **Walgreens** · 1500 W Wilson Dr
- **Walgreens** · 4720 N Marine Dr

Pizza

- **Bo Jono's Pizzeria** · 4185 N Clarendon Ave
- **Domino's** · 1415 W Irving Park Rd
- **Fornello** · 1011 W Irving Park Rd
- **Gigio's Pizzeria** · 4643 N Broadway Ave
- **Godfather's Pizza** · 1265 W Wilson Ave
- **Laurie's Pizzeria & Liquors** · 5153 N Broadway Ave
- **Michael's Pizzeria & Sports** · 4091 N Broadway Ave
- **Pizza Factory** · 4443 N Sheridan Rd
- **Ranalli's Up North** · 1522 W Montrose Ave
- **Rosati's Pizza** · 4863 N Broadway St
- **Uptown Pizza** · 1031 W Wilson Dr

Post Offices

- 1343 W Irving Park Rd
- 4850 N Broadway Ave
- 1343 W Irving Park Ave

Schools

- **American Islamic College** · 640 W Irving Park Rd
- **Arai Middle School** · 900 W Wilson Ave
- **Day School** · 800 W Buena Ave
- **Goudy Elementary School** · 5120 N Winthrop Ave
- **Joseph Brennemann School** · 4251 N Clarendon Ave
- **Lakeview High School** · 4015 N Ashland Ave
- **McCutcheon Elementary School** ·
  4865 N Sheridan Rd
- **McCutcheon School** · 4850 N Kenmore Ave
- **Our Lady of Lourdes School** · 4641 N Ashland Ave
- **St Augustine College** · 1333 W Argyle St
- **St Mary of The Lake School** · 4201 N Kenmore Ave
- **St Thomas of Canterbury** · 4827 N Kenmore Ave
- **Stewart Elementary School** · 4525 N Kenmore Ave
- **Stockton Elementary School** · 4420 N Beacon St
- **Truman College** · 1145 W Wilson Ave
- **Van Nail School** · 1108 W Leland Ave
- **Walt Disney School** · 4140 N Marine Dr

 Supermarkets

- **Aldis** · 4440 N Broadway Dr

Map 40 · **Uptown**

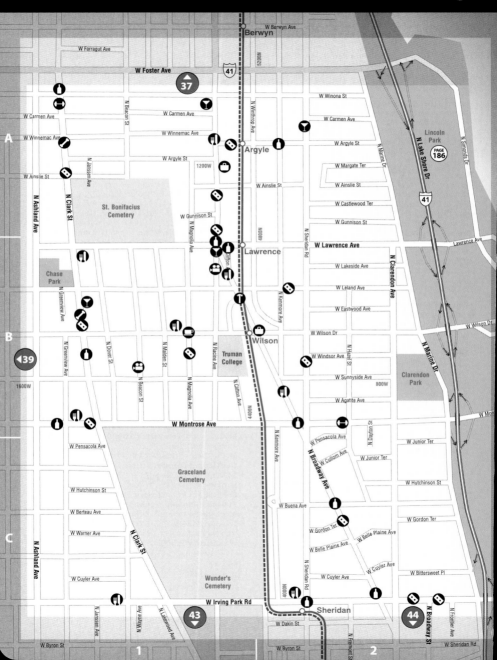

What do you expect in a neighborhood called the Psychiatric Ghetto? Thankfully, classic speakeasy Green Mill Pub, which opened in 1907, hasn't lost its vibe. Patronized by John Dillinger and Al Capone, this Chicago performance institution on Broadway specializes in live jazz and swing. If you haven't been to the Mill's Uptown Poetry Slam on Sundays, you must go.

Bars

- **Big Chicks** · 5024 N Sheridan Rd
- **Carols Pub** · 4659 N Clark St
- **Green Mill Pub** · 4802 N Broadway Ave
- **Lakeview Lounge** · 5110 N Broadway Ave

Coffee

- **Starbucks** · 4600 N Magnolia Ave

Gyms

- **Know No Limits** · 5121 N Clark St
- **World Gym Fitness Center** · 909 W Montrose Ave

 Hardware Store

- **Uptown Ace Hardware** · 4654 N Broadway Ave

Liquor Stores

- **Able Food & Liquor** · 4808 N Broadway Ave
- **Discount Food & Liquor** · 4007 N Broadway Ave
- **Foremost Liquor Stores** · 1040 W Argyle St
- **H Heinze Cut Rate Liquor** · 1021 W Montrose Ave
- **Hopleaf Bar** · 5148 N Clark St
- **Manhattan Food & Liquors** ·
  4200 N Broadway Ave
- **Rayan's Discount Liquors** · 1532 W Montrose Ave
- **Rayan's Liquor** · 4553 N Clark St
- **Saxony Liquor & Lounge** · 1136 W Lawrence Ave
- **Sheridan-Irving Liquor** · 3944 N Sheridan Rd

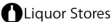 Movie Theaters

- **Black Ensemble Theatre** · 4520 N Beacon St
- **Riviera Night Club** · 4746 N Racine Ave

Pet Shops

- **Chicago Aquarium** · 5028 N Clark St
- **M & V Pet Shop** · 4623 N Clark St

Restaurants

- **Andies** · 1467 W Montrose Ave
- **Bale French Bakery** · 5018 N Broadway Ave
- **Don Quijote** · 4761 N Clark St
- **Frankie J's An American Theatre and Grill** ·
  4437 N Broadway St
- **Golden House Restaurant** ·
  4744 N Broadway Ave
- **Holiday Club** · 4000 N Sheridan Rd
- **Magnolia Café** · 1224 W Wilson Dr
- **Smoke Country House** · 1465 W Irving Park Rd

Shopping

- **Tai Nam Market Center** · 4925 N Broadway Ave
- **Wilson Broadway Mall** · 1114 W Wilson Dr

Video Rental

- **Albert Video** · 1435 W Montrose Ave
- **Bankok Video & Grocery** · 4617 N Clark St
- **Critic's Choice** · 655 W Irving Park Rd
- **Hollywood Video** · 4883 N Broadway Ave
- **Line Video** · 4554 N Magnolia Ave
- **Nationwide Video** · 736 W Irving Park Rd
- **Neehas Video Record Rental** ·
  1026 W Leland Ave
- **Power Video** · 4132 N Broadway St
- **United Video** · 4519 N Sheridan Rd
- **Video Express** · 1139 W Argyle St
- **Vietnam Video** · 4820 N Broadway Ave
- **World of Video** · 4923 N Clark St

Map 41 · **Avondale/Logan Square**

If hipster sightings are any indication, blue-collar Avondale is positioning itself as the new frontier in North Side urban gentrification. Roscoe Villagers and Logan Square residents branch ever outward searching for that elusive street parking.

$ Banks

- **Firstar Bank** · 3611 N Kedzie Ave
- **Harris Trust & Savings Bank** · 2927 W Addison St
- **North Community Bank** · 2800 W Belmont Ave

Car Washes

- **Gilbert's Carwash** · 3635 N Kedzie Ave
- **Tropical Car Wash** · 2933 N Elston Ave

Fire Department

- **Chicago District Fire Chiefs** · 3401 N Elston Ave

Gas Stations

- **Addison & Kedize Shell Service Station** · 3159 W Addison St
- **Citgo** · 3001 W Belmont Ave
- **Clark Station** · 2811 N Sacramento Ave
- **Fuel Express** · 2920 N California Ave
- **James Standard Service** · 3201 W Addison St

Pharmacies

- **Osco Drug** · 3572 N Elston Ave
- **Walgreens** · 3302 W Belmont Ave

Pizza

- **Little Caesar's** · 3135 W Addison St

Post Office

- 3750 N Kedzie Ave

Schools

- **DeVry Institute of Technology** · 3300 N Campbell Ave
- **Gordon Technical High School** · 3633 N California Ave
- **Grover Cleveland School** · 3121 W Byron St
- **Lane Tech Band** · 2501 W Addison St
- **Linne Elementary School** · 3221 N Sacramento Ave
- **Resurrection Catholic Academy** · 2845 W Barry Ave

Supermarkets

- **Carnicerias Guanajuato** · 3140 N California Ave
- **Dominicks** · 3300 W Belmont Ave
- **Hidalgo Supermercado** · 3705 N Kedzie Ave
- **Jewel** · 3572 N Elston Ave
- **Supermarcado** · 3001 W Diversey Ave

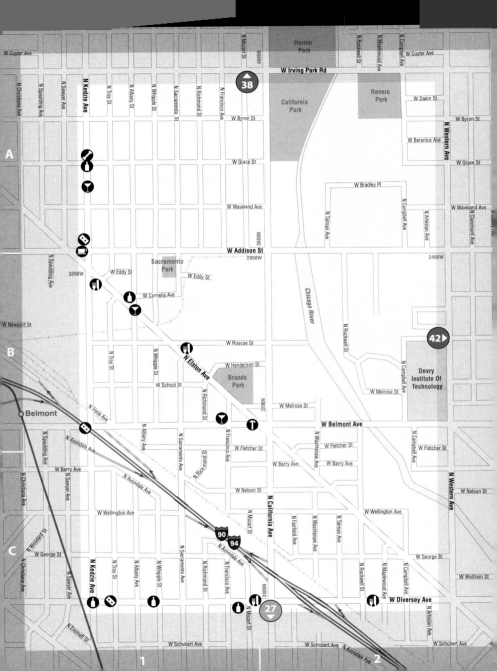

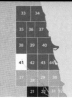
Corner taverns are still the entertainment as well as community centers. Residents rely on Dunkin Donuts for java. When Starbucks finally arrives, the real neighborhood will be lost.

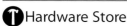 Bars
- **Chief O'Neill's** · 3471 N Elston Ave
- **Christine's Place** · 3759 N Kedzie Ave
- **Mycroft's** · 2900 W Belmont Ave

Coffee
- **Dunkin Donuts** · 3210 W Addison St

Hardware Store
- **Elston Ace Hardware** · 2825 W Belmont Ave

Liquor Stores
- **7-Eleven** · 3800 N Kedzie Ave
- **Discount Store** · 3457 N Albany Ave
- **JJ Peppers** · 3201 W Diversey Ave
- **Logan Square Liquor** · 2857 W Diversey Ave
- **Ramallah Foods & Liquor** · 3056 W Diversey Ave

Pet Shops
- **Harmony House for Cats** · 3809 N Kedzie Ave
- **Pet Supplies Plus** · 3640 N Elston Ave
- **VCA North Animal Hospital** · 3631 N Elston Ave

Restaurants
- **IHOP** · 2818 W Diversey Ave
- **La Finca** · 3361 N Elston Ave
- **Rancho Luna del Caribe** · 2554 W Diversey Ave
- **Sunshine Grill** · 3523 N Elston Ave

Video Rental
- **Blockbuster Video** · 3326 W Belmont Ave
- **Blockbuster Video** · 3233 W Addison St
- **Leo's Video** · 3151 W Diversey Ave

Map 42 · **North Center / West Lakeview**

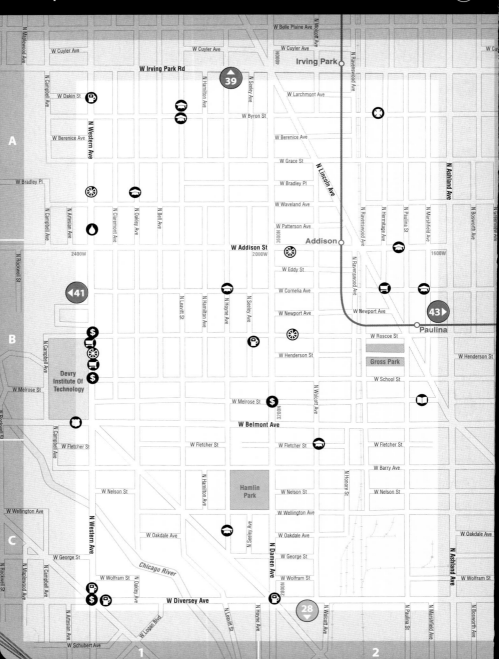

Map

The busy intersection of Western and Belmont was the grounds for Riverview Park, once the world's largest amusement park. Now it's a playground filled with funky bars, clubs and trendy restaurants. Within this recently gentrified area is small but popular Roscoe Village.

Banks

- **Lincoln Park Savings Bank** ·
  W Damen Ave & W Melrose St
- **North Community Bank** · 2800 N Western Ave
- **North Community Bank** · 3324 N Western Ave
- **North Community Bank** · 3401 N Western Ave

 Car Wash

- **Ultra Sonic Car Wash** · 3650 N Western Ave

 Fire Department

- **Chicago Fire Dept** · 1732 W Byron St

Gas Stations

- **Citgo** · 2401 W Diversey Ave
- **Gas For Less** · 2801 N Damen Ave
- **Speedway** · 3354 N Damen Ave
- **Western & Irving Amoco** · 3955 N Western Ave

Library

- **Lincoln-Belmont Library** · 1659 W Melrose St

Pizza

- **Carreno's Pizza** · 1955 W Addison St
- **Pete's Pizza & Restaurant** · 3737 N Western Ave
- **Robey Pizza Co.** · 1958 W Roscoe St

Police

- **Chicago District Police Dept** ·
  2452 W Belmont Ave

Schools

- **Alexander Hamilton Elementary School** ·
  1650 W Cornelia Ave
- **Bell Elementary School** · 3730 N Oakley Ave
- **Friedrich L Jahn School** · 3149 N Wolcott Ave
- **George Schneider School** · 2957 N Hoyne Ave
- **John L Audubon Elementary School** ·
  3500 N Hoyne Ave
- **St Andrew School** · 1710 W Addison St
- **St Benedict Grade School** · 3920 N Leavitt St
- **St Benedict High School** · 3900 N Leavitt St

Supermarkets

- **Dominicks** · 3350 N Western Ave
- **Jewel-Osco** · 3400 N Western Ave
- **Paulina Meat Market** · 3501 N Lincoln Ave

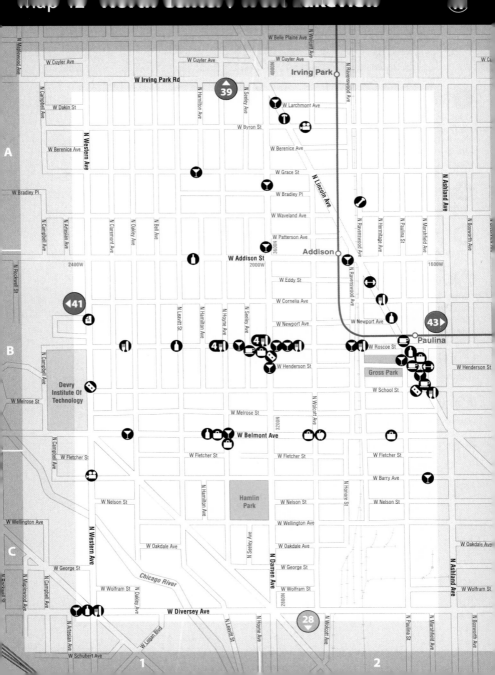

Restaurant Row is Roscoe Ave. between Damen and Western. While there are lots of new eateries to choose from, we still like the Village Tap. Pull up a bar stool for good grease, cold beer and jaw a while. Belmont Ave between Ashland and Western is lined with antique shops. Toy Town is our top pick.

Bars
- **Art of Sports** • 2444 W Diversey Ave
- **Beat Kitchen** • 2100 W Belmont Ave
- **Benedict's** • 3937 N Lincoln Ave
- **Black Rock** • 3614 N Damen Ave
- **Cody's Public House** • 1658 W Barry Ave
- **Four Moon Tavern** • 1847 W Roscoe St
- **Four Treys** • 3333 N Damen Ave
- **G & L Fire Escape** • 2157 W Grace St
- **JT Collins** • 3358 N Paulina St
- **Mulligan's Public House** • 2000 W Roscoe St
- **Riverview Tavern & Restaurant** • 1958 W Roscoe St
- **Tavern 33** • 3328 N Lincoln Ave
- **The Hungry Brain** • 2319 W Belmont Ave
- **The Village Tap** • 2055 W Roscoe St
- **Tiny Lounge** • 1814 W Addison St
- **Xippo** • 3759 N Damen Ave

Coffee
- **Dinkel's Bakery** • 3329 N Lincoln Ave
- **Starbucks** • 2023 W Roscoe St
- **Starbucks** • 3350 N Lincoln Ave
- **Su Van's Café and Bake Shop** • 3405 N Paulina St

Copy Shop
- **Kinko's** • 3435 N Western Ave

Farmer's Market
- **Roscoe Village** • W Belmont Ave & N Wolcott Ave

Gyms
- **Know No Limits** • 3530 N Lincoln Ave
- **Lakeview YMCA** • 3333 N Marshfield Ave

Hardware Store
- **Staubers Ace Hardware** • 3911 N Lincoln Ave

Liquor Stores
- **J R Food & Liquors** • 3356 N Paulina St
- **Miller's Tap & Liquor Store** • 2204 W Roscoe St
- **Miska's Liquor Store** • 2156 W Belmont Ave
- **Pelly's Liquors** • 3444 N Lincoln Ave
- **R & S Liquor** • 2425 W Diversey
- **West Lakeview Liquors** • 2156 W Addison St

Movie Theaters
- **American Blues Theatre** • 1909 W Byron St
- **Chicago Underground Film Festival** • 3109 N Western Ave

Pet Shop
- **Lucky Dog Pet Service** • 3729 N Ravenswood Ave

Restaurants
- **Brett's Café Americain** • 2011 W Roscoe St
- **Costello Sandwich & Sides** • 2015 W Roscoe St
- **El Tinajon** • 2054 W Roscoe St
- **Four Moon Tavern** • 1847 W Roscoe St
- **Hot Doug's** • 2314 W Roscoe St
- **Kitsch'n on Roscoe** • 2005 W Roscoe St
- **La Mora** • 2132 W Roscoe St
- **Lee's Chop Suey** • 2415 W Diversey Ave
- **Piazza Bella Trattoria** • 2116 W Roscoe St
- **Riverview Tavern** • 1958 W Roscoe St
- **Thai Linda Café** • 2022 W Roscoe St
- **The Village Tap** • 2055 W Roscoe St
- **Victory's Banner** • 2100 W Roscoe St
- **Wild Onion** • 3500 N Lincoln Ave
- **Wishbone** • 3300 N Lincoln St

Shopping
- **Antique Resources** • 1741 W Belmont Ave
- **Father Time Antiques** • 2108 W Belmont Ave
- **Good Old Days Antiques** • 2138 W Belmont Ave
- **Lynn's Hallmark** • 3353 N Lincoln Ave
- **Serendipity** • 2010 W Roscoe St
- **Toy Town** • 1903 W Belmont Ave

Video Rental
- **Blockbuster Video** • 1645 W School St
- **Blockbuster Video** • 3322 N Western Ave
- **Hard Boiled Records and Video** • 2008 W Roscoe St

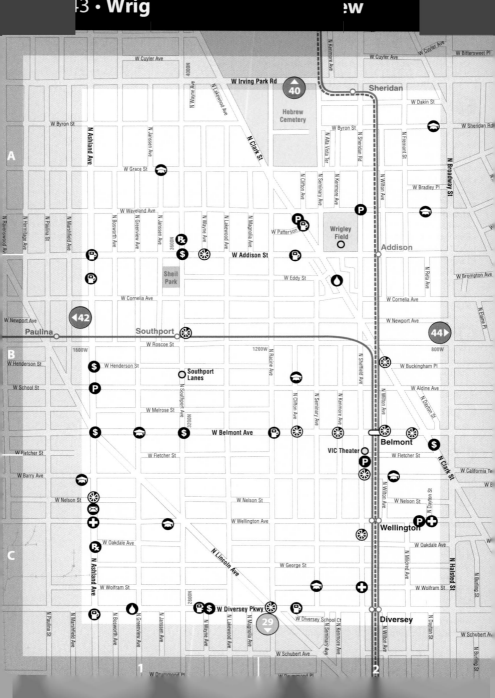

The Wrigleyville and East Lakeview neighborhoods rival Lincoln Park when it comes to a pleasant place to live. The area boasts a classic ballpark. Although upscale with rents and real estate values to prove it, the neighborhoods haven't lost what keeps them interesting. Corner taverns are second homes to ballpark denizens.

Map

Banks

- **BankOne** · 3335 N Ashland Ave
- **Corus Bank** · 3179 N Clark St
- **Corus Bank** · 3604 N Southport Ave
- **First American Bank** · 1345 W Diversey Pkwy
- **La Salle Bank** · 3201 N Ashland Ave
- **North Community Bank** · 1401 W Belmont Ave

Car Washes

- **Krystal's Hand Car Wash** · 3518 N Clark St
- **We'll Clean** · 1515 W Diversey Pkwy

Gas Stations

- **Addison & Ashland Shell** · 3552 N Ashland Ave
- **Ashland Diversey Shell** · 2801 N Ashland Ave
- **Auto Expert** · 1150 W Addison St
- **Bel Ray Amoco** · 1200 W Belmont Ave
- **Cub's Park Service Station** · 3648 N Clark St
- **S & D Amoco** · 1355 W Diversey Pkwy
- **Shell** · 1160 W Diversey Pkwy
- **Val's Amoco** · 3600 N Ashland Ave

Hospitals

- **Illinois Masonic Medical Center** · 3002 N Ashland Ave
- **Illinois Masonic Hospital** · 2835 N Sheffield Ave
- **Illinois Masonic Medical Center** · 836 W Wellington Ave

Landmarks

- **Southport Lanes** · 3325 N Southport Ave
- **Vic Theater** · 3145 N Sheffield Ave
- **Wrigley Field** · 1060 W Addison Ave

Parking

- 3650 N Clark St
- 3701 N Sheffield Ave
- 3138 N Sheffield Ave
- 836 W Wellington Ave
- 3300 N Ashland Ave

Pharmacies

- **Osco Drug** · 2940 N Ashland Ave
- **Osco Drug** · 3637 N Southport Rd

Pizza

- **Art Of Pizza** · 3033 N Ashland Ave
- **D'Agostino Pizzeria** · 1351 W Addison St
- **Gino's East Of Chicago** · 2801 N Lincoln Ave
- **Giordano's** · 1040 W Belmont Ave
- **Homemade Pizza Co** · 1137 W Belmont Ave
- **Logalbo's Pizzeria** · 3417 N Southport Ave
- **Marisa's Pizza** · 3341 N Clark St
- **Pat's Pizzeria** · 3114 N Sheffield Ave
- **Philly's Best** · 855 W Belmont Ave
- **Pizza Capri** · 964 W Belmont Ave
- **Pompei Bakery** · 2955 N Sheffield Ave

✉ Post Office

- 3026 N Ashland Ave

🎓 Schools

- **Augustus H Burley School** · 1630 W Barry Ave
- **Horace Greeley School** · 832 W Sheridan Rd
- **Inter-American Magnet School** · 919 W Barry Ave
- **James G Blaine School** · 1420 W Grace St
- **John V Le Moyne School** · 851 W Waveland Ave
- **Louis J Agassiz School** · 2851 N Seminary Ave
- **Nathaniel Hawthorne School** · 3319 N Clifton Ave
- **St Alphonsus School** · 1439 W Wellington Ave
- **St Luke Lutheran School** · 1500 W Belmont Ave

175

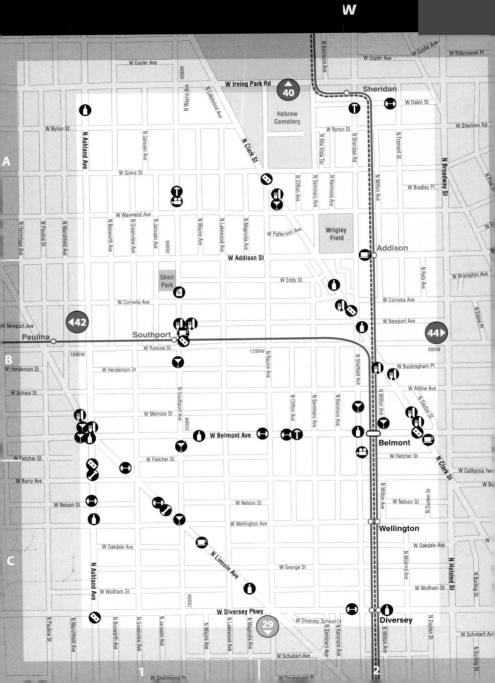

Bowling alley Southport Lanes still has pin boys. Metro is perhaps the City's best live music venue. We recommend the Brew & View movie nights at the vintage Vic Theater for cheap beers and good flicks. Go to the classic Music Box Theater built in 1929 on Southport for independent, underground films and foreign language movies.

Bars

- **Bungalow Bar and Lounge** ·
  1622 W Belmont Ave
- **Fizz Bar and Grill** · 3220 N Lincoln Ave
- **Justin's** · 3358 N Southport Ave
- **Lakeview Links** · 3206 N Wilton St
- **Lincoln Tap Room** · 3010 N Lincoln Ave
- **Metro** · 3730 N Clark St
- **Schuba's** · 3159 N Southport Ave
- **Sheffield's** · 3258 N Sheffield St

Coffee

- **Bean Caffe** · 2965 N Lincoln Ave
- **Caribou Coffee** · 3424 N Southport Ave
- **Coffee Craze** · 950 W Addison St
- **Starbucks** · 3184 N Clark St

Copy Shop

- **Kinko's** · 3524 N Southport Ave

Gyms

- **Chicago Fitness Center** · 3131 N Lincoln Ave
- **From the Center** · 3047 N Lincoln Ave
- **Lincoln Park Athletic Club** ·
  1019 W Diversey Pkwy
- **Rock Bodies Personal Training** ·
  1156 W Belmont Ave
- **Thousand Waves Spa for Women** ·
  1212 W Belmont Ave
- **Walk-a-Bye Baby Fitness** · 909 W Dakin St
- **Youthercise** · 3053 N Ashland Ave

Hardware Stores

- **Ace Hardware** · 3921 N Sheridan Rd
- **Klein True Value Hardware** ·
  3737 N Southport Ave
- **Tenenbaum Hardware & Paint** ·
  1138 W Belmont Ave

Liquor Stores

- **1000 Liquors** · 1000 W Belmont Ave
- **Ace Liquor Store** · 3949 N Ashland Ave
- **Bel-Port Food & Liquor** · 1362 W Belmont Ave
- **Courtesy Liquors** · 1622 W Belmont Ave
- **Foremost Liquor Stores** · 3014 N Ashland Ave
- **Gilday Liquors** · 946 W Diversey Pkwy
- **Gold Crown Liquors Store** · 3425 N Clark St
- **Kent Certified Wine Cellar** ·
  2860 N Lincoln Ave
- **Wrigleyville Food & Liquor** · 3515 N Clark St

Movie Theaters

- **Brew & View At The Vic** · 3145 N Sheffield Ave
- **Music Box Theatre** · 3733 N Southport Ave

Pet Shops

- **Aquatic World** · 3039 N Lincoln Ave
- **Petco** · 3122 N Ashland Ave

Restaurants

- **Bistro Zinc** · 3442 N Southport Ave
- **Heaven on Seven** · 3478 N Clark St
- **Mama Desta's Red Sea** · 3218 N Clark St
- **Mia Francesca** · 3311 N Clark St
- **Mongolian BBQ** · 3330 N Clark St
- **Shiroi Hana** · 3242 N Clark St
- **Technicolor Kitchen** · 3210 N Lincoln Ave
- **Tombo Kitchen** · 3244 N Lincoln Ave
- **Viennese Kaffee-Haus Brandt** ·
  3423 N Southport Ave
- **Wrigleyville Dog** · 3735 N Clark St

Video Rental

- **Blockbuster Video** · 2803 N Ashland Ave
- **City Lights Video** · 3761 N Racine Ave
- **Hollywood Video** · 3128 N Ashland Ave
- **Movie City** · 3456 N Clark St
- **Nationwide Video** · 843 W Belmont Ave
- **Southport Video** · 3408 N Southport Ave

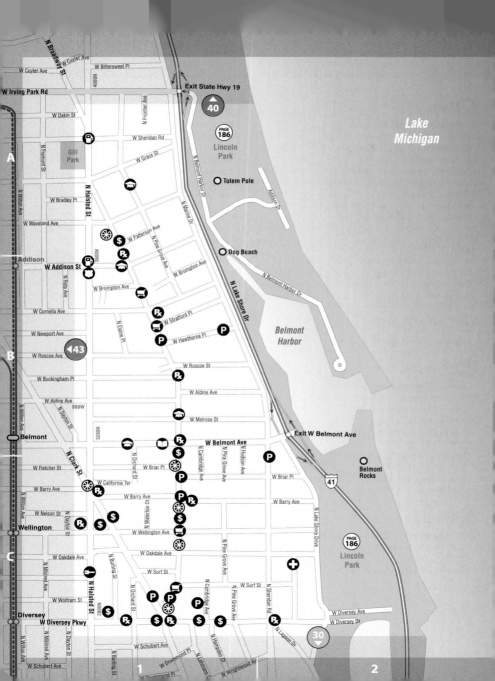

Lake Michigan

N Broadway St
W Cuyler Ave
W Cuyler Ave
W Bittersweet Pl
N 4000
Exit State Hwy 19
W Irving Park Rd
40
W Dakin St
PAGE 186
Lincoln Park
N Frontier Ave
W Sheridan Rd
A
Gill Park
W Grace St
N Fremont St
N Halsted St
N Marina Dr
Totem Pole
W Bradley Pl
N Belmont Harbor Dr
W Waveland Ave
W Patterson Ave
N Pine Grove Ave
Addison
W Addison St
W Brompton Ave
Dog Beach
N Reta Ave
W Brompton Ave
N Lake Shore Dr
N Belmont Harbor Dr
W Cornelia Ave
W Newport Ave
N Elaine Pl
W Stratford Pl
Belmont Harbor
B
W Roscoe Ave
143
W Hawthorne Pl
W Roscoe St
W Buckingham Pl
N Wilton Ave
N Dayton St
W Aldine Ave
800W
W Aldine Ave
N Clark St
3200N
W Melrose St
Belmont
W Belmont Ave
Exit W Belmont Ave
W Fletcher St
N Orchard St
W Briar Pl
N Cambridge Ave
N Pine Grove Ave
N Hudson Ave
W Briar Pl
41
Belmont Rocks
W Barry Ave
N Wilton Ave
W California Ter
W Barry Ave
N Dayton St
W Barry Ave
N Waterloo Ct
W Nelson St
Wellington
W Wellington Ave
N Lake Shore Drive
C
W Oakdale Ave
W Oakdale Ave
N Burling St
W Surf St
N Orchard St
N Cambridge Ave
N Pine Grove Ave
PAGE 186
Lincoln Park
N Mildred Ave
W Wolfram St
W Surf St
N Halsted St
W Surf St
N Sheridan Rd
Diversey
W Diversey Pkwy
N Wilton Ave
N Mildred Ave
N Dayton St
N Burling St
N Orchard St
W Diversey Ave
W Diversey Dr
30
N Lagoon Dr
W Schubert Ave
W Schubert Ave
W Drummond Pl
N Hampden Ct
N Lehmann Ct
W Wrightwood Ave
W Drummond Pl
1
2

The southeast section of East Lakeview is called Boystown, home of the Gay Pride parade and the equally flamboyant Halsted Street Market Days. Chicagoans of all stripes and from every strata flock to this hip lakefront neighborhood for entertainment. They drive around for hours looking for street parking.

Banks

- **BankOne** • 3032 N Clark St
- **Central Savings** • 2800 N Broadway St
- **La Salle Bank** • 3051 N Clark St
- **La Salle Bank** • 538 W Diversey Pkwy
- **Mid America Bank** • 3020 N Broadway St
- **North Community Bank** • 3180 N Broadway St
- **North Community Bank** • 3639 N Broadway St
- **North Community Bank** • 742 W Diversey Pkwy
- **St Paul Federal Bank-Savings** •
  664 W Diversey Pkwy

Car Rental

- **Budget** • 2901 N Halsted St •

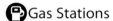 Gas Stations

- **Marathon** • 3901 N Broadway St
- **Somboon's Shell Service Station** •
  801 W Addison St

Hospital

- **St. Joseph's Hospital** •
  2913 N Commonwealth Ave

Landmarks

- **Belmont Rocks** • Briar Pl & Lake Michigan
- **Dog Beach** • Northern tip of Belmont Harbor
- **Totem Pole** • Waveland Ave& Belmont Harbor Dr

Library

- **John Merlo Public Library** • 644 W Belmont Ave

Parking

- Between Roscoe St & Buckingham Pl
- 2848 N Broadway St
- 3440 N Broadway St
- 3115 N Broadway St
- 3157 N Broadway St
- 600 W Diversey Pkwy
- 2836 N Clark St
- 3170 N Sheridan Rd
- 525 W Hawthorne Pl

Pharmacies

- **CVS Procare Pharmacy** • 3337 N Broadway St
- **CVS Procare Pharmacy Broadway** •
  N Broadway St & W Barry Ave
- **Osco Drug** • 3101 N Clark St
- **Osco Drug** • 3531 N Broadway St
- **Stone Medical Pharmacy** • 2800 N Sheridan
- **Walgreens** • 3046 N Halsted St
- **Walgreens** • 3201 N Broadway St
- **Walgreens** • 3646 N Broadway St
- **Walgreens** • 740 W Diversey Pkwy
- **Walgreens** • 2801 N Broadway St

Pizza

- **Domino's** • 3103 N Clark St
- **Mac's Pizza** • 606 W Briar Pl
- **Nancy's Pizza** • 2930 N Broadway St
- **Pizza Hut** • 3034 N Broadway St
- **Pizza Primavera** • 3702 N Broadway St
- **Renaldi's Pizza Pub** • 2827 N Broadway St

Police

- **Chicago District Stations** • 3600 N Halsted St

 Schools

- **Bernard Zell Anshe Emet Day School** •
  3760 N Pine Grove Ave
- **Lake View Academy** • 716 W Addison St
- **Louis Nettelhorst School** • 3252 N Broadway St
- **Mt Carmel Academy** • 720 W Belmont Ave

Supermarkets

- **Dominicks** • 3012 N Broadway St
- **Jewel** • 3531 N Broadway St
- **Treasure Island** • 3460 N Broadway St

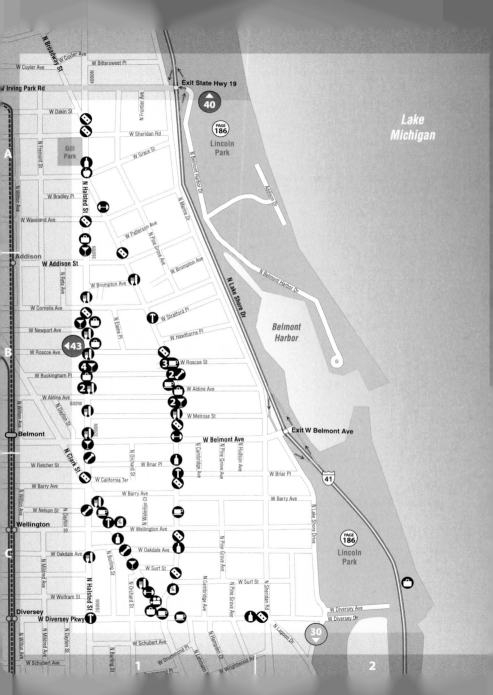

Posh restaurants and high-end shops mingle with the neighborhood's tattoo parlors and sex shops. The Melrose is a classic diner slinging good grease and hearty breakfasts. Yoshi's Café on Halsted is everybody's favorite Asian restaurant; try the wontons. Dog Beach at Belmont Harbor's sandbox is always packed with pooches and their socializing owners.

Bars

- **Circuit** · 3641 N Halsted St
- **Cocktail** · 3359 N Halsted St
- **Duke of Perth** · 2913 N Clark St
- **Manhole** · 3458 N Halsted St
- **Roscoe's** · 3354-56 N Halsted St
- **Sidetrack** · 3345-55 N Halsted St
- **Spin** · 3201 N Halsted St
- **The Closet** · 3251 N Broadway St
- **Town Hall Pub** · 3340 N Halsted St

Coffee

- **Borders** · 2817 N Clark St
- **Caribou Coffee** · 3025 N Clark St
- **Caribou Coffee** · 3300 N Broadway St
- **Coffee & Tea Exchange** · 3311 N Broadway St
- **Intelligentsia Coffee Roasters** · 3123 N Broadway St
- **Seattle's Best** · 2951 N Broadway St
- **Starbucks** · 3358 N Broadway St
- **Starbucks** · 617 W Diversey St

Copy Shops

- **Kinko's** · 3001 N Clark St
- **Office Max** · 2832 N Broadway St

Farmer's Market

- **North Halsted** · W Broadway St & N Halsted St

Gyms

- **Bally's Total Fitness** · 2828 N Clark St
- **Chicago Sweat Shop** · 3215 N Broadway St
- **Quads Gym** · 3727 N Broadway St

Hardware Stores

- **Clark Street Ace Hardware** · 3011 N Clark St
- **Edwards True Value Hardware** · 2804 N Halsted St
- **Lehman's True Value Hardware** · 3473 N Broadway St
- **Midtown True Value Hardware** · 3130 N Broadway St

Liquor Stores

- **Binny's Beverage Depot** · 3000 N Clark St
- **Broadway Food & Liquor** · 3158 N Broadway St
- **Eastgate Wine & Spirits** · 446 W Diversey Pkwy
- **Gold Medal Liquors** · 3823 N Broadway St
- **Paradise Liquors** · 2934 N Broadway St

Movie Theater

- **Landmark Century Cinema** · 2828 N Clark St

Pet Shops

- **Barker & Meowsky** · 3319 N Broadway St
- **Groomingdales Pet Salon** · 3165 N Halsted St
- **Happy Tails** · 3335 N Broadway St
- **Petco** · 3046 N Halsted St
- **Scrub Your Pup** · 2935 N Clark St

Restaurants

- **Angelina** · 3561 N Broadway St
- **Arco de Cuchilleros** · 3445 N Halsted St
- **Chicago Diner** · 3411 N Halsted St
- **Clark Street Dog** · 3040 N Clark St
- **Erwin** · 2925 N Halsted St
- **Jack's on Halsted** · 3201 N Halsted St
- **La Creperie** · 2845 N Clark St
- **Las Mananitas** · 3523 N Halsted St
- **Mark's Chop Suey** · 3343 N Halsted St
- **Nookie's Tree** · 3334 N Halsted St
- **The Melrose** · 3233 N Broadway St
- **Yoshi's Café** · 3257 N Halsted St

Shopping

- **Century Mall** · 2828 N Clark St
- **Evil Clown Compact Discs** · 3418 N Halsted St
- **Gallimaufry Gallery** · 3345 N Halsted St
- **GayMart** · 3457 N Halsted St
- **The Brown Elephant Resale** · 3651 N Halsted St
- **Toyscape** · 2911 N Broadway St
- **Unabridged Bookstore** · 3251 N Broadway St

Video Rental

- **Blockbuster Video** · 3120 N Clark St
- **Broadway Video** · 3916 N Broadway St
- **Golden Video** · 3619 N Broadway St
- **Hollywood Video** · 2868 N Broadway
- **Mr Video** · 3356 N Broadway St
- **Nationwide Video** · 2827 N Broadway St
- **Nationwide Video** · 3936 N Clarendon Ave
- **R J's Video** · 3452 N Halsted St
- **Specialty Video** · 3221 N Broadway St
- **Video Island** · 440 W Diversey Pkwy
- **West Coast Video** · 3114 N Broadway St
- **Windy City Video** · 3701 N Halsted St

Grant Park · Parks & Places

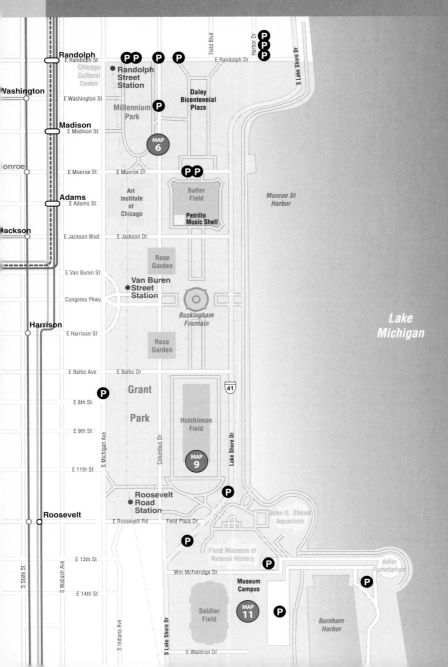

Randolph
E Randolph St
Chicago Cultural Center

Washington
E Washington St

Madison
E Madison St

onroe
E Monroe St

Adams
E Adams St

Jackson
E Jackson Blvd

E Van Buren St

Harrison
E Harrison St

E Balbo Ave

E 8th St

E 9th St

E 11th St

Roosevelt

E 13th St

S State St
S Wabash Ave

E 14th St

Field Blvd
Harbor Dr
E Randolph Dr

Randolph Street Station

Daley Bicentennial Plaza

Millennium Park

E Washington St

E Madison St

MAP 6

E Monroe Dr

Art Institute of Chicago

Butler Field

Petrillo Music Shell

Monroe St Harbor

E Jackson Dr

Rose Garden

Van Buren Street Station

Buckingham Fountain

Rose Garden

E Balbo Dr

Grant Park

Hutchinson Field

41

S Michigan Ave

Columbus Dr

Lake Shore Dr

MAP 9

Roosevelt Road Station

E Roosevelt Rd
Field Plaza Dr

John G. Shedd Aquarium

Field Museum of Natural History

Wm McFetridge Dr

Museum Campus

Soldier Field

MAP 11

S Indiana Ave
S Lake Shore Dr

E Waldron Dr

Adler Planetarium

Burnham Harbor

Lake Michigan

S Lake Shore Dr

Overview

Grant Park is Chicago's favorite place to promenade, picnic, protest, party and play. Art permeates the park year-round from landscaped gardens, sculpture and Buckingham Fountain to concerts, the Art Institute of Chicago and Museum Campus - all on Grant Park's 319 acres.

Called Chicago's "front lawn," Grant Park stretches along the lakeshore from Randolph St. south to Roosevelt Rd. and west to Michigan Ave. where grass meets glass. Although the City's massive Summer Festivals turn the park into Chicago's doormat, Grant Park is usually a quiet place with open space to relax and play.

Architect Daniel Burnham laid the groundwork for the park. However, thank Chicago catalog king Aaron Montgomery Ward for pressuring the State of Illinois in 1911 to preserve the land as "public ground forever to remain vacant of buildings." Grant Park's development dragged on till 1934. History repeats itself. Traffic-traumatized Chicagoans pray that construction of the new Millennium Park complex at Grant Park's northwest corner will be complete by next century.

Nature

Grant Park's lawns, gardens, lakefront and bench-lined paths attract office workers on break, including runners, bicyclists, readers and thinkers (some disguised as snoozing homeless). South of Buckingham Fountain are the formal Music Garden and Rose Gardens. Near Daley Bicentennial Plaza is the riotously colorful Wildflower Garden recalling Illinois' prairies past. These gardens are butterfly and bird havens. Throughout the park are 18 sculptures created between 1893 and 1988.

Sports

Chicagoans play in Grant Park like kids in their back yards. After work, balls, kites and Frisbees fly across Butler and Hutchinson Fields. Summer softball leagues fill baseball diamonds in the park's south end near the first-come-first-serve free tennis courts. Picnics for 50 or more people and tent set-up require permits from the Chicago Park District, 312-742-7529; www.chicagoparkdistrict.com.

On the park's north side is Daley Bicentennial Plaza, 337 E. Randolph St., 312-742-7648, with a fitness center, skating rink and 12 outdoor tennis courts. Year-round tennis hours are weekdays, 7 a.m. to 10 p.m.; weekends, 8 a.m. to 5 p.m. Court time costs $7 an hour (2 hour limit); reservations recommended, 312-742-7650. The rink is open daily November to March for ice skating ($2, skate rental available), and free in-line skating on off-ice months.

Buckingham Fountain

Buckingham Fountain is Grant Park's spouting centerpiece at the intersection of Congress Pkwy. and Columbus Dr. Designed by Edward Bennett and first operational in 1927, Buckingham Fountain showers onlookers with wind-blown spray April through October from 10 a.m. to 11 p.m. daily. For 20 minutes every hour on the hour the center basin jettisons water 150 feet. Beginning at dusk at the same times, the skyrocketing water display is accompanied by lights and music. Food concessions and restrooms are nearby.

Art Institute of Chicago

The Art Institute has 12 extensive, permanent collections, plenty of exhibitions, and also hosts interesting public programs daily, even on the free day- Tuesday. Other days, a $10 donation is requested. The handy "Pocketguide" breaks collections down into hour-at-a-time visits, perfect and impressive for Loop lunch dates. Open June through September, the outdoor Garden Restaurant has live music some evenings. The museum is open weekdays 10:30 a.m. to 4:30 p.m. (Tuesdays open till 8 p.m.), and weekends 10 a.m. to 5 p.m. 111 S. Michigan Ave., 312-443-3600; www.artic.edu.

Festivals & Events

Chicagoans gather at the Petrillo Music Shell, Jackson Blvd. and Columbus Dr., for free Grant Park Orchestra and Chorus concerts June through August on Wednesday and Sunday evenings, (312-742-4763); www.grantparkmusicfestival.com. You can't always pass up a free headliner concert at Grant Park's monstrous Summer Festivals. Avoid the gut-to-gut, al fresco feeding frenzy at 10-day Taste of Chicago by going, if you must, on a weekday. Contact the Mayor's Office of Special Events for a complete event schedule, 312-744-3315; www.cityofchicago.org/SpecialEvents.

How to Get There

By Car: Exits off Lake Shore Dr. west to Grant Park are Randolph St., Monroe Dr., Jackson Dr., Balbo Dr. and Roosevelt Rd. Also, enter the park from Michigan Ave. heading east on the same streets. The underground East Monroe Garage is off Monroe Dr. Columbus Dr. runs through Grant Park's center, and has metered parking.

By Train: From the Richard B. Ogilvie Transportation Center, travel east to Michigan Ave. and Grant Park on CTA buses 56, 20 and 157 ($1.50 one way). From Union Station board CTA buses 60, 157, 123 and 151.

Metra trains coming from the south stop at the Roosevelt Rd. station on the south end of Grant Park before terminating travel at the underground Randolph St. station below Millennium Park.

By El: Get off at any El stop in the Loop between Randolph St. and Van Buren St. ($1.50 one way). Walk two blocks east to Grant Park.

By Bus: CTA buses 151, 145, 146, 147, 3 and 10 (weekends only) stop along Michigan Ave. in front of Grant Park ($1.50 one way).

Millennium Park · Parks & Places

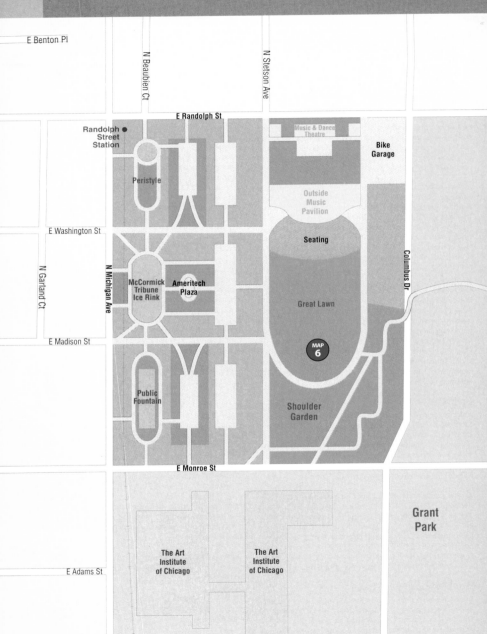

E Benton Pl

N Beaubien Ct

N Stetson Ave

E Randolph St

Randolph Street Station

Peristyle

Music & Dance Theatre

Bike Garage

Outside Music Pavilion

Seating

E Washington St

N Garland Ct

N Michigan Ave

McCormick Tribune Ice Rink

Ameritech Plaza

Great Lawn

Columbus Dr

MAP 6

E Madison St

Public Fountain

Shoulder Garden

E Monroe St

The Art Institute of Chicago

The Art Institute of Chicago

Grant Park

E Adams St

Overview

It seems like centuries of construction since Mayor Daley unveiled the grandiose Millennium Park plan for Grant Park's northwest corner. The 24-acre cultural and recreational complex bounded by Michigan Ave., Columbus Dr., Randolph Dr. and Monroe St. will eventually include landscaped gardens, sculpture, performance venues, restaurants and a 400-space indoor bicycle parking facility. The ice rink and underground garages are open now.

The park's master plan is as ambitious as it is behind schedule and over budget. The price tag has soared from $150 million to almost $400 million. Private donations exceeding $100 million will help pay for the project, whose target completion date was originally summer 2000. Now the goal is 2004.

Millennium Park officials keep promising it will be worth the pounding headaches construction has caused. But as the project drags on, we're asking the same question as Frank Gehry, architect of the park's music pavilion, did in a 2001 Chicago Tribune interview: "Why is it taking so [expletive] long?"

Music Pavilion

The park's 4,000-seat music pavilion, intended to replace the Petrillo Band Shell, was designed by renowned architect Frank Gehry. In keeping with his steely design for the Guggenheim Museum in Bilbao, Spain, the Millennium Park outdoor concert hall's roof is made of unfurling stainless steel bands curlicue-ing 40 feet into the sky. The stage faces south towards the 95,000-square-foot Great Lawn that will seat up to 7,000. All pavilion events will be free.

Music & Dance Theatre

The underground 1,500-seat theatre is located behind the pavilion and will become home to nonprofit performing arts groups. A restaurant is on the drawing board. Two underground parking garages flank the theatre.

Nature & Sculpture

Gardens with sculpted hedges and flowing water designed by Kathyrn Gustafson are planned for the park's southeast corner bordered by Monroe St. Slated to open by 2006, the Art Institute's proposed, pricey addition by architect Renzo Piano will overlook them. A replica of Grant Park's original Peristyle of Greek Columns from 1917 anchors Millennium Park's northwest corner. A dramatic fountain will grace the southwest corner. On top of a proposed 300-seat restaurant next to the ice rink on Michigan Ave. will be Ameritech Plaza, featuring a 66-foot long, 100-ton, jelly bean-shaped sculpture of polished stainless steel by Anish Kapoor, his first public work installed in the United States. Mayor Daley's graffiti busters better be ready to blast that bean once it arrives.

Sports

While Millennium Park's construction moves at glacial speed, the McCormick Tribune Ice Rink has been operational since December, 2001. The 15,910 square-foot rink is open daily starting in November. Admission is free; skate rental available ($3 per session). In summer, the rink doubles as a dance floor and activity center. 55 N. Michigan Ave., 312-742-5222; www.chicagoparkdistrict.com.

How to Get There

No matter your mode of travel, approach the area around Millennium Park with patience and allow extra time. For train, El and bus transportation recommendations see NFT's Grant Park section. Metra's Randolph St. train station servicing only south-bound trains is located under Millennium Park. Contact the RTA Information Center, 312-836-7000; www.rtachicago.com; for schedules and fares.

The park's garages are open. Access the Grant Park North Garage from Michigan Ave. Enter Millennium Park Garage from the lower levels of Randolph St. and mid-level of Columbus Dr. (12 hours or less, $10).

Additional Information

Public Building Commission Chicago, 312-744-3090; www.pbcchicago.com

Lincoln Park · Parks & Places

Overview

The largest of Chicago's 552 parks, Lincoln Park stretches 1,208-acres along the lakefront from North Ave. to Hollywood Ave. Sports enthusiasts and culture seekers find satisfaction indoors and out. Public buildings including animal houses at the Lincoln Park Zoo, Café Brauer, Peggy Notebaert Nature Museum and vintage beach bath houses make the park as architecturally attractive as it is naturally beautiful.

Nature

Much of southern Lincoln Park is open green space popular for football, soccer, dog play and barbeques. Paths shaded by mature trees lead to stoic statues. Until the 1860's, portions of this area were municipal cemetery populated with cholera and small pox victims buried in shallow graves. Although the City attempted to relocate all the bodies in the cemetery-to-park conversion, digging doggies may unearth more than picnickers' chicken bones.

In Spring, bird watchers flock to Lincoln Park's ponds and nature trails. Addison Bird Sanctuary Viewing Platform north of Belmont Harbor overlooks five fenced-in acres of wetlands and woods. Birding programs are held around Montrose Point, 312-742-7529; www.chicagoparkdistrict.com. The Chicago Ornithological Society, 312-409-9678; www.chicagobirder.org, leads walks around North Pond. The Fort Dearborn Chapter of the Illinois Audubon Society, 847-675-3622, hosts free park and zoo bird walks. Migratory birds gather around the revamped 1889 lily pond at Fullerton Ave. and N. Cannon Dr.

Sports

Baseball diamonds on the park's south end are bordered by La Salle Dr. and Lake Shore Dr. next to the newly renovated field house and NorthStar Eatery. Upgrades planned for the area include a running track, soccer field, basketball and volleyball courts. Bicyclists and runners race along Lincoln Park Lagoon to the footbridge over Lake Shore Dr. to North Ave. Beach, Chicago's volleyball mecca. To reserve courts and rent equipment, go to the south end of the landmark, boat-shaped bath house, 312-742-3224. The upper deck of Chicago Beach Café rocks on weekends with live music. Just north of the bath house is a seasonal rollerblade rink and fitness club.

Nine-hole Sydney R. Marovitz Public Golf Course, 3600 N. Recreation Dr., 312-742-7930, hosts hackers year-round. Snail-slow play allows plenty of time to enjoy skyline views from this lakefront cow pasture that is

always crowded, thanks to bargain pricing ($7 to $17; club rental, $10). Reserve tee times, 312-245-0909, or show up at sunrise. The starter sits in the northeast corner of the clock tower field house.

Twenty first-come-first-served free tennis courts are on Recreational Dr. north of Belmont Harbor beside baseball diamonds, playing fields and a playground. Four courts are next to the new Diversey Miniature Golf Course. Also nearby is the year-round Diversey Golf Range, 141 W. Diversey Pkwy, 312-742-7929. Tennis courts are open 8 a.m. to 8 p.m. and for May through October, reservations are recommended, 312-742-7821 ($12 per hour). The Lincoln Park Tennis Association plays on six neighboring courts, 773-929-3671.

Members of the Lincoln Park Boat Club row in Lincoln Park Lagoon. Rowing classes for the public are offered May through September, 773-549-2628; www.lpbc.net. Ply whimsical swan-shaped paddleboats at South Pond next to Café Brauer, 2021 N. Stockton Dr., a restored Prairie School national landmark, housing seasonal restaurants and an upstairs ballroom. Fishermen frequent South Pond and the lagoon. Belmont, Montrose and Diversey Harbors allow shore fishing. North of Montrose Harbor on lakefront N. Wilson Dr. is a new, free skateboard park.

Lincoln Park Zoo

Address: *2200 N. Cannon Dr.*
Phone: *312-742-2000*
Website: *www.lpzoo.com*
Hours: *Daily, 8-6 p.m.; animal buildings 10-5 p.m.*

Established in 1868, Lincoln Park Zoo is the nation's oldest free zoo. National television shows "Zoo Parade" and Ray Rayner's Show "Ark in the Park" were filmed here. Supported by big corporate sponsorships and private funds, new Zoo improvements include "Farm in the Zoo" and "African Journey," opening Spring 2003. The Zoo's elephants, giraffes, hippos and rhinos will return and be joined in the new exhibit by other species native to the continent's natural habitats. Flanking the Zoo's northwest side is the free Lincoln Park Conservatory.

Peggy Notebaert Nature Museum

Address: *2430 N. Cannon Dr.*
Phone: *773-755-5100*
Website: *www.naturemuseum.org*
Hours: *M-F 9-4:30 p.m.; S-S 10-5 p.m.*
Admission: *$6, Tuesdays free*

The Peggy Notebaert Nature Museum succeeds at making Illinois' level landscape interesting. The contemporary version of the 1857 Chicago Academy of Sciences, this hands-on museum depicts the close connection between urban and natural environments. A flowing water lab and flitting butterfly haven invite return visits.

Chicago Historical Society

Address: *Clark St. & North Ave.*
Phone: *312-642-4600*
Website: *www.chicagohistory.org*
Hours: *Mon-Sat 9:30-4:30 p.m.; Sun: 12-5 p.m.*
Admission: *$5, Mondays free*

The Chicago Historical Society preserves the life and times of Chicago's citizens. Exhibits on the City's pioneer roots, architecture, music, fashion, neighborhoods and windy politics breathe life into otherwise dry history. Chicagoans access the excellent free research center (open Tuesday through Saturday) for genealogical information and housing history. Big Shoulders Café is a good, light lunch spot.

Performances

Lincoln Park Cultural Center, 2045 N. Lincoln Park West, 312-742-7726, produces plays, theater workshops and family performances year-round. Theater on The Lake, Fullerton Ave. and Lake Shore Dr., 312-742-7994, performs nine weeks of alternative drama in summer ($12). Lincoln Park Zoo has outdoor summer concerts. Call events hotline, 312-742-2283.

How to Get There

By Car: Lake Shore Dr. exits to Lincoln Park are Bryn Mawr Ave., Foster Ave., Lawrence Ave., Wilson Dr., Montrose Dr., Irving Park Pkwy., Belmont Ave., Fullerton Ave. and North Ave.

Free parking lots are at Recreational Dr. near Belmont Harbor and Simonds Dr. near Montrose Harbor. Paid lots are at North Ave. Beach, Chicago Historical Society, Lincoln Park Zoo and Grant Hospital Garage. Stockton Dr. and Cannon Dr. have free street parking. A metered lot is on Diversey Pkwy. next to the golf range.

By Bus: CTA buses 151, 156, 77, 146 and 147 travel through Lincoln Park ($1.50 one way). For schedules and fares, contact the RTA Information Center, 312-836-7000; www.rtachicago.com.

By El: Get off the Red Line at any stop between Fullerton Ave. and Bryn Mawr Ave. ($1.50 one way). Head one mile east.

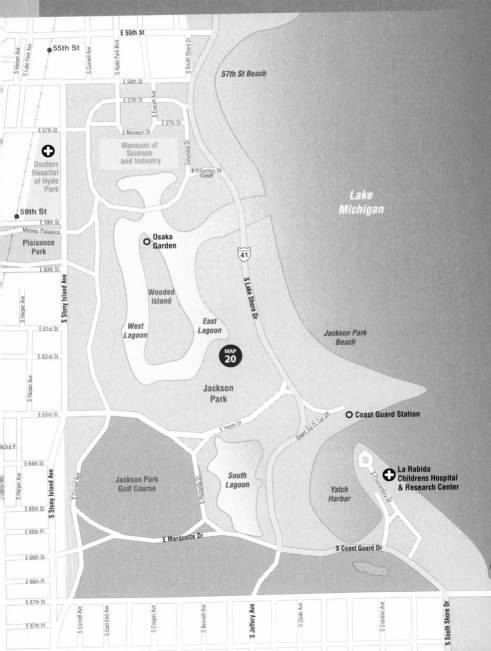

Overview

The South Side's answer to Lincoln Park, historic Jackson Park forms the eastern edge of Hyde Park, the diverse neighborhood of the University of Chicago.

Jackson Park's history is rooted in humankind's quest for discovery. It was the site of the 1893 World's Columbian Exposition. Architect Daniel Burnham, chief of construction for the Exposition, transformed the windswept lakefront into a shimmering "White City" with lagoons, landscaped gardens, sculpture, harbors and ornate, landmark buildings to house exhibits from around the world. Today, the Museum of Science and Industry and La Rabida Children's Hospital and Research Center occupy two former Fair structures.

Until recently, Jackson Park had gone to seed. But things are coming up roses again, thanks to clean and green Mayor Daley's passion for the City's parks. Major improvements to the area's lakefront, bike path and beaches have Jackson Park shimmering again.

Museum of Science and Industry

Address: *57th St. and Lake Shore Dr.*
Phone: *773-684-1414*
Website: *www.msichicago.org*
Hours: *M-F 9:30am-4 pm; Sa-Su 9:30am-5:30pm*
Admission: *Adults $9; Chicagoans $8*

The 1893 Exhibition's original Arts Palace is now the 350,0000-square foot Museum of Science and Industry. Generations of Chicagoans have been wowed by the Human Body Slices, U-505 (the only World War II German submarine captured), 3,000-square foot Model Railroad and Walk-Through Heart. "Genetics: Decoding Life", the museum's newest permanent exhibit, explores cloning, genetic engineering and the human genome project. For relief from brain freeze, check out the fast food toy exhibit, early spacecrafts that look like toys, and the Fairy Castle.

Nature

The East and West Lagoons surround Wooded Island, also called Paul H. Douglas Nature Sanctuary. On the Island's northern tip is Osaka Garden, a serene Japanese garden with an authentic tea house and entrance gate. The ceremonial garden, like the golden Statue of The Republic on Hayes Ave., recalls the park's 1893 Exposition origins. The Chicago Audubon Society, 773-539-6793, conducts bird walks here and in nearby Bob-O-Link Meadow. These sites and the Perennial Garden at 59th St. and Cornell Dr. are butterfly havens.

Sports

When Jackson Park Golf Course opened in 1899 it was the Midwest's first public course. Certified by the Audubon Cooperative Sanctuary, the 18-hole course has wilderness habitats - or are those scruffy fairways? Weekend greens fees are $20. A driving range is adjacent to the course. 312-245-0909.

Jackson Park field house has a weight room and gymnasium. From Hayes Dr. north along Cornell Dr. are outdoor tennis courts, baseball diamonds and a running track. Tennis courts are on the west side of Lakeshore Dr. at 63rd St. Jackson Park's beaches are at 57th St. and 63rd St. (water playground too). Inner and Outer Harbors allow shore fishing. 6401 S. Stony Island Ave., 312-747-6187.

Neighboring Parks

North of Jackson Park at 55th St. and Lake Shore Dr. is Promontory Point, a scenic lakeside picnic spot. Harold Washington Park, 51st St. and Lake Shore Dr., has a model yacht basin and eight tennis courts on 53rd St.

To the west, 460-acre Washington Park, 5531 S. Martin Luther King Dr., 312-747-6823, has an outdoor swimming pool, playing fields, nature areas, Lorado Taft's 1922 Fountain of Time sculpture and the DuSable Museum of African American History, 740 E. 56th Pl., 773-947-0600; www.dusablemuseum.org.

At 71st St. and South Shore Dr. are South Shore Beach, a harbor, bird sanctuary and South Shore Cultural Center, 7059 S. Shore Dr., 312-747-2536. South Shore Golf Course is a nine-hole, public course, 312-245-0909.

How to Get There

By Car: From the Loop, drive south on Lake Shore Dr. exit west on 57th St. From the south, take I-94 west. Exit on Stony Island Ave. heading north to 57th Dr. The museum's parking garage entrance is on 57th Dr. The Music Court lot is behind the museum. A free parking lot is on Hayes Dr.

By Bus: From the Loop, CTA buses 6 and 10 (weekends and daily in summer) stop by the museum.

By El: (the quickest way to get to Jackson Park): Take the Red or Green Lines to the Garfield Blvd. (55th St.) station stop ($1.50 one way); walk two blocks east or transfer to the eastbound 55 bus ($1.80 one way).

By Train: Sporadic service. From the Loop's Randolph St. and Van Buren St. stations, take Metra Electric service ($1.95 one way). Trains stop at the 55th, 56th and 57th St. station platform (maybe under construction). Walk two blocks east. From Richard B. Ogilvie Transportation Center, walk two blocks south to Union Station on Canal St. and catch CTA bus 1.

Museum Campus · Parks & Places

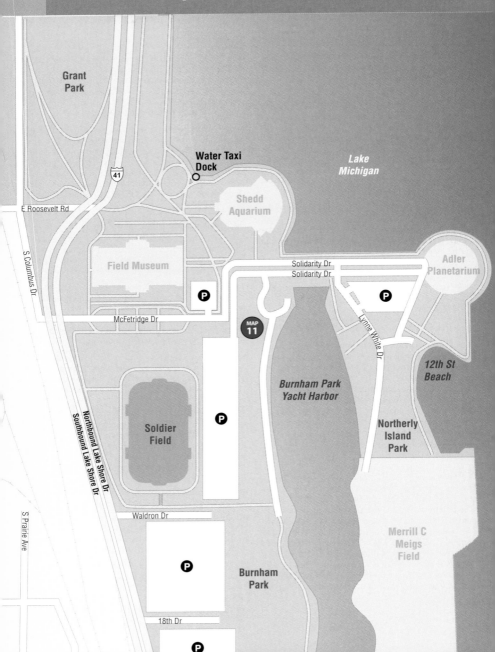

Grant Park

Water Taxi Dock

Lake Michigan

41

E Roosevelt Rd

Shedd Aquarium

Solidarity Dr
Solidarity Dr

Adler Planetarium

Field Museum

P

McFetridge Dr

P

Lynne White Dr

MAP 11

12th St Beach

Burnham Park Yacht Harbor

Northbound Lake Shore Dr
Southbound Lake Shore Dr

Soldier Field

P

Northerly Island Park

S Columbus Dr

Waldron Dr

Merrill C Meigs Field

S Prairie Ave

P

Burnham Park

18th Dr

P

Overview

The Museum Campus is the ultimate educational field trip. South of Grant Park at the intersection of Roosevelt Rd. and Lake Shore Dr., visitors can walk through uninterrupted lakefront parkland among three world-renowned institutions - Field Museum, Shedd Aquarium and Adler Planetarium. However, it wasn't always a sprawling grassy peninsula on Burnham Park's northern edge. Mayor Daley championed the rerouting of Lake Shore Dr. to create the Museum Campus, which opened in 1998.

Field Museum of Natural History

Address:	1400 S. Lake Shore Dr.
Phone:	312-922-9410
Website:	www.fieldmuseum.org
Hours:	M-F 10-5 p.m.; S-S 9-5 p.m.
Admission:	$8

Approach the Field Museum of Natural History as though it were a smorgasbord. The massive, classical Greek architectural-style museum constructed in 1921 houses over 20 million artifacts. From dinosaurs, diamonds and earthworms to man-eating lions, totem poles and mummies, there is just too much to savor in a single sitting. Some temporary exhibits and the Underground Adventure cost an additional $6. Free museum tours are weekdays at 11 a.m. and 2 p.m.

John G. Shedd Aquarium

Address:	1200 S. Lake Shore Dr.
Phone:	312-939-2438
Website:	www.shedd.org
Hours:	M-F 10-6 p.m.; S-S 9-5 p.m.
Admission:	$15 (30% discounts for Chicagoans)

In Spring 2003, the John G. Shedd Aquarium will unveil an extremely cool underwater exhibit, Philippine Island, a coral reef shark habitat. Visitors walk through 385,000 gallons of water where sharks cruise. The ten-room, $45 million addition showcases Indo-Pacific animals, corals and tropical fish. Opened in 1929, the Beaux Arts architectural-style aquarium's six wings radiate from a giant, circular coral reef tank.

Adler Planetarium

Address:	1300 S. Lake Shore Dr.
Phone:	312-922-7827
Website:	www.adlerplanetarium.org
Hours:	M-F 10-4:30 p.m.; S-S 9-5 p.m.
Admission:	$7

Adler Planetarium & Astronomy Museum has interactive exhibits explaining space phenomena and intergalactic events. The museum's 2,000 historic astronomical and navigational instruments is the Western Hemisphere's largest collection. Chicago skyline views from Planetarium grounds are out of this world.

Burnham Park

Burnham Park, the site of the 1933 Century of Progress exhibition, encompasses McCormick Place, Burnham Harbor, Merrill C. Meigs Airport and Soldier Field. At Lake Shore Dr. and 31st St. is a free skateboard park. The 12th St. Beach is on Northerly Island. Other beaches are at 31st St. and 49th St. Outdoor basketball courts are east of Lake Shore Dr. around 35th St. and 47th St. Along Solidarity Dr. and Burnham Harbor shore fishing is welcome. The wilderness Nature Area at 47th St. attracts butterflies and birds.

How to Get There

By Car: From the Loop take Columbus Dr. south; turn east on McFetridge Dr. From the south, take Lake Shore Dr. to McFetridge Dr. Area parking lots are near Soldier Field, Field Museum, Adler Planetarium and McCormick Place. Metered parking lines Solidarity Dr.

By Bus: CTA buses 2, 6, 10, 12, 14, 127, 130 and 146 serve the area ($1.50 one way). For schedules and fares, contact the RTA Information Center, 312-836-7000; www.rtachicago.com.

By El: Ride the Orange, Red or Green Lines to the Roosevelt Rd. stop ($1.50). Walk east through the pedestrian underpass at Roosevelt Rd.

By Train: From Richard B. Ogilvie Transportation Center, travel east on CTA bus 20 to State St.; transfer to the 146 ($1.80 one way). From Union Station take CTA bus 1, 151 or 126; transfer at State St. to the 146 or 10. From La Salle St. station, take the 146 ($1.50 one way). South Shore and Metra trains stop at the Roosevelt Rd. station.

By Trolley: Free trolleys travel to the Museum Campus from public transportation stations and some parking lots. See www.cityofchicago.org/Transportation/trolleys/.

On Foot: Walk south through Grant Park past bobbing boats and Buckingham Fountain to the Museum Campus.

Water Taxis: Seasonally, water taxis operate between Navy Pier and the Museum Campus, 312-222-9328; www.shorelinesightseeing.com.

West Kinzie St

Carroll Dr

Carroll Ave

N St Louis Ave

N Homan Ave

W Fulton St

N Avers Ave

Garfield Park Conservatory

W Fulton Blvd

Pulaski

N Pulaski Rd

N Harding Ave

Conservatory Dr

North Central Park Ave

Gold Dome

Walton St

Conservatory Central Park Drive

West Lake St

North Hamilton Ave

W Maypole Ave

W Schrader Dr

W Maypole Ave

North Central Park Av.

W End St

ALL MAPS

Lagoon

W Washington Blvd

Garfield

W Warren Ave

W Washington Blvd

Park

W Madison St

S Pulaski Rd

S Springfield Ave

South Hamilton Blvd

Music Court Dr

Woodard Dr

South Central Park Ave

S St Louis Ave

S Homan Ave

S Spaulding Ave

W Monroa St

W Monroa St

Wilcox Ave

W Adams Ave

W Adams St

Independence Blvd

Baseball Field

W Jackson Blvd

W Jackson Blvd

S Christiana Ave

Baseball Field

Baseball Field

S Trumbull Ave

W Gladys Ave

W Glady Ave

W Van Buren St

Fifth Ave

S Millard Ave

Pulaski

W Congress St

290

Dwight D Eisenhower Expressway

W Harrison St

Ke

Overview

Until recently, the slowly gentrifying West Side had the city's best kept secret garden—Garfield Park Conservatory in Garfield Park. The Chicago Park District invested over $12 million to restore this national landmark. The 185-acre park's outdoor attractions include fishing lagoons, a swimming pool, an ice rink, baseball diamonds and basketball and tennis courts. Garfield Park's landmark Gold Dome houses a fitness center, a basketball court and the Peace Museum.

Garfield Park and its sister parks—Humboldt Park, 1400 N. Sacramento Ave., 312-742-7549, and Douglas Park, 1401 S. Sacramento Ave., 312-747-7670—compose a grand system of sprawling green spaces linked by broad boulevards designed in 1869 by William Le Baron Jenney. However, Jenney's plan didn't bear fruit until almost forty years later (after corrupt park officials were uprooted) when Danish immigrant and former park laborer Jens Jensen became chief landscape architect. In 1908, Jensen completed the parks and consolidated their three small conservatories under the 1.8-acre Garfield Park Conservatory's curvaceous glass dome, designed to resemble a "great Midwestern haystack."

Garfield Park Conservatory

Address:	*300 N. Central Park Ave.*
Phone:	*312-746-5100*
Website:	*www.garfield-conservatory.org*
Hours:	*Daily 10-5 p.m.*

One of the nation's largest conservatories, Garfield Park's has six thematic plant houses enclosing 1,000 species and over 10,000 individual plants from around the world. Plants Alive!, a 5,000-square foot children's garden, has touchable plants, a soil pool for digging, a Jurassic Park-sized bumble bee and a two-story, twisting flower stem that doubles as a slide. School groups often book the garden, so call first to determine public access hours. Annual Conservatory events include the Spring Flower Show, Azalea/Camellia Show, Chocolate Festival, Summer Tropical Show, Chrysanthemum (Chicago's city flower) Show and Holiday Garden Show. A snack-café cart operates weekends.

Peace Museum

Address:	*100 N. Central Ave.*
Phone:	*773-638-6450*
Website:	*www.peacemuseum.org*
Hours:	*T-F 10-5 p.m*

Located on the top floor of the landmark Garfield Park Gold Dome is the Peace Museum. The tiny museum's collection of 10,000 artworks, photographs and artifacts promoting non-violence are displayed through rotating, thematic exhibits. Special exhibits include a John Lennon guitar, original U2 song sheet and moving drawings by Nagasaki and Hiroshima survivors. Call for information on current and traveling exhibits.

Fishing

Garfield Park's two lagoons at Washington Blvd. and Central Park Ave. and those at Douglas and Humboldt Parks are favorite West Side fishing holes. Seasonally, they are stocked with Bluegill, Crappie, Channel Catfish and Largemouth Bass. Review your health insurance plan before eating what you hook. Weekdays June through August at park lagoons, the Chicago Park District sponsors free fishing instruction for all ages, 312-747-6067, as does the Illinois Department of Natural Resources' Urban Fishing Program, 847-294-4132.

Nature

The Chicago Park District hosts free nature walks and has created marked trails with information plaques at the city's bigger parks, Garfield and Humboldt Parks included. Seasonally, view as many as 100 species of colorful butterflies at the formal gardens of Garfield Park (Madison St. and Hamlin Ave.), Humboldt Park (Humboldt Ave. and Division St.) and Douglas Park (Ogden Ave. and S. Sacramento Ave.). The parks' lagoons are designated Chicago "birding parks." Free bird walks are offered by the Chicago Audubon Society, 773-539-6793; www.audubon.or/chapter/il/chicago. Picnics for 50 people or more and tent set-up require permits issued by the Chicago Park District.

How To Get There

By Car: Garfield Park is ten minutes from the Loop. Take I-290 west; exit on Independence Blvd. and travel north. Turn east on Washington Blvd. to Central Park Ave. Go north on Central Park Ave. two blocks past the Golden Dome field house and Lake St. to the Conservatory. A free parking lot is on the building's south side just after Lake St. Street parking is available on Central Park Ave., Madison St. and Washington Blvd.

By El: From the Loop, take the Green Line west ($1.50 one way) to the new Garfield Park Conservatory stop, a renovated Victorian train station at Lake St. and Central Park Ave.

By Bus: From the Loop, board CTA 20 Madison St. bus westbound ($1.50 one way). Get off at Madison and Central Park Ave. Walk four blocks north to the Conservatory.

Additional Information

Chicago Park District, 312-742-7529; www.chicagoparkdistrict.com
Nature Chicago Program - City of Chicago and Department of the Environment, 312-744-7606; www.cityofchicago.org
Chicago Ornithological Society, 312-409-9678; www.chicagobirder.org

Navy Pier · Parks & Places

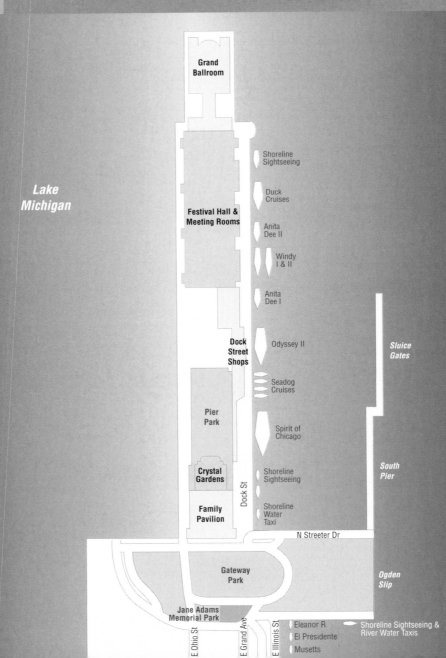

Grand Ballroom

Lake Michigan

Shoreline Sightseeing

Duck Cruises

Festival Hall & Meeting Rooms

Anita Dee II

Windy I & II

Anita Dee I

Dock Street Shops

Odyssey II

Sluice Gates

Seadog Cruises

Pier Park

Spirit of Chicago

Crystal Gardens

Shoreline Sightseeing

South Pier

Family Pavilion

Dock St

Shoreline Water Taxi

N Streeter Dr

Gateway Park

Ogden Slip

Jane Adams Memorial Park

E Ohio St

E Grand Ave

E Illinois St

Eleanor R

El Presidente

Musetts

Shoreline Sightseeing & River Water Taxis

Overview

Navy Pier is a destination that attracts visitors and Chicagoans alike-the visitors go to the trade shows and conventions and the locals swig pints at the outdoor beer garden.

Built in 1916 as a municipal wharf, the pier has also done time as a) the University of Illinois at Chicago's campus, b) a hospital, c) a military training facility, d) a concert venue and e) a white elephant. In 1989, the Metropolitan Pier and Exposition Authority invested $150 million to transform the crumbling pier into a peninsular entertainment-exhibition complex that attracts 8 million people a year. In addition to convention space, Navy Pier has two museums, the Shakespeare Theater, the Crystal Gardens, an ice rink, outdoor concert pavilion, vintage grand ballroom, 15-story Ferris wheel, IMAX Theatre, and, just for the hell of it, a radio station.

General Information

Location:	600 E. Grand Ave.
Phone:	312-595-7437
Website:	www.navypier.com
Pier Hours:	Opens at 10 a.m. daily. Pier closing times and hours of restaurants, shops and attractions vary by season, holiday and public exhibitions/events
Skyline Stage:	1,500-seat, outdoor performance pavilion in Pier Park; performances are May through September, 312-595-7437
IMAX Theatre:	312-595-0090
Free Fireworks Displays:	Memorial Day to Labor Day evenings, Wednesdays (9:30 p.m.) and Saturdays (10:15 p.m.)
Ice Rink:	Open seasonally in Pier Park; free ($3.50 skate rental)
WBEZ Radio:	National Public Radio's local station, 312-832-9150; www.wbez.org.
Exhibit Space:	Festival Hall, Lakeview Terrace, Ballroom Lobby, Grand Ball Room; 36 meeting rooms

Chicago Shakespeare Theater

The professional Chicago Shakespeare Theater has a 510-seat, courtyard-style theater and 185-seat studio theater that are Chicago's sole venues dedicated to performing only wordsmith Willy's works. In addition to the season's plays, the theater produces Shakespeare "shorts" for younger patrons. A bookstore and Teacher Resource Center are on-site. 312-595-5600; www.chicagoshakes.com.

Chicago Children's Museum

The Chicago Children's Museum features daily activities, a creative crafts studio and 15 inter-active exhibits ranging from dinosaur digs and waterworks to a toddler tree house, safety town and construction zone. Generally, hours are 10 a.m. to 5 p.m. daily. Admission is $6.50; free Thursdays 5 p.m. to 8 p.m. 312-527-1000; www.chichildrensmuseum.org.

Smith Museum of Stained Glass Windows

This is the first stained glass-only museum in the country. The 150 windows installed in the lower level of Festival Hall are mostly from Chicago-area buildings and the City's renowned stained glass studios. Windows representing over a century of artistic styles include works by Louis Comfort Tiffany, Frank Lloyd Wright, Louis Sullivan and John LaFarge. The free museum is open pier hours, 312-595-5024.

Getting There

By Car: From the north, exit Lake Shore Dr. at Grand Ave.; proceed east. From the southeast, exit Lake Shore Dr. at Illinois St; go east. Three garages are on the pier's north side and plenty of parking lots are just west of Lake Shore Dr. in Streeterville (Map 3).

By Bus: CTA busses 29, 56, 65, 66, 120 serve Navy Pier.

By El: Take the Green or Red Line to Grand Ave. stop ($1.50 one way). Board eastbound CTA Bus 29 (.30 additional) or take the free trolley.

By Train: From Richard B. Ogilvie Transportation Center take CTA buses 56 or 120. From Union Station board bus 121.

By Trolley: Daily, free trolleys travel between Navy Pier, State St. and along Grand Ave. and Illinois St. See www.cityofchicago.org/Transportation/trolleys/.

By Boat: Seasonal water shuttles travel between Navy Pier and the Museum Campus and along the Chicago River to Sears Tower, 312-222-9328; www.shorelinesightseeing.com.

General Information

Address:	78 E. Washington St.
Phone:	312-744-6630
Website:	www.cityofchicago.org/Tour/CulturalCenter/
Hours:	M-W:10-7; Th: 10-9; F: 10-6; Sa: 10-5, Su: 11-5.

Overview

The Chicago Cultural Center is the Loop's public arts center. Free concerts, theatrical performances, films, lectures and exhibits are offered daily. Admission to the Cultural Center, its art galleries and Museum of Broadcast Communications are free too. Call for weekly event updates, 312-346-3278.

The building itself is a neoclassical landmark constructed in 1897. It features Carrara marble and intricate mosaics of glass and marble covering walls and grand stairways. Once the City's central public library, the Cultural Center boasts the world's largest Tiffany Dome in Preston Bradley Hall and the Renaissance-style Grand Army of the Republic Exhibition Hall. Free architectural tours are Wednesdays, Fridays and Saturdays at 1:15 p.m.

Performances

Weekday "LunchBreak" concerts are in the Randolph Cafe. Classical concerts and opera are performed Wednesdays at 12:15 p.m. in Preston Bradley Hall. Call for information on frequently scheduled special programs. Off-Loop theater productions appear regularly in the Studio Theater. The seasonal ShawChicago series features plays by Bernard Shaw on Saturdays, Sundays and Mondays. Reservations recommended, 312-409-5605; www.shawchicago.org.

Art Galleries

A permanent exhibit in the Landmark Gallery, Chicago Landmarks Before the Lens is a stunning black and white photographic survey of Chicago architecture. Five additional galleries regularly rotate exhibits showcasing work in many mediums by renowned and local artists. Tours of current exhibits are Thursdays at 12:15 p.m.

Museum of Broadcast Communications

Chicago's contributions to air wave history come alive at the free Museum of Broadcast Communications 312-629-6000; www.Museum.TV. Chicago television studios spawned national programs including Bozo's Circus and Kukla, Fran & Ollie. Footage and memorabilia are displayed. Visitors tape a play-by-play of historic sporting events, recreate radio shows and produce television newscasts. Breakthrough advertising commercials are exhibited. The museum is home to America's only Radio Hall of Fame; www.radiohof.org; preserving 50,000 hours of broadcasts. Teachers can tap into museum resources, 312-629-6047, including the killer research center (closed Sundays). Museum hours: Monday through Saturday, 10 a.m. to 4:30 p.m.; Sunday noon to 5 p.m. Tours are weekdays from 10 a.m. and 4:30 p.m. ($2).

How to Get There

By Car: Travel down Michigan Ave. to Randolph St. From Lake Shore Dr., exit at Randolph St. For parking garages in the area, see NFT Map 6.

By Train: From the Richard B. Ogilvie Transportation Center, travel east to Michigan Ave. on CTA buses 157, 20, 56 and 127. From Union Station take CTA buses 60, 157, 151 and 123. From the Randolph St. station below Millennium Park, walk west across Michigan Ave. For schedules and fares, contact the RTA Information Center, 312-836-7000; www.rtachicago.com.

By El: Take the Green Line to the Randolph-Wabash stop. Walk east one block.

By Bus: CTA buses 151, 145, 146, 147, 3 and 10 (weekends only) stop on Michigan Ave. in front of the Cultural Center.

General Information

Address: 400 S. State St.
Phone: 312-542-7279
Website: www.chipublib.org

Overview

Harold Washington Library Center is the world's largest public library. Named after Chicago's first African American mayor, the 756,640 square-foot facility has over 70 miles of shelves storing 9 million books, microforms, serials and government documents. Over 50 works of notable sculpture, paintings and mosaics adorn the free library visited by over 6,000 patrons daily.

Collections are on floors three through eight. Roam the outer walls for a windowed alcove to read, write and snooze in blissful quiet. The Winter Garden, a welcome bad-weather escape, is on the ninth floor next to the Beyond Words Café (open for lunch and afternoon tea Monday through Saturday). A coffee shop and used bookstore are on the first floor. Frequent free public programs are held in the lower level's 385-seat auditorium, video theater, exhibit hall and meeting rooms, 312-747-4649.

Library hours are Monday through Thursday 9 a.m. to 7 p.m.; Friday and Saturday 9 a.m. to 5 p.m.; Sunday 1 to 5 p.m. Free library tours starting from the third floor Orientation Theater are Thursdays at 2 p.m., 312-747-4136.

Research Services

To check availability or location of an item, call Catalog Information, 312-747-4340, or search the library's Online Catalog www.chipublib.org. The Email Reference Service responds to information requests within a week. For quick answers to common research questions, check out the handy Virtual Library Service called "Reference Shelf."

Computer Services

The library's 32 computers with Internet access and 24 more with word processing, desktop publishing, graphic presentation and spreadsheet applications are in the fifth floor Computer Connection Department. Computer use is free and available on a first-come-first-serve basis. Reserve computers for up to 2 hours per day based on walk-in availability. Limited time slots available via phone reservation, 312-747-4540. For downloads, bring your own formatted diskette or purchase one ($2). Free laser printing provided. Closed Sunday.

Thomas Hughes Children's Library

The 18,000-square foot Thomas Hughes Children's Library serves children through age 14. In addition to 120,000 books representing 40 foreign languages, there is a reference collection on children's literature for adults. Twenty free computers, two with internet connections, are available. Children's programs hosted weekly, 312-747-4647.

Special Collections

The library's Special Collections & Preservation Division's highlights include: Harold Washington Collection, Civil War & American History Research Collection, Chicago Authors & Publishing Collection, Chicago Blues Archives, Chicago Theater Collection, World's Columbian Exposition Collection and Neighborhood History Research Collection. The reading room is closed Sundays.

How to Get There

By Car: The library is at the intersection of State St. and Congress Pkwy. in South Loop. Take I-290 east into the Loop. See NFT Map 5 for area parking garages.

By El: The Brown Line, Purple Line and Orange Line stop at the Library station. Exit the Red Line and O'Hare Airport Blue Line at Van Buren Station; walk one block south. Change from the Harlem/Lake St. Green Line to the northbound Orange Line at Roosevelt Rd. station; get off at Library station.

By Bus: CTA busses that stop on State St. in front of the library are the 2, 6, 29, 36, 62, 151, 145, 146 and 147.

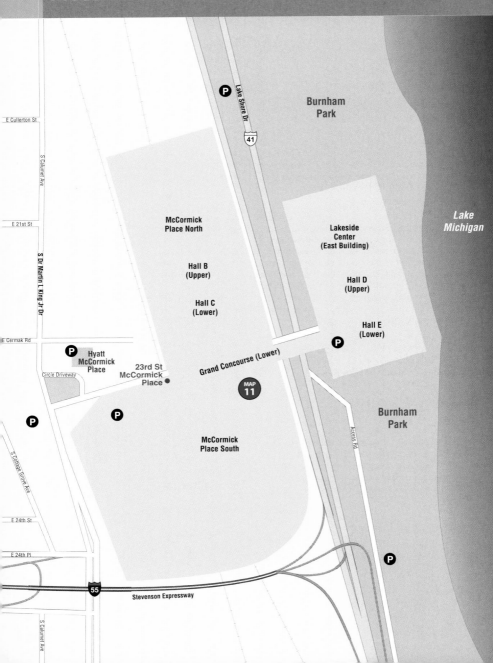

E Cullerton St

S Calumet Ave

Lake Shore Dr

Burnham
Park

41

E 21st St

S Dr. Martin L King Jr Dr

McCormick
Place North

Lake
Michigan

Lakeside
Center
(East Building)

Hall B
(Upper)

Hall D
(Upper)

Hall C
(Lower)

Hall E
(Lower)

E Cermak Rd

Hyatt
McCormick
Place

Circle Driveway

23rd St
McCormick
Place

Grand Concourse (Lower)

MAP
11

Burnham
Park

McCormick
Place South

Access Rd

S Cottage Grove Ave

E 24th St

E 24th Pl

55

Stevenson Expressway

S Calumet Ave

General Information

Mailing Address:	McCormick Place
	2301 S. Lake Shore Dr.
	Chicago, IL 60616
Phone:	312-791-7000
Website:	www.mccormickplace.com
South Building:	Exhibit Hall A; charter bus stop
North Building:	Exhibit Halls B and C; Metra train station
Lakeside Center:	Exhibit Halls D and E; 4,249-seat Arie Crown Theater (Level 2); underground parking garage

Overview

When it comes to the convention business, size does matter. With 2.2 million square feet of exhibit space spread among three buildings, McCormick Place is the largest convention center in North America. Annually, over three million visitors attend its trade shows and public exhibitions in the South Building, North Building and Lakeside Center (East Building). Apparently the City's colossal cash cow is about to get even bigger with the addition of a new $800 million West Building. Slated for completion in 2007, the expansion will add 600,000 square feet of exhibit space and 200,000 square feet of meeting rooms.

McCormick Place's growth continues to bolster the rapid gentrification of South Loop, and with each expansion, the complex's overall aesthetic appeal steadily improves. However, despite major renovations to Lakeside Center, Chicagoans still call it "the mistake on the lake." Wedged between the water and Lake Shore Dr. in Burnham Park, Mayor Daley refers to the black boxy behemoth as the "Berlin Wall" separating Chicagoans from their beloved lakefront.

Finding Your Way Around

Getting to McCormick Place is easy compared to finding your way around inside. The main entrance is off Martin Luther King Dr. next to the Hyatt Hotel. Here's how to crack the code names for meeting rooms and exhibit halls:

All meeting room locations start with E (Lakeside Center/East Building), N (North Building) or S (South Building). The first numeral is the floor level. The last two digits specify which room. No room numbers are duplicated among the complex's three buildings.

Exhibit halls are named by consecutive letters starting with the South Building where Hall A (Level 3) is located. North Building houses Halls B (Level 3) and C (Level 1). Exhibit Halls D (Level 3) and E (Level 2) are in Lakeside Center.

Restaurants & Services

In addition to the complex's concessions, Connie's Pizza and McDonald's Express are in the North Building (Level 2). The Plate Room food court can be found in the South Building (west side of Level 2.5) where Starbucks, shops, a shoe shine and massage services are also located. Business Centers and ATMs are in the Grand Concourse (Level 2.5), North Building (Level 2) and Lakeside Center (Level 2).

How To Get There

By Car: From the Loop, take Lake Shore Dr. south; from the southeast travel north on Lake Shore Dr. Signage to McCormick Place on the Drive is frequent and clear. Parking garages are in Lakeside Center and the Hyatt. Lots are at 31st St. and Lake Shore Dr. and at Martin Luther King Dr. across from the South Building. Additional lots are north of McCormick Place at Burnham Harbor and Soldier Field.

By Bus: From the Loop, CTA buses 3 and 4 stop in front of the South Building. From Richard B. Ogilvie Transportation Center, take buses 122, 125 or 157 to Michigan Ave.; transfer to a southbound 3 or 4 ($1.80 one way). From Union Station, board eastbound bus 1 to Michigan Ave.; transfer to a southbound 3 or 4.

During major shows, countless charter buses circle downtown hotels transporting conventioneers to McCormick Place for free. With the new express busway, charter buses travel from Randolph St. to the South Building in less than 10 minutes. For schedules, check with the hotels and at McCormick Place information desks. A 2003 expansion of the busway will connect it to 18th St. providing closer access to the North Building and Lakeside Center.

By Train: Metra Electric Trains from the Loop's Randolph St. and Van Buren St. stations to the 23rd St. stop under the North Building take 9 minutes ($1.75 one way). The escalators to the train platform are on the west side of the Grand Concourse (Level 2.5).

Evanston · Parks & Places

Overview

Just 13 miles from Chicago's bustling Loop, Evanston seems a world away. Spacious Victorian and Prairie-style homes with mini-vans and Mercedes parked on tree-lined streets overlook Lake Michigan and surround the quaint college town's downtown.

Evanston was founded in 1850 by a group of Methodists. They established prestigious Northwestern University five years later on the lake's shores, once home to Potawatami Indians. Today, residents are as devoted to cultural and intellectual pursuits as the morally-minded patriarchs were to enforcing prohibition. The sophisticated, racially diverse suburb of over 74,000 packs a lot of business and entertainment into its 8.5 square mile radius. Superb museums, many national historic landmarks, parks, artistic events, eclectic shops and theaters make up for the poor sports performances by Northwestern University's Wildcats in recent Big Ten football and basketball seasons.

Culture

Evanston has several museums and some interesting festivals that definitely warrant investigation. Besides Northwestern's Block Museum of Art (see Northwestern University pages), the impressive Mitchell Museum of the American Indian at Kendall College, 2600 Central Park Ave., 847-475-1030, showcases life of the Midwest's Native Americans. The 1865 home of Frances E. Willard, founder of the Women's Christian Temperance Union and women's suffrage leader, is at 1730 Chicago Ave., 847-328-7500.

Festivals & Events

December: First Night, city-wide arts celebration rings in the New Year, 847-328-5864; May: Evanston goes Baroque during Bach Week, 847-236-0452; June: Fountain Square Arts Festival, 847-328-1500, and free Starlight Concerts hosted in many of the city's 80 parks through August, 847-448-8058; July: Ethnic Arts Festival, 847-448-8058; September: Town architectural walking tour, 312-922-3432.

Nature

Evanston is blessed with six public beaches open June 10th through Labor Day. For hours, fees and boating information, contact the City of Evanston's Recreation Division, 847-866-2910; www.cityofevanston.org. The town's most popular parks encircle its beaches: Grosse Point Lighthouse Park, Centennial Park, Burnham Shores Park, Dawes Park and South Blvd. Beach Park. All are connected by a bike path and fitness trail. On clear days, Chicago's skyline is visible from Northwestern's Lakefill Park. West of downtown McCormick, Twiggs and Herbert Parks flank the North Shore Channel. Bicycle trails thread along the shore from Green Bay Rd. south to Main St. North of Green Bay Rd. is Peter N. Jans Community Golf Course, a short 18-hole, par 60 public links at 1019 Central Ave., 847-866-2910, and the Ladd Memorial Arboretum and Ecology Center, 2024 McCormick Blvd., 847-864-5181.

Where to Eat

- **Trio**, 1625 Hinman Ave. in the Homestead Hotel, 847-733-8746. French. Deep-pocketed regulars gush about the daring food combinations. A favorite for foodies.
- **Blind Faith Café**, 525 Dempster St., 847-328-6875. Vegetarian. Healthy, fiber-filled fare for the Birkenstock set. Food so earthy, you need to floss dirt from your teeth.
- **Va Pensiero**, 1566 Oak Ave. in the Margarita Inn, 847-475-7779. Italian. Classy, romantic super club offering over 250 Italian wines. A "pop the question" kind of place.
- **The Dining Room at Kendall College Culinary Institute**, 2408 Orrington Ave. , 847-866-1399. Eclectic. Charlie Trotter hopefuls dish up lunch and dinner. Four star dining hall eats.
- **Pet Miller's Original Steakhouse**, 1557 Sherman Ave., 847-328-0399. American. Beef bubbas stake out this joint as one of Chicago's best for red meat served in a cozy dining room; fist-thick burgers slung in live jazz lounge.
- **Tapas Barcelona**, 1615 Chicago Ave., 847-866-9900. Spanish. Lick your fingers with friends over tasty tapas and sangria.

How to Get There

By Car: Lake Shore Dr. to Sheridan Rd. is the most direct and scenic route. Drive north on LSD which ends at Hollywood; jog west to Sheridan and continue north. Near downtown, Sheridan becomes Burnham Pl. briefly, then Forest Ave. Go north on Forest, which turns into Sheridan again by lakefront Centennial Park.

By Train: Metra's Union Pacific North Line departing from the Richard B. Ogilvie Transportation Center in West Loop stops at the downtown Davis Street CTA Center station, 25 minutes from the Loop ($2.55 one way). This station is the town transportation hub where Metra and El trains and buses interconnect. For all Metra, El and CTA bus schedules contact the RTA Travel Information Center, 312-836-7000; www.rtachicago.com.

By El: The CTA Purple Line Express El train travels direct to and from the Loop during rush hours ($1.50 one way). Other hours, ride the Howard-Dan Ryan Red Line to Howard St., transfer (additional .30) to Purple Line.

By Bus: From Chicago's Howard St. station, CTA and Pace Suburban buses service Evanston ($1.50 rush hours one way; other, $1.25).

Additional Information

Evanston Convention & Visitors Bureau, 847-328-1500; www.evanston-illinois.org
Evanston Public Library, 847-866-0300; www.epl.org

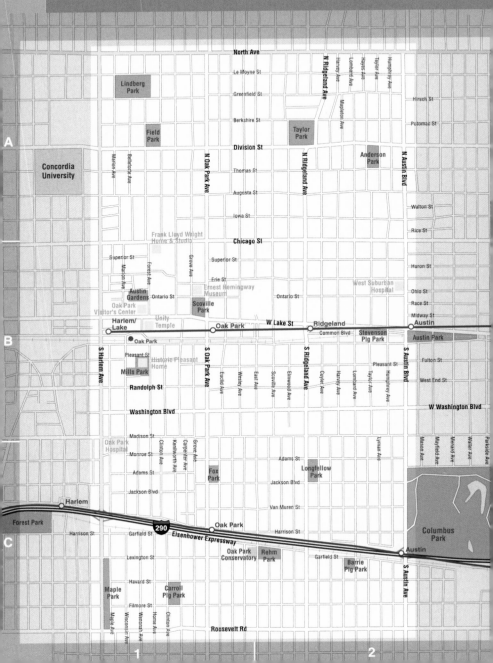

Oak Park · Parks & Places

Concordia University

Lindberg Park

Field Park

Taylor Park

Anderson Park

North Ave
Le Moyne St
Greenfield St
Berkshire St
Division St
Thomas St
Augusta St
Iowa St
Chicago St
Superior St

N Ridgeland Ave
Harvey Ave
Lombard Ave
Hayes Ave
Taylor Ave
Humphrey Ave

N Austin Blvd

Hirsch St
Potomac St
Walton St
Rice St
Huron St

Mapleton Ave

N Oak Park Ave

Marion Ave
Belleforte Ave

Frank Lloyd Wright Home & Studio

Grove Ave
Superior St
Erie St

Forest Ave
Marion Ave

Austin Gardens

Oak Park Visitor's Center

Ernest Hemingway Museum

West Suburban Hospital

Ohio St
Race St
Midway St

Scoville Park

Ontario St
Ontario St

Harlem/Lake
Unity Temple
Oak Park
W Lake St
Ridgeland
Austin

Oak Park
Common Blvd
Stevenson Plg Park
Austin Park

S Harlem Ave

Pleasant St
Historic Pleasant Home

Mills Park

Randolph St

Washington Blvd

S Oak Park Ave

Euclid Ave
Wesley Ave
East Ave
Scoville Ave
Elmwood Ave

S Ridgeland Ave

Cuyler Ave
Hardy Ave
Lombard Ave
Taylo Ave
Humphrey Ave

Pleasant St

S Austin Blvd

Fulton St
West End St

W Washington Blvd

Madison St
Oak Park Hospital
Monroe St
Adams St
Jackson Blvd

Clinton Ave
Kenilworth Ave
Carpenter Ave
Grove Ave

Fox Park

Adams St
Jackson Blvd
Van Buren St

Longfellow Park

Lyman Ave

Mason Ave
Mayfield Ave
Menard Ave
Waller Ave
Parkside Ave

Harlem
Forest Park

Harrison St
Garfield St

290
Eisenhower Expressway

Oak Park
Harrison St

Columbus Park

Austin

Lexington St
Oak Park Conservatory
Rehm Park
Garfield St
Barrie Plg Park

S Austin Ave

Maple Park

Havard St
Carroll Plg Park
F 1lmore St

Maple Ave
Wisconsin Ave
Wenonah Ave
Home Ave
Clinton Ave

Roosevelt Rd

A

B

C

1

2

General Information

Oak Park Visitors Bureau, 708-524-7800; visitoakpark.com
Oak Park Tourist, www.oprf.com

Overview

Thank Oak Park for McDonald's, Tarzan, A Moveable Feast and Prairie Style architecture. Their creators called the charming suburb their home: Ray Kroc, Edgar Rice Burroughs, Ernest Hemingway and Frank Lloyd Wright.

Best known for its architectural gems and strong public schools, Oak Park is a happy hunting ground for home buyers seeking an upscale, integrated suburb 10 miles from the Loop. Less impressed than most with his picture-perfect hometown of 52,500, Hemmingway described Oak Park as "a village of wide lawns and narrow minds."

Village trustees must still be smarting from Hemmingway's crack because they publicize an official policy on maintaining diversity. The "diversity statement" sounds like a disclaimer or zealot's vision for heaven on Earth: "Ours is a community that encourages contributions of all citizens regardless of race, gender, ethnicity, sexual orientation, disability, religion . . ."

Architecture

Oak Park harbors the nation's largest concentration of Frank Lloyd Wright buildings, 25 in the village and another six in neighboring River Forest. The village's must-see sites are located in a compact area bordered by Division St., Lake St., Forest Ave. and Ridgeland Ave. Designs by Wright, William Drummond, George W. Maher, John Van Bergen and E.E. Roberts are represented.

Ground yourself in Prairie Style architectural principles at the Frank Lloyd Wright Home and Studio, 951 Chicago Ave., 708-848-1976, daily at 11 a.m., 1 p.m. and 3 p.m. ($9). Only 15 people are allowed per tour and tickets are bought on-site; early arrival recommended. Worthwhile walking tours of surrounding streets are offered ($9). A combined ticket covers the home-studio site and a walking tour ($16).

Unity Temple, 875 Lake St., 708-383-8873, was Wright's first public building. Open daily for self-directed tours and weekend guided tours ($6). Designed by George W. Maher, Historic Pleasant Home, 217 S. Home Ave., 708-383-2654, aptly illustrates the architectural evolution from Victorian design to early Prairie Style. Tours: Thursday through Sunday at 12:30 p.m., 1:30 p.m. and 2:30 p.m. ($5, Fridays free).

Oak Park Visitors Center, 158 N. Forest Ave., 708-848-1500; www.visitoakpark.org, offers maps and an audio walking tour of the Ridgeland Historic District featuring 15 Victorian painted ladies ($6).

Culture & Events

Once a year in May, the public gets to snoop inside Wright-designed homes that are private residences during the popular Wright Plus Tour ($85). His home-studio and Robie House in Hyde Park (shuttle provided) are included, 708-848-9518; www.wrightplus.org.

Get your fill of he-man author Hemingway at the Ernest Hemingway Museum, 200 N. Oak Park Ave., 708-386-2952; www.hemingway.org, open Thursday through Sunday ($6). His birthplace is at 339 N. Oak Park Ave., 708-848-2222.

Summer evenings see Shakespeare's works performed outdoors in Austin Gardens by Festival Theatre, 708-524-2050. The lush Oak Park Conservatory, built in 1929, is at 615 Garfield St., 708-386-4700; free admission.

Where to Eat

- **Petersen Ice Cream**, 1100 Chicago Ave., 708-386-6131. American. Comfort food and silky ice cream make this diner a popular destination.
- **Cucina Paradiso**, 814 North Blvd., 708-848-3434. Italian. Fork-twirling Oak Parkers patronize this friendly pasta place.
- **Khyber Pass**, 1031 Lake St., 708-445-9032. Indian. Taxi drivers and curry-loving locals fill up on lunch and dinner buffets.
- **Philander's Oak Park** in the Carleton Hotel, 1120 Pleasant St., 708-848-4250. Seafood. Marine cuisine served in handsome atmosphere; nightly fishtail to live jazz.

How to Get There

By Car: From Loop, drive west on I-90; exit Harlem Ave. Travel north to Lake St. and head east to historic sites and downtown. Close to architectural sites is inexpensive garage parking: Lake & Forest Garage, 938 W. Lake St. (above the Oak Park Visitors' Center); Holly Court Garage, 1125 Ontario St.

By Train: Metra's Union Pacific West Line travels to Oak Park in 15 minutes from Chicago's Richard B. Ogilvie Transportation Center ($1.95 one way). From the Oak Park stop, walk north up Oak Park Ave. to Lake St. For schedules, contact the RTA Travel Information Center, 312-836-7000; www.rtachicago.com.

By El: CTA Green Line service is frequent ($1.50 one way). From the Oak Park station walk north up Oak Park Ave. to Lake St.

By Bus: From Chicago's Union Station take the 60 Blue Island bus west to 24th St. and Cicero Ave. Pick up 312 Pace Suburban west to Ogden Ave. and Oak Park Ave. Transfer to 311. Off at Lake St. and Oak Park Ave. ($1.80 including all transfers).

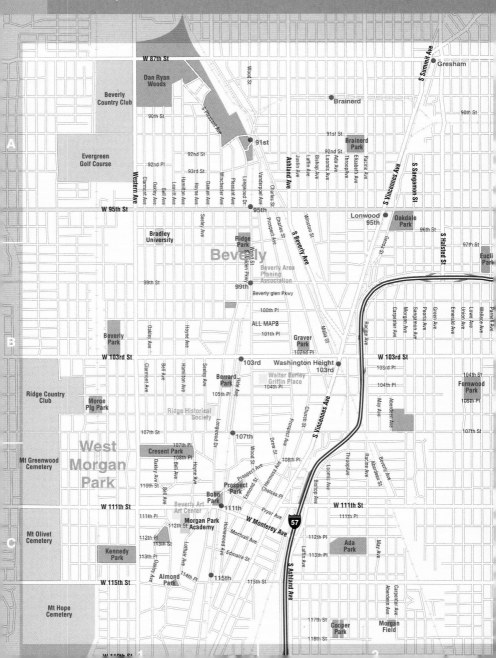

Overview

Beverly Hills, best known simply as Beverly, is the stronghold of Chicago's heralded "South Side Irish" community. An authentic medieval castle, baronial mansions, rolling hills and plenty of pubs compose Chicago's Emerald Isle of 39,000 residents.

Once populated by Illinois and Potawatomi Indian tribes, Beverly is now home to clans of Irish-American families who moved here after the Great Chicago Fire. Famous residents: Andrew Greeley, Brian Piccolo, George Wendt, the Schwinn Bicycle family and decades of loyal Chicago civil servants.

Proud and protective of their turf, these close-knit South Siders call Beverly and its sister community Morgan Park "The Ridge." The somewhat integrated neighborhood occupies the highest ground in Chicago, 30 to 60 feet above the rest of the city atop Blue Island Ridge.

Although The Ridge is just 15 miles from the Loop, most North Siders never venture south of Cermak Rd except to invade Beverly on St. Patrick's Day weekend to see the parade and guzzle green beer at pubs lining Western Ave. Chicago playwright Mike Houlihan called the strip the "South Side Irish Death March."

But there are better than a six pack of reasons to visit Beverly. The Ridge Historic District is one of the country's largest urban areas on the National Register of Historic Places. Surprised, huh?

Architecture

Sadly, many Chicagoans are unaware of the rich architectural legacy on the city's far South Side. Beverly and Morgan Park encompass four landmark districts including The Ridge Historic District, three Chicago Landmark Districts and over 30 Prairie Style structures.

Within approximately a nine-mile radius, from 87th St. to 115th St. and Prospect. Ave. to Hoyne Ave., view a vast collection of homes and public buildings representing American architectural styles developed between 1844 and World War II. Like an outdoor museum, designs by Chicago's prominent residential architects, including Frank Lloyd Wright, stand side-by-side.

The 109th block of Prospect Ave., every inch of Longwood Dr. and Victorian train stations at 91st St., 95th St., 99th St., 107th St., 111th St. and 115th St. are Chicago landmarks. Walter Burley Griffin Place on W. 104th has Chicago's largest concentration of Prairie School houses built between 1909 and 1913 by Griffin, a student of Frank Lloyd Wright and designer of the city of Canberra in Australia.

Beverly Area Planning Association (BAPA), 10233 S. Wood St., 312-233-3100; www.bapa.org, provides a good architectural site map plus events and shopping information. The Ridge Historical Society and museum is open Sundays and Thursdays, 2 p.m. to 5 p.m. 1016 S. Longwood Ave., 773-881-1675; www.ridgehistoricalsociety.org.

Culture & Events

The new Beverly Art Center is the epicenter of Ridge culture. The $8 million facility hosts Chicago's only contemporary Irish Film Festival the first week of March. 2153 W. 111th St., 773-445-3838; www.beverlyartcenter.org.

Historic Ridge homes open their doors to the public every May during the annual Home Tour, Chicago's oldest such tour. Sites represent diverse architectural styles. Tour hours: 11 a.m. to 5 p.m.; guided trolley tours offered. Purchase tickets through BAPA or Beverly Art Center ($25 advance; $30 day-of).

A Chicago must-see, the infamous South Side Irish Parade marches down Western Ave. from 103rd to 112th St. on the Sunday nearest St. Patrick's Day. Contact BAPA, 312-233-3100.

Where to Eat

- **Franconello's**, 10222 S. Western Ave. at 103rd St., 773-881-4100. Italian. Perhaps the only pure Italians in Beverly make pasta dishes at this authentic Roma restaurant.
- **Rainbow Cone**, 9233 S. Western Ave., 773-238-7075. Ice Cream. On summer nights more than 50 folks line up for sweet treats at this 76- year old soda fountain.
- **Café Luna**, 1742 W. 99th St., 773-239-8990. Eclectic. Sink your teeth into heart-healthy sandwiches and sinful desserts.

How to Get There

By Car: From Loop, take Lake Shore Dr. south to I-55 and follow signs "To Indiana" that lead to I-90/94. Travel south on I-90-94 to I-57; exit Halsted St. Head south on frontage road to 99th St. Turn west on 99th St. to Beverly.

By Train: Metra's Rock Island Line departs from the Loop's LaSalle St. Station, 414 S. LaSalle St. The 20-minute ride runs through Ridge historic districts stopping at seven stations in Beverly and Morgan Park ($2.75 one way).

By Bus: From Loop, board the El Red Line heading south to the end at 95th St. CTA busses 119 and 114 and 96 Pace suburban bus serve The Ridge ($1.80 one way fare including transfer).

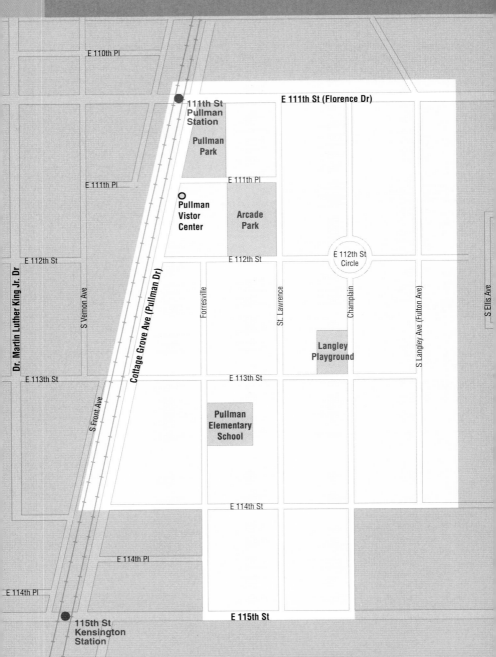

Historic Pullman • Parks & Places

E 110th Pl

E 111th St (Florence Dr)

111th St Pullman Station

Pullman Park

E 111th Pl

E 111th Pl

Pullman Vistor Center

Arcade Park

E 112th St

E 112th St Circle

E 112th St

S Vernon Ave

Dr. Martin Luther King Jr. Dr

Cottage Grove Ave (Pullman Dr)

Forresville

St. Lawrence

Champlain

S Langley Ave (Fulton Ave)

S Ellis Ave

Langley Playground

E 113th St

E 113th St

S Front Ave

Pullman Elementary School

E 114th St

E 114th Pl

E 114th Pl

115th St Kensington Station

E 115th St

Overview

Although railroad magnate George Pullman's utopian community went belly-up, the Town of Pullman he founded 14 miles south of the Loop survives as a National Landmark Historic District. Built between 1880 and 1885, Pullman is one of America's first planned, model industrial communities.

The workers' paradise earned Pullman humanitarian hoorahs, as well as a 6 per cent return on his investment. Pullman believed that if laborers and their families lived in comfortable housing with gas, plumbing and ventilation, their productivity would increase, as would his profits. Pullman was voted "the world's most perfect town" at the Prague International Hygienic and Pharmaceutical Exposition of 1896.

All was perfect in Pullman until a depression incited workers to strike in 1894. The idealistic industrialist refused to negotiate with his workers. While George Pullman's dream of a model community died with him in 1897, hatred for him lived on. Pullman's tomb at Graceland Cemetery is more like a bomb shelter. To protect his corpse from irate labor leaders, Pullman was buried under a forest of railroad ties and concrete.

So, let Pullman's tale of perfection found and paradise lost be a lesson to today's industry leaders. Ex-Enron Chairman Ken Lay's grave is already deeper than an oil well. When the time comes, how many tons of pipeline will it take to keep Ken laid?

Architecture & Events

Architect Solon Beman and landscape architect Nathan Barrett based Pullman's design on French urban plans. Pullman had mostly brick rowhouses (95 per cent still in use) and several parks, shops, schools, churches, and a library plus health, recreational and cultural facilities.

The compact community's borders are 111th St. (Florence Dr.), 115th St., Cottage Grove Ave. (Pullman Dr.) and S. Langley Ave. (Fulton Ave.). For sightseeing, start at the Pullman Visitor Center, 11141 S. Cottage Grove Ave. (773-785-8901); www.pullmanil.org. The 20 minute film provides a good historical overview. Free self-guided walking tour brochures are available. Call the center for lecture and additional specialty tour information.

The annual House Tour on the second weekend in October is a popular Pullman event. Eight private residences open their doors from 11 a.m. to 5 p.m. ($12). May through October, the center offers a two-hour First Sunday Guided Walking Tour, 12:30 and 1:30 p.m. ($4). Key tour sites: Hotel Florence, Greenstone Church (interior), Market Square, the stables and fire station. Hotel Florence's interior is being restored, as well as the fire-damaged Clock Tower Administration Building.

How to Get There

By Car: Take I-94 south to the 111th St. exit. Go west to Cottage Grove Ave. and turn south driving one block to 112th St. to the Visitor Center surrounded by a large, free parking lot.

By Train: The Illinois Central Metra Electric Line departs from Randolph St. Station (underground) at Michigan Ave. between S. Water St. and Randolph St. Ride 30 minutes to Pullman Station at 111th St. ($2.75 one way). Walk east to Cottage Grove Ave. and head south one block to 112th and the Visitor Center.

By El: From the Loop, take the Red Line to the 95th St. station. Board CTA 111 Pullman bus going south ($1.80 with transfer).

By Bus: CTA 4 bus from the Randolph St. Station travels south to the 95th St. and Cottage Grove stop. Transfer to 111 Pullman bus heading south ($1.80 with transfer).

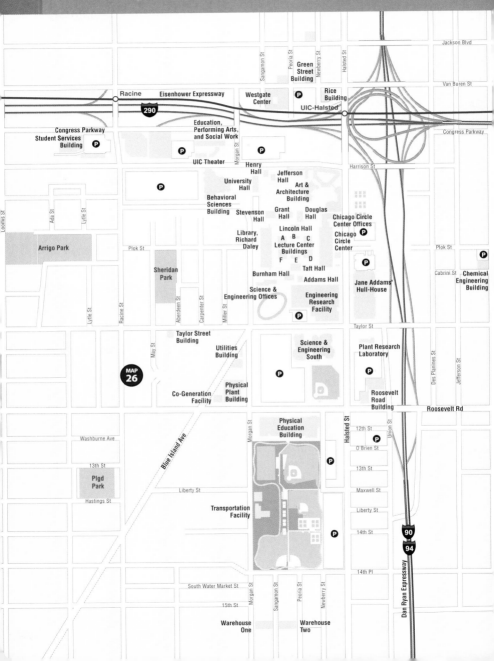

University of Illinois at Chicago

General Information

Mailing Address: University of Illinois at Chicago,
601 S. Morgan St., Chicago, IL 60607
Phone: 312-996-7000
Website: www.uichicago.edu

Overview

With 25,000 students, the University of Illinois at Chicago (UIC) is the largest university in Chicago. Located on the City's Near West Side, UIC is ethnically diverse and urban to the core. It is a leading public research university and home to the nation's largest medical school.

However, its legacy as a builder in Chicago is a bit spotty. In the mid 1960s, the school leveled most of what was left of a vibrant Italian-American neighborhood to build its campus next to the Eisenhower. During current development of the South Campus, UIC is consuming city blocks south of Roosevelt Rd. UIC's expansion all but erased the colorful, landmark Maxwell Street flea market area. The saving grace about UIC's construction craze is that many of the original campus's ugly, cement slab structures designed by Walter Netsch are kissing the wrecking ball and being replaced with more inspired buildings. But even with the multi-million dollar improvements, the campus still doesn't ignite a desire to visit. Other than going to class or the doctor, a lone trip to UIC to see the Jane Addams Hull House Museum is sufficient.

Tuition

In the 2002-2003 academic year, an Illinois resident, undergraduate student's tuition and fees will be $6,520; room and board will cost $6,428. These figures do not include books, supplies, lab fees or personal expenses.

Sports

In recent years, the Division I Flames have been hot. The men's basketball team's first appearance in the NCAA Tournament was 1997. They returned in 2002 after winning their first-ever Horizon League Tournament. Additionally, last season the Flames women's gymnastics, tennis squad and softball teams all advanced to NCAA Tournament play.

Other Flames men's and women's teams are swimming & diving and cross country/track & field. UIC also has men's tennis, gymnastics, baseball and soccer, plus women's basketball and volleyball. Basketball games and women's volleyball matches are played at the recently renovated UIC Pavilion at the corner of Racine Ave. and Harrison St. For tickets, call 312-413-8421; www.uicflames.com.

Too bad the NCAA doesn't have a bowling tournament because UIC would be a strong contender. The campus has two alleys. The public is welcome to sling balls and swig beers with students. The larger alley is at 750 S. Halsted St., 312-413-5170; the other is at 828 S. Walcott St., 312-413-5268.

Culture on Campus

Jane Addams Hull House, 800 S. Halsted St., 312-413-5353; www.uic.edu/jaddams/hull; was America's first settlement house opened in 1889. The free museum documents the pioneering organization's social welfare programs supporting the community's destitute immigrant workers. Museum hours are 10 a.m. to 4 p.m. Monday through Saturday and noon to 5 p.m. on Sunday.

Department Contact Information

All area codes are 312 unless otherwise noted
Admissions and Records .996-4350
Graduate College 413-2550
College of Architecture & The Arts 996-3337
College of Applied Health Sciences 996-6695
College of Dentistry 996-7520
College of Business Administration 996-2700
College of Education 996-4532
College of Engineering .996-3463
College of Liberal Arts and Sciences 996-3366
College of Medicine 996-5635
College of Nursing 996-7800
College of Pharmacy 996-7240
College of Public Health 996-6620
College of Social Work .996-7096
University of Illinois Medical Center 1-800-842-1002
College of Urban Planning & Public Affairs . . .996-5240
Office of Continuing Education 355-0423

University of Chicago

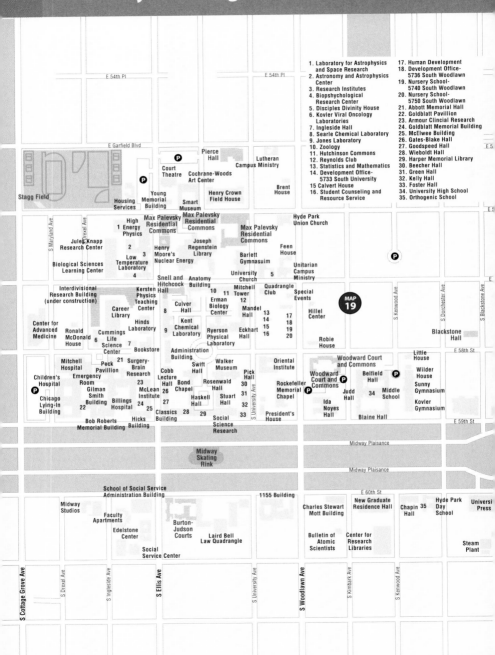

1. Laboratory for Astrophysics and Space Research
2. Astronomy and Astrophysics Center
3. Research Institutes
4. Biopsychological Research Center
5. Disciples Divinity House
6. Kovler Viral Oncology Laboratories
7. Ingleside Hall
8. Searle Chemical Laboratory
9. Jones Laboratory
10. Zoology
11. Hutchinson Commons
12. Reynolds Club
13. Statistics and Mathematics
14. Development Office-5733 South University
15. Calvert House
16. Student Counseling and Resource Service
17. Human Development
18. Development Office-5736 South Woodlawn
19. Nursery School-5740 South Woodlawn
20. Nursery School-5750 South Woodlawn
21. Abbott Memorial Hall
22. Goldblatt Pavillion
23. Armour Clincial Research
24. Goldblatt Memorial Building
25. McElwee Building
26. Gates-Blake Hall
27. Goodspeed Hall
28. Wieboldt Hall
29. Harper Memorial Library
30. Beecher Hall
31. Green Hall
32. Kelly Hall
33. Foster Hall
34. University High School
35. Orthogenic School

General Information

Mailing Address: DePaul University - Loop Campus
Mailing Address: University of Chicago Administration Building,
                   5801 S. Ellis Ave., Chicago, IL 60637
Phone: 773-702-1234
Website: www.uchicago.edu
Campus Visitors Center: Ida Noyes Hall, 1st Floor,
                   1212 E. 59th St.,
                   773-702-9739
                   Guest Parking: Lot located between 58th and
                   59th Sts. Enter off Woodlawn Ave. Meters are
                   north of Ida Noyes Hall

Overview

University of Chicago is a world-renowned research institution with a winning tradition in Nobel Prizes. Seventy-three Nobel laureates have been associated with the university as faculty, students or researchers. More importantly (for some people) is the fact that University of Chicago helped found the Big 10 Conference and created "the world's first controlled release of nuclear energy"- uh, for us regular folks, that's the atomic bomb.

Besides hordes of brainy gurus of economics, business, law, and medicine, University of Chicago graduates include artists, writers, politicians, film directors and actors. To name a few: Studs Terkel, Sara Paretsky, Carol Mosely-Braun, Kurt Vonnegut, Susan Sontag, John Ashcroft, Ed Asner, Saul Bellow, Katharine Graham, Philip Glass, Sherry Lansing, Martin Marty and co-creators of Chicago's Second City comedy troupe, Bernard Sahlins and Mike Nichols.

Established in 1890, University of Chicago was founded and funded by John D. Rockefeller. Built on 200 acres donated by Marshall Field and designed by architect Henry Ives Cobb, the university's English Gothic buildings of ivy-clad limestone ooze old money and intellectual achievements. Rockefeller described the university as "the best investment I ever made." We just hope parents footing the bill for their kids' education feel the same.

Tuition

University of Chicago's academic year is three quarters. In the 2002-2003 academic year, an undergraduate student will pay approximately $27,324 for tuition and fees and an additional $8,727 for room and board. Add on costs for books, lab fees and personal expenses. Costs for graduate students vary based on the school. Chicago has 13,000 students, 4,000 of them undergraduate students. About 2,000 of the graduate students attend classes at the downtown riverfront campus' Gleacher Center, 450 N. Cityfront Plaza Dr., 312-464-8740, where the popular Graham School of General Studies holds most of its continuing education classes.

Sports

At one time, University of Chicago racked up football trophies as well as Nobel Prizes. In 1935, the first Heisman Trophy winner was senior Jay Berwanger. The Maroons won seven Big Ten football championships between 1899 and 1924 followed by a steady loosing streak. In 1946 the university threw in the proverbial towel, resigning from the Big 10 in favor of developing students' brains instead of brawn.

But the school hasn't totally marooned sports. A member of the University Athletic Association, Chicago has women's volleyball and softball teams and men's baseball, football and wrestling squads. There are men's and women's basketball, cross country, soccer, swimming, tennis and track & field teams. And, hey, the Maroons must have a killer College Bowl team because a university contestant was the 1999 Jeopardy College Champion.

Culture on Campus

Located at 5757 S. Woodlawn Ave., Robie House, 773-834-1361, Frank Lloyd Wright's Prairie Style residential masterpiece, is a must-see for architecture fans, although it will be much more impressive once renovations are completed. Two must-see but often overlooked free museums on campus are the Oriental Institute, 1155 E. 58th St., 773-702-9514; www.oi.uchicago.edu, and Smart Museum of Art, 5550 S. Greenwood Ave., 773-702-0200; smartmuseum.uchicago.edu. Showcasing archeological finds from university digs since the 1900s, the Oriental Institute has treasures from the ancient Near East dating from 9000 BC to AD 900. The Smart Museum displays 8,000 fine arts items with strong collections in painting and sculpture spanning centuries and continents.

Now in its 48th season, the university's professional Court Theatre presents fresh interpretations of classic dramas, 773-753-4472. For information on additional professional arts organizations' performances, including Contemporary Chamber Players, Pacifica String Quartet and University of Chicago Presents, go to the school website.

University of Chicago's campus is considered a botanic garden. Grand plans are underway to revitalize the Midway Plaisance parkway. In addition to a permanent ice skating rink, the plan envisions an urban horticultural center, children's garden, canals, and a healing garden.

Department Contact Information

Log onto www.uchicago.edu/uchi/directories/ for a university directory and links to division and department web pages. The area code for the following numbers is 773, unless otherwise noted.

Undergraduate Student Admissions 702-8650
Biological Sciences 834-2105
Humanities 702-1552
Physical Sciences 702-8789
Social Sciences 702-8415
Divinity School 702-8217
Graduate School of Business 702-7369
Graduate Affairs 702-7813
Harris Graduate School of Public Policy Studies 702-8401
Law School 702-9484
Pritzker School of Medicine 702-1939
School of Social Service Administration 702-1492
Continuing Education-Graham School of General Studies
....702-1726
Graham School Master of Liberal Arts Program 312-464-8652

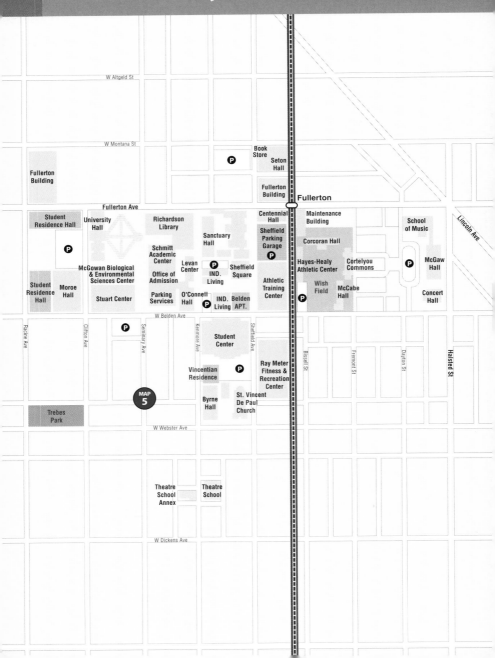

DePaul University

W Altgeld St

W Montana St

Book Store

Seton Hall

Fullerton Building

Fullerton Building

Fullerton Ave

Fullerton

Student Residence Hall

University Hall

Richardson Library

Centennial Hall

Maintenance Building

School of Music

Sheffield Parking Garage

Corcoran Hall

Sanctuary Hall

Schmitt Academic Center

Levan Center

McGowan Biological & Environmental Sciences Center

IND. Living

Sheffield Square

Hayes-Healy Athletic Center

Cortelyou Commons

McGaw Hall

Office of Admission

Wish Field

McCabe Hall

Student Residence Hall

Moroe Hall

Athletic Training Center

Concert Hall

Stuart Center

Parking Services

O'Connell Hall

IND. Living

Belden APT.

W Belden Ave

Student Center

Ray Meter Fitness & Recreation Center

Vincentian Residence

MAP 5

Byrne Hall

St. Vincent De Paul Church

Trebes Park

W Webster Ave

Theatre School Annex

Theatre School

W Dickens Ave

Racine Ave

Clifton Ave

Seminary Ave

Kenmore Ave

Sheffield Ave

Bissell St

Fremont St

Dayton St

Halsted St

Lincoln Ave

DePaul University

General Information

Mailing Address:	DePaul University - Loop Campus 1 E. Jackson Blvd. Chicago, IL 60604
Phone:	312-362-8000
Lincoln Park Campus:	DePaul University Schmitt Academic Center 2320 N. Kenmore Ave. Chicago, IL 60614-3298
Phone:	773-325-7000
Website:	www.depaul.edu
Suburban Campuses:	Barat College, 847-295-4260; Lake Forest, 847-604-8220; Naperville, 630-548-9378; Oak Forest, 708-633-9091; O'Hare 847-296-5348; Rolling Meadows, 847-437-9522

Overview

Established in 1898 by the Vincentian Fathers, DePaul is the largest Catholic university in the country and biggest private educational institution in Chicago. Total enrollment last year was approximately 21,400 students. According to The Princeton Review's recent survey of college students nationwide, "DePaul students were the happiest in the nation." It must be all the bars near campus on Halsted St. and Lincoln Ave.

DePaul has eight campuses in the Chicago area, but the Lincoln Park and Loop campuses are the university's core locations. The highly acclaimed Theatre School, College of Liberal Arts and Sciences, School of Music and School of Education are on the 36-acre Lincoln Park campus amidst renovated, vintage homes on tree-lined streets. Prominent DePaul alumni include Chicago father-son mayors Richard M. Daley and his dad, late Richard J. Daley; McDonald's Corporation's CEO Jack Greenberg; Pulitzer Prize-winning composer George Perle, and actress Gillian Anderson.

DePaul's Loop Campus at Jackson Blvd. and State St. is where the College of Commerce, College of Law and School of Computer Science, Telecommunications, Information Systems are located. So are the nationally respected Kellstadt Graduate School of Business and DePaul's thriving continuing education program, the "School of New Learning." The heart of the Loop campus is DePaul Center, located in the old Goldblatt Brothers Department Store.

Tuition

Each college has its own tuition; room and board costs depend on the residence facility and meal plan chosen by the student. In the 2002-2003 academic year, undergraduate tuition and fees will be approximately $17,880 plus an average room and board cost of $7,455. Add on books, lab fees and personal expenses. Graduate student tuition, fees and expenses vary by college.

Sports

DePaul's Blue Demons men's basketball team teased Chicago with an NCAA Division I Championship in 2000 when the team appeared in its first tournament since 1992. Newly appointed in 2002, Coach Dave Leitao plans to reinstate the Demons' winning record. The Blue Demons play at United Center, 1901 W. Madison St., www.unitedcenter.com, and Allstate Arena, 6920 N. Mannheim Rd. in Rosemont, www.allstatearena.com. For tickets, call Ticketmaster, 312-559-1212; www.ticketmaster.com; go to the stadiums' box offices; or visit the DePaul Athletic Center box office, 2323 N. Sheffield Ave., 773-325-7526; www.depaulbluedemons.com.

Blue Demons men's and women's teams include basketball, cross country, soccer, tennis and track & field. DePaul also has a men's golf team as well as women's softball and volleyball squads. For stats and schedules, visit the Blue Demons' website.

Culture On Campus

DePaul's vibrant Theatre School is the oldest in the Midwest. Founded in 1925 as the Goodman School of Drama, the respected school produces over 200 performances during its Showcase, Chicago Playworks, New Directors Series and School Workshop seasons. The Theatre School Showcase performs contemporary and classic plays at its 1,325-seat Merle Reskin Theatre, 60 E. Balbo Dr. in South Loop. The Chicago Playworks for Families and Young Audiences and the School of Music's annual opera are also performed at the Merle Reskin Theatre, a French Renaissance-style theatre built in 1910. For tickets ($8-$12), directions and parking garage locations call 312-922-1999; www.theatreschool.depaul.edu. Take the Red Line to the Harrison St. or Jackson St. stops just southwest of the theatre. CTA buses 29, 62 and 146 stop near the theatre. Check the Theatre School website for New Directors Series and School Workshop productions, theater locations and ticket prices.

DePaul University Art Gallery is located in the John T. Richardson Library, 2350 N. Kenmore Ave. (773-325-7506). Permanent collections of sculpture and oils from local and international artists adorn the free gallery. A pay parking lot is one block east of the library on Sheffield Ave. DePaul's John T. Richardson Library and Loop campus library in DePaul Center are open to the public year-round. Take plenty of change for the copy machines as check-out privileges are reserved for students and faculty.

Department Contact Information

Lincoln Park Campus Admissions Office 773-325-7500
Loop Campus Admissions Office 312-362-8300
College of Commerce 312-362-6783
School of Computer Science, Telecommunications
 and Information Systems 312-362-8381
College of Education 773-325-7740
Kellstadt Graduate School of Business 312-362-8810
College of Law 312-362-8701
College of Liberal Arts and Sciences 773-325-7310
John T. Richardson Library 773-325-7862
Loop Campus Library 312-362-8433
School for New Learning 312-362-8001
School of Music 773-325-7260
Theatre School 773-325-7917

213

Northwestern University (Evanston Campus)

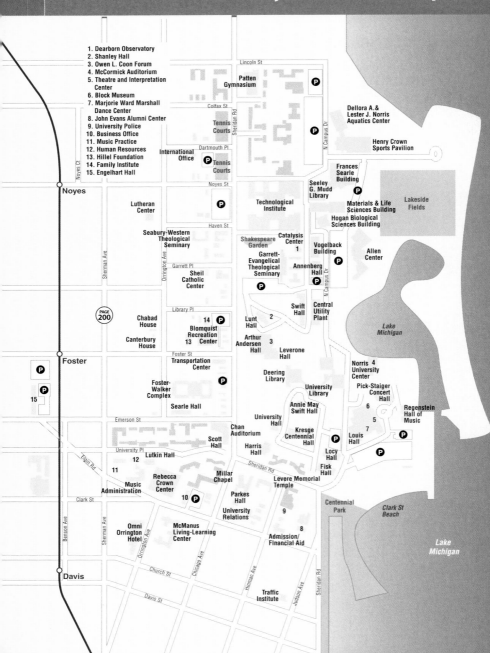

1. Dearborn Observatory
2. Shanley Hall
3. Owen L. Coon Forum
4. McCormick Auditorium
5. Theatre and Interpretation Center
6. Block Museum
7. Marjorie Ward Marshall Dance Center
8. John Evans Alumni Center
9. University Police
10. Business Office
11. Music Practice
12. Human Resources
13. Hillel Foundation
14. Family Institute
15. Engelhart Hall

Lincoln St

Patten Gymnasium

Dellora A. & Lester J. Norris Aquatics Center

Colfax St

Henry Crown Sports Pavilion

Tennis Courts

Sheridan Rd

N Campus Dr

Dartmouth Pl

Frances Searle Building

International Office

Tennis Courts

Seeley G. Mudd Library

Noyes St

Lakeside Fields

Noyes

Technological Institute

Materials & Life Sciences Building

Hogan Biological Sciences Building

Lutheran Center

Haven St

Shakespeare Garden

Catalysis Center 1

Vogelback Building

Allen Center

Seabury-Western Theological Seminary

Garrett-Evangelical Theological Seminary

Annenberg Hall

Sherman Ave

Orrington Ave

Garrett Pl

Sheil Catholic Center

Swift Hall

Central Utility Plant

Lake Michigan

PAGE 200

Library Pl

14

Chabad House

Blomquist Recreation Center
13

Lunt Hall 2

Arthur Andersen Hall 3

Canterbury House

Foster St

Leverone Hall

Norris 4 University Center

Foster

Transportation Center

Deering Library

Pick-Staiger Concert Hall

Foster-Walker Complex

University Library

6

Regenstein Hall of Music

15

Searle Hall

Emerson St

Annie May Swift Hall

5

7

University Hall

Kresge Centennial Hall

Louis Hall

Chan Auditorium

Scott Hall

University Pl

Lutkin Hall

12

Harris Hall

Locy Hall

Benson Ave

Sherman Ave

11

Music Administration

Rebecca Crown Center

Millar Chapel

Fisk Hall

Clark St

10

Parkes Hall

Levere Memorial Temple

Centennial Park

Clark St Beach

Elgin Rd

Omni Orrington Hotel

McManus Living-Learning Center

University Relations

9

8

Orrington Ave

Chicago Ave

Admission/Financial Aid

Lake Michigan

Davis

Church St

Hinman Ave

Judson Ave

Sheridan Rd

Davis St

Traffic Institute

General Information

Evanston Campus
Administrative Offices: Northwestern University
633 Clark St.
Evanston, IL 60208
Phone: 847-491-3741
Chicago Campus
Administrative Offices: Abbot Hall
710 N. Lake Shore Dr.
Chicago, IL 60611
Phone: 312-503-8649
Website: www.northwestern.edu

Northwestern University's wealth and influence is evident by its lakefront campuses in Evanston and downtown Chicago. About 15,800 full and part-time students attend Northwestern's 11 colleges and schools. The private research university is known nationally for its strong Liberal Arts undergraduate program and for its highly-ranked graduate schools in law, medicine, journalism and business.

Opened in 1855, Northwestern University was established in Evanston by many of the same Methodist founding fathers of the town itself. The 380-acre lakefront campus is bordered roughly by Central Ave. on the north and Sheridan Rd. to the south and west. The Evanston campus houses the College of Arts and Sciences; Schools of Engineering, Music, Speech, Education and Social Policy; the Graduate School, Medill School of Journalism and J.L. Kellogg School of Management.

Northwestern's Chicago campus opened in 1920. Located between the Lake and Michigan Ave. in the Streeterville neighborhood, it houses the Schools of Law, Medicine and Continuing Studies. Graduate school and Kellogg courses are offered here as well. Several excellent hospitals and medical research institutions affiliated with the university dominate the northern edge of Streeterville. In 2004, construction of the Robert H. Lurie Medical Research Center at Fairbanks Ct. and Superior St. will be completed. The new women's hospital across from it will be finished in 2007.

Tuition

The tuition and fees for an undergraduate to attend Northwestern University during the 2002-2003 school year will be $27,327 and $8,147 for room and board. Books, lab fees and personal expenses are additional. Graduate school expenses vary by school.

Sports

Like all Big Ten Conference schools, Northwestern has football and basketball teams-but that's all we can really say of the Wildcats lately. There was more to talk about in the 1990s with back-to-back bowl appearances in the 1996 Rose Bowl (their first bowl appearance and only bowl win since 1949) and the1997 Citrus Bowl. After Nebraska de-clawed, skinned and gutted the Wildcats at the 2001 Alamo Bowl, it seems the team has been licking its wounds ever since. (The trouncing is conveniently not listed on the university's sports website in the bowl games summary.)

The Wildcat's home field is Ryan Field at 1501 Central Ave., about three blocks east of the Central Ave. stop on the Purple El Line ($1.50 one way). Basketball games are at Welsh-Ryan Arena behind the stadium. For football and basketball tickets, call 847-491-2287. All sports contests are listed at www.nusports.com.

Northwestern also has men's wrestling and baseball teams plus men's and women's basketball, golf, soccer, tennis, field hockey and swimming and diving teams. Additional sports Wildcat women compete in are X-country, fencing, softball, lacrosse and volleyball. Purchase tickets at the door for volleyball, baseball and wrestling events.

Culture on Campus

The Mary and Leigh Block Museum of Art on the Evanston campus, 1967 S. Campus Dr., 847-491-4001; www.blockmuseum.northwestern.edu, has 4,000 items in its permanent collection including Old Masters' prints, architectural drawings and contemporary photographic images. The Block also has a 1,000-seat concert hall and other performance spaces. The free museum is open to the public Tuesdays and Wednesdays, 12 p.m. to 5 p.m.; Thursday through Sunday, 12 p.m. to 8 p.m.

The Pick-Staiger Concert Hall, 1977 S. Campus Dr., 847-491-5441; www.northwestern.edu/pick-staiger, is not only the stage for the university's musical and theatrical performances, but is also home to several professional performance organizations: Chicago Chamber Musicians, Symphony of the Shores, Chicago String Ensemble, Performing Arts Chicago and others. Call 847-467-4000 to purchase tickets.

Department Contact Information

General Information/Switchboard:	312-503-8649
Undergraduate Admissions	847-491-7271
Graduate School	847-491-7264
College of Arts and Sciences	847-491-7559
School of Continuing Education	312-503-8649
	847-491-3741
School of Continuing Studies	312-503-6950
	847-491-5611
School of Education and Social Policy	847-491-8193
School of Engineering and Applied Sciences	847-491-3345
School of Medicine	312-503-8206
School of Music	847-491-7575
School of Speech	847-491-7241
Kellogg Graduate School of Management	847-491-3300
Medill School of Journalism	847-491-5228
School of Law	312-503-3100

Loyola University (Rogers Park Campus)

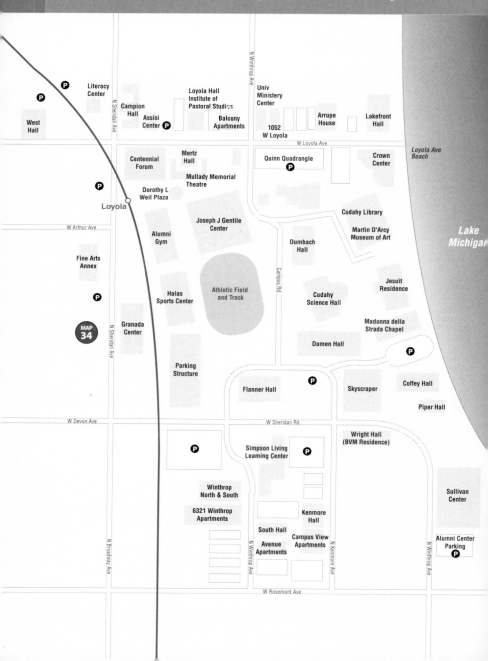

West Hall

Literacy Center

Campion Hall

Assisi Center

Loyola Hall Institute of Pastoral Studies

Balcony Apartments

Univ Ministery Center

1052 W Loyola

Arrupe House

Lakefront Hall

W Loyola Ave

Loyola Ave Beach

Centennial Forum

Mertz Hall

Mullady Memorial Theatre

Dorothy L Weil Plaza

Quinn Quadrangle

Crown Center

Loyola

Cudahy Library

W Arthur Ave

Alumni Gym

Joseph J Gentile Center

Dumbach Hall

Martin D'Arcy Museum of Art

Lake Michigan

Fine Arts Annex

Athletic Field and Track

Cudahy Science Hall

Jesuit Residence

MAP 34

Halas Sports Center

Granada Center

Madonna della Strada Chapel

Damen Hall

N Sheridan Ave

Campus Rd

Parking Structure

Flanner Hall

Skyscraper

Coffey Hall

Piper Hall

W Devon Ave

W Sheridan Rd

Simpson Living Learning Center

Wright Hall (BVM Residence)

Winthrop North & South

6321 Winthrop Apartments

Kenmore Hall

Sullivan Center

N Broadway Ave

South Hall

Avenue Apartments

Campus View Apartments

N Winthrop Ave

N Kenmore Ave

N Winthrop Ave

Alumni Center Parking

W Rosemont Ave

N Winthrop Ave

General Information

Lake Shore Campus:	Loyola University
	6525 N. Sheridan Rd.
	Chicago 60626
Phone:	773-274-3000
Water Tower Campus:	Loyola University - Lewis Towers
	820 N. Michigan Ave.
	Chicago 60611
Phone:	312-915-6000
Medical Center Campus:	Loyola University Medical Center
	2160 S. First Ave.
	Maywood, IL 60153
Phone:	708-216-9000
Website:	www.luc.edu

Overview

Loyola University, one of the largest Jesuit universities in the United States, is known throughout the Midwest for its undergraduate and graduate Schools of Business, School of Law and the University of Loyola Medical Center, a respected medical research institution. Approximately 13,400 students attend the university.

Lake Shore Campus, the largest campus of Loyola's four campuses, is on the lake in Rogers Park, and houses The College of Arts and Sciences, The Graduate School, Niehoff School of Nursing, Mundelein College Adult Education Program and Cudahy Library. The university's Water Tower campus downtown on Michigan Ave. is home to the Schools of Business, Education, Law, Social Work and some College of Arts and Sciences courses. Loyola operates the Stritch School of Medicine and the master's degree programs through the Niehoff School of Nursing at its suburban Maywood campus. The university also has a campus in Rome, one of the largest American campuses in Western Europe.

Tuition

In the 2002-2003 academic year, undergraduate tuition and fees amounted to $20,086 plus an average room and board cost of $7,500. Add on books, lab fees and personal expenses. Graduate student tuition, fees and expenses vary by college.

Sports

Loyola is the only Illinois school to win a Division I National Championship basketball tournament. The year 2003 marks the fortieth anniversary of the Loyola Ramblers' 1963 NCAA men's basketball championship. The Ramblers' most recent tournament appearance was in 1985. They play at the Joseph J. Gentile Center on the Lake Shore Campus. For tickets, visit the box office or call 773-508-2569; www.ramblermania.com.

Loyola University has men's and women's basketball, cross country, track, soccer and volleyball teams. The women also have a softball squad. Last year, the men's volleyball team was ranked as one of the top 10 in the nation.

Culture on Campus

The Martin D'Arcy Museum of Art at the Cudahy Library, 773-598-2679, on Lake Shore Campus is Chicago's only museum specializing in Medieval, Renaissance and Baroque art. Paintings by Masters Tintoretto, Guercino, Bassano and Stomer plus sculpture, furniture, jewelry, decorative arts and liturgical vessels are part of the over 500-piece collection dating from 1150 to 1750. Admission is free. Museum hours are Tuesday through Saturday 12 p.m. to 4 p.m. during the school year. Call for summer hours. Take the Red Line El to the Loyola stop. CTA buses 151 and 147 travel to campus from downtown. The Cudahy Library, Water Tower Campus Library, and Graduate Business School Library welcome the public to use their resources; however, checkout privileges are for students and faculty only.

The Loyola University Theatre performs four classic dramas a season at the Kathleen Mullady Theatre, 1125 W. Loyola Ave., 773-508-3847, in the Centennial Forum/Mertz Hall building on the Lake Shore campus. Tickets are $15 for the general public and available for purchase through the box office open Monday through Friday 2:30 p.m. to 5:30 p.m.

Department Contact Information

Undergraduate Admissions	773-508-3075
Adult Continuing Education, Mundelein College	312-915-6501
College of Arts and Sciences	773-508-3500
School of Business Administration	312-915-6113
School of Education	847-853-3000
School of Law	312-915-7120
Stritch School of Medicine	708-216-3223
Niehoff School of Nursing	773-508-3249
Rome Center of Liberal Arts	773-508-2760
School of Social Work	312-915-7005
Graduate School of Business	312-915-6120
The Graduate School	773-508-3396
University Libraries	773-508-2632

O'Hare Airport · Transit

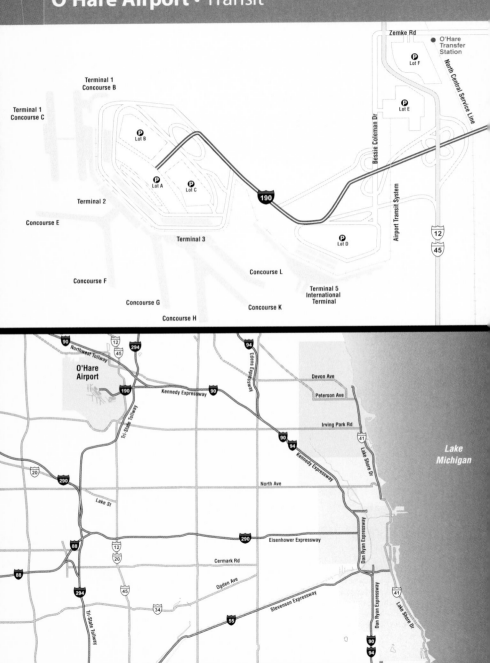

Zemke Rd

O'Hare Transfer Station

Lot F

Terminal 1 Concourse B

Terminal 1 Concourse C

Lot E

Bessie Coleman Dr

North Central Service Line

Lot B

Lot A

Lot C

190

Airport Transit System

12

45

Terminal 2

Concourse E

Terminal 3

Lot D

Concourse L

Concourse F

Terminal 5 International Terminal

Concourse G

Concourse K

Concourse H

90 Northwest Tollway

45

294

94

O'Hare Airport

190

Kennedy Expressway

90

Edens Expressway

Devon Ave

Peterson Ave

Irving Park Rd

90

94

Kennedy Expressway

41

Lake Shore Dr

Lake Michigan

Tri-State Tollway

20

290

Lake St

North Ave

88

12

20

290

Eisenhower Expressway

Dan Ryan Expressway

88

Cermark Rd

294

45

Ogden Ave

34

55

Stevenson Expressway

Dan Ryan Expressway

41

Tri-State Tollway

Lake Shore Dr

90

94

General Information

Location:	10000 W. O'Hare
	Chicago, IL 60666
Phone:	773-686-2200; 800-832-6352
Website:	www.ohare.com
Ground Transportation:	773-686-8040
Lost and Found:	773-686-2201
Parking:	773-686-7530
Traveler's Aid:	773-894-2427
Police:	773-686-2385
Customs Information:	773-894-2900

Overview

O'Delay might be a better name for O'Hare. What else can we say about the nation's busiest airport? To its credit, O'Hare serves 174,000 travelers daily in one of the most unpredictable weather zones in the country. Although located just 17 miles northwest of the Loop, sometimes it can take the better part of a day to get to your departure gate. Commuter traffic, airline snafus, parking, security checks, snowstorms, airport construction and roadwork can make the O'Hare leg of your journey as pleasurable as a migraine.

Expansion spells relief, according to Mayor Daley and Governor Ryan, who have joined forces to push through a $6.6 billion controversial plan designed to double O'Hare's capacity and secure its "busiest" title for the duration of the 21st Century. The plan calls for building another runway, reconfiguring the other seven, building an additional entrance on the airport's west side and spending millions in soundproofing area homes and schools. In addition, O'Hare's World Gateway Program proposes development of two new passenger terminals, renovation of existing ones and two new federal customs inspection facilities. Recently, political opposition has thrown up hefty lawsuits to block legislation that would cement the Daley-Ryan deal into federal law.

Meanwhile, the rest of us are stuck in traffic, in line, on the runway, etc...

How to Get There

By Car: If you must drive, pack aspirin in your glove compartment along with favorite CDs because the crawl down the Kennedy can often equate to a grueling road trip. To be safe, allow over an hour just for the drive, more during rush hours between 6 a.m. to 9 a.m. and 3 p.m. to 7 p.m. From the Loop to O'Hare, take the I-90 West. From the North Suburbs, take I-294 South. From the South Suburbs, take I-294 North. From the West Suburbs, take I-88 East to I-294 North. Get off all of the above highways at I-190, which will lead you directly to the airport. All of the major routes have clear signage easily legible at a snail's pace.

Parking: O'Hare Airport's parking garage reflects its hometown's passion for sports. All levels are "helpfully" labeled with Chicago sports teams' colors and larger-than-life logos (Wolves, Bulls, Blackhawks, White Sox, Bears, Cubs). From floor to floor, annoying elevator musak whines each team's fight song. If this isn't enough to guide you to your car, we can't help you because the garage's numbering-alphabetical system is more frustrating than the tinny elevator tunes.

If parking for less than three hours, go to Level 1. It costs $3 for the first hour, $21 for up to 4 hours, and a deterring $50 per day. Overnight parking close to Terminals 1, 2 and 3 on Levels 2 through 6 of the garage or in outside lots B and C costs $23 a day. For flyers with cash to burn, valet parking is available on Level 1 of the garage for $10 per hour or $32 per day. Parking in the International Terminal 5's designated Lot D costs $3 for the first hour; the daily rate is $30. Know that incoming international passengers always disembark in Terminal 5 (even if the airline departs from another terminal) because passengers must clear customs.

Long-term parking lots are Economy Lots E and F costing $2 for the first hour; $13 per day. From Lot E, walk or take the free shuttle to the free Airport Transit System (ATS) train station servicing all terminals. From Lot G, the shuttle will take you to the ATS stop in Lot E. Frequent flyers that are budget-conscious may want to purchase a prepaid Lot E "ExpressLane Parking" windshield tag for hassle-free, speedy departure from the airport.

By Bus: CTA buses 220 and 330 stop at the airport. If you're not near either of those bus lines, your best bet is to take your nearest bus line north or south to one of the O'Hare Blue Line train stations. The CTA also offers a special door-to-door service to and from the airport for Chicago-area residents and out-of-towners needing extra assistance. Call 312-917-4357 or 312-917-1338 (TTY) for additional information. All shuttles to airport hotels depart from the Bus Shuttle Center in front of the O'Hare Hilton Hotel in the center of the airport.

By Train: Take the Metra train only if you seek a transportation challenge above and beyond what your airline will provide. The Wisconsin North Central Line departs Union Station for Antioch with a stop at the

O'Hare Transfer station five times a day starting in the afternoons on weekdays only ($3.30 one way). Travel time is 30 minutes. Then add time to hop on the free Airport Transit System (ATS) to get to your terminal. Needless to say, the odds of the Metra's schedule conveniently coinciding with your flight schedule are only slightly better than those of the Bulls winning the championship this year.

By El: We recommend the Blue Line as the best transportation method if you don't have several large bags or dependents in tow. The train runs between downtown Chicago and O'Hare 24 hours a day every 8 to 10 minutes ($1.50 one way). Travel time to the Loop is 45 minutes. The train station is on the lowest level of the airport's main parking garage. Walk through the underground pedestrian tunnels to Terminals 1, 2 and 3. If you're headed for the International Terminal 5, walk to Terminal 3 and board the free Airport Transit System (ATS) train.

By Cab: Join the cab queue at the lower level curb-front of all terminals. Metered cab fares from O'Hare to downtown run up to $40. Some cab companies servicing O'Hare include: American United, 773-248-7600, Flash Cab Co., 773-561-1444, King Drive Cab, 773-487-9000, and Yellow Cab, 312-829-4222. Share-ride fares are a flat $15 a head to the Loop. Check with the cab starter to confirm current pricing.

By Kiss 'n' Fly: The Kiss 'n' Fly is a convenient drop-off and pick-up point for "chauffeurs" who wisely want to avoid the terminal curb-side chaos. But the flyer needs to build in more time for the ATS transfer to his or her terminal. The Kiss 'n' Fly zone is off Bessie Coleman Dr. Take I-190 to the International Exit, and then to Bessie Coleman Dr. Turn left at the light and follow Bessie Coleman Dr. north to the Kiss 'n' Fly entrance and ATS stop.

By Shuttle: Continental Airport Express, 312-454-7800 or 800-654-787, provides a shuttle service between O'Hare and downtown Chicago from 6 a.m. until 11.30 p.m. with departures approximately every 15 minutes. Shuttles stop at all major downtown hotels. Tickets are $20 one way ($36 return) for individuals, $15 per person for pairs going to the same destination and $12 per person for three or more going to the same downtown destination. Shuttle ticket counters are located in the baggage claim areas of Terminal 1 by Door 1E and Terminal 3 at Door 3E; however, shuttles pick up passengers at Terminals 1, 2, 3 and 5. Look for the shuttle stop identification signage curb-side. If you haven't pre-purchased a ticket at a counter, have cash ready for the driver. To calculate a shuttle fare to North Suburb locations, go to www.airportexpress.com and use their online fare calculator.

Omega Airport Shuttle offers service between O'Hare and Midway every 45 minutes beginning around 6:40 a.m. each day till about 11:45 p.m. The shuttle leaves from the International Terminal's outside curb by Door 5E and from the airport's Bus Shuttle Center in front of the O'Hare Hilton Hotel by Door 4. Allow at least an hour for travel time between the airports. Expect to pay $20 for a one way fare. Omega also has over 20 pickup and drop-off locations on the South Side serving O'Hare and Midway Airports. Contact Omega for information on current schedules, to make reservations and to prearrange home pickups, 773-483-6634; www.omegashuttle.com.

By Limousine: Sounds pricey, but depending on where you're going and how many people you are traveling with, it may be cheaper to travel by limo than cab or shuttle. Advance reservations recommended. Limo services include: O'Hare-Midway Limousine Service, 312-558-1111, www.ohare-midway.com; My Chauffeur/American Limo, 630-920-8888, www.americanlimousine.com; Sundling Limousine, 800-999-7552, www.limousineservicecorp.com; D & D Limousine, 888-277-7999, www.ddlimo.com.

How to Get There—Really

Taking surface roads is an option, but you can relieve yourself of any O'Hare hassles by spending the night before your flight at one of the airport hotels. Otherwise get to O'Hare in plenty of time to work out at the O'Hare Hilton Hotel fitness center ($9) and pray for the expansion to get approved at the airport's Interfaith Chapel (free).

O'Hare International Airport (ORD)

Airline	Terminal	Phone	Airline	Terminal	Phone
Aer Lingus	5	888-474-7424	Korean Airlines	5	800-438-5000
Aeromexico	5	800-237-6639	Kuwait Airways	5	800-458-9248
Air Canada	2	888-247-2262	LOT Polish Airlines	5	800-223-0593
Air France	5	800-237-2747	Lufthansa German Airlines	1/5 int arr	800-645-3880
Air Jamaica	2 dep/5 arr	800-523-5585	Mexicana Airlines	5	800-531-7921
Alaska Airlines	3	800-426-0333	National Airlines	2	888-757-5378
Alitalia	5	800-223-5730	Northwest Airlines	2	800-225-2525
All Nippon Airways (ANA)	5	800-235-9262	Royal Jordanian	5	800-223-0470
America West Airlines	2	800-235-9292	Ryan Air	3/5 int arr	800-942-6735
American Airlines Domestic	3	800-443-7300	Sabena	5	800-955-1980
Americal Airlines International	3/5 int arr	800-443-7300	Scandinavian Airlines SAS	5	800-221-2350
American Eagle	3	800-443-7300	Singapore Airlines	5	800-742-3333
British Airways	5	800-247-9297	Spirit Airlines	5	800-772-7117
BMI British Midland	5	800-241-6522	Sun Country Airlines	5	800-359-6786
Continental Airlines	2	800-525-0280	Swissair	5	800-221-4750
Delta Airlines	3	800-221-1212	Trans World Airlines TWA	3	800-221-1980
El Al	5	800-223-6700	Turkish Airlines	5	800-874-8875
Iberia Airlines	3 dep/5 arr	800-772-4642	United Airlines	2/5 int arr	800-241-6522
Japan Air Lines	5	800-525-3663	United Express	1,2	800-241-6522
KLM Royal Dutch Airlines	5	800-374-7747	US Airways	2	800-428-4322

Car Rental

On-site

Alamo	800-327-9633	Budget	800-527-0700	Hertz	800-654-3131
Avis	800-331-1212	Dollar	800-800-4000	National	800-227-7368

Off-site

Enterprise	800-867-4595	Thrifty	847-928-2000
Payless	800-PAY-LESS		

Hotels

Amerisuites - 8101 W. Higgins Rd.	773-867-0000	Hyatt Regency O'Hare - 9300 W. Bryn Mawr Ave.	847-696-1234
Best Western at O'Hare - 10300 W. Higgins Rd.	847-296-4471	LaQuinta Inn - 1900 E. Oakton Ave.	847-439-6767
Comfort Inn O'Hare - 2175 E. Touhy Ave.	847-635-1300	Marriott Suites O'Hare - 6155 North River Rd.	847-696-4400
Courtyard by Marriott - 2950 S River Rd.	847-824-7000	O'Hare Marriott Hotel - 8535 W. Higgins Rd.	773-693-4444
Days Inn O'Hare International - 1920 E. Higgins Rd.	847-437-1650	Radisson Hotel O'Hare - 6810 N. Mannheim Rd.	847-297-1234
DoubleTree Club Chicago O'Hare - 5460 N. River Rd.	847-292-9100	Ramada Hotel O'Hare - 6600 N. Mannheim Rd.	847-827-5131
Embassy Suites - 5500 N. River Rd.	847-678-4000	Residence Inn by Marriott - 7101 Chestnut St.	847-725-2210
Four Points Hotel Sheraton - 10249 Irving Park Rd.	847-671-6000	Sheraton Gateway Suites - 6501 N. Mannheim Rd.	847-699-6300
Hilton Chicago O'Hare - at the airport	773-686-8000	Super 8 - 2951 Touhy Ave.	708-456-3600
Holiday Inn O'Hare International - 5440 N. River Rd.	847-671-6350	Travelodge Chicago O'Hare - 3003 Mannheim Rd.	847-296-5541
Hotel Sofitel Chicago - 5550 N. River Rd.	847-678-4488	Westin Hotel, O'Hare - 6100 N. River Rd.	847-698-6000

Midway Airport (MDW)

Airline	Concourse	Phone
Air Tran	G	800-825-8538
American Airlines	C	800-433-7300
ATA	A	800-225-2995
ATA Connections/Chicago Express	A	800-264-3929
ComAir	C	800-927-0927
Continental Airlines	C	800-525-0280
Delta Airlines	C	800-221-1212
Frontier Airlines	C	800-432-1359
Indigo Aviation		773-585-5155
Mexicana Airlines	A	800-531-7921
National Airlines	B	888-757-5387
Northwest Airlines	B	800-225-2525
Southwest Airlines	F,G	800-435-9792
Vanguard	G	800-VANGUARD

Car Rental

Alamo		800-327-9633
Avis		800-831-2847
Budget		800-517-0700
Dollar		800-800-4000
Enterprise		800-566-9249
Hertz		800-654-3131
National		800-227-7368
Thrifty		800-527-7075

Hotels

Best Western Inn	8220 S. Cicero Ave.	708-497-3000
Fairfield Inn	6630 S. Cicero Ave.	708-594-0090
Four Points Sheraton	7353 S.Cicero Ave.	773-581-5300
Hampton Inn	6540 S. Cicero Ave.	708-496-1900
Hampton Inn	13330 S. Cicero Ave.	708-597-3330
Hilton	9333 S Cicero Ave.	708-425-7800
Holiday Inn Express	6500 S. Cicero Ave.	708-458-0202
Holiday Inn	6520 S. Cicero Ave.	708-594-5500
Marriott Courtyard	6610 S. Cicero Ave.	708-563-0200
Sleep Inn	6650 S. Cicero Ave.	708-594-0001

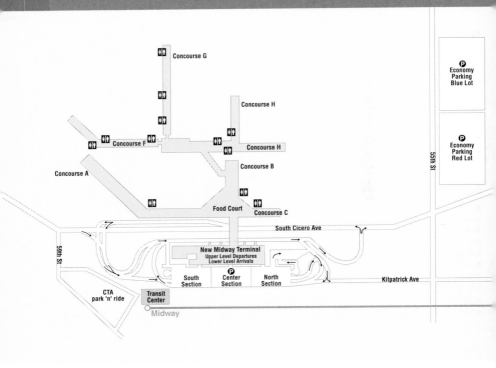

General Information

Address:	5700 S. Cicero Ave.
	Chicago, IL 60638
Phone:	773-838-0600
Website:	www.ohare.com/midway
Police:	773-838-3003
Parking:	773-838-0756

Overview

Just ten miles southwest of downtown Chicago, Midway is one of the fastest growing airports in the country, serving 47,000 passengers daily. Considered Chicago's outlet mall of airports, Midway primarily provides service from budget carriers, especially Southwest Airlines.

However, expect Midway to gain altitude in national airport rankings in 2004 when the $793 million Terminal Development Plan is completed. Plans include a swank new Terminal Building, new

concourses, a 3,000-space parking facility, food court, retail corridor and customs facility to facilitate international jumbo jet arrivals and departures. In 2003, part of Concourse H is closed while additional gates are being built. When all the dust settles, Midway will have upped its jet gate count from 29 to 41. Anticipating increased passenger traffic, several prominent hotel chains have built new properties close to Midway.

How to Get There

By Car: From Downtown, take I-55 South. From the Northern Suburbs, take I-290 South to I-55 North. From the Southern Suburbs, take I-294 North to I-55 North. From the Western Suburbs, take I-88 East to I-294 South to I-55 North. Whether you're traveling North or South along I-55, look for the Cicero Ave./South/Midway Airport exit. Passenger drop-off is on the upper level and pick-up on the bottom level of the new terminal building.

By Bus: CTA buses 55, 59 and 63 all run from points

East to the airport. Take the Green Line or the Red Line to the Garfield station and transfer to bus 55 heading west ($1.80 one way including transfer). If you're coming from the South on the Red Line, get off at the 63rd St. stop and take bus 63 westbound ($1.80 one way). Other buses that terminate at the airport include 54B, 379, 382, 383, 384, 385, 386, 831 and 63W.

By El: The Orange Line is the most convenient and cost-effective method for travel between the Loop and Midway Airport, especially since the train's operational hours were extended ($1.50 one way). The Orange Line's first train of the day departs from Midway Station (last stop on the line's southern end) for the Loop at 3:55 a.m. daily and 7a.m. on Sundays and holidays. The trip to the Loop is 30 minutes. The first train of the day departing south from the Loop's Adams/Wabash station at 4:32 a.m. arrives at Midway at 4:57a.m., well in advance of the airport's first early bird flight. The Orange Line's Loop-bound owl service ends at 12:51 a.m. when the last train leaves Midway arriving at the Library station by 1:18 a.m. The final Midway-bound owl train departs from the Adams/Wabash stop southbound around 1:29 a.m. arriving at Midway by 1:53 a.m. Trains run every 5 to 7 minutes during rush hours, 10 minutes most other times and 15 minutes late evenings. We recommend that wee hours travelers stay alert at all times.

By Cab: Cabs depart from the lower level of the main terminal and are available on a first-come, first-served basis. You can expect to pay around $20 to the Loop. Some cab companies servicing Midway include: American United, 773-248-7600, Flash Cab Co., 773-561-1444, King Drive Cab, 773-487-9000, and Yellow Cab, 312-829-4222. Share-ride fares are a flat $15 a head to the Loop. Check with the cab starter to confirm current pricing.

By Shuttle: Continental Airport Express, 312-454-7800; 800-654-7871, travels between Midway and downtown and some northern suburbs locations from 6 a.m. until 11.30 p.m. Departures are approximately every 15 minutes. Shuttles stop at all major downtown hotels. Tickets are $15 one way ($27 return) for individuals, $12 per person for pairs going to the same destination, and $10 per person for three or more going to the same downtown destination. The ticket counter and loading zone are in the terminal's lower level across from the baggage claim area by door D3. To calculate a shuttle fare to North Suburb locations, go to www.airportexpress.com and use their online fare calculator.

Omega Airport Shuttle, 773-483-6634; www.omegashuttle.com offers service leaving every 45 minutes or so between Midway and O'Hare beginning around 7 a.m. each day with the final shuttle departing around 10 p.m. The shuttle's information desk and boarding area is on the terminal's lower level across from baggage claim. Allow at least an hour for travel time between the airports, and expect to pay $20 one way. Contact Omega for information on over 20 pickup locations on the South Side, to confirm schedules, make reservations and to prearrange home pickups.

By Limousine: Sounds pricey, but depending on where you're going and how many people you are traveling with, it may be cheaper to travel by limo than by cab or shuttle. Advance reservations recommended. Limo services include: O'Hare-Midway Limousine Service, 312-558-1111, www.ohare-midway.com; My Chauffeur/American Limo, 630-920-8888, www.americanlimousine.com; Sundling Limousine, 800-999-7552, www.limousineservicecorp.com; D & D Limousine, 888-277-7999, www.ddlimo.com.

Parking

Short term parking in the new garage is on the 3rd floor. It costs $3 for the first hour and $2 for every hour thereafter, up to $50 for 24 hours. Overnight parking is $22 in the daily parking sections on Levels 1, 4, 5 and 6 (Level 2 is for rental car pick-up and drop-off). The economy lot for $9 a day is located on Cicero Ave. at 55th St., a quarter mile away. Allow extra time to take the free shuttle between the lot and the terminal.

General Information

RTA Mailing Address:	Regional Transportation Authority
	181 W. Madison St., Ste. 1900
	Chicago, IL 60602
Phone	312-917-7000
RTA Information Center:	312-836-7000
RTA Website:	www.rtachicago.com
CTA Phone:	1-888-YOUR-CTA (968-7282)
CTA Website:	www.transitchicago.com
Pace Phone:	847-364-7223
Pace Website:	www.pacebus.com
Greyhound Phone:	1-800-229-9424
Greyhound Website:	www.greyhound.com

Overview

Three major bus networks contribute to the mobility of Chicagoans, and are the perfect compliment to the rail system—CTA, Pace and Greyhound. The RTA oversees the Chicago Transit Authority (CTA) that operates Chicago's buses as well as Pace, the suburban bus service.

CTA Buses

The CTA's buses cart 1 million passengers around Chicago daily. CTA's 134 bus routes mirror Chicago's efficient grid system. The majority of CTA routes run north-south or east-west and, in areas where the streets are numbered, the bus route is usually the same as the street.

Bus Stops: CTA stops are clearly marked with blue and white signs displaying the name and number of the route, as well as the final destination. Most routes operate from the early morning until 10:30 p.m. Night routes called "Night Owls" are identified on bus stop signage by an owl picture. Owl service runs approximately every half hour through the night.

Fares: Exact fare is required for individual bus rides. A regular one way fare is $1.50. A transfer slip, good for two additional rides on either different CTA buses or CTA El/Subway trains within two hours of issuance, costs an additional 30¢, making the total fare $1.80 for up to three legs of a single journey. Transfers must be purchased with the base fare on the first leg of your journey. An "express surcharge" of 25¢ is required (in addition to a valid transfer card) when you board buses 2, 14, 16 and 147 downtown in designated pickup zones.

Reduced Fares of 75¢ per individual trip and 15¢ for a transfer are available for riders who qualify. These include children 7-11, seniors aged 65+ with an RTA Reduced Fare Riding Permit, and riders with disabilities showing a permit and their companion. Grade and high school students with a CTA Student Riding Permit ($5 per semester; $2 summer school) pay reduced fares on weekdays from 5:30 a.m. and 8:00 p.m. Children aged six and under ride free with a fare-paying customer, as do "other uniformed or ID-bearing categories authorized by the Chicago Transit Board."

The CTA offers a number of different fare packages. These include:
- For the convenience of not having to fish for exact change, purchase Ten Packs of one way tickets for $15.
- Unlimited Ride Passes: 1-Day ($5), 2-Day ($9), 3-Day ($12) and 5-Day ($18).

Frequent CTA riders prefer Monthly Passes with unlimited rides for $75 or Transit Cards sold through vending machines at all CTA rail stations. Transit Cards are available in various increments up to $100. For every $10 you put on your card, the CTA will contribute an extra $1 free. Transit Cards are sold in $10 and $20 increments at currency exchanges, Jewel and Dominick's stores, via the Internet and at many other City locations.

Bicycles Onboard: Designated CTA buses are equipped with bike racks to carry a maximum of two bikes. Bike racks are mounted on the buses' front grills. Generally speaking, CTA bike buses are those that travel to lakefront beaches. They include the 63rd St. and 72 North Ave. buses. Others with bike racks are the 75th St. and 65 Grand buses. During the summer season and special events downtown, additional buses with bike racks may be added. Check the website for an update on bike buses as the service may be expanding.

Here is how to load your bike on a CTA bus:
- If your bike is the first to be loaded, lower the rack and place it in position with the front wheel facing the curb.
- If there is already a bike on the rack, place your bike's rear wheel toward the curb.
- If two bikes are already loaded the rack is full, wait for the next bus.

Pace Suburban—Chicago Buses

Pace buses serve over 37 million passengers in the Chicago suburbs and some parts of the City. With 248 routes covering 3,446 square miles, Pace provides a vital transportation service to commuters traveling between suburbs, within their suburbs, to Metra train stations and into the City. Buses usually run every 20-30 minutes. Generally, service stops by mid-evening. Special express service is offered to Chicago-area entertainment and cultural venues. Contact Pace for specific bus route and schedule information.

Park-n-Ride Stations: Pace has eleven Park-n-Ride stations located throughout Pace's six-county coverage area. Check the Pace website for addresses.

Fares: Pace fares vary according to the route: $1.25 for local service and $1.50 for expanded service. The one way fare on express routes 210, 355, 737, 855 and 1018 is $3.00. CTA transit cards may be used on Pace buses. Pace offers qualified discounts and several bus pass package purchase options. Contact Pace for a full menu of choices; however, here is a sampling of what's available for purchase:

Pace offers discounts for students, seniors, children and disabled riders. Passengers must display an RTA Reduced Fare Card Permit to enjoy discounts.

Pass options include the Pace 30-Day Commuter Club Cards (CCC) allowing unlimited Pace rides for $50.00. A combined Pace/CTA 30-day unlimited pass is $75 and can be used on all Pace buses and CTA trains and buses. The PlusBus Sticker (sold by Metra with a Metra Monthly Train Pass) is $30 and allows unlimited Pace bus use.

Greyhound Buses

Greyhound is the rock-bottom travelers' best friend. Called "The Dog" by its patrons, Greyhound offers dirt cheap fares, the flexibility drifters prefer, basic station amenities (toilets and vending machines), and the gritty, butt-busting experience of traveling America's scenic blue-line highways and rural by-ways along with some very colorful characters.

Here are some tips on taking "The Dog" out of town:
- Even though bathrooms are onboard, pack your own toilet paper and Wet Ones.
- Air freshener, deodorant, a pillow and earplugs make being bused more bearable.
- Pack a cooler. Then padlock it.
- Wear padded bicycle shorts or bring a cushion.
- Get your shots.

Stations: Greyhound's main train station is south of Union Station at 630 W. Harrison St. at S. Desplaines Ave. in West Loop, 312-408-5980. CTA buses 60, 125, 156 and 157 stop near the terminal. The closest El stop is on the Blue Line's Forest Park Branch at the Clinton St. Station on Congress Pkwy. Additional Chicago-area Greyhound stations are located within El train stations: 14 W. 95th St. in the Red Line's 95th St./Dan Ryan station, 312-408-5999, and 5800 N. Cumberland Ave. on the Blue Line's O'Hare Branch in the Cumberland station, 773-693-2474. Contact Greyhound to determine which routes best suit your regional and national travel requirements.

Shipping Services: Greyhound Package Express offers commercial and personal shipping services and is available at all three Chicago bus stations. Packages are held at the station for pick-up. The main terminal in South Loop also houses a UPS shipping office that provides door-to-door package delivery. Call the stations for shipping office hours and rates.

Fares: To purchase tickets, call the toll-free number and pay by credit card, book online with a credit card through Greyhound's website or visit a station where cash, travelers checks and major credit cards are accepted.

Regular fare pricing applies for both individual advance ticket sales and minutes-before-departure sales as Greyhound does not reserve seats. Tickets can be used for travel to the designated destination on any day or at any departure time. Boarding is first-come-first-served, so get in line at the boarding zone for a choice seat. However, Greyhound's bark is bigger than its bite-if a significant number of passengers are abandoned, Greyhound rolls another bus, or two, or three, out on the spot. Good dog.

Discounts are given for children under 12 (50%), seniors 62 and older (10%), military (10%) and patients of Veteran's Administration Hospitals (25%). The cost for an individual return ticket is deeply discounted if it is purchased at the same time as a departure ticket.

Traveling companions can save money. Purchase a ticket three days in advance and earn a free ticket for your companion (no age restrictions). Passengers accompanying someone with a disability always ride free.

Super Friendly Fares offer the greatest savings for travelers who can purchase seven days in advance of travel. For example, a regular one way ticket from Chicago to New York City is $90 and a regular fare round-trip ticket costs $159. However, if you book a round-trip Super Friendly Fare the ticket costs only $89. You do the math.

Metra Train Lines · Transit

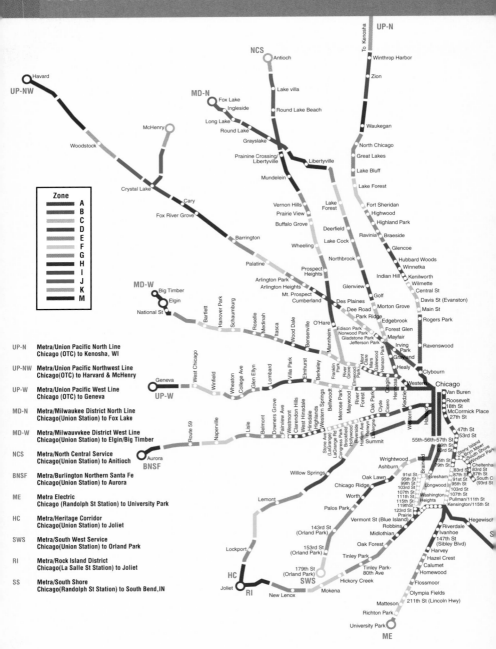

Zone
A
B
C
D
E
F
G
H
I
J
K
M

UP-NW   Havard

UP-N   To Kenosha   UP-N
         Winthrop Harbor
         Zion

NCS   Antioch

MD-N   Fox Lake
         Ingleside
         Lake villa
         Round Lake Beach
         Long Lake
         Round Lake
         McHenry   Grayslake   Waukegan
         Woodstock   Prainine Crossing/ North Chicago
                          Libertyville   Great Lakes
                          Libertyville   Lake Bluff
                          Mundelein   Lake Forest
         Crystal Lake   Fort Sheridan
                          Vernon Hills   Lake Forest   Highwood
                   Cary   Prairie View   Highland Park
         Fox River Grove Buffalo Grove   Deerfield Ravinia Braeside
                                          Lake Cock   Glencoe
                   Barrington   Wheeling   Hubbard Woods
                          Palatine   Northbrook   Winnetka
                                   Prospect   Indian Hill Kenilworth
MD-W   Heights   Wilmette
         Big Timber   Arlington Park   Glenview   Golf Central St
         Elgin   Arlington Heights   Des Plaines Davis St (Evanston)
National St   Mt. Prospect Cumberland   Morton Grove Main St
                         Bartlett Roselle   O'Hare Dee Road Edgebrook Rogers Park
                         Hanover Park Medinah   Park Ridge Forest Glen
         West Chicago   Schaumburg Itasca Wood Dale Edison Park Mayfair
                                          Bensenville Norwood Park Forest Glen Ravenswood
UP-W   Gladstone Park Irving
         Geneva   Winfield Glen Ellyn Villa Park Mannheim Jefferson Park Park Grayland
                   Wheaton College Ave Lombard Elmhurst Franklin Park Mont Clare Healy
UP-W   Geneva   Berkeley River Grove   Western Clybourn
                                                   Grand Elmwood Galewood
MD-N   Maywood River Oak Park Hanson Park Chicago
                                  Melrose Park Forest Clyde Ragin Van Buren
MD-W   River Forest Cicero Kedzie Hermosa Roosevelt
         Route 59 Naperville Bellwood   Halsted 18th St
NCS   Lisle Belmont Fairview Ave Berwyn McCormick Place
                   Downers Grove Western Springs Lavergne 27th St
         Aurora   Clarendon Hills Highlands Summit
BNSF   West Hinsdale Brookfield   47th St
                   Hinsdale Congress Park Riverside 53rd St
BNSF   Stone Ave Hollywood Wrightwood 55th-56th-57th St
                   LaGrange Harlem Ave Ashburn   59th St
ME   Willow Springs   91st St   63rd St Stony Island
HC   Oak Lawn 95th St 79th St South Shore
                   Chicago Ridge 99th St 91st St Windsor Park
SWS   Lemont   Worth 103rd St 95th St Cheltenham
         Palos Park 107th St 103rd St 83rd St
RI   111th St 107th St 87th St South C
                     115th St Washington 91st St (93rd St)
SS   119thSt   Heights 95th St
                     123rd St
                     Prairie Pullman/111th St
                     143rd St Kensington/115th St
                     (Oland Park) Robbins
                     Vermont St (Blue Island) Ivanhoe Riverdale
         Lockport   153rd St Midlothian 147th St
                     (Oland Park) Oak Forest (Sibley Blvd)
                     Tinley Park Harvey
                     179th St Tinley Park- Hazel Crest
                     (Oland Park) 80th Ave Calumet
HC   Joliet New Lenox Mokena Homewood
RI   SWS   Hickory Creek Flossmoor
                 Matteson Olympia Fields
                 Richton Park 211th St (Lincoln Hwy)
                 University Park
                 ME   Hegewisch

UP-N   Metra/Union Pacific North Line
         Chicago (OTC) to Kenosha, WI

UP-NW   Metra/Union Pacific Northwest Line
         Chicago(OTC) to Harvard & McHenry

UP-W   Metra/Union Pacific West Line
         Chicago (OTC) to Geneva

MD-N   Metra/Milwaukee District North Line
         Chicago(Union Station) to Fox Lake

MD-W   Metra/Milwauvvkee District West Line
         Chicago(Union Station) to Elgin/Big Timber

NCS   Metra/North Central Service
         Chicago(Union Station) to Anitioch

BNSF   Metra/Burlington Northern Santa Fe
         Chicago(Union Station) to Aurora

ME   Metra Electric
         Chicago (Randolph St Station) to University Park

HC   Metra/Heritage Corridor
         Chicago(Union Station) to Joliet

SWS   Metra/South West Service
         Chicago(Union Station) to Orland Park

RI   Metra/Rock Island District
         Chicago(La Salle St Station) to Joliet

SS   Metra/South Shore
         Chicago(Randolph St Station) to South Bend,IN

General Information

Metra Address:	Metra Passenger Services
	547 W. Jackson Blvd., 14th Fl.
	Chicago, IL 60661
Phone:	312-322-6777
Website:	www.metrarail.com
Metra Passenger Service:	312-322-6777
South Shore Metra Lines:	800-356-2079
RTA Information Center:	836-7000; www.rtachicago.com

Overview

With a dozen lines and roughly 495 miles of track, Metra does its best to service Cook, DuPage, Lake, Will, McHenry and Kane counties with 230 stations scattered throughout the City and burbs. The rails emanating from four major downtown stations are lifelines for commuters traveling to and from the Loop.

The good news for Metra is that ridership is strong. The bad news for the riders is trying to find station parking. In an attempt to resolve its parking issues, Metra is purchasing land surrounding many suburban stations and constructing new parking facilities. See Metra's website for development plans.

Loop Stations

There are four major Metra train stations in the Loop from which twelve train lines emanate. To try and make everyone slightly less confused, here's a chart:

Station	Line
Richard B. Ogilvie	Union Pacific North
Transportation Center	Union Pacific West
	Union Pacific Northwest
Union Station	Milwaukee District North
	Milwaukee District West
	North Central Service
	Southwest Service
	Burlington Northern
	Heritage Corridor
	Amtrak
La Salle St. Station	Rock Island Line
Randolph St. Station	South Shore Railroad
	Metra Electric—3 Branches:
	• Main Line
	• South Chicago
	• Blue Island

Fares

Fares are calculated according to the number of Metra zones traversed during your journey. one way, full-fare tickets range in price from $1.85 to $6.95. To calculate a base one way fare, visit http://metrarail.com/Data/farechk.html. Tickets may be purchased through a ticket agent or onboard the train ($2 more if the ticket windows were open at the time you boarded the train). There is no reserved seating.

Metra offers a number of reasonably-priced ticket packages, including a 10-Ride Ticket (which saves 15% off one way fares) and a Monthly Unlimited Ride Ticket (the most economical choice for commuters who use Metra service daily). If your commute includes CTA and/or Pace bus services, consider purchasing the Link-Up Sticker ($36) for unlimited connecting travel on CTA and Pace buses. If you only use the Pace suburban buses, purchase the Metra/Pace PlusBus Pass ($30) for unlimited travel on all Pace suburban buses. Metra's Weekend Pass is ideal for urbanites to visit the 'burbs on the weekend or suburbanites to spend the weekend in the City. It's only $5 and includes unlimited rides on both Saturday and Sunday. Metra's South Shore route is not included. You can buy all the aforementioned tickets in person, through the mail or online at http://metrarail.com/TBI/index.html.

Metra makes travel by rail attractive through discounted fares, which include children under 7, riding free. On weekdays, Children 7-11 ride for half price, while on weekends they ride free. On weekends, Children 12-17 ride the rails for half price on a regular one way fare. Full time students enrolled in an accredited grade school or high school enjoy Student Fares that are approximately 50% off the cost of regular one way fares.

Additionally, Senior Citizens/Disability Fares are approximately half of the regular fare. To qualify, riders must present an RTA Reduced Fare Riding Permit ID card. U.S. Military Personnel in uniform ride Metra for approximately half the regular one way fare.

CTA Rush Shuttles and Wendella RiverBuses

If you're traveling to the downtown stations on CTA buses at rush hours, CTA offers $1 cash shuttle fares on many of its routes. Check the Metra website for a comprehensive list of participating buses and the latest on road construction that may affect those routes.

Spring through fall, commuters can get to N. Michigan Ave. quickly on a RiverBus plying the Chicago River during rush hours. Operated by Wendella, boats leave from Transportation Center at the dock on the northwest corner of Madison St. RiverBuses run daily from April 1 through November 29. The trip takes 9 minutes one way. The first boat leaves the train station dock at 7 a.m.; the last boat departs from the 400 N. Michigan Ave. dock at the base of the Wrigley Building at 7 p.m. The fare is $2 one way. Discounted Monthly and Ten-Ride fares are available. 312-337-1446; www.wendellariverbus.com.

Baggage & Pets

While Metra may be "the way to really fly," your carry-on train baggage is more limited than on an aircraft. Bicycles, skis, golf clubs, non-folding carts and other large luggage items cannot be transported on trains at any time. This is one more reason, besides the limited schedules, not to take Metra to O'Hare. The pet rules are as prohibitive as the baggage rules. No pets are allowed unless they are trained guide animals assisting the disabled.

South Shore Train Lines · Transit

General Information

Loop Station Address: Randolph St. Station
    151 E. Randolph St.
    Underground at N. Michigan
    Ave. and E. Randolph St.
    Chicago, IL 60601
Phone: 312-782-0676
Website: www.nictd.com
Lost and Found: 219-874-4221 x205

Overview

Although the historic South Shore train lines were built in 1903, they still get you from the Loop to Indiana's South Bend Airport in just 2.5 hours. The Northern Indiana Commuter Transportation District (NICTD) oversees the line and its modern electric trains, which serve as a vital transportation link for many Northwest Indiana residents working in the Loop.

The South Shore's commuter service reflects its Indiana ridership. Outbound heading from the Loop, there are limited stops before the Hegewisch station, close to the Indiana state line. If traveling by train to Chicago's South Side, you're better off on an outbound Metra Electric Line train departing from the Randolph St. Station (see Metra page).

The underground Randolph St. Station at the corner of N. Michigan Ave. and E. Randolph St. is feeling the jackhammers of Millennium Park's construction overhead as well as within its own confines. Currently the station is undergoing massive construction improvements, slated for completion sometime before 2004.

Fares

Regular one way fares can be purchased at the stations or on the train. Tickets purchased onboard the train cost .50 more if the station's ticket windows were open at the time of departure.

Special South Shore fares and packages include commuter favorites: 10-Ride and 25-Ride Tickets and the Monthly Pass, which is good for unlimited travel. These can be purchased in person at stations staffed with ticket agents, station vending machines and via the mail. Senior Citizens/Disability Fares offer savings for persons aged 65 and older with valid identification and for disabled passengers. Students with school identification qualify for Student Fares, including reduced one way tickets and discounted 25-Ride Tickets good for travel during weekdays. Youth Fares range from free passage for infants under two (who must sit in a paying passenger's lap) and half off a regular fare for children aged two to 13 years. On weekends and holidays Family Fares are available. Each fare paying adult (minimum age 21) may take two children (age 13 and under) with them free of charge. Additional children will be charged the youth fare. There are no published fare discounts for military personnel.

Baggage & Pets

Any accompanying baggage must be placed in the overhead racks. No bicycles are permitted onboard. Apart from small animals in carry-on cages, the only other pets allowed onboard are service dogs accompanied by handlers or passengers with disabilities. Animals must not occupy seats.

General Information

Amtrak Reservations: 1-800-USA-Rail (872-7245)
Website: www.amtrak.com
Union Station: 210 S. Canal St.
                      Chicago, IL 60661
Phone: 312-322-6900

Overview

Chicago is the nucleus for Amtrak's national rail network comprised of over 500 stations in 46 states (not including Alaska, Hawaii, South Dakota and Wyoming). Departing from Chicago's Union Station, Amtrak trains head west to Seattle and Portland, east to New York City and Boston, north to Ontario and south to New Orleans, San Francisco and San Antonio.

Fares

Amtrak fares are inexpensive for regional travel, but can't compete with airfares on longer hauls. But, just as airlines deeply discount, so does Amtrak. And like booking an airline ticket, you have to ask Amtrak's sales agents about special fares and search Amtrak's website for the best deals (booking in advance does present some savings). We recommend the website route as you could be on hold longer than it takes to get from Chicago to Los Angeles on Amtrak.

Amtrak offers special promotional fares year-round targeting seniors, veterans, students, children under 16 and two or more persons traveling together. The "Rail SALE" page on Amtrak's website lists discounted fares between certain city pairs. Amtrak has hooked its sleeper cars up with plenty of travel partners to create interesting packages. The Air-Rail deals whereby you rail it one way and fly back the other are attractive for long distance destinations. Call 1-877-937-7245 and surf the "Amtrak Partners" website page for more partner promotional fares.

Service

No one we know can claim to have ever arrived on time travelling Amtrak, so tell whoever is picking you up you'll just call them on your cell phone when you're close. And here's another tip: Pack food because dining car fare is just fair, and pricey. But Amtrak's seats are comfortably roomy, some have electric sockets for computer hookup and bathrooms are in every car.

Within Illinois: Three main Amtrak lines travel south through Illinois on a daily basis: The "State House" travels to St. Louis, MO; the "Illinois Zephyr" travels to Quincy, IL; and the "Illini Service" travels daily between Chicago and Carbondale, IL.

Going to New York City or Boston: If you're heading east, the "Lake Shore Express" breaks off at Albany and goes to New York (21 hours) and Boston (24 hours). one way tickets range from $90 to $110.

Going to Seattle or Portland: The "Empire Builder" takes passengers to Seattle and Portland and everywhere in between. With the journey to Seattle taking around 44 hours, we definitely recommend dropping some additional dollars on a sleeper car. A one way fare costs between $130 and $195.

Going to San Francisco: You'll spend two solid days and then some riding the rails during the 52-hour journey on the "California Zephyr" to San Francisco (Emeryville). The fare is approximately $165 one way. "Zephyr" passes through Lincoln, Denver, Salt Lake City and makes a whole host of small town America stops along the way.

Going to New Orleans: The "City of New Orleans" line goes from Chicago via Memphis to New Orleans in roughly 20 hours. The fair is approximately $125 one way.

Going to San Antonio: The mighty "Texas Eagle" shoots across the Alamo and stops at 40 cities on its way from the Midwest to the South. The 32-hour trip will cost approximately $130 each way.

Going to Milwaukee: "Hiawatha" runs six times daily to Milwaukee: 8:25 a.m., 10:20 a.m., 1 p.m., 3:15 p.m., 5:08 p.m. and 8:05 p.m. The 90-minute trip costs $20 each way. This is a viable alternative to driving from Chicago on busy weekends and rush hours.

Going to Kansas City: The "Missouri Routes" line terminates in Kansas City while the "Southwest Chief" passes through it on the way to Los Angeles. "Missouri" departs daily at 8:30 a.m. and travels via St. Louis to Kansas City in just over 12 hours. The fare is $50 one way; $95 return. "Southwest Chief" departs daily at 3:15 p.m. and reaches Kansas City in just over seven hours. The fare is $63 one way.

Going to Los Angeles: The "Southwest Chief" departs for Los Angeles, travels via Albuquerque, takes almost 42 hours, and costs $165 one way.

Union Station

210 S. Canal St. at E. Adams St. and E. Jackson Blvd.
312-322-4269

Designed by the architects Graham, Anderson, Probst and White, monumental and massive Union Station is a national railroad hub. In its peak in the 1940s, 100,000 passengers passed through the terminal daily, while today's volume is half that. Despite the number of times you rush through Union Station, the magnificent, light-swathed Great Hall is impressive. It is the surviving half of the original 1925 station and a favorite site for black-tie soirees.

Both Metra's and Amtrak's train services are on the ground floor (or "Concourse Level") of the station. This level is then further divided into the North Concourse and South Concourse. An information booth is between the concourses on this level, although not always staffed. While there is signage throughout Union Station, the many escalators can make navigating the block-long building with multiple entrances and exits a challenge.

Ticket Windows: The easiest way to get to Metra ticket agents is to enter Union Station at the Clinton St. entrance near E. Jackson Blvd. and go down into and through the Grand Hall. Metra's ticket agents will be on your left in the North Concourse. Metra's ticket office is open from 6 a.m. to 11:30 p.m. weekdays, 6:30 a.m. to 11:30 p.m. on Saturday and 7 a.m. to 11:30 p.m. on Sunday. Metra Lines that terminate at Union Station are: Milwaukee District East and West Lines, North Central Service, Burlington Northern Santa Fe, Heritage Corridor, and South West Service.

To get to the Amtrak action, enter Union Station off Canal St., take the escalator down into the Grand Hall and turn left. Amtrak's attractive, vintage ticket agent desk straddles the two concourses and is open daily from 6:30 a.m. to 9 p.m. Amtrak's waiting rooms and baggage claim are in the South Concourse. For more detail on Amtrak service, call 1-800-872-7245.

Services: On the Mezzanine/Street Level there is a plethora of convenience stores, newsstands and eateries including Connie's Pizza, Snuggery, Corner Bakery and Kelly's Cajun Grill. ATMs are in both concourses on this level.

Public Transportation: The closest El station to Union Station is the Blue Line, which stops two blocks south of the station at the Clinton St. stop on Congress Pkwy. The Orange, Brown and Purple Lines stop three blocks east of the station at the Quincy stop on Wells St. CTA buses 1, 51 and 60 all stop at Union Station. Most commuters heading to work in the Loop enter and exit the station from the Madison St., Adams St. and Jackson Blvd. doorways where cabs line up.

Richard B. Ogilvie Transportation Center

500 W. Madison St. at S. Canal St.
312-496-4777

Metra's Union Pacific Lines emanate from the Richard B. Ogilvie Transportation Center, which Chicagoans commonly call Northwestern Station, its former name. Sterile by comparison to Union Station, the tall, smoky glass-and-green-steel-girder building replaced a classic, grand train station. Oh well. Roughly 40,000 passengers pass through the Richard B. Ogilvie Transportation Center daily.

Ticket Windows: Metra's ticket office is on the Upper Level, across from the entrance to the train platform, and is open from 5:30 a.m. until 12:40 a.m. Monday to Saturday, and 7:15 a.m. to 12:40 a.m. on Sundays. ATMs can be found on the Upper Level at Citibank and next to the currency exchange. Public phones are also by the currency exchange in the south-east corner of the Upper Level. Trains depart from this level, and the smoking waiting room looks out onto the platform.

Services: There are a lot of fast junky options on the Street Level food court, which also serves as a de facto waiting room. If you want healthier fare, try the Rice Market and Boudin Sourdough Bakery on the

east side of the building. There is a selection of stores to wander through if you're killing time or to pick up a last-minute gift. These include several women's career clothing and shoe shops, Bath and Body Works, Waldenbooks, Dakota Watch Company, Claire's Accessories, Petite Sophisticate and Carlton Cards. Annoyingly enough, the only restrooms in the station are on the Street Level, which is a long escalator ride from the train platform.

Public Transportation: The closest El station is the Green Line's Clinton St. stop at Lake St. several blocks north of the station. CTA buses 14, 20, 56 and 157 board at Washington and Canal Sts. and travel to N. Michigan Ave. and the Loop. Coming from the Loop, take the same bus lines west across Madison St. If you're after a cab you'll find other like-minded commuters lining up in front of the main entrance on Madison St. between Canal and Clinton Sts.

Randolph St. Station

151 E Randolph St. at N. Michigan Ave.
312-322-7819

The underground Randolph St. Station is the Loop station from which Metra Electric's three-branches of service to Chicago's South Side and the South Shore Line to South Bend, Indiana depart. Schedules are somewhat sporadic for both except during weekday rush hours. The Van Buren St. Station also serves both the Metra Electric and South Shore lines and is located at E. Jackson Blvd. and Van Buren St., 312-322-6777. When planning train travel from the Randolph St. and Van Buren St. Stations, it is wise to double check schedules and stops with the RTA Information Center, 312-836-7000; www.rtachicago.com.

Ticket Windows: Enter the Randolph St. Station at E. Randolph St. and N. Michigan Ave. or from Metra's South Water St. Station via the Randolph St. platform. The ticket office is immediately visible upon descending the steps off Michigan Ave. or entering via the Pedway which tunnels around the Loop and east under Michigan Ave. ending at the station. Ticket office hours are 6 a.m. to 10:20 a.m. daily. The waiting room is open 5 a.m. to 12:50 a.m. daily.

Services: As the Randolph St. Station undergoes a massive reconstruction effort, the best way to describe amenities is "self-serve." There is no end date for construction in sight as the station's final configuration and appearance is influenced by the seemingly never-ending Millennium Park development overhead.

Public Transportation: Randolph St. Station is served by CTA buses 56, 151, 157 and, on days when there are events at the United Center, Express bus 19. A little over one block west of the train station in the Loop is the Randolph St. El station, which the Orange, Green, Purple and Brown Lines service.

LaSalle St. Station

414 S. LaSalle St. at E. Congress Pkwy.
312-322-8957

The La Salle St. Station located underneath the Chicago Stock Exchange serves the Metra Rock Island District Line's 15,000 commuters daily. The service has 11 mainline stops and 10 south suburban stops on its way to Joliet.

Ticket Windows: Enter the station off La Salle St., take the escalator one floor up, walk through the lobby past the bar to an open area where there are tracks and the ticket office. Agents are on duty from 7 a.m. to 8 p.m. weekdays and 10:30 a.m. to 6:30 p.m. on Saturday.

Services: There are no shops to speak of, but at least there's a bar. During the week, the small waiting room is less crowded than the bar (duh), especially after the markets close. The waiting room is open daily from 6 a.m. to midnight.

Public Transportation: The Blue Line's La Salle St. stop at Congress Pkwy. and the Orange, Purple and Brown Lines' La Salle St. stop at Van Buren St. all drop El riders right in front of the train station. CTA buses 145 and 147 stop in front of the station as well.

The "El" • Transit

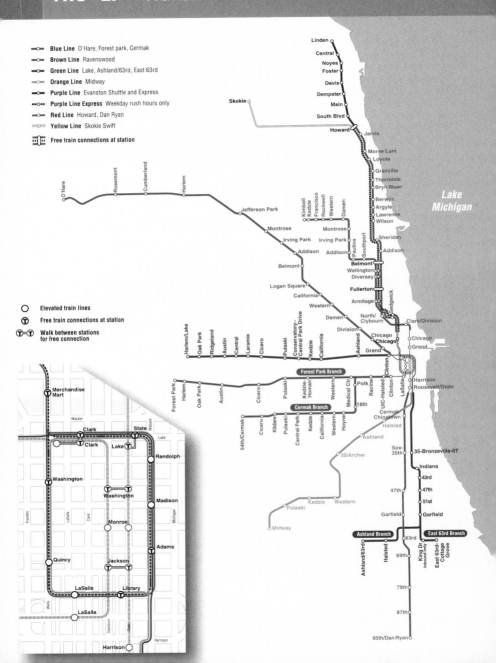

Blue Line O'Hare, Forest park, Cermak
Brown Line Ravenswood
Green Line Lake, Ashland/63rd, East 63rd
Orange Line Midway
Purple Line Evanston Shuttle and Express
Purple Line Express Weekday rush hours only
Red Line Howard, Dan Ryan
Yellow Line Skokie Swift
Free train connections at station

○ Elevated train lines
Ⓣ Free train connections at station
Ⓣ–Ⓣ Walk between stations for free connection

Lake Michigan

General Information

CTA Mailing Address:	Chicago Transit Authority
	Merchandise Mart Plaza, 7th Fl.
	P.O. Box 3555, Chicago, IL 60654
Phone:	312-664-7200
CTA Information:	1-888-YOUR-CTA (968-7282)
Website:	www.transitchicago.com
Email:	ctahelp@transitchicago.com

Overview

Whether traveling underground, street level or above the sidewalk, Chicagoans call their rapid transit system the "El." The name says Chicago as loud and clear as the high-pitched whine, guttural grumble and steely grind of the train itself. El tracks lasso Chicago's heart creating The Loop, where six of the seven El lines ride side-by-side above the pulsating business and financial district.

CTA riders herd onto the El trains and buses roaming about the City. CTA trains make 1,452 trips each day and serve 143 stations in the Chicago Metropolitan Area. Daily, thousands of Chicagoans rely on the system to transport them to and from work, home and entertainment.

Fares

The standard full-fare on CTA trains is $1.50. A 30¢ transfer slip allows two additional rides within two hours of issuance and can be used for transferring from rail to bus (or vice versa), and also between buses. Transfers must be purchased with the base fare on the first leg of the journey. Transferring within the rail network is free.

Avoid fishing for exact change by purchasing a Transit Card at vending machines located in all El stations. Cards are available in various increments up to $100. For every $10 you put on your card, the CTA will contribute an extra $1 free. Transit Cards are also sold for $10 and $20 at currency exchanges, Jewel and Dominick's stores, online and at many other city locations. CTA also offers a 10-Pack of one way tickets for $15, no savings but no change hassle either. A $75 Monthly Pass is good for unlimited rides. Day Passes are 1-Day ($5), 2-Day ($9), 3-Day ($12) and 5-Day ($18).

Reduced Fares cost 75¢ for the base trip and 15¢ for a transfer for riders who qualify: children ages seven to 11 years; seniors age 65+ with an RTA Reduced Fare Riding Permit; and riders with disabilities (with an RTA permit) and their companion. Grade school students with CTA Student Riding Permits ($5 per semester; $2 summer school) pay reduced fares on weekdays from 5:30 p.m. to 8:00 p.m. Free Rides are reserved for children aged six and under. Riders that are in "other uniformed or ID-bearing categories authorized by the Chicago Transit Board" (whatever that means) also enjoy free rides. You might want that stinking badge after all…

Frequency of Service

CTA publishes schedules that say trains run every 3 to 12 minutes during weekday rush hours and every 6 to 20 minutes at other times. But service can be irregular, especially during non-rush hours, after hours and in bad weather. While the system is relatively safe late at night, stick to stations in populated areas as much as possible. Buses with owl service may be better options in the wee hours.

El Lines

For ease of navigation, the El's seven lines are color-coded: Blue, Red, Brown, Orange, Green, Purple and Yellow. While we provide general schedule information for each line, contact the RTA Information Center for detailed schedule information.

Blue Line: Comprised of the O'Hare, Forest Park and Cermak branches traveling west, O'Hare and Forest Park run 24-hours while Cermak is operational only on weekdays.

Red Line: Runs north-south from the Howard St. station down to the 95th St./Dan Ryan station; operates 24-hours.

Brown Line: Starts from the Kimball St. station and heads south with service to the Loop and sometimes just to Belmont Ave. On weekdays and Saturdays, the first Loop-bound train leaves Kimball St. at 4:45 a.m.; the last train to leave the Loop is at 12:105 a.m. Sundays service begins at 6:50 a.m. and ends at 11:50 p.m. After that, take the Red Line to Belmont Ave. and transfer to the Brown Line where the last train leaves at 2:25 a.m. (12:55 a.m. on Sundays). The Brown Line also runs between Kimball St. and Belmont Ave. from 4:00 a.m. to 2:25 a.m. weekdays and Saturdays; and from 5:05 a.m. to 12:55 a.m. on Sundays.

Orange Line: Travels from Midway Airport to the Loop and back. Trains depart from Midway beginning at 4:35 a.m. weekdays and Saturdays and at 7 a.m. on Sundays; the last train leaves the Loop for the airport at 11:45 p.m. daily.

Green Line: Covers portions of west and south Chicago. The Harlem/Lake St. branch travels straight west. The Ashland Ave./63rd St. and E.63rd St./Cottage Grove branches go south and split east and west. Depending on the branch, service begins around 4 a.m. weekdays with the last trains running around 1 a.m. Weekend schedules vary.

Purple Line: Shuttles north-south between Linden Pl. in suburban Evanston and Howard St., Chicago's northernmost station. Service starts at 4:35 a.m. and ends at 12:55 a.m. weeknights, 1:45 a.m. on weekends and 12:55 a.m. Sundays. Weekdays, an express train runs between Linden Pl. and the Loop between 6:25 a.m. and 10:10 a.m. and then again between 2:55 p.m. and 6:15 .p.m. At all other times, take the Purple Line Shuttle to the Howard St. station and transfer to the Red Line to reach the Loop.

Yellow Line: Runs between the north suburban Skokie station and Chicago's Howard St. station on weekdays from 4:50 a.m. to 10:15 p.m. On weekends, take CTA bus 97 from the Skokie station to Howard St. and catch the Red Line to the Loop.

Bicycles

Bicycles ride free and are permitted onboard at all times except weekdays from 7 a.m. to 9 a.m. and 4 p.m. to 6 p.m. Only two bikes are allowed per car, so survey the platform for other bikes and check out the cars as they pull into the station for two-wheelers already onboard. When entering a station, either use the turnstile or ask an attendant to open the gate. Don't try to take your bike through the tall steel gates—it WILL get stuck!

Free Trolleys · Transit

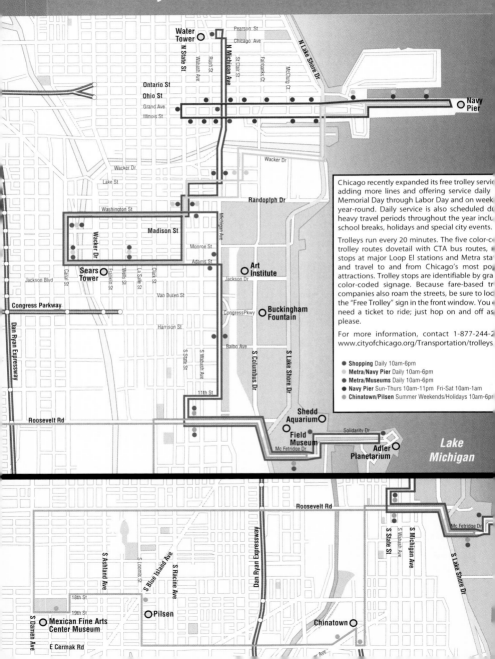

Chicago recently expanded its free trolley servic
adding more lines and offering service daily
Memorial Day through Labor Day and on week
year-round. Daily service is also scheduled du
heavy travel periods throughout the year inclu
school breaks, holidays and special city events.

Trolleys run every 20 minutes. The five color-c
trolley routes dovetail with CTA bus routes,
stops at major Loop El stations and Metra sta
and travel to and from Chicago's most po
attractions. Trolley stops are identifiable by gra
color-coded signage. Because fare-based tr
companies also roam the streets, be sure to loc
the "Free Trolley" sign in the front window. You
need a ticket to ride; just hop on and off as
please.

For more information, contact 1-877-244-2
www.cityofchicago.org/Transportation/trolleys

- ● **Shopping** Daily 10am-6pm
- ● **Metra/Navy Pier** Daily 10am-6pm
- ● **Metra/Museums** Daily 10am-6pm
- ● **Navy Pier** Sun-Thurs 10am-11pm Fri-Sat 10am-1am
- ● **Chinatown/Pilsen** Summer Weekends/Holidays 10am-6pr

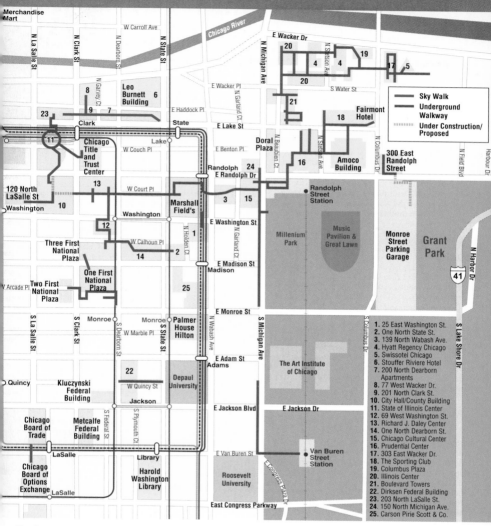

The downtown underground Pedway keeps Chicagoans moving throughout the central business district. An over 40-block network of tunnels and overhead bridges connects important public, government and private sector buildings with retail stores, major hotels, rapid transit stations and commuter rail stations. A subterranean city with shops, restaurants, services and public art works, the Pedway is a welcome alternative to navigating trafficked intersections on foot and walking outdoors in Chicago's below wind-chill winters. The underground walkway system is open 24 hours; however access to a number of the buildings is limited after standard business hours. The first Pedway links were built in 1951 to connect the State St. and Dearborn St. subways at Washington St. and Jackson Blvd. Today, Chicago's Pedway continues to grow as City government and the private sector cooperate to expand it.

General Information

Chicago Park District:	*www.chicagoparkdistrict.com*
	312-742-PLAY
Chicagoland Bicycle	*www.chibikefed.org*
Federation:	*312-42-PEDAL*
Chicago Area Runner's	*203 N Wabash Ave.*
Association:	*312-666-9836*

Overview

Greater Chicago offers dozens of recreational off-road paths that allow users to bike, skate, walk and jog without the worry of vehicular traffic - now if only we could get dogs off the paths! In addition to recreational paths in the city's parks, designated off-street trails exist along the Lakefront, North Shore Channel, the North Branch Trail along the Chicago River, Burnham Greenway and the Major Taylor Trail.

Lakefront Trail

Chicago has one of the prettiest and most accessible shorelines of any city in the U.S. (aside from having to first cross treacherous Lake Shore Drive to get to there). Use one of the over/underpasses and you'll discover 15 miles of bathing beaches and 18 miles of bike paths-just don't anticipate being able to train for the Athens Olympics during the Summer months, when the sheer numbers make it impossible to advance along the path beyond a snail's pace during peak times. Thankfully for Chicagoans, in 1909, Daniel Burnham and Edward Bennett created the "Plan for Chicago," which included deeming that the shoreline be used as a public, non-commercial space where the city has paid plans for cycling, jogging, blading, skating and swimming.

Major Taylor Trail

If you've ever wanted to take in a slice of Chicago's southwestern-most corner (and let's face it, who hasn't?) a new bike route, which incorporates an abandoned railroad right of way begins at Dawes Park at 81st and Hamilton Sts., near Western Ave. The 6-mile trail runs to the southeast through Beverly and Morgan Park, ending up at the Cook County Forest Preserve near 130th and Halsted Streets. The trail was named in honor of cycling legend Marshall "Major" Taylor, an African-American who competed in the early years of cycle racing and lived out the final years of his life in a YMCA in Chicago.

Burnham Greenway

The following information was present in a Trust For Public Land report on the state of the proposed route of the Burnham Greenway Trail before it was paved:

Site History: Five-mile Conrail right-of-way between Chicago and the south suburbs, running through both industrial and natural areas.
Contamination: Phase II indicated pollution from adjacent uses, including fly dumping, railroad pollutants, and some unnatural coloration in adjacent water. Assessment determined no risk as long as the soil remains undisturbed.
REMEDIATION: Corridor will be paved.

So, as long as you stick to the paved trail and don't feel the desire to go digging around off the path, you should remain in good health! The path is suitable for riding, skating, rollerblading and pedestrian activity.

North Branch Trail

To access the northern end of the trail, take Lake Cook Road to the Chicago Botanic Garden, located east of I-94. Starting from any of the forest preserves as the path winds southward is also an option. To access the southern end of the trail in Chicago, take Milwaukee Avenue to Devon Avenue and head a short way east to the Caldwell Woods Preserve. The North Branch winds along the Chicago River and the Skokie Lagoons but, unlike most of the other trails, this one crosses streets so be careful and look out for cars as you approach.

North Shore Channel Trail

This trail follows North Shore Channel of the Chicago River from Lawrence Ave. through Lincolnwood, Skokie and Evanston to Green Bay Rd. at McCormick Blvd. Not all of the seven miles of the trail are paved bike paths and you'll have to endure the hassle of switching between path and street. Skokie recently paved the trail segment between Oakton and Howard Sts. but there are still many missing links in the route, much to the chagrin of Friends of the Chicago River (FOCR), who are trying to extend and improve the Channel Trail.

Chicago Park District

Many of the parks under the jurisdiction of the Chicago Park District have paths dedicated to cycling, jogging, walking, rollerblading and skating. The Chicago Area Runner's Association is so committed to lobbying for runners' rights that it successfully petitioned to have the Lincoln Park running paths ploughed through the winter so they could continue their running activities. This calls into question the sanity of such sadistic dedication but we can only assume that the entire year is needed to prepare for the Chicago Marathon, held annually on the last Sunday in October. Check out the chart on the pacing page to determine Chicago Parks that designate jogging/walking and cycling/skating paths.

Park District—North Region	Address	Phone	Jog/Walk	Bike/Skate	Map
Brooks Park	7100 N Harlem Ave	312-742-7855	■		
Emmerson Park	1820 N Granville Ave	312-742-7877	■		36
Eugene Field Park	5100 N Ridgeway Ave	312-742-7591		■	
Indian Boundary Park	2500 W Lunt Ave	312-742-7887	■		33
Oz Park	2021 N Burling St	312-742-7898	■		30
Peterson Park	5801 N Pulaski Ave	312-742-7584	■		
Portage Park	4100 N Long Ave	312-742-7634	■		
River Park	5100 N Francisco Ave	312-742-7516		■	38
Shabbona Park	6935 W Addison St	312-742-7608	■		
Warren Park	6601 N Western Ave	312-742-7888	■	■	33
Wilson Park	4630 N Milwaukee Ave	312-742-7616	■		
Winnemac Park	5100 N Leavitt St	312-742-5101	■		39

Park District—Central Region	Address	Phone	Jog/Walk	Bike/Skate	Map
Columbus Park	500 S Central Ave	312-746-5046	■	■	
Douglas Park	1401 S Sacramento Blvd	312-747-7670	■	■	
Dvorak Park	1119 W Cullerton St	312-746-5083	■		
Humboldt Park	1400 N Sacramento Blvd	312-742-7549	■		26
Piotrowski Park	4247 W 31st St	312-745-4801	■	■	
Riis Park	6100 W Fullerton Ave	312-746-5363	■	■	
Rutherford Sayre Park	6871 W Belden Ave	312-746-5368	■		
Union Park	1501 W Randolph St	312-746-5494	■		24

Park District—Southwest Region	Address	Phone	Jog/Walk	Bike/Skate	Map
Bogan Park	3939 W 79th St	312-747-6056	■		
Cole Park	361 E 85th St	312-747-6063	■		
Cornell Square Park	1809 W 50th St	312-747-6097	■		
Hayes Park	2936 W 85th St	312-747-6177	■		
LeClaire Hearst Park	5120 W 44th St	312-747-6438	■		
Mount Greenwood Park	3721 W 111th St	312-747-6564	■		
Rainey Park	4350 W 79th St	312-747-6630	■		
Senka Park	5656 S St. Louis Ave	312-747-7632	■		
Sherman Park	1301 W 52nd St	312-747-6672	■		
Avalon Park	1215 E 83rd St	312-747-6015	■		
Bradley Park	9729 S Yates Ave	312-747-6022	■		
Gately Park/Wendell Smith School Park	810 E 103rd St	312-747-6155	■		
Hamilton Park	513 W 72nd St	312-747-6174	■		
Lake Meadows Park	3117 S Rhodes Ave	312-747-6443	■	■	14
Meyering Park	7140 S Martin Luther King Dr	312-747-6545	■		
Palmer Park	301 E 111th St	312-747-6576	■		
Rosenblum Park/ Horace Mann School	7547 S Euclid Ave	312-747-6649	■		
Washington Park	5531 S Martin Luther King Dr	312-747-6823	■	■	

Park District—Lakefront Region	Address	Phone	Jog/Walk	Bike/Skate	Map
Calumet Park	9801 S Avenue G	312-747-6039		■	
Jackson Park	6401 S Stony Island Ave	312-747-6187		■	
Lincoln Park	2045 N Lincoln Park West	312-742-7726	■	■	
Loyola Park	1230 W Greenleaf Ave	312-742-7857	■	■	34
Rainbow Park & Beach	3111 E 77th St	312-745-1479		■	
South Shore Cultural Center	7059 S South Shore Dr	312-747-2536		■	

General Information

Chicagoland Bicycle Federation: 650 S. Clark St., #300, 312-427-3325, www.biketraffic.org
Chicago Park District: www.chicagoparkdistrict.com, 312-742-PLAY
Chicago Transit Authority: www.transitchicago.com
DOT Bikes Page: http://www.ci.chi.il.us/Transportation/Bikes/

For some, bike riding in Chicago is a means of transit while, for others, it presents an enjoyable way to tour Chicago and get some fresh air! Regardless of your motivation for riding, we don't need to remind you that head injuries are the leading cause of fatality among bicyclists—but we will anyway. If you are a recreational rider, see Page 237 for information on bicycle paths.

For those who are not rubbernecking, consider the following to make your transit more pleasurable: Wherever possible stick to roads with designated bike lanes including King Dr., Wells St. from the Chicago River to Lincoln Park, Elston/Milwaukee Ave., Canal St. from 18th St. to Walnut St., Halsted St. from Diversey Pkwy to Fulton St. and Roosevelt Rd. from Grant Park to California Ave. The Skyway, which will be undergoing major construction in 2003, also has a bike lane that connects with King Dr. There are other "recommended bike routes" with lanes that are wider to accommodate riders and cars. Get a copy of Chicago's free bike map for a comprehensive listing - www.cityofchicago.org/transportation. Wherever possible stick close to the right hand curb and make sure if you leave home early or your office late, you have the appropriate evening gear. Unless you have a secure place to store your bike, invest in the heaviest chain and lock you can find (and carry). Don't leave your bike unattended for a second!

Bikes Onboard Mass Transit

Bicycles are permitted (free) on all El trains at all times except 7am–9am and 4pm–6pm weekdays. Use the accessible turnstile or ask an attendant to open an access gate. Don't try to take your bike through the tall steel gates—it will get stuck! Only two bikes per carriage are allowed so check for other bikes before you get on. The following CTA Buses are equipped with bike racks: 63rd St., 72 North Ave., 75th St. and 65 Grand buses. If your bike is the first to be loaded, lower the rack and place it in position with the front wheel facing the curb. If there is already a bike on the rack, place your bike's rear wheel toward the curb. If two bikes are already loaded, wait for the next bus. Plan on taking the Metra? Leave your bike at home! Items larger than a briefcase are not permitted on Metra Trains.

Bike Shops	Address	Phone	Map
Art's Cycle	1646 E 55th St	773-363-7524	20
Atlantic Cyclery Inc	3001 N Broadway St	773-244-1079	44
Baron Von Scoot	1706 W North Ave	773-252-5800	21
Bicycle Garage	11 E Jackson Blvd	800-300-1993	5
Bike Chicago	600 E Grand Ave	312-755-0488	3
Bike Source	1600 W Beach Ave	773-327-2706	22
Bike Stop	1626 Ogden Ave	630-936-4616	24
Bike Stop Cycles	1034 W Belmont Ave	773-868-6800	43
Chicagoland Bicycle	3107 N Rockwell St	773-478-1659	41
Cyclone Sports	2468 N Clark St	773-281-0444	30
Easy Rider Bike Shop	3103 N Ashland Ave	773-348-8200	43
Edgebrook Cycle & Sport	4119 N Lincoln Ave	773-549-1240	39
International Bike Shop	1435 W Fullerton Ave	773-472-7433	29
Johnny Sprocket's	1725 S Racine Ave	312-226-6330	26
Johnny Sprocket's North	1052 W Bryn Mawr	773-293-1695	37
Kozy Cyclery	1451 W Webster Ave	773-528-2700	29
Kozy Cyclery	3712 N Halstead St	773-281-2263	44
Mission Works	738 W Randolph St	312-466-9111	4
Monkeyworks	1800 W Cornelia Ave	773-935-5948	42
On The Route Bicycle	3146 N Lincoln Ave	773-477-5066	43
Oscar Wastyn Cycles	2634 W Fullerton Ave	773-384-8999	27
Out Spoken	1113 W Belmont Ave	773-404-2919	43
Performance Bicycle Shop	2720 N Halsted St	773-248-0107	30
Quick Release Bike Shop	1623 N Halsted St	773-871-3110	31
Rapid Transit Cycle Shop	1900 W North Ave	773-227-2288	21
Recycle Bike Shop	1465 S Michigan Ave	312-987-1080	11
Roberts Cycle	7054 N Clark St	773-274-9281	34
Sportmart Inc	3134 N Clark St	312-337-6151	44
Sportmart Inc	620 N La Salle Dr	773-871-8500	2
Trek Of Chicago	1337 N Wells St	312-726-2453	31
Upgrade Cycle Works	1128 W Chicago Ave	312-226-8650	24
Urban Bikes	4653 N Broadway St	773-728-5212	40
Village Cycle Center	1337 N Wells St	312-726-2453	31
Wheels & Things	5210 S Harper Ave	773-493-4326	19

General Information

Chicago Park District: www.chicagoparkdistrict.com
312-742-PLAY (7529)

Overview

Due to the temperature extremes that Chicago experiences, its residents can enjoy both ice skating and inline skating at various times of the year. Ice skating can be a fun, free winter activity if you have your own skates and if you don't, many rinks rent them. Skateboarding is also a popular pastime and a number of parks throughout the city are equipped with skating facilities.

Inline Skating

Similar to bike riding, inline skating in Chicago serves dual purposes. If you plan on strapping on the blades to get you from A to B, be super-careful navigating the streets. As it is, Chicago drivers tend to have difficulty seeing bicycle riders and, chances are, they won't notice you until you've slammed into the inside of their car door. Wear protective gear whenever possible, especially a helmet, and learn to shout loudly so that people can anticipate your approach. If recreational skating is more your speed, check out the Recreational Paths page for cool places to skate. If you'd like to join the hundreds of skaters on the paths in summer and you don't have your own gear, the following places offer skate rental: Londo Mondo, 1100 N Dearborn St. at W Maple St., 312-751-2794; Rainbo Sports Shop, 4836 N Clark St., 773-275-5500; Bike Chicago at Navy Pier, 800-915-BIKE; City Sweats, 2467 N Clark St. at Fullerton Ave., 773-348-2489. Hourly rates range from $7-$10, while daily rates are from $20-$30.

Skate Parks

If what you're after is a phat jam session, grab your blades or board and a couple of buddies and head down to the magnificent Burnham Skate Park (East of Lake Shore Drive at 31st St.). With amazing grinding walls and rails, vert walls and banks, Burnham Park presents hours of fun and falls. Less intense, but equally fun, are the two skate parks with ramps, quarter pipes and grind rails. One can be found at West Lawn Park, 4233 W 65th St., 312-747-7032, the other at Oriole Park, 5430 N Olcott Ave., 312-742-7852.

Ice Skating

The long-running and popular Skate on State was canceled due to the opening of two new ice rinks: the McCormick-Tribune Ice Rink at Millennium Park and the Midway Plaisance ice rink.

The Millennium Park rink is a beautiful place to skate during the day or evening, with Chicago's glorious skyline in the background. In summer months, the area becomes home to al fresco dining and entertainment. Located at 55 N. Michigan Ave., enter on the east side of Michigan Ave. between Monroe Dr. and Randolph St. Parking is available for $10 at the Grant Park North Garage (enter from Michigan Ave. median at Washington or Madison Sts.). Skate rental is $3 for adults and children and if you have your own and want them sharpened it's $5, 312-742-7529.

The new Olympic-sized skating rink and warming house complex at Midway Plaisance is the alternative to to Millenium Park. The construction of the permanent skating rink was a joint effort by the University of Chicago, the City of Chicago, and the Chicago Park District. Located at 59th and Woodlawn Ave., entry costs between $3-$5. During summer the facility is used for roller-skating and entertainment, 312-747-0233.

Other ice-skating rinks are located seasonally at:
McFetridge Sports Complex (year-round),
3843 N. California Ave., 312-742-7585
($1.50-$2.50 admission + rental)
Daley Bicentennial Plaza Rink,
337 E. Randolph St., 312-742-7650
($1-$2 admission + rental)
McKinley Park,
2210 W. Pershing Rd., 312-747-5992 ($3-$5 rental)
Mt. Greenwood Park,
3721 W. 111th St., 312-747-2200 ($2-$3 rental)
Navy Pier Ice Rink,
600 E Grand Ave., 312-595-5100 ($3-$4 rental)
Riis Park,
6100 W. Fullerton Ave., 312-746-5735 ($2-$3 rental)
Rowan Park,
11546 S. Avenue Ln., 312-747-2200 ($2-$3 rental)
Warren Park, 6601 N. Western Ave., 312-742-6600
West Lawn Park, 4233 W. 65th St., 312-747-8500
The Rink (rollerskating), 1122 E 87th St, 773-221-2600 ($1)
USA-Rainbo Roller Skating Center,
4836 N Clark St., 773-271-5668 ($4-$10)

Gear

If you're after skateboard gear, check out Affiliate Skateboards at 431 N Wolcott Ave., 312-633-0777, Air Time Skate Boards at 3315 N Clark St.,773-248-4970, and Uprise Skateboard Shop at 1357 N Milwaukee Ave.,773-342-7763.

For skating equipment, Air Time (above) also does inline skates as does Londo Mondo which has two locations: 1100 N Dearborn St. at W Maple St.,312-751-2794, and Rainbo Sports Shop at 4836 N Clark St.,773-275-5500.

For all your ice-skating needs, try the Skater's Edge store in the McFetridge Sports Complex. They deal in hockey skates and equipment as well as inline skates and accessories such as sequined dresses! (3843 N. California, 312-742-7585)

Chicago is blessed with a number of golf courses within the City limits. Many courses offer discounts for residents and seniors, so be sure to ask. We couldn't possibly list all the great links in the surrounding suburbs so we picked a few close to NFT's coverage area. Our Chicago favorites include: Jackson Park for being the closest 18 holes to the Loop; Sydney R. Marovitz executive course for beautiful lake views; Harborside International for a challenging Scottish-links experience; and Family Golf Center for a lunchtime 9.

Golf Courses

	Phone	Map	Holes	Fees
Family Golf Center				
221 N Columbus Dr	312-616-1236	6	9	$15
Robert A. Black Golf Course				
2045 West Pratt Ave	312-245-0909	34	9	$11.50 weekdays/ $13 weekends
Sydney R Marovitz Golf Course				
3600 N Recreation Dr	312-245-0909	43	9	$14 weekdays/ $16.50 weekends
Columbus Park Golf Course				
5700 W Jackson Blvd	312-245-0909		9	$10 weekdays/ $11.50 weekends
Edgebrook Golf Course				
5900 N. Central Ave	773-763-8320		18	$13 weekdays/ $16 weekends
Glencoe Park District Course				
621 Westley Rd., Glencoe	847-835-0250		18	$36 weekdays/ $42 weekends
Harborside International Golf Center				
11001 S Doty Ave	312-STARTER		18	$76 weekdays/ $87 weekends
Indian Boundary Golf Course				
8600 W Forest Preserve Ave	773-625-9630		18	$23 weekdays/ $26 weekends
Jackson Park Golf Course				
6400 Richards Dr	312-245-0909		18	$10 weekdays/ $20 weekends
Marquette Park Golf Course				
6700 S Kedzie Ave	312-747-2761		9	$10.75 weekdays/ $12 weekends
Peter N. Jans Community Golf Course				
1019 Central Ave, Evanston	847-866-2910		18	$15 weekdays/ $17 weekends
Riverside Golf Club				
2320 Desplaines Ave	708-447-1049		18	$65 weekdays/ $75 weekends
South Shore Country Club				
7059 South Shore Dr	312-245-0909		9	$10 weekdays/ $11.50 weekends
The Glen Club				
2901 West Lake Ave, Glenview	847-724-7272		18	$110 weekdays/ $135 weekends
Winnetka Park District Course				
1300 Oak St, Winnetka	847-501-2050		18	$28 weekdays/ $34 weekends

Driving Ranges

	Phone	Map	Fees
Diversey Driving Range			
455 N. Cityfront Plaza Dr.	312-742-7929	3	$7/65 balls, $2 clubs
Family Golf Center			
221 N Columbus Dr.	312-616-1236	6	$10/100 balls, $3 clubs
Harborside International Golf Center			
11001 S Doty Ave	312-STARTER	18	$10/100, $3 clubs
Jackson Park Golf Course			
6400 Richards Dr	312-245-0909	18	$6-50/65 balls, $2 clubs

312-742-PLAY (general info); 312-747-2474 (Lake Front Region Office). All tennis courts (except Daley Bicentennial Plaza in Grant Park, Diversey Park and Waveland Park) are free to the public and first come, first served. Courts are open daily, check each park for individual hours.

Tennis Courts

Armour Square Park	3309 S Shields Ave	312-747-6012
Ashe Beach Park	2701 E 74th St	
Athletic Field Park	3546 W Addison St	
Brands Park	3259 N Elston Ave	312-742-7582
California Park	3843 N California Ave	312-742-7585
Chase Park	4701 N Ashland Ave	312-742-7518
Clemente Park	2334 W Division St	
Cornell Square Park	1809 W 50th St	312-747-6097
Daley Bicentennial Plaza		
	337 E Randolph St	312-742-7650
$7/hr; reservations must be made in person. 7am-10pm.		
David Square Park	4430 S Marshfield Ave	312-747-6107
Douglas Park Cultural & Community Center		
	1401 S Sacramento Ave	312-747-7670
Dunham Park	4638 N Melvina Ave	
Ellis Park	648 E 37th St	312-747-6122
Emmerson Playground Park		
	1820 W Granville Ave	
Eugene Field Park	5100 N Ridgeway Ave	
Fuller Park	331 W 45th St	312-747-6144
Gompers Park	4222 W Foster Ave	312-742-7628
Grant Park	331 E Randolph St	
Green Briar Park	2650 W Peterson Ave	
Hamilton Park	513 W 72nd St	312-747-6174
Hamlin Park	3035 N Hoyne Ave	312-742-7785
Harrison Park	1824 S Wood St	312-746-5491
Hollywood Park	3312 W Thorndale Ave	
Horner Park	2741 W Montrose Ave	
Humboldt Park	1400 N Sacramento Ave	312-742-7549
Independence Park	3945 N Springfield Ave	312-742-7590
Indian Boundary Park	2500 W Lunt Ave	312-742-7887
Jackson Park	6401 S Stony Island Ave	312-747-2763
Jefferson Park	4822 N Long Ave	312-742-7609
Jensen Playground Park		
	4600 N Lawndale Ave	
Jonquil Park	1023 W Wrightwood Ave	
Kenwood Community Park		
	1330 E 50th St	312-747-6285
Kosciuszko Park	2732 N Avers Ave	312-742-7546
Lake Shore Park	808 N Lake Shore Dr	

Legion Park	W Peterson Ave to	
	W Foster Ave at the Chicago River	
Lerner Park	7000 N Sacramento Ave	
Loyola Park	1230 W Greenleaf Ave	
Mandrake Park	900 E Pershing Rd	
Mather Park	5941 N Richmond St	312-742-7501
McFetridge Sports Center (California Park)		
	3843 N California Ave	312-742-7585
McGuane Park	2901 S Poplar Ave	
McKinley Park	2210 W Pershing Rd	312-747-6527
Metcalfe Park	4134 S State St	
Nichols Park	1300 E 55th St	
Oz Park	2021 N Burling St	
Piotrowski Park	4247 W 31st St	312-747-6608
Pottawattomie Park	7340 N Rogers Ave	
Rainbow Park & Beach		
	2873 E 76th St	
Revere Park	2509 W Irving Park Rd	312-742-7594
River Park	5100 N Francisco Ave	312-742-7516
Rogers Park	7345 N Washtenaw Ave	
Roosevelt Park	62 W Roosevelt Rd	
Senn Park	1550 W Thorndale Ave	
Sheridan Park	910 S Aberdeen St	312-746-5369
Sherman Park	1307 W 52nd St	312-747-6672
Smith (Joseph Higgins) Park		
	2526 W Grand Ave	312-742-7534
South Shore Culture Center		
	7059 S Shore Dr	
Taylor Park	41 W 47th St	312-747-6728
Touhy Park	7348 N Paulina St	
Union Park	1501 W Randolph St	312-746-5494
Warren Park	6601 N Western Ave	312-742-7879
Washington Park	5531 S Martin Luther	
	King Dr	312-747-6823
Welles Park	2333 W Sunnyside	
	Ave	312-742-7511
Frank J. Wilson Park	4630 N Milwaukee Ave	
Lincoln Park-Diversey Tennis Center		312-742-7821
$12/hr; reservations must be made in person. Clay courts.		
Lincoln Park-Waveland Tennis Center		312-742-7674
$12/hr; reservations must be made in person.; 7:30am-8pm		

Volleyball Courts

Lincoln Park/ North Avenue Beach   312-74-BEACH (reservations and price info.)
101 courts—12 are always open to the public. Much league play and reserved courts.
Office hours: 1pm-9pm Mon-Fri; 8am-5pm weekends.

Lincoln Park/ Montrose Beach   312-742-1976 (reservations and price info.)
45 courts—first come, first served. League play in the evening.

Jackson Park/ 63rd Street Beach
4 courts—first come, first served. Free.

Swimming & Bowling · Sports

312.742.PLAY (general park info number); 312.742.5121 (Department of Beaches and Pools). All outdoor pools are free for the summer (Memorial Day-Labor Day). During the year, all lap swim fees are for 10-week sessions. $20 before 9am; $10 after 9am.

Outdoor Pools

Avondale Park	3516 W School St	312-742-7581
Chase Park	500 N Ashland Ave	312-742-7518
Douglas Park Cultural & Community Center	1401 S Sacramento Ave	312-747-7670
Dvorak Park	1119 W Cullerton St	312-746-5083
Franklin Park	4320 W 15th St	312-747-7676
Gompers Park	4222 W Foster Ave	312-742-7628
Hamlin Park	3035 N Hoyne Ave	312-742-7785
Humbolt Park	1400 N Sacramento Ave	312-742-7549
Jefferson Park	4822 N Long Ave	312-742-7609
McFetridge Sports Center (California Park)	3843 N California Ave	312-742-7585
Piotrowski Park	4247 W 31st St	312-747-6608
Pulaski Park	1419 W Blackhawk St	312-742-7559
River Park	5100 N Francisco Ave	312-742-7516
Sherman Park	1307 W 52nd St	312-747-6672
Sherwood Park	5705 S Shields Ave	
Smith (Joseph Higgins) Park	2526 W Grand Ave	312-742-7534
Taylor Park	41 W 47th St	312-747-6728
Union Park	1501 W Randolph St	312-746-5494
Washington Park	5531 S Martin Luther King Dr	312-747-2490
Wentworth Gardens Park	3770 S Wentworth Ave	312-747-6996
Wrightwood Park	2534 N Greenview Ave	312-742-7816

Indoor Pools

Altgeld Park	515 S Washtenaw Ave	312-746-5001
Clemente Park	2334 W Division St	312-742-7466
Eckhart Park	1330 W Chicago Ave	312-746-5553
Gill Park	825 W Sheridan Rd	312-742-5807
Harrison Park	1824 S Wood St	312-421-8572
Independence Park	3945 N Springfield Ave	312-742-7530
Kosciuszko Park	2732 N Avers Ave	312-742-7556
Leone Park & Beach	1222 W Touhy Ave	
Mather Park	5941 N Richmond St	312-742-7513
McGuane Park	2901 S Poplar Ave	312-747-7463
Sheridan Park	910 S Aberdeen St	312-746-5370
Stanton Park	618 W Scott St	312-742-9553
Washington Park	5531 S Martin Luther King Dr	
Welles Park	2333 W Sunnyside Ave	312-742-7515

Bowling Alleys

Diversey-River Bowl Inc	2211 W Diversey Ave	773-227-5800	Sun-Thurs: $19/hr per lane, $3 for shoes; Fri-Sat: $26/hr per lane, $3 for shoes
Drake Bowl	3550 W Montrose Ave	773-463-1377	$1.50-2 per game; $2 for shoes
Habetler Bowl Inc	5250 N Northwest Hwy	773-774-0500	$4 per game, $2.50 for shoes; Tuesdays $1 per game
Lucky Strike	2747 N Lincoln Ave	773-549-2695	$15/hr per lane, $2 for shoes
Marigold Bowl	828 W Grace St	773-935-8183	$1.75-3.25 per game; $2 for shoes
Southport Lanes & Billiards	3325 N Southport Ave	773-472-6600	$16/hr per lane, $2 for shoes
Timber Lanes Inc	1851 W Irving Park Rd	773-549-9770	$2.50 per game, $2 for shoes
Waveland Bowl Inc	3700 N Western Ave	773-472-5900	$3-6 per game, $4 for shoes

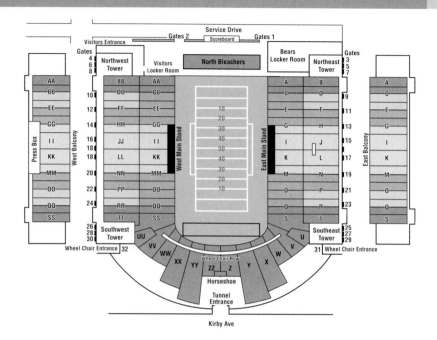

General Information

Location: 200 E. Florida Ave.
Champaign, IL 61820
Bears Sales Office (Champaign): 888-79-BEARS (792-3277)
Bears website: www.chicagobears.com
Bears email: stadiumsales@bears.nfl.com
Ticketmaster: 312-559-1212; www.ticketmaster.com
Fighting Illini: 217-333-3470
Fighting Illini website: http://fightingillini.fansonly.com

Overview

While Solider Field is being rebuilt, the Chicago Bears and their fans will migrate 141 miles south to Memorial Stadium at the University of Illinois at Urbana-Champaign, where the Bears will play the 2002-2003 season and 2003-2004 pre-season games. The Fighting Illini's stadium holds 70,000. Provided that construction proceeds as planned, The Bears will play their 2003-2004 season at Chicago's new Solider Field.

How to Get Tickets

Purchase individual tickets through Ticketmaster. Contact the Bears sales office in Champaign for 10-game ticket packages starting at $400. University of Illinois students get 10-game packages with end zone seating for $200.

How to Get There

By Car: Your wisest choice. From Chicago, drive east on I-57 to the University Ave. exit. Turn right onto Mattis Ave. to Kirby Ave. Turn left on Kirby Ave. and follow the clear signage to the parking lots that charge minimal fees. Most of the stadiums lots are located south of Kirby Ave. Season ticket parking permit holders should follow signs to designated lots. If Kirby Ave. is backed up, continue south on Mattis Ave. to Windsor Rd. Turn left on Windsor Rd. and left again on either First St. or Lincoln Ave. to reach the lots.

By Train: Although Amtrak's Illinois and City of New Orleans services departing from Union Station downtown both go to Champaign, their limited schedules require leaving the day before and overnighting in Champaign to make kickoff for most games. The 2.5 hour journey costs $16 to $32 each way.

By Bus: Greyhound takes 3 hours one-way to Champaign Urbana and buses depart fairly regularly. Roundtrip tickets costs approximately $54. Upon arrival at the Champaign bus station, catch a cab or local bus to the stadium. Call Chicago-area Greyhound bus stations for schedules and fares. Stations are located at 630 W. Harrison St. in South Loop , 312-408-5980; 95th St. in the El's Red Line Dan Ryan station, 312-408-5999, and 5800 N. Cumberland Ave. in the El's Blue Line Cumberland station, 773-693-2474.

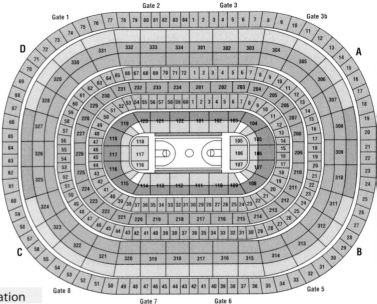

General Information

Location:
 1901 W. Madison St., Chicago, IL 60612
Phone: 312-455-4500
Website: www.unitedcenter.com
Ticketmaster: 312-559-1212; www.ticketmaster.com
Chicago Bulls: 312-455-4000 • Bulls website: www.bulls.com
Chicago Blackhawks: 312-455-7000
Blackhawks website: www.chicagoblackhawks.com

Overview

Looming over the West Side, United Center is home to the NHL's Blackhawks and the NBA's Chicago Bulls. The glitzy stadium is also the City's premier concert venue. Opened in 1994, the $175 million stadium was privately funded by deep-pocketed Blackhawks owner William Wirtz and penny-pinching Bulls majority owner Jerry Reinsdorf.

The Bulls still sell out even though the team with the six-pack of NBA championship trophies is history. It must be the ingenious half-time antics drawing the crowds because, despite Coach Bill Cartwright's efforts in the 2001-2002 season, the Bulls finished last in the Central Division.

Although it's been an ice age since the Blackhawks won the Stanley Cup (1961), the team enjoys unwavering support by boisterous fans. Last season showed signs of thaw when the Blackhawks made it to the playoffs. Coach Brian Sutter hopes to heat things up in the 2002-2003 season.

How to Get Tickets

Book tickets over the phone or online with Ticketmaster, by United Center mail order, or visit the United Center box office at Gate 4 next to the soaring, tongue-wagging statue of Michael Jordan. Box office hours are Monday to Saturday, 11am to 6pm. For Bulls and Blackhawks season tickets and group bookings call the phone numbers above.

How to Get There

By Car: From the Loop, drive west on Madison St. to United Center. From the north take I-90/94 exit at Madison St; head west to the stadium. From the southwest, take I-55 north to the Damen/Ashland exit; head north to Madison St. From the west, take I-290 east to the Damen Ave. exit; go north to Madison St.

Parking lots surround United Center, as do countless cops. General public parking is in Lot B on Warren Blvd. (cars, $13-16; limo, R.V. and bus parking, $21). Lot H on Wood St. is closest to the stadium and is reserved for VIPs. Disabled parking is in Lots G and H on Damen Ave. Additional lots within easy walking distance of the stadium are on Damen Ave., Madison St., Adams St. Wood St., Paulina St. and Warren Blvd.

By El: Take the Forest Park Branch of the Blue Line to the Medical Center-Damen Ave. station. Walk two blocks north to the United Center.

By Bus: CTA bus #19 United Center Express is the most intelligent and safest choice. In service only on event and game days, this express bus travels from Chicago Ave. south down Michigan Ave., then west along Madison St. to the United Center. Michigan Ave. stops are at Chicago Ave., Illinois St. and Randolph St. On Madison St. stops are at State St., Wells St. and Clinton St. ($1.50 one-way). Service starts two hours before an event and runs up to 30 minutes before it starts. After events, bus service continues for 45 minutes. CTA bus 20 also travels Madison St. beginning at Wabash Ave. and has "owl service" but travel is slow, schedules sometimes erratic, and even with cops circling the stadium, the neighborhood's level of safety is questionable. Contact the RTA Information Center for schedules, 312-836-7000; www.rtachicago.com.

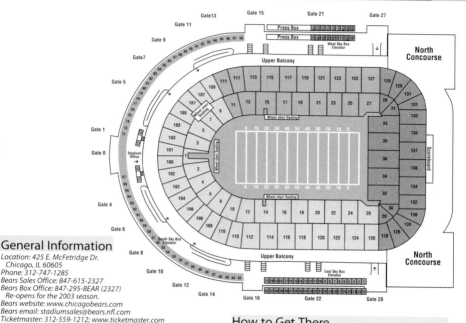

General Information

Location: 425 E. McFetridge Dr.
  Chicago, IL 60605
Phone: 312-747-1285
Bears Sales Office: 847-615-2327
Bears Box Office: 847-295-BEAR (2327)
  Re-opens for the 2003 season.
Bears website: www.chicagobears.com
Bears email: stadiumsales@bears.nfl.com
Ticketmaster: 312-559-1212; www.ticketmaster.com

Overview

Construction of the new Soldier Field in 2002 is best described as the ultimate political football. When the final buzzer rang, Soldier Field stayed put and all but the signature colonnade from the original stadium built in 1924 met the wrecking ball. In 2003 when the new stadium (we hope) opens in time for the regular season, fierce Chicago Bears fans will judge, whether, harangue and traffic hang-ups on Lake Shore Dr. delivers not only a better den for their beloved Bears, but helps stir them from hibernation since their only Super Bowl win in 1985.

The new Soldier Field is a key player in a $587 million Lakefront Improvement Plan for the shoreline between Navy Pier and McCormick Place. An estimated $365 million went towards the 61,000-seat stadium. The new underground garage cost $75 million and another $147 million was spent on outside parking facilities, infrastructure, road improvements and 17 acres of parkland with memorials to war veterans and Chicago's Finest. Tree-hugger victories include a winter garden, children's park and sledding hill.

How to Get Tickets

Contact Ticketmaster to purchase individual game tickets. Season tickets in the new stadium are already sold out. So, your best bet to get good seats is to get top billing on somebody's will or work with a licensed ticket broker. Fans marked their territory early by purchasing a one-time Permanent Seat License (PSL). In exchange for paying big premiums to help cover construction expenses, PSL holders were promised first choice of ticket seating each year. Of the stadium's 61,000 seats, 27,500 are PSL zones and the remaining 33,500 are non-licensed seats in the stadium's higher altitudes. Call the Bears sales office to get on the season ticket wait list.

How to Get There

By Car: From the north or south, take Lake Shore Dr.; follow the signs to Soldier Field. For parking lots, exit at E. McFetridge, E. Waldron, E. 14th Blvd. and E. 18th Dr. From the west, take I-55 east to Lake Shore Dr., turn north and follow the signs. Travel east on I-290, then south on I-90/94 to I-55; get on I-55 heading east to Lake Shore Dr.

Parking lots surrounding Soldier Field cost between $6 and $12, including the new underground North Parking Garage. Two parking and game-day tailgating lots are south of Waldron Dr. There are lots on the Museum Campus off McFetridge Dr. and near McCormick Place off 31st St. and E. 18th St.

By Train: On game days, CTA Soldier Field Express bus 128 runs non-stop between the Ogilvie Transportation Center and Union Station to Soldier Field ($1 one-way). Service starts two hours before the game; runs up to 45 minutes before kickoff; and up to 45 minutes post-game.

By El: Take the Red, Orange or Green Lines to the Roosevelt Rd. station stop ($1.50 one way; 30¢ additional for bus transfer). Either board eastbound CTA bus 12, or the free green trolley to the Museum Campus. Walk south to Soldier Field.

By Bus: CTA buses 12, 127 and 146 stop on McFetridge Dr. near Soldier Field. Contact the RTA Information Center for routes and schedules, 312-836-7000; www.rtachicago.com.

By Trolley: The Green Trolley travels along Michigan Ave., Washington St., Canal St. and Adams St. to the Museum Campus. From there, walk south to the field. For routes and schedules, visit www.cityofchicago.org/Transportation/trolleys/.

General Information

Location:
  1060 West Addison St.
  Chicago, IL 60613-4397
Cubs Box Office Phone:
  773-404-CUBS (2827)
Tickets.com: 800-THE-CUBS (843-2827)
Lost and Found: 773-404-4185
Website: www.cubs.com

Overview

Wrigley Field draws worshipers of America's favorite pastime like St. Peter's draws Catholics to Rome. Built in 1914, and the Cubs' home field since 1916, Wrigley Field is the second-oldest ball park in Major League Baseball (Boston's Fenway is from 1912). Called the "Friendly Confines," Wrigley Field's ivy-strewn walls, classic grass-field design and hand-turned scoreboard transcend time and technology. Lights for night games were not installed until 1988 when the League threatened to force the Cubbies into playing their post-season games in St. Louis, nesting grounds of the arch-rival Cardinals.

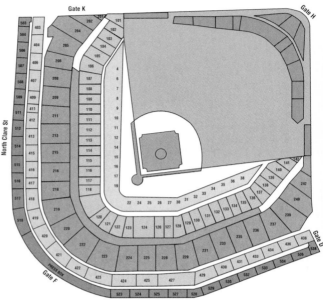

Today, nostalgia for the cherished, landmark ballpark limits the number of night games and is leading the charge against recent proposals to expand the bleachers. A sacred section of Wrigley Field, the bleachers are fiercely protected by park denizens who defiantly toss opposing teams' homerun balls back onto the field. And just like God-fearing folk, fervent Cubs fans believe in a Second Coming. Although the Cubbies haven't won a World Series since their back-to-back wins over Detroit in 1907 and 1908, the loveable losing team has one of the most impressive attendance records in league history. Perhaps in 2003, the Cubs' 90th season at Wrigley Field, faithful fans' prayers will be answered...then again, perhaps not.

How to Get Tickets

Individual game tickets can be purchased from the Cubs' website, by calling Tickets.com or in person at some Chicagoland Sears and Sears Hardware stores. Also, buy tickets at the Wrigley Field Box Office which is open weekdays from 8 a.m. to 6 p.m.; weekends from 9 a.m. to 4 p.m. Generally, seats are discounted April, May and September for Monday through Thursday afternoon games. A purchase of 20 or more tickets is a group sale; purchase them at the box office, by phone or mail order. Children age 2 years and over require tickets. Call Tickets.com Customer Service (1-800-955-5566) to change previously purchased tickets.

How to Get There

By Car: If you must...From the Loop or South, take Lake Shore Dr. north; exit at Irving Park Rd. and head west to Clark St.; turn south on Clark St. to Wrigley Field. From the North, take Lake Shore Dr. to Irving Park Rd.; head west to Clark St. and turn south. From Chicago's West Side, take I-290 east or I-55 north to Lake Shore Dr. Follow directions above. From the Northwest, take I-90 east exiting at Addison St.; travel east three miles. From the Southwest side, take I-55 north to I-90/94 north. Exit at Addison St.; head east to the park.

Street parking around Wrigley Field is heavily restricted. The Cubs operate a garage at 1126 W. Grace St. Purchase parking passes through the mail or at the Wrigley Field Box Office. On game nights, tow trucks cruise Wrigleyville's streets nabbing cars without a resident permit sticker. So park smart at the DeVry Institute, 2600 W. Rockwell, because CTA bus 154 Wrigley Express shuttles patrons to and from the park (just $5 covers parking and roundtrip shuttle per carload).

By El: Riding the Howard/Dan Ryan Red Line is the fastest and easiest way to get to Wrigley Field ($1.50 one-way). Get off at the Addison St. stop one block east of the field.

By Bus: CTA buses 22, 8 and 152 stop closest to Wrigley Field ($1.50 one-way). For schedules, contact the RTA Information Center, 312-836-7000; www.rtachicago.com.

General Information

Location:
333 W. 35th St.
Chicago, IL 60616
Chicago White Sox:
312-674-1000; tickets@chisox.com
Tickets.com:
1-866-SOX-GAME (769-4263)
Lost and Found:
312-674-1000
Website: www.whitesox.com

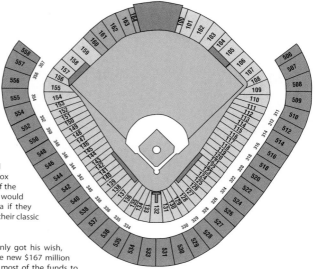

Overview

It was a sad day for baseball when "Old Comiskey Park" became a deal breaker. In 1988, Chicago White Sox owner Jerry Reinsdorf (also owner of the Bulls) threatened that the ChiSox would abandon the South Side for Florida if they didn't get a new stadium to replace their classic but crumbling 1910 ballpark.

Notoriously stingy Reinsdorf not only got his wish, but got someone else to pay for the new $167 million Comiskey Park. The state collected most of the funds to build the sleek, stylish, sterile stadium from an additional hotel tax. The new park opened in 1991. In anticipation of hosting the All-Star Game in July, 2003, "new" Comiskey Park was recently renovated.

But, there is one thing new construction and team ownership just can't change tradition. Raunch and paunch still go together like a beer and hotdog at Comiskey Park. Bawdy bards of baseball, White Sox fans shout creative strings of expletives between beer guzzles and finger flip offs. Nothing and no one is spared their gritty, expressive slurs—their beloved players and their mothers, the team's cretin owner, the opponent, the park, its burritos or the weather. But under all the crass commentary burns a fierce love for a tough ball club that has given their passionate fans plenty to cheer about since their last World Series win in 1917.

How to Get Tickets

Purchase tickets over the website or at the Comiskey Park Box Office, open weekdays 10 a.m. to 6 p.m. and till 4 p.m. on weekends. Tickets.com also sells seats over the phone and at their retails outlets in Chicagoland Sears and Sears Hardware stores. Children shorter than the park's turnstile arm (approximately 36 inches so let 'em slouch for once!) are admitted free, but share your seat. Ballpark bargains include Half-Price Mondays for all regular seats, and Willy Wonka's Kids Days on select Sundays when children 14 and under get in for $1. Wonka tickets must be purchased at park ticket windows on game day. Check the website for Wonka schedules.

How to Get There

By Car: Comiskey Park is located at the 35th St. exit off the Dan Ryan Expressway. From the north or south, take I-90/94, stay in the local lanes and exit at 35th St. If you possess a green parking coupon or plan on paying cash for parking ($13), exit at 35th St. Follow signs to "Sox Parking" at lots E, F and L on the stadium's south side. Fans with red, prepaid season parking coupons* exit at 31st St. and follow signs for "Red Coupons" to lots A, B and C just north of the stadium. If the 35th St. exit is closed due to heavy traffic, which is often the case on game days, proceed to the 39th St. exit; turn right for "Sox Parking" and left for "Red Coupons." The handicapped parking and stadium drop-off area is in Lot D, west of the field and accessible via 37th St. All lots open two hours prior to the opening pitch and close right after the game. Additional public parking lots with shuttle service to and from Comiskey Park are at the Illinois Institute of Technology, 3300 S. Federal St.

By Bus: CTA buses 24 and 35 stop closest to the park. Others stopping in the vicinity are the 29, 44 and 39. Armies of cops surround Comiskey Park on game days because the neighborhood is rough, especially at night.

By El: Ride the Red Line to the Sox-35th St. stop just west of the ballpark. If taking the Green Line, get off at the 35th-Bronzeville-IIT station.

Police Departments

	Address	Phone	Map
Chicago District Police Department	2452 W Belmont Ave	312-744-5983	42
Chicago District Station	3600 N Halsted St	312-744-8320	44
Chicago District Station	113 W Chicago Ave	312-744-8230	2
Chicago Law Dept Investigation	30 N La Salle St #1720	312-744-1882	5
Chicago Police Department	1121 S State St	312-744-8320	8
Chicago Police Department	1718 S State St	312-747-6230	11
Chicago Police Department	3501 S Lowe Ave	312-747-8227	13
Chicago Police Department	300 E 29th St	312-747-8340	14
Chicago Police Department	4947 S Federal St #715	312-791-4650	15
Chicago Police Department	5101 S Wentworth Ave	312-747-8366	15
Chicago Police Department	937 N Wood St	312-746-8350	21
Chicago Police Department	2150 N California Ave	312-744-8290	27
Chicago Police Department	6464 N Clark St	312-744-5907	34
Chicago Police Department	100 S Racine Ave	312-746-8396	24
Chicago Police Pension Board	221 N La Salle St #1626	312-744-3891	5
Chicago Police Pro Standards	1130 S Wabash Ave #400	312-747-6307	8
Chicago Police Training Division	1300 W Jackson Blvd	312-746-8310	24
Chicago Police-Gun Registration	50 W Washington St #Cl-90	312-744-8100	5
Chicago Police-Public Housing	365 W Oak St #1	312-744-8392	31
Cook County Criminal Court	155 W. 51st St	773-373-8875	15
EAP	407 S Dearborn St #800	312-747-1371	5
Emergency Patrol-II Traffic	3501 S Normal Ave	773-624-0470	13
Near North Police Station	1160 N. Larrabee		31

Firehouses

	Address	Phone	Map
Chicago Breathing Apparatus	1044 N Orleans St	312-744-3209	31
Chicago District Fire Chiefs	3401 N Elston Ave	312-744-8741	41
Chicago Fire Department	202 E Chicago Ave		3
Chicago Fire Department	1732 W Byron St	312-744-8847	42
Chicago Fire Dept-Public Education	1010 S Clinton St	312-747-1699	7
Chicago Fire Dept-Paramedic	1338 S Clinton St	312-746-5841	10
Chicago Fire Prevention Bureau	2100 W Eastwood Ave	312-744-1089	39
Chicago Fire Prevention Bureau	444 N Dearborn St	312-744-4723	2
Engine Co. 14, CFD	1129 W Chicago Ave		24
Engine Co. 30, CFD	1125 N Ashland Blvd		22
Fire Suppression & Rescue	558 W De Koven St	312-747-7241	7

Map 2
222 Merchandise Mart Plz 312-321-0386 60654
540 N Dearborn St   312-644-3919 60610
Map 3
227 E Ontario St   312-642-7698 60611
Map 4
168 N Clinton St   312-906-8051 60661
222 S Riverside Plz   312-669-5663 60606
300 S Riverside Plz #1480S
                         312-627-2990 60606
433 W Van Buren St   312-654-3895 60607
Map 5
100 W Randolph St   312-263-7811 60601
150 S Wacker Dr #200   312-424-2443 60606
233 S Wacker Dr   312-876-1670 60606
Map 6
200 E Randolph St   312-861-1210 60601
Map 7
740 S Canal St   312-983-8765 60607
Map 10
2345 S Wentworth Ave   312-326-6441 60616
19 W 16th St   312-225-8093 60616
Map 11
2035 S State St   312-225-9110 60616
Map 15
4101 S Halsted St   773-247-6901 60609
Map 16
4601 S Cottage Grove Ave
                         773-924-9221 60653
Map 18
700 E 61st St   773-493-3124 60637
Map 19
1526 E 55th St   773-324-0363 60615
956 E 58th St   773-324-2723 60637
Map 22
1635 W Division St   773-278-1919 60622
Map 23
2419 W Monroe St   312-243-1603 60612
Map 26
1859 S Ashland Ave   312-733-1156 60608
Map 27
2339 N California Ave   773-489-1474 60647
Map 30
2643 N Clark St   773-525-5959 60614
Map 34
1723 W Devon Ave   773-508-1200 60660
7056 N Clark St   773-764-3120 60626
7617 N Paulina St   773-743-5240 60626
Map 38
2522 W Lawrence Ave   773-561-9294 60625
Map 39
2011 W Montrose Ave   773-472-8230 60618
Map 40
1343 W Irving Park Rd   773-327-2932 60613
4850 N Broadway St   773-561-8916 60640
1343 W. Irving Park Ave
Map 41
3750 N Kedzie Ave   773-478-6714 60618
Map 43
3026 N Ashland Ave   773-248-8494 60657

Hospitals • General Information

Chicago is home to some of the nation's leading research and teaching hospitals. Encompassing several hospitals and medical institutions, the Illinois Medical District is one of the largest health-care centers in the world. Cook County Hospital established the nation's first emergency trauma unit in 1966.

Hospital	Address	Phone	Map
Advocate Health Care Center	2400 N Lincoln Ave		30
Advocate Health Centers-Logan Square	2511 N Kedzie Blvd	773-292-2700	27
Advocate Ravenswood Med Center	4550 N Winchester Ave	773-878-4300	39
Augustana Hospital & Health	2035 N Lincoln Ave	773-975-5128	30
Bernard Mitchell Hospital	5815 S Maryland Ave	773-702-1000	19
Bronzeville's Medical Center	300 E Pershing Rd		14
California Devon Medical Center	6420 N California Ave	773-973-6100	33
Chen's Medical Center	100 E 35th St		14
Chicago Institute-Neurosurgery	2515 N Clark St	773-388-7600	30
Children's Memorial Dialysis	2611 N Halsted St	773-549-9410	30
Columbia Chicago Lakeshore	4840 N Marine Dr	773-878-9700	40
Columbia Grant Hospital	550 W Webster Ave	773-883-2000	30
Columbia Michael Reese North	60 E Delaware Pl	312-440-5100	32
Columbus Hospital	2520 N Lakeview Ave	773-388-7300	30
Columbus Maryville Clinic	810 W Montrose Ave	773-728-2356	40
Cook County Hospital	1835 W Harrison St	312-633-6000	25
Doctors Hospital of Hyde Park	5800 S Stony Island Av	773-643-9200	20
Duchossois Center for Advanced Medicine (DCAM)	5758 S. Maryland Ave	773-702-1000	19
Foot Ankle Clinics of America	1001 N Dearborn St	312-751-0378	32
Herron Medical Center Ltd	1150 N State St	312-337-6072	32
Ill Masonic Medical Center	3002 N Ashland Ave	773-525-7755	43
Illinois Masonic Hospital	2835 N Sheffield Ave	773-755-1483	43
Illinois Masonic Medical Center	836 W Wellington Ave	773-975-1600	43
Johnston R Bowman Health Center	710 S Paulina St	312-942-7000	25
Kindred Chicago Lakeshore	6130 N Sheridan Rd	773-381-1222	37
Kindred Hospital	2544 W Montrose Ave	773-267-2622	38
La Rabida Children's Hospital & Research Center	E 65th St at Lake Michigan Ave	773-363-6700	20
Louis A Weiss Memorial Hosp	4646 N Marine Dr	773-878-8700	40
Mercy Hospital & Medical Center	2525 S Michigan Ave	312-567-2000	11
Methodist Hospital Of Chicago	5025 N Paulina St	773-271-9040	39
Michael Reese Hospital & Medical Center	2929 S Ellis Ave	312-791-2000	14
National Jewish Center	100 N La Salle St	312-920-1798	5
Nazareth Family Center	1127 N Oakley Blvd	312-770-2391	21
Northwestern Hospital	Oak/Dearborn		32
Northwestern Memorial Hospital	251 E Huron St	312-944-2358	3
Prentice Women's Hospital	333 E Superior St	312-908-7580	3
Provident Hospital	500 E 51st St	773-572-2000	16
Ravenswood Hospital Medical	2312 W Irving Park Rd	773-866-6990	39
Ravenswood Hospital Medical	4055 N Western Ave	773-728-3737	39
Ravenswood Hospital Medical	4753 N Broadway St	773-561-3400	40
Rush Presbyterian Hospital	1653 W Congress Pkwy	312-942-5000	26
Rush-Presbyterian St Luke's	1725 W Harrison St	312-942-5983	25
Schwab	2020 N Clybourn Ave	773-404-5277	29
Shaare Zedek Medical Center	101 W Grand Ave	312-527-0972	2
St Elizabeth's Hospital	1431 N Claremont Ave	773-278-2000	21
St Elizabeth's Hospital Family	1431 N Western Ave	312-491-5050	21
St. Josephs Hospital	2913 N Commonwealth Ave	773-665-3000	44
St Mary Of Nazareth Hospital	2233 W Division St	312-770-2000	21
Swedish Covenant Hospital	5145 N California Ave	773-878-8200	38
Swedish Covenant Prepaid Mdcl	2740 W Foster Ave	773-271-0880	35
Thorek Hospital & Medical Center	850 W Irving Park Rd	773-525-6780	40
Thorek Hospital Medical Office	4945 N Sheridan Rd	773-275-4920	40
Univ. of Chicago Children's Hospital	5839 S Maryland Ave		19
University Of Chicago Hospital	5841 S Maryland Ave	773-702-1000	19
University Of Chicago Hospital	901 E 58th St	773-702-6250	19
University of Chicago Physicians Group	1301 E 47th St	773-624-0777	17
University Of Illinois at Chicago Hospital	1740 W Taylor St	312-996-7000	25
University-Chicago Hospital Empl	800 E 55th St	773-753-8587	19
US Veterans Medical Center	820 S Damen Ave	312-666-6500	25

The Chicago Public Library System has 75 branches and two regional libraries serving Chicago citizens. In the midst of a huge capital improvement program, the City expects to have built or renovated 55 neighborhood branch libraries by the end of 2004.

Families and schools should take advantage of the Chicago Public Library System's "Imagination on Loan" pass, which is available to library cardholders who are Chicago residents. You can check-out the free Pass using your library card, just like you would any other item, and the loan is good for two weeks. The Pass entitles entry for up to 8 people to the Chicago Children's Museum at Navy Pier. For more information, call your local library or the Museum on 312-527-1000.

Chicago has many excellent research libraries and university libraries, one of which is the independent Newberry Library, established in 1887. It shelves rare books, manuscripts and maps. Generally, Chicago's universities and colleges welcome the public to their libraries during specified hours, but it's best to call first and check.

Hospital	Address	Phone	Map
Asher Library-Spertus Institute	618 S Michigan Ave	312-922-8248	9
Bessie Coleman Library	731 E 63rd St	312-747-7760	18
Canaryville Library	642 W 43rd St	312-747-0644	15
Chicago Bee Library	3647 S State St	312-747-6872	14
Chicago Bezazian Library	1226 W Ainslie St	312-744-0019	40
Chicago Eckhart Park Library	1371 W Chicago Ave	312-746-6069	24
Chicago Public Library	400 S State St	312-747-4999	5
Chicago Public Library	1605 N Troy St	312-744-2244	27
Chicago Public Library	6435 N California Ave	312-744-2292	33
Chicago Public Library, Eckhart Pk Branch	1371 W Chicago Ave		24
Chicago Robert Taylor Library	5120 S Federal St	312-747-2828	15
Chinatown Library	2353 S Wentworth Ave	312-747-8013	10
Conrad Sulzer Regional Library	4455 N Lincoln Ave	312-744-7616	39
Daley Public Library	3400 S Halsted St	312-747-8990	13
Damen Avenue Library	2056 N Damen Ave	312-744-6022	28
Edgewater Branch	1210 W Elmdale St		37
Hall Public Library	4801 S Michigan Ave	312-747-2541	16
Harper Memorial Library	1116 E 59th St		19
Illinois Regional Library	1055 W Roosevelt Rd	312-746-9210	26
John Merlo Public Library	644 W Belmont Ave	312-744-1139	44
Library	600 S Michigan Ave	312-344-7906	9
Lincoln Park Public Library	1150 W Fullerton Ave	312-744-1926	29
Lincoln-Belmont Library	1659 W Melrose St	312-744-0166	42
Lozano Library	1805 S Loomis St	312-746-4329	26
Mabel Manning Public Library	6 S Hoyne Ave	312-746-6800	23
Midwest Public Library	2335 W Chicago Ave	312-744-7788	23
Municipal Reference Library	121 N La Salle St	312-744-4992	5
Near North Branch Library	310 W Division St	312-744-0992	31
Newberry Library	60 W Walton St	312-943-9090	32
Northtown Public Library	6435 N. California Ave	312-744-2292	33
Rogers Park Public Library	6907 N Clark St	312-744-0156	34
Roosevelt Branch Library	1101 W Taylor St	312-746-5656	26
University Of Chicago Illinois	801 S Morgan St	312-996-2724	26
Uptown Library	929 W Buena Ave	312-744-8400	40
US Library	77 W Jackson Blvd	312-353-2022	5
West Town Public Library	1271 N Milwaukee Ave	312-744-1473	21

FedEx Locations · General Information

* Pick-up time, p.m.

Map 1 · River North/Fulton *

Drop box	600 W Fulton St	7:45
Drop box	600 W Chicago Ave	7:30
Drop box	400 W Erie St	7:30
Drop box	430 W Erie St	7:30
Drop box	401 W Superior St	7:00
Drop box	445 W Erie St	7:00
Drop box	700 N Green St	7:00
Drop box	770 N Halsted St	7:00
Drop box	727 N Hudson Ave	6:00

Map 2 · Near North/River North *

Drop box	77 W Wacker Dr	9:00
Service Center	350 N Clark St	9:00
Service Center	222 Merchandise Mart Plaza	9:00
Drop box	205 W Wacker Dr	8:00
Drop box	211 W Wacker Dr	8:00
Drop box	308 W Erie St	8:00
Drop box	320 W Ohio St	8:00
Kinko's	444 N Wells St	8:00
Drop box	56 W Illinois St	8:00
Drop box	515 N State St	8:00
Drop box	54 W Hubbard St	8:00
Drop box	1 E Erie St	8:00
Drop box	330 N Wabash Ave	8:00
Drop box	730 N Franklin St	7:30
Drop box	311 W Superior St	7:30
Drop box	343 W Erie St	7:30
Drop box	1 W Superior St	7:30
Drop box	414 N Orleans St	7:30
Drop box	405 N Wabash Ave	7:30
Drop box	420 N Wabash Ave	7:30
Drop box	401 N Wabash Ave	7:30
Drop box	223 W Erie St	7:15
Drop box	225 W Wacker Dr	7:00
Image Direct Express	211 W Wacker Dr	7:00
Drop box	225 W Ohio St	7:00
Drop box	20 W Kinzie St	7:00
Drop box	100 E Huron St	7:00
Drop box	444 N Wabash Ave	7:00
Drop box	68 Wacker Place	6:30
Drop box	1 E Wacker Dr	6:30
Drop box	55 W Wacker Dr	6:30
Drop box	540 N Dearborn St	6:30
Drop box	350 N Orleans St	6:00
Mail Boxes Etc	446 N Wells	5:00

Map 3 · Streeterville/Mag Mile *

Service Center	500 N Michigan Ave	9:00
Drop box	737 N Michigan Ave	8:00
Drop box	400 N Michigan Ave	8:00
Drop box	401 N Michigan Ave	8:00
Drop box	211 E Ontario St	7:45
Drop box	251 E Huron St	7:30
Drop box	233 E Erie St	7:30
Drop box	240 E Ontario St	7:30
Drop box	333 E Ontario St	7:30
Drop box	303 E Ohio St	7:30
Drop box	676 N Saint Clair St	7:30
Drop box	150 E Huron St # 160	7:30
Drop box	645 N Michigan Ave	7:30
Drop box	625 N Michigan Ave	7:30
Drop box	211 E Chicago Ave	7:30

Drop box	680 N Lake Shore Dr	7:00
Drop box	400 N McClurg Court	7:30
Drop box	444 N Michigan Ave	7:30
Drop box	142 E Ontario St	7:00
Drop box	676 N Michigan Ave	7:00
Drop box	440 N McClurg Court	7:00
Drop box	435 N Michigan Ave	7:00
Drop box	430 N Michigan Ave	7:00
Kinko's	540 N Michigan Ave	6:00
Mail Boxes Etc	207 E Ohio St	5:00
Drop box	227 E Ontario St	5:00

Map 4 · West Loop Gate *

Drop box	222 S Riverside Plaza	8:00
Kinko's	843 W Van Buren St	7:45
Drop box	300 S Riverside Plaza	7:35
Drop box	833 W Jackson Blvd	7:30
Drop box	555 W Madison St	7:30
Drop box	10 S Riverside Plaza	7:00
Drop box	2 N Riverside Plaza	7:00
Drop box	100 N Riverside Plaza	7:00
Drop box	120 S Riverside Plaza	7:00
Kinko's	128 S Canal St	7:00
Drop box	322 S Green St	7:00
Drop box	850 W Jackson Blvd	7:00
Drop box	820 W Jackson Blvd	7:00
Drop box	550 W Washington Blvd	7:00
Drop box	500 W Monroe St	7:00
Drop box	547 W Jackson Blvd	7:00
Drop box	600 W Jackson Blvd	6:30
Drop box	651 W Washington Blvd	6:00
Drop box	130 S Jefferson St	6:00
Drop box	641 W Lake St	6:00
Drop box	118 S Clinton St	6:00
Drop box	216 S Jefferson St	5:30
Drop box	168 N Clinton St	4:00

Map 5 · The Loop *

Service Center	136 S Dearborn	9:00
Service Center	101 N Wacker Dr	9:00
Service Center	227 W Monroe St	9:00
Drop box	333 W Wacker Dr	9:00
Service Center	200 W Jackson Blvd	9:00
Kinko's	6 W Lake St	8:00
Drop box	29 E Madison St	8:00
Drop box	100 W Monroe St	8:00
Drop box	210 S Clark St	8:00
Drop box	175 W Jackson Blvd	8:00
Drop box	1 N Franklin St	8:00
Drop box	125 S Wacker Dr	8:00
Drop box	200 W Monroe St	8:00
Drop box	150 S Wacker Dr	8:00
Drop box	205 W Randolph St	8:00
Drop box	200 W Madison St	7:45
Drop box	311 S Wacker Dr	7:45
Drop box	180 N Wabash Ave	7:30
Drop box	105 W Madison St	7:30
Drop box	55 E Monroe St	7:30
Drop box	36 Wabash Ave	7:30
Drop box	2 S Dearborn St	7:30
Drop box	135 S La Salle St	7:30
Drop box	407 S Dearborn St	7:30
Drop box	1 N Wacker Dr	7:30
Drop box	123 N Wacker Dr	7:30

Drop box	150 N Wacker Dr	7:30
Drop box	250 S Wacker Dr	7:30
Drop box	70 E Lake St	7:00
Drop box	35 Wacker Dr	7:00
Drop box	171 N Clark St	7:00
Drop box	33 N Dearborn St	7:00
Drop box	1 N State St	7:00
Drop box	11 E Adams St	7:00
Drop box	30 W Monroe St	7:00
Drop box	247 S State St	7:00
Drop box	230 S Dearborn St	7:00
Drop box	219 S Dearborn St	7:00
Drop box	111 W Jackson Blvd	7:00
Drop box	401 S State St	7:00
Drop box	29 N Wacker Dr	7:00
Drop box	1 S Wacker Dr	7:00
Drop box	20 N Wacker Dr	7:00
Drop box	303 W Madison St	7:00
Drop box	309 W Washington St	7:00
Drop box	30 S Wacker Dr	7:00
Drop box	230 W Monroe St	7:00
Drop box	155 N Wacker Dr	7:00
Drop box	200 S Wacker Dr	7:00
Drop box	200 W Adams St	7:00
Drop box	300 S Wacker Dr	7:00
Drop box	203 N Wabash Ave	6:30
Drop box	65 Wacker Dr	6:30
Drop box	188 W Randolph St	6:30
Drop box	243 S Wabash Ave	6:30
Drop box	100 W Randolph St	6:00
Kinko's	55 E Monroe St	6:00
Drop box	211 S Clark St	5:00
Service Center	400 S La Salle	5:00
Mail Boxes Etc	27 N Wacker Dr	5:00

Map 6 · The Loop/Grant Park *

Service Center	130 E Randolph St	9:00
Service Center	34 S Michigan Ave	9:00
Drop box	200 E Randolph St	8:00
Drop box	300 E Randolph St	8:00
Drop box	30 N Michigan Ave	8:00
Drop box	332 S Michigan Ave	7:45
Drop box	8 S Michigan Ave	7:30
Drop box	180 Michigan Ave	7:00
Drop box	155 N Michigan Ave	7:00
Service Center	150 N Michigan Ave	7:00
Drop box	307 N Michigan Ave	7:00
Drop box	333 N Michigan Ave	7:00
Drop box	20 N Michigan Ave	7:00
Drop box	310 S Michigan Ave	7:00
Drop box	224 S Michigan Ave	7:00
Drop box	200 S Michigan Ave	7:00
Drop box	430 S Michigan Ave	7:00
Service Center	205 N Michigan Ave	5:00
Sullivan's Order	111 E Wacker Dr Ste LI9	5:00

Map 8 · Dearborn Park *

Drop box	536 S Clark St	7:30
Drop box	800 S Wells St	7:30
Drop box	47 W Polk St	7:00
Drop box	600 S Federal St	7:00
Drop box	542 S Dearborn St	7:00
Drop box	33 E Congress Pkwy	6:00
Drop box	819 S Wabash Ave	5:30
Mail Boxes Etc	47 W Polk St	5:00

Map 9 · S Michigan Ave *
Drop box	1000 N Lake Shore Dr	7:00

Map 10 · East Pilsen/Chinatown *
Kinko's	1242 S Canal St	8:00
Drop box	2345 S Wentworth Ave	5:00

Map 11 · McCormick Place *
Drop box	1347 S State St	7:30
Drop box	1211 S Michigan Ave	7:00
Drop box	2035 S State St	5:00

Map 12 · Bridgeport (West) *
Drop box	3757 S Ashland Ave	6:30
Mail Boxes Etc	1341 W Fullerton St	5:30

Map 14 · Prairie Shores *
Drop box	3200 S Wabash Ave	6:30
Mail Boxes Etc	3473 S King Dr	6:00

Map 16 · Bronzeville *
Drop box	4601 S Cottage Grove	5:30

Map 17 · Kenwood *
Co-op Markets Mailing & B		
	1300 E 47th St Fl 2	5:00

Map 18 · Washington Park *
Drop box	700 E 61st St	6:00

Map 19 · Hyde Park *
Drop box	1525 E 53rd St	7:00
Drop box	1155 E 60th St	7:00
Drop box	5801 S Ellis Ave	7:00
Kinko's	1315 E 57th St	7:00
Drop box	800 E 55th St	6:30
Drop box	1554 E 55th St	6:30
Drop box	1126 E 59th St	6:30
Drop box	956 E 58th St	6:30
Drop box	5841 S Maryland Ave	6:30
Drop box	59th & Kimbark	6:30
Drop box	57th & University	6:30
Mail Boxes Etc	1507 E 53rd St	5:00

Map 20 · Jackson Park *
Post Link	1634 E 53rd St	5:30

Map 21 · Wicker Park *
Kinko's	1800 W North Ave	8:00
Drop box	2233 W Division St	7:30
Drop box	1608 N Milwaukee Ave	7:00
CopyMax	1573 N Milwaukee	6:00

Map 22 · Noble Square *
Service Center	875 W Division	9:45
Service Center	875 W Division St	9:45
Drop box	935 W Chestnut St	7:30
Drop box	848 W Eastman St	7:30
The Box Shoppe	1001 W North Ave	6:00

Map 23 · West Town *
Drop box	1700 W Van Buren St	6:30
Packaging & Shipping Specialists	2002 W Chicago Ave	6:00
Drop box	2023 W Carroll Ave	5:30
Drop box	2419 W Monroe St	4:00

Map 24 · River West/West Town *
Service Center	1260 W Madison	9:00
Drop box	1017 W Washington Blvd	8:30

Drop box	1260 W Madison St	7:30
Drop box	901 W Jackson Blvd	7:00
Drop box	38 S Peoria St	7:00
Drop box	216 N May St	7:00
Drop box	1550 W Carroll Ave	6:30
Drop box	1438 W Kinzie St	6:00
Mail Boxes Etc	910 W Van Buren St	5:00
Drop box	1030 W Chicago Ave	5:00

Map 25 · Illinois Medical District *
Drop box	840 S Wood St	7:00
Drop box	1725 W Harrison St	6:30
Drop box	820 S Damen Ave	6:00
Drop box	715 S Wood St	4:00

Map 26 · University Village *
Drop box	1201 W Harrison St	6:30
Drop box	1100 W Cermak Rd	6:30
Drop box	851 S Morgan St	5:30

Map 27 · Logan Square (North) *
Post Net	2820 W North Ave	5:00

Map 28 · Bucktown *
Drop box	1644 N Honore St	7:30
Drop box	1735 N Paulina St	7:30
Drop box	2525 N Elston Ave	7:30
CopyMax	1829 W Fullerton Ave	7:00
Drop box	2355 N Damen Ave	7:00
Mail Boxes Etc	1658 N Milwaukee Ave	7:00
Drop box	1965 N Milwaukee Ave	4:00

Map 29 · DePaul/Wrightwood *
Kinko's	2300 N Clybourn Ave	8:00
Drop box	1870 N Clybourn Ave	7:45
Drop box	990 W Fullerton Ave	7:00
Drop box	2000 N Racine Ave	7:00
Drop box	1925 N Clybourn Ave	7:00
Drop box	2323 N Seminary Ave	6:30
Mail Boxes Etc	858 W Armitage Ave	5:30

Map 30 · Lincoln Park *
Drop box	1749 N Wells St	8:00
Drop box	802 W Belden Ave	5:00
Drop box	2506 N Clark St	6:00
Mail Boxes Etc	2038 N Clark St	6:00

Map 31 · Old Town/Near North *
Drop box	1333 N Kingsbury St	8:30
Drop box	900 N Franklin St	8:00
Drop box	820 N Orleans St	7:30
Drop box	213 W Institute Pl	7:30

Map 32 · Gold Coast *
Service Center	875 W Michigan Ave	9:00
Kinko's	1201 N Dearborn St	8:00
Drop box	919 N Michigan Ave	8:00
Drop box	163 E Walton St	7:30
Drop box	980 N Michigan Ave	7:30
Drop box	100 E Walton St	7:30
Drop box	1 E Delaware Pl	7:30
Drop box	900 N Michigan Ave	7:00
Drop box	1165 N Clark St	6:30
Drop box	875 N Michigan Ave	6:30
Postal Plus	1151 N State St	6:00
Drop box	844 N Rush St	6:00
Mail Boxes Etc	60 E Chestnut St	6:00
Packaging Store	58 W Maple St	3:00

Map 33 · West Rogers Park *
Drop box	7555 N California Ave	7:15
Unik Business	2337 W Devon Ave	7:15
OfficeMax	2255 W Howard St, Evanston	7:00

Map 34 · East Rogers Park *
Drop box	1723 W Devon Ave	7:00
Caribbean Shipping & Post	721 Howard St, Evanston	6:00
Drop box	7056 N Clark St	6:00
Drop box	1400 W Devon Ave	6:00

Map 37 · Edgewater *
Drop box	5419 N Sheridan Rd	7:30
Mail Boxes Etc	5315 N Clark St	5:00

Map 38 · Ravenswood Manor *
Drop box	2522 W Lawrence Ave	7:00

Map 39 · Ravenswood *
Drop box	1807 W Sunnyside Ave	7:30
Remesas	1924 W Montrose Ave	6:00
Mail Boxes Etc	4514 N Lincoln Ave	6:00
Drop box	2011 W Montrose Ave	3:30

Map 40 · Uptown *
Drop box	4600 N Clarendon Ave	7:30
Drop box	4850 Broadway	6:30
Drop box	4753 N Broadway St	6:30
Mailstop & More	1338 W Irving Park Rd	5:30

Map 41 · Logan Square (South) *
Drop box	3611 N Kedzie Ave	7:00
Drop box	3401 N California Ave	7:00
Drop box	2630 W Bradley Pl	6:30

Map 42 · North Center *
Kinko's	3435 W Western Ave	7:45
Drop box	1800 W Larchmont Ave	7:00
Drop box	3717 N Ravenswood Ave	7:00
Mailbox Plus	2154 W Addison St	6:00

Map 43 · Wrigleyville/Lakeview *
Kinko's	3524 N Southport Ave	7:30
Drop box	1300 W Belmont Ave	7:00
Mail Boxes Etc	3540 N Southport Ave	7:00
Mail Boxes Etc	3105 N Ashland Ave	6:00
Drop box	3024 N Ashland Ave	4:00
Drop box	2835 N Sheffield	7:30 am

Map 44 · East Lakeview *
Kinko's	3001 N Clark St	8:00
Drop box	2800 N Sheridan Rd	7:00
Mail Boxes Etc	3712 N Broadway St	6:00
PostNet	636 W Diversey Pkwy	6:00
Postal Plus	559 W Diversey Pkwy	6:00
Postal Place	3304 N Broadway St	6:00
Pak Mail	3176 N Broadway St	5:30
Postage & More	3906 N Broadway St	5:00
Mail Boxes Etc	3023 N Clark St	5:00

Gay & Lesbian • General Information

Websites

Out Chicago: http://www.outchicago.org
Check this out for comprehensive listings of community organizations and nonprofit resources, entertainment and nightlife, business and commercial services, calendars and announcements, media and publications and Out Chicagoans.

Pride Time: http://www.pridetime.com
Chicago gay and lesbian information and resource guide for bars and restaurants, music and theater, health and fitness, style, current events and free weekly prizes.

Horizons Community Services: http://www.horizonsonline.org
Horizons is the Midwest's largest lesbian, gay, bisexual, and transgendered social service agency.

LesBiGay Radio: http://www.lesbigayradio.com
Daily drive time radio show for Les/Bi/Gay listeners and their friends. Real Audio enabled. AM 750.

Chicago Area Gay and Lesbian Chamber of Commerce:
http://www.glchamber.org/
Chicago's online gay and lesbian business guide offers an index of members, membership info and supportive businesses.

Chicago's Gay and Lesbian Professional Networking Association: http://www.cpna.org/
Check out the regular events for Chicago's professional gay and lesbian community, join the club, find a job or read articles about important issues.

Alternative Phone Book: http://www.prairienet.org/apb/
Chicago's Lesbigay Yellow Pages.

About Face Theatre: http://www.aboutfacetheatre.com
About Face Theatre is a group of gay, lesbian, and straight artists committed to the creation of performances that examine queer lives, histories, and experiences. Check their website for performance schedule, tickets and subscription details. They also have a Youth Theatre group and to be eligible youth must be between the ages of 14 and 20, and must be able to participate in the weekly workshops. Check the site for details.

Alternative Connections: http://www.mygaypartner.com
Your online Chicago gay and lesbian dating service.

Dyke Diva: http://www.dykediva.com
Up-to-date info about what's going on in the lesbian scene in Chicago.

SANGAT: http://hometown.aol.com/youngal/sangat.html
Gay and lesbian organization and support group for the people from India, Pakistan, Bangladesh, SriLanka, Nepal, Afghanistan, Iran, Burma, and the rest of the Sub-Continent.

Fairy Gardeners Guild: http://www.fairygardeners.org
Website with resources for gay and lesbian gardeners.

Chicago Gay Golf Club:
http://members.aol.com/chgogga/myhomepage/
Golf club for gay men and women. Check the website for membership, events, links and photos.

Gay, Lesbian and Straight Education Network (GLSEN):
http://members.aol.com/glsenchgo/index.html
This group brings together a wide variety of people who actively care about ending homophobia in schools. Everyone (regardless of occupation or sexual orientation) is welcome to get involved so check out their site for more info.

Early2Bed: http://www.early2bed.com/pages/home.html
Woman-owned sex shop online; store location at 5232 Sheridan Rd.

Women in the Director's Chair: http://www.widc.org
This organization features lots of lesbian and transgender films and events.

Thousand Waves Spa: http://www.thousandwaves.com/twspa/
This is a women-only spa with a strong lesbian presence (not to be confused with the proverbial "bathhouse.")

Windy City Radio: http://www.windycityradio.com/home.html
Gay radio program on WCKG-Radio, 105.9 on Sunday nights at 10:30 p.m. to midnight

Publications

Pick up a copy of the following publications to find out what's happening around town, from the current political headlines to the most happening clubs. They can be found in gay-friendly bookstores, cafes, bars and various shops.

Windy City Times: http://www.wctimes.com
Gay and Lesbian news weekly—check this site for happenings around town.

En La Vida: http://www.outlineschicago.com/enlavida.html
Monthly gay, lesbian, bisexual and transgender publication for Latinos.

Black Lines: http://www.outlineschicago.com/blacklines.html
Expressions from Black gay, lesbian, bisexual and transgendered life featuring news articles reflections, calendar, arts and advertising.

Nightspots: http://www.outlineschicago.com/nightlines.html
Articles, astrology and happenings around town.

The Out!:
http://www.windycitytimes.com/Ooutguide/out1.html
Comprehensive GLBT resource guide with listings for services including carpenters, real estate brokers, accounting services, social services, media, computers, bars, bowling alleys and restaurants.

Chicago Free Press: http://www.chicagofreepress.com/
Popular publication with features on political issues, arts, culture, spiritual life, entertainment and resources lists.

Gay Chicago: http://www.gaychicagomag.com/
One of the city's oldest gay publications with events listings, columns, news, astrology and reviews.

Bookstores

Women & Children First Books:
5233 N. Clark St., 773-769-9299
20 year-old lesbian resource in Andersonville.
Unabridged Books: 3251 N. Broadway St., 773-883-9119
Located in the heart of the North Side gay community, you will find a plethora of local resources as well as general books and magazines.
Gerber/Hart Gay and Lesbian Library and Archives:
1127 W. Granville St., 773-381-8030
While not actually a "bookstore," this amazing library houses more than 10,000 books, magazines, newspapers and videos. For special events including readings and screenings, check the website at www.gerberhart.org.
Barbara's Bookstore: 1110 N. Lake St, Oak Park
Gay-friendly bookstore with a large selection of gay and lesbian fiction and non-fiction titles.
Seminary Cooperative Bookstore:
5757 University Ave., 773-752-4381
Located in Hyde Park, this bookstore has sections on GLBT studies.
57th Street Books: 1301 E. 57th St., 773-684-1300
Another Hyde Park bookstore with a strong GLBT section.
Borders Books and Music:
Clark St. and Diversey Pkwy., 773-935-3909
This Borders store hosts Outbound, a gay literature discussion group.

Health Center & Support Organizations

Horizons Community Services: The Midwest's largest lesbian, gay, bisexual, and transgendered social service agency. http://www.horizonsonline.org
Lesbian and Gay Help Line: 773-929-HELP (6pm until 10pm)
The Crisis Hotline/Anti-Violence Project: 773-871-CARE
Legal Services: 773-929-HELP, legal@horizonsonline.org
Mature Adult Program: 773-472-6469 ext. 245, perryw@horizonsonline.org
Psychotherapy Services: 773-472-6469 ext. 261, sarag@horizonsonline.org
Youth Services: 773-472-6469, ext. 252, premp@horizonsonline.org
Illinois State HIV/AIDS/STD Hotline: 772-AID-AIDS
AIDS Foundation of Chicago: 411 Wells St., Ste 300, Chicago, IL 60607, 312-922-2322
AIDSCARE: 315 W. Barry, Chicago, IL 60657, 773-935-4663
GLAAD Chicago: P.O. Box 46343, Chicago, IL 60614, 773-871-7633
PFLAG Chicago: P.O. Box 11023, Chicago, IL 60611, 773-472-3079
Northstar Medical Center: 2835 N. Sheffield Ave., #104, Chicago, IL 60657, 773-296-2400 (General Physicians, psychological counseling, nutrition)
Northwestern Memorial Physicians Group: 3245 N. Halsted St., Chicago, IL 60657, 312-926-3627 (General Physicians, affiliated with Northwestern Hospital)
Brasch Medical Center: 2360 N. Clark St. Chicago, 773-281-0511 (Onsite pharmacy, HIV treatment)
Howard Brown Health Center: 4025 N. Sheridan Rd., 773-388-8882 (anonymous, free AIDS testing and GLBT Domestic Violence Counseling and Prevention Program)
Support Groups: http://www.prairienet.org/apb/Frames.html
Many support groups exist for men, women and families in Chicago. Check out the LesBiGay Yellow Pages for more information about the groups.

Venues

Gay

Anvil - 1137 W. Granville St. 773-973-0006
Bucks Saloon - 3439 N. Halsted St., 773-525-1125
Cell Block - 3702 N. Halsted St., 773-665-8064
Charlie's - 3726 N. Broadway St., 773-871-8887
Charmers - 1502 W. Jarvis St., 773-465-2811
Circuit / Rehab - 3641 N. Halsted St., 773-325-2233
Hideaway - 7301 W. Roosevelt Rd., Forest park, 708-771-4459
Hunter's - 1932 E. Higgins Rd., Elk Grove Village, 847-439-8840
Legacy '21 - 3042 W. Irving Park Rd., 773-588-9405
Little Jims - 3501 N. Halsted St., 773-871-6116
Lucky Horseshoe - 3169 N. Halsted St., 773-404-3169
Manhandler - 1948 N. Halsted St., 773-871-3339
Manhole - 3458 N. Halsted St., 773-975-9244
North End - 3733 N. Halsted St., 773-477-7999
Nutbush - 7201 W. Franklin St., Forest Park, IL, 708-366-5117
Rails, The - 1675 N. Elston Ave., 708-802-1705
Second Story Bar - 157 E. Ohio St., 312-923-9536
Sidetrack - 3349 N. Halsted St., 773-477-9189
Touche - 6412 N. Clark St., 773-465-7400

Lesbian

The Closet - 3325 N. Broadway St., 773-477-8533
Club Intimus - 312 W. Randolph St., 312-901-1703
Girlbar - 2625 N. Halsted St., 773-871-4210
Lost & Found - 3058 W. Irving Park Rd., 773-463-7599
Patch, The - 201 155th St., Calumet City, 708-891-9854
Pour House - 103 155th St., Calumet City, 708-891-3980
Temptations - 10235 W. Grand Ave., Franklin Park, IL, 847-455-0008

Both

Berlin - 54 W. Belmont Ave., 773-348-4975
Bungalow - 1622 W. Belmont Ave, 773-244-0400
Big Chicks - 5024 N. Sheridan Rd., 773-728-5511
Bobby Loves - 3729 N. Halsted St., 773-525-1200
Buddies' Bar & Restaurant - 3301 N. Clark St., 773-477-4066
Chicago Eagle - 5015 N. Clark St., 773-728-0050
Clark's On Clark - 5001 N. Clark St., 773-728-2373
Club Escape - 1530 E. 75th St., 773-667-6454
Cocktail - 3359 N. Halsted St., 773-477-1420
Different Strokes - 4923 N. Clark St., 773-989-1958
Gentry On Halsted - 3320 N. Halsted St., 773-348-1053
Gentry On State - 440 N. State St., 312-836-0933
Madrigal's - 5316 N. Clark St., 773-334-3033
Jeffery Pub - 7041 S. Jeffery St., 773-363-8555
Roscoe's - 3356 N. Halsted St., 773-281-3355
Scot's - 1829 W. Montrose Ave., 773-528-3253
Spin Nightclub - Halsted St. & Belmont Ave., 773-327-7711
StarGaze Nightlclub - 5419 N. Clark St., Chicago, IL 60640, 773-561-7363
T's Bar & Restaurant- 5025 N. Clark St., 773-784-6000

Map 1 · River North / Fulton Market District

The Blommer Chocolate Co.	600 W Kinzie	312-226-7700	Opened in 1939. Eventually became largest commercial chocolate manufacturer in the U.S.

Map 2 · Near North / River North

House of Blues	329 N Dearborn St	312-923-2000	Concert venue, hotel, and bowling alley.
Merchandise Mart Mart Plz	222 Merchandise	312-527-7600	Houses furniture showrooms and a small mall.
Sotheby's	215 W Ohio St	312-396-9599	Renowned auction house

Map 3 · Streeterville / Mag Mile

Navy Pier	600 E Grand Ave	312-595-5300	A bastion of Chicago tourism.
Tribune Tower	435 N Michigan Ave	312-222-3994	Checkout the stones from famous buildings around the world.

Map 4 · West Loop Gate / Greek Town

Dugans Drinking Emporium	128 S Halsted	312-421-7191	Sports bar in Greektown fantastic beer garden and favorite cop hangout.
Union Station	200 S Canal St		Built in 1925, the architecture is not to be missed!
Zorba's House Restaurant	301 S Halsted	312-454-1397	24 hour Greek food—hangout for cops and hospital workers; everybody ends up here sooner or later.

Map 5 · The Loop

Chicago Board of Trade	141 W Jackson Blvd	312-435-3500	This building is a unique blend of the past and the future, with its telecommunications network and its gorgeous architecture.
Chicago Board Options Exchange	400 S LaSalle St	312-431-9729	The biggest option exchange in the world.
Chicago Cultural Center	78 E Washington	312-744-FINEART	The spot for free lectures, exhibits, concerts and movies.
Chicago Mercantile Exchange	20-30 S Wacker Dr	312-207-0588	A global marketplace that started out as the Chicago Butter and Egg Board.
Chicago Stock Exchange	440 S LaSalle St	312-663-2222	Founded in 1882 and one of the most important exchanges around.
Daley Civic Plaza	50 W Washington		Home of Picasso sculpture, Christmas tree ceremony and alfresco lunches
Harold Washington Library Center	400 S State	312-747-4300	The world's largest public library building, nearly 100 works of art on every floor.
Sears Tower	233 S Wacker	312-875-9696	World's tallest building, cool skydeck

Map 6 · The Loop / Grant Park

Art Institute of Chicago	111 S Michigan Ave	312-443-3600	World-class art museum.
Auditorium Building	430 S Michigan Ave		Designed by Louis Sullivan; on National Register of Historic Places.
Fine Arts Building	410 S Michigan Ave	312-913-0537	Frank Lloyd Wright had an office here.
Symphony Center	22 S Michigan Ave	312-294-3000	Classical music headquarters.

Map 7 · South Loop / River City

Old Post Office	404 W Harrison		Straddling 90/94 and 290 as they enter downtown, this massive edifice continues to act as a benchmark for traffic reports.
River City	800 S Wells St		A fluid cement design flop by architect Bartrand Goldberg.
U.S. Postal Distribution Center	433 W Harrison		The city's main mail routing center, employing over 6,000 people and operating 24 hours a day

Map 8 · South Loop / Dearborn Park

Columbia College Center for Book & Paper Arts	1104 S Wabash, 2nd Floor	312-344-6630	Two galleries feature changing exhibits of handmade books, paper, letterpress, and related objects.
Former Eliot Ness Building	618 S Dearborn St		Former headquarters of Eliot Ness, head of the Untouchables. Ness arranged Al Capones delivery to prison at the Dearborn Station just down the street, so he could personally view his exit from Chicago. Now it's an insurance agency.
Old Dearborn Train Station	47 W Polk St		Beautiful turn of the century train station with a lighted clocktower visible for several blocks at the end of Dearborn and Polk. Rich history includes being the station Al Capone was sent from Chicago to prison. (see next landmark)

Map 9 · South Loop / S Michigan Ave

Buckingham Fountain	Columbus Dr & East Congress Pkwy	312-747-2474	Built of pink marble; inspired by Versailles.
Chicago Hilton and Towers	720 S Michigan Ave	312-922-4400	Check out the frescoes in the lobby; sneak a kiss in the palatial ballroom.

Julian & Doris Wineberg Sculpture Garden	681 S Michigan Ave		A tranquil spot to ponder traffic on Michigan Ave.
Shedd Aquarium	1200 South Lake Shore Dr	312-939-2435	Marine and freshwater creatures from around the world are on view in this 1929 Classical Greek-inspired Beaux Arts structure.

Map 10 · East Pilsen / Chinatown

Chinatown Square	S Archer Ave		near S. Wentworth in the Chinatown Square Plaza.

Map 11 · South Loop / McCormick Place

America's Courtyard	South of Adler Planetarium on the lakefront		A spiral of stones that echoes both the milky way and ancient structures. Artists: Denise Milan and Ary R. Perez.
Chicago Meigs Airport	1500 South Lake Shore Dr	312-744-4787	The mayor is fighting to close this small airport-used mainly by owners of private jets-so the lakefront space it occupies will be open to the public.
Clarke House	1827 S Indiana Ave	312-745-0040	Built c. 1836 by an unknown architect, this Greek Revival-style home has been relocated twice and is now a designated Chicago landmark. Part of the Prairie Avenue Historic District.
Hillary Rodham Clinton Women's Park and Gardens of Chicago	1800-1900 S Prairie Ave		This park celebrates everything female, named in honor of the U.S. Senator.
Hyatt Regency McCormick Place	2233 S Martin Luther King Dr	312-567-1234	A direct link to the McCormick Place Convention Center.
McCormick Place	2301 South Lake Shore Drive		
Monument to the Great Northern Migration	MLK Drive, just before Stevenson Expressway		Statue depicts man standing on pile of worn shoes, representing the journey of African-Americans from the south. Artist: Alison Saar
National Vietnam Veterans Art Museum	1801 S Indiana Ave.	312-326-0270	Features art about the war created by Vietnam veterans from all sides of the conflict.
Quinn Chapel, African Methodist Episcopal Church	2401 S Wabash Ave	312-791-9710	Built in 1892, this Victorian Gothic-style church houses Chicago's oldest African-American congregation. The chapel has been host to famous speakers and performers, including George Washington Carter, Martin Luther King, and Patti LaBelle.
Raymond Hilliard Homes	2030 S State St		Designed by Bertrand Goldberg (also the designer of the nearby River City apartments), this public housing complex has long been admired by architects. Plans are underway to rehab the buildings into upscale rental apartments.
Second Presbyterian Church	1936 S Michigan Ave	312-225-4951	This Gothic Revival-style church, frequented by the wealthy denizens of Prairie Avenue, was built in 1874 by James Renwirk and reconstructed in 1900 by Howard Van Doren Shaw.
Soldier Field	425 E McFetridge Dr	312-747-1285	This concert venue and Chicago Bears stadium is under renovation until 1997.
Streetwise offices	1331 S Michigan Ave		Chicago's homeless newspaper
The Chicago Daily Defender	2400 S Michigan Ave	312-225-5656	Founded in 1905, this became the country's most influential black newspaper through the 1950s. Still in operation, the much-diminished Defender has been at the center of an ownership battle since 1997.
The Wheeler Mansion	2020 S Calumet Ave	312-945-2020	This Second Empire-style mansion now houses a Boutique Hotel for high-end travelers.
Willie Dixon's Blues Heaven Foundation	2120 S Michigan Ave	312-808-1286	Located in the former Chess Records Studio, where several influential 1960s blues and rock albums were recorded, this foundation offers tours, exhibits, and performances, along with workshops and support for emerging musicians. Call for hours.
Women Made Gallery	1900 S Prairie Ave	312-328-0038	This gallery and gift shop, located in the historic Keith House, showcases contemporary women's art Wed, Th, Fri: Noon-7pm; Sat, Sun: Noon-4pm

Map 12 · Bridgeport (West)

Library Fountain	W 34th & Halsted		
Monastery of the Holy Cross	3111 S Aberdeen St	773-927-7424	Home of Benedictine Monks with a bed and breakfast.
Wilson Park	S May & W 34th Pl	312-747-7002	

Map 13 · Bridgeport (East)

McGuane Park	W 29th St & S Halsted		
Richard J. Daley House	3536 S Lowe Ave		Childhood home of Mayor Richard J. Daley.
The Old Neighborhood Italian American Club	3031 S Shields	312-326-6420	Cultural gathering place.

Map 14 • Prairie Shores / Lake Meadows

Benches	S King Dr btn E 33rd-E 35th St	
Douglas Tomb State Historical Site	E 35th St & Lake Park	Entrance on east side of Lake.
Dunbar Park	S Indiana & E 31st St	
Mandrake Park	E Pershing Rd & S Cottage Grove Ave	
Mandrake Park & Track	King Dr btn. E Pershing & E Oakwood	
McCormick Tribune Campus Center	S State St & E 33rd St	A brand-new building at the Illinois Institute of Technology, designed by famous Dutch architect Rem Koolhaas.
Robert Taylor Homes	E 35th St & S State St 773-924-1203	One of the first public housing projects in the country.

Map 15 • Back of the Yards/Canaryville

Union Stockyard Gate	Exchange Ave & Peoria St	This limestone gate marks the place that made Chicago Hog Butcher to the World.

Map 16 • Bronzeville

Fountain	S Drexel Blvd. @ E Oakwood Blvd
Historic Walk	S Drexel Blvd & E Hyde Park Blvd
Metcalf Park	S. State St & E 43rd St
Mural	S Cottage Grove Ave & E 41st St
Murals	S King Dr & E 40th St
Track	S Cottage Grove Ave & E Oakwood Blvd

Map 17 • Kenwood

South Kenwood Mansions	Between S. Dorchester (east) and S Ellis (west), and S Hyde Park Blvd (south) and E 47th (north)	Built in the early 1900s by wealthy businessmen who wanted to flee the cramped North Side. Once in a state of disrepair, the mansions have (mostly) been rehabbed, and are once again the Jewels of the South Side.

Map 18 • Washington Park

DuSable Museum of African-American History	740 E 56th Pl	773-947-0600	Founded in 1961 and dedicated to preserving and honoring African-American culture, the museum is the oldest not-for-profit institution of its kind.
Former Home of Jesse Binga	5922 S. King Dr.		Home of nation's first African-American banker.
Interesting House	6215 S. Prairie		
United Center	1901 W Madison St	312-455-4500	Popular music and sports venue.
Washington Park	5531 S King Dr	312-747-6823	
Washington Park Aquatic Center & Refectory	5531 S Russell Dr	312-747-7618	

Map 19 • Hyde Park

Frederick C. Robie House	5757 S Woodlawn Ave		Designed by Frank Lloyd Wright, preservation trust property.
Midway Plaisance Park & Skating Rink	S Ellis Ave & S University Ave- Between E 59th St & E 60th St		
Rockefeller Memorial Chapel	1156 E 59th Ave	773-702-7059	Authentic English cathedral built in 1928.

Map 20 • East Hyde Park / Jackson Park

Osaka Garden/ Wooded Island	Just south of the Museum of Science and Industry, between the West Lagoon and East Lagoon	
Promontory Point Park	5491 S Shore Dr 773-747-6620	

Map 21 • Wicker Park / Ukrainian Village

Division Street Russian Bath	1916 W Division St	773-384-9671	Treat yourself to an old-school style day at the spa, complete with Swedish massages and granite heating room.
Holy Trinity Orthodox Cathedral and Rectory	1121 N Leavitt St	773-486-4545	Designed by Louis Sullivan to look like Russian provincial cathedrals known to churchgoers when it was built in 1903.
The Coyote Building	1600 N Milwaukee Ave		This 12-story Art Deco building was built in 1929.
The Flat Iron Building	1579 N Milwaukee Ave		This distinct triangular-shaped building is a part of the Chicago Coalition of Community Cultural Centers and houses artist studios.
Wicker Park District	Pierce and Hoyne Streets		The homes in this district reflect the style of Old Chicago.

Map 22 • Noble Square / Goose Island

Morton Salt Elston Facility	1357 N Elston St	773-235-1010	Has a painting of the famous salt girl.
Nelson Algren Fountain	Division St & Ashland Blvd		Recent, and controversial, addition.
North Avenue Bridge			Wretched traffic jams; river view.

Polish Museum of America	984 N Milwaukee Ave	773-384-3352	Right to life painting on the side.
Pulaski Park/ Pulaski Fieldhouse	Blackhawk St & Cleaver St		Has an outdoor swimming pool.
St. Stanislaus Kostka Church	1351 W Evergreen Ave	773-278-2470	One of the oldest in Chicago.
Weed St. District	Between Chicago River & Halsted St		Several bars and clubs in one area.

Map 23 · West Town / Near West Side

First Baptist Congregational Church	60 N Ashland Ave		Official Chicago Landmark.
Metropolitan Missionary Baptist Church	2151 W. Washington Blvd.		Official Chicago Landmark
Ukrainian Cultural Center	2247 W Chicago Ave	773-384-6400	A gathering place to share and celebrate Ukrainian culture.
Ukrainian National Museum	721 N Oakley Blvd	312-421-8020	Museum, library and archives detail the heritage, culture and people of Ukraine.

Map 24 · River West / West Town

Eckhart Park/Ida Crown Natatorium	Noble St & Chicago Ave		One of two swimming pools in the area.
Goldblatt Bros. Department Store	1613-35 W Chicago Ave		Official Chicago Landmark.

Map 27 · Logan Square

Illinois Centennial Monument	3100 W Logan Blvd		A well-known landmark to orient visitors, some neighbors feel that this eagle-topped obelisk stands for Logan Square.

Map 28 · Bucktown

Crumbling Bucktown	1579 N Milwaukee Ave		Structural icon seen from miles away; nucleus of Around the Coyote Arts Festival
Margie's Candies	1960 N. Western Ave.		This old-fashioned ice cream shop is known all over the world for its nostalgic charm and awesome homemade goodies.

Map 29 · DePaul/Wrightwood/Sheffield

Courtland Street Drawbridge	1440 W Cortland		Built in 1902 by John Ernst Erickson, this innovative leaf-lift bridge changed the way the world built bridges.
Mc Cormick Row House District			800 blocks of Chalmers, Fullerton, and Belden Streets.

Map 30 · Lincoln Park

Dewes Mansion	503 N Wrightwood Ave.	773-477-3075	Ornate historic home done in the German baroque style and built in 1896.
Kauffman Store and Flats	2312-14 N Lincoln Ave		One of the oldest existing buildings designed by Adler and Sullivan. It's amazing that its characteristic features have survived.
Lincoln Park Boat Club	Cannon Dr. & Fullerton Ave.	773-549-2628	
Lincoln Park Conservatory	2400 N. Stockton Dr.	312-742-7736	Sister to Garfield Park Conservatory. Built in 1891.
Lincoln Park Cultural Center	2045 N. Lincoln Park West	312-742-7726	
Lincoln Park Zoo	Cannon Dr & Fullerton Pkwy	312-742-2000	Oldest free zoo in the U.S.
Peggy Notebaert Nature Museum	2430 N Cannon Dr	312-652-6524	An oasis for adults and kids to reconnect with nature by playing with wildflowers and butterflies.
Theurer-Wrigley House	2466 N Lakeview		Early Richard E. Schmidt (and maybe Hugh H.G. Garden) based on late-Italian Renaissance architecture. Also famous because it was later sold to William Wrigley Jr, chewing gum king.

Map 32 · Gold Coast/Mag Mile

Water Tower and Park	Michigan btw. Chicago & Chestnut	Water tower that survived the Chicago Fire of 1871.

Map 33 · Rogers Park West

Bernard Horwich JCC	3003 W Touhy Ave	773-761-9100	Community center, programming for kids/adults, pool / fitness center, senior center, sports leagues.
Croatian Cultural Center	2845 W Devon Ave	773-338-3839	A place where families can relax, socialize and congregate. Intended to benefit the Croatian community in Chicago.
High Ridge YMCA	2430 W Touhy Ave	773-262-8300	Community center, programming for kids/adults, summer activities, child care programs, sport teams, pool.

259

Indian Boundary Park	2500 W Lunt	773-742-7887	Petting zoo, tennis courts, chess tables, ice rink, tennis courts, skate park, batting cages, spray pool, community center classes seasonally
Rogers Park / West Ridge Historical Society	6424 N Western	773-764-4078	Photos / memorabilia / historical documents of the community's history, details it's ethnic diversity, open Wed / Fri 10-5, Th 7pm-9pm, and by appointment.
Thillen's Stadium	Devon and Kedzie		Chicago landmark, 16 softball field, features little league baseball and various other games and benefits.
Warren Park	6601 N Western Ave	312-742-7888	Seasonal free entertainment, pony rides, ethnic food festivals, amusement park rides, arts & crafts, Winter sledding hill, baseball diamond, picnic pavilions, dog play areas.

Map 34 • Rogers Park East

| Robert A. Black Golf Course | 2045 W Pratt | 773-764-4045 | The newest of Chicago Park District courses; 2,300 yard, par 33 layout, great choice for all skill levels, perfect for group outings and golf leagues, nine-hole daily fee. This short-distance course plays more difficult that most players predict. |

Map 35 • Arcadia Terrace

| India Town | Devon street Indian strip | | Devon street features Indian and Pakistani shops, grocery stores, restaurants, and more. |

Map 36 • Bryn Mawr

| Rosehill Cemetery and Mausoleum | 5800 N Ravenswood Ave | 773-561-5940 | Chicago's historical glitterati entombed among unsurpassed sculpture and architecture. |

Map 37 • Edgewater / Andersonville

Ann Sather's Restaurant	5207 N Clark St	773-327-9522	More than a restaurant, a cultural field trip.
Philadelphia Church	5437 N Clark St	773-728-5106	Can't miss neon sign.
Swedish American Museum	5211 N Clark St	773-728-8111	Everything you want to know about Swedish culture, which is more than you thought.
The Belle Shore Hotel Building	1062 W Bryn Mawr Ave	312-337-5339	Once homes to roaring 1920s nightlife, now historic landmarks, restored to their former glory as apartments.

Map 38 • Ravenswood / Albany Park

North Branch Pumping Station	Lawrence and the River		With its 1930s Art Deco façade, it seems like something prettier should be happening here than pumping most of the North Side's sewage.
Paradise	2910 W Montrose Ave	773-588-1989	It's a sushi restaurant. It's a beauty shop. It's a sauna ($12 for as long as you want). It's paradise. Of course, it's a neighborhood landmark.
Ravenswood Manor Park	4626 N Manor Ave	312-742-7572	It's just a tiny triangle wedged between the non-elevated El and several streets, but it is ground zero for garden sales, neighborhood associations, dogs, kids and any community activity.
River Park	5100 N Francisco Ave	312-742-7594	More than 30 acres of park including one of the few city canoe launches.

Map 39 • Ravenswood / North Center

| St. Benedict's Church | 2215 W Irving Park Rd | 773-588-6484 | The namesake of the St. Ben's neighborhood. |

Map 40 • Uptown

Graceland Cemetary	4001 N Clark	773-525-1105	Chicago famous buried in masterpiece of landscape architecture
Green Mill Pub	4802 N Broadway	773-878-5552	Live jazz 7 nights a week. Dillinger drank here.
Lakeview Lounge	5110 N Broadway St	773-769-0994	Old School Bar—live music weekends. John Dillinger used to drink here—shot and a beer type of joint.
Rainbow Roller Rink	4826 N Clark St	773-271-5668	Adult Midnight Rumble on Skates.
Tattoo Factory	4408 N Broadway	773-989-4077	Tattoos for famous and infamous.
Uptown Theatre	4707 N. Broadway	773-561-5700	An acre of seats in a magic city-scheduled to reopen 2004

Map 43 • Wrigleyville / East Lakeview

Southport Lanes	3325 N Southport Ave	773-472-1601	Formerly a brothel.
Vic Theater	3145 N Sheffield Ave	773-472-0366	Drink, watch films and take in an occasional band at this old theater.
Wrigley Field	1060 W Addison Ave	773-404-CUBS	Legendary neighborhood ballpark claims full houses whether the team wins or loses.

Map 44 • East Lakeview

Belmont Rocks	Briar at the lake		Popular lakefront hangout.
Dog Beach	northern tip of Belmont Harbor		Fun and frolic with your pup.
Totem Pole	Waveland & Belmont Harbor Drive		Where did it come from? Why is it there? Nobody knows.

Make no bones about it, Chicago is a dog's kind of town. Over 750,000 canines live and play in the Windy City. Dogs socialize and exercise their owners daily at designated DFAs (dog friendly areas), shady parks and sprawling beaches.

Dog Friendly Areas

Dog Friendly Areas (DFAs) are parks reserved just for canines. DFA amenities vary by park, but they include doggie drinking fountains, agility equipment, grass, wood chip, pea pebble and green asphalt surfaces, "time out" fenced-in areas for shy or bad dogs to chill, trash receptacles and doggie bags for, well, not take-out; and bulletin boards and information kiosks to post animal lovers' announcements.

DFAs are managed by the neighborhood's dog owners' council and the Chicago Park District. Chicago Police, who have the authority to ticket dog owners who don't leash their pooches or pick up their piles ($500 fine), recognize DFAs as legal areas to let canines run free and poop as they please. However, dog owners must abide by the DFA rules which include cleaning up after your pooch, ensuring that your dog is fully immunized, de-wormed, licensed and wearing ID tags, and not bringing puppies under four months and dogs in heat into the park. Chicago has seven DFAs.

- **Coliseum Park**, 14th St. & Wabash Ave.
  Long, narrow and fenced-in park where dogs race the passing trains.
- **Dog Lot**, Orleans St. and Ohio Sts. (southwest corner)
  This park is as creative as its name. Next to the I-90/94 exit ramp, the fenced-in strip of concrete flanked by bushes is better used for rat races than dog exercise.
- **Hamlin Park**, 3035 N. Hoyne Ave. at Wellington Ave. (Map 42). Located in the shady southwest corner, this active L-shaped park appeals to tennis-ball chasers and fetching owners.
- **Margate Park**, 4921 N. Marine Dr. (Map 40)
  Called "pup town" by the canine community, this beloved DFA tends to be grass-worn because of all the doggone fun. Plans are to add trees and a drinking fountain.
- **Walsh Park**, 1722 N. Ashland Ave.; walshparkdogs@aol.com (Map 29). A 4,500 square foot park with grassy area for fetching, with pea gravel and shade.
- **Wicker Park**, 1425 N. Damen Ave. (Map 21)
  Popular pooch as well as dog owner pick-up park. Often packed with dog-walkers wrangling fleets of frisky canines.
- **Wiggley Field**, 2645 N. Sheffield Ave. (Map 29)
  Shaded by El tracks and trees, this model DFA built in 1997 with all the pawpular amenities was Chicago's pilot pooch park: It has a fenced-in doggy obstacle course, a green asphalt surface; drinking fountain; "time out" area; and info kiosk.

Creating a DFA takes a serious grass-roots effort spearheaded by the neighborhood's dog owners. They must organize themselves into an official dog owner council (DOW), get the community to bow to their desires through several surveys and meetings and, most importantly, unleash the support of their alderman, police precinct and park district. For more DFA information call the Park District's Dog Hot Line 312-744-DOGS (3647). Chicago's Dog Advisory Work Group (DAWG) assists neighborhood groups in establishing DFAs, 312-409-2169.

Top Dog Parks and Beaches

Basically, dogs and well-behaved owners are welcome in most of Chicago's parks and on its beaches. Here are some local canines' top picks.

- **Lincoln Park**
  Paws down, the best dog park in town for romping, fetch and Frisbee. Unofficial "Bark Park" where pet lovers congregate is a grassy area south of Addison St. bound by a fence on the west and the lake's rocky shoreline.
- **Warren Park**
  Rogers Park dogs give a waggly tails up for this DFA's big hill for sprints and lake views.
- **Dog Beach**
  A crescent of sand at the north corner of Belmont Harbor separated from the bike path by a fence, this unofficial dog sand box is always crowded with frolicking Fidos.
- **Horner Park**
  Dog heaven with lots of trees, grass, squirrels to chase and other pups to meet.
- **Montrose/Wilson Ave. Beach**
  Perfect for pooches to practice dogpaddling as lake water is shallow.
- **Loyola Beach**
  Decent breakwaters for serious paddlers and pooches that dig body surfing.
- **Ohio St. Beach and Olive Park**
  The perfect combo for cross-training canines: Olive Park's fenced-in grassy areas for running and neighboring Ohio St. Beach's calm waters for swim.
- **Promontory Point**
  Radical dog run for daring, buff dogs that dive off the scenic picnic area's rocks into the deep water below.

More Doggone Information

Chicago's canine community keeps up to sniff on doggie doings through *Chicago Tails Magazine* produced by DAWG and *Pet Times* newspaper, 312-337-6976. The definitive dog resource for Chicagoans is Steve Dale's book *Doggone Chicago*.

Hotels · General Information

Map 1 · River North/Fulton Market

Acacia Hotel	725 W Grand Ave	312-421-4597

Map 2 · Near North / River North

Best Western Inn	125 W Ohio St	312-467-0800
Comfort Inn	15 E Ohio St	312-494-1515
Courtyard By Marriott	30 E Hubbard St	312-329-2500
Embassy Suites Hotel	600 N State St	312-943-3800
Great Lakes Spa Suites	15 W Hubbard St	312-527-1311
Hampton Inn	33 W Illinois St	312-832-0330
Hilton Garden Inn	10 E Grand Ave	312-595-0000
Holiday Inn Mart Plaza	350 N Orleans St	312-836-5000
Homewood Suites	40 E Grand Ave	312-644-2222
Hotel 71	71 E Wacker Dr	312-346-7100
Hotel Wacker	111 W Huron St	312-787-1386
House Of Blues Hotel	333 N Dearborn St	312-245-0333
Lenox House Suites	616 N Rush St	312-337-1000
Ohio East Inn	15 E Ohio St	312-644-8222
Ohio House Motel	600 N La Salle Dr	312-943-6000
Penisula Chicago Hotel	745 N Rush St	312-337-2888
Renaissance Chicago Hotel	1 W Wacker Dr	312-372-7200
Westin River North	320 N Dearborn St	312-744-1900

Map 3 · Streeterville / Mag Mile

Allerton Crowne Plaza	701 N Michigan Ave	312-440-1500
Best Western Inn	162 E Ohio St	312-787-3100
Embassy Suites Lakefront	511 N Columbus Dr	312-836-5900
Fairfield Inn	216 E Ontario St	312-787-3777
Holiday Inn City Center	300 E Ohio St	312-787-6100
Hotel Inter-Continental	505 N Michigan Ave	312-944-4100
Kapalua Bay Hotels & Villas	625 N Michigan Ave	312-751-4299
Kirkpatrick Hotel	166 E Superior St	312-787-6000
Le Meridien	520 N Michigan Ave	312-645-1500
Marriott Chicago Downtown		
	540 N Michigan Ave	312-836-0100
Motel 6	162 E Ontario St	312-787-3580
Omni Chicago Hotel	676 N Michigan Ave	312-944-6664
Park Hyatt Hotel	800 N Michigan Ave	312-335-1234
Radisson Hotel	160 E Huron St	312-787-2900
Sheraton Chicago	301 E North Water	312-464-1000
W Lakeshore	644 N Lake Shore Dr	312-943-9200
Wyndham Chicago	633 N Saint Clair St	312-573-0300

Map 4 · West Loop Gate / Greek Town

New Jackson Hotel	768 W Jackson Blvd	312-372-8856
Quality Inn	1 S Halsted St	312-829-5000

Map 5 · The Loop

Crowne Plaza Silversmith	10 S Wabash Ave	312-372-7696
Ewing Annex Hotel	426 S Clark St	312-939-9120
Fairmont Hotel	200 N Columbus Dr	312-565-8000
Hotel Allegro	171 W Randolph St	312-236-0123
Hotel Burnham	1 W Washington Blvd	312-782-1111
Hotel Monaco	225 N Wabash Ave	312-960-8500
Hyatt Regency Chicago		
	151 E Wacker Dr	312-565-1234
Inn On Mackinac	111 W Monroe St	312-558-5367
Marriott Hotels & Resorts	333 N Michigan Ave	312-214-8923
Palmer House Hilton	17 E Monroe St	312-726-7500
Swissotel Chicago	323 E Wacker Dr	312-565-0565
W City Center	172 W Adams St	312-332-1200

Map 7 · South Loop / River City

Holiday Inn-Downtown West Loop		
	506 W Harrison St	312-957-9100

Map 8 · South Loop / Dearborn Park

Chicago Travelodge Downtown		
	65 E Harrison St	312-427-8000
Ho Jo Inn	720 N La Salle St	312-664-8100
Hotel Roosevelt	1152 S Wabash Ave	312-427-7582
Hyatt Printers Row	505 S Dearborn St	312-986-1234
St James Hotel	1234 S Wabash Ave	312-427-7013

Map 9 · South Loop / S Michigan Ave

Best Western Inn	1100 S Michigan Ave	312-922-2900
Congress Plaza Hotel	520 S Michigan Ave	312-427-3800
Essex Inn	800 S Michigan Ave	312-939-2800
Hilton & Towers Chicago	720 S Michigan Ave	312-922-4400

Map 11 · South Loop/McCormick Place

Hyatt McCormick Place	2233 S Dr Martin L King Jr Dr	312-567-1234

Map 14 · Prairie Shores/Lake Meadows

Amber Inn	3901 S Michigan Ave	773-285-1000
Bronzeville's First Bed & Breakfast		
	3911 S King Dr	773-373-8081
Michigan Plaza Motel	2600 S State St	312-791-1110
Royal Michigan Motel	3756 S Michigan	
Royal Michigan Motel	3756 S Michigan Ave	773-536-4100
Tortoise Inn	3747 S Michigan Ave	773-285-5151
Zanzibar Motel 5	453 E Pershing Rd	773-373-6100

Map 15 · Back of the Yards/Canaryville

Root Inn	234 W Root St	773-285-5280

Map 16 · Bronzeville

Booker Hotel	753 E 47th St	773-924-5400
Callo Hotel	4822 S Michigan Ave	773-536-6420
Central Arms Hotel	520 E 47th St	773-624-6500
Fox's Inn	4719 S Indiana Ave	773-268-9200
Harlem Hotel	5020 S Michigan Ave	773-536-1640
Lodging House Hotel	4905 S Michigan Ave	773-924-0600
Ritz Hotel	409 E Oakwood Blvd	773-536-6000
Zanzibar III	5040 King Dr	773-373-8302

Map 18 · Washington Park

Hudson Hotel	5522 S Indiana Ave	773-363-8422
Jackson Hotel	5615 S Prairie Ave	773-288-6973
The New Hudson Hotel	5522 S Indiana Ave	773-493-5028

Map 19 · Hyde Park

Hyde Park Arms Hotel	5316 S Harper Ave	773-493-3500
Ramada Inn Lakeshore	4900 S Lakeshore Dr	773-288-5800

2

2

Map 23 • West Town / Near West Side

Vel Mar Hotel	2120 W Washington Blvd	312-733-3624

Map 24 • River West / West Town

Rosemoor Hotel	1622 W Jackson Blvd	312-243-2900
Viceroy Hotel	1519 W Warren Blvd	312-421-4611

Map 25 • Illinois Medical District

Hyatt at University Village	625 S Ashland	312-243-7000

Map 27 • Logan Square

Milshire Hotel	2525 N Milwaukee Ave	773-384-7611
North Hotel	1622 N California Ave	773-278-2425

Map 28 • Bucktown

Dogs Day Inn	1719 W Wrightwood Ave	773-868-4001

Map 30 • Lincoln Park

Covent Hotel	2653 N Clark St	773-549-3399
Days Inn	1816 N Clark St	312-664-3040

Map 31 • Old Town / Near North

Carling Hotel	1512 N La Salle Dr	312-664-6660
Marshall Hotel	1232 N La Salle Dr	312-664-3080

Map 32 • Gold Coast/Mag Mile

Cedar Hotel	1118 N State St	312-787-5560
Claridge Hotel	1244 N Dearborn St	312-787-4980
Doubletree Guest Suites	198 E Delaware Pl	312-664-1100
Drake Hotel	140 E Walton St	312-787-2200
Elms Hotel	18 E Elm St	312-787-4740
Four Seasons Hotel Chicago		
	120 E Delaware Pl #1	312-280-8800
Mark Twain Hotel	111 W Division St	312-642-7150
Omni Ambassador East Hotel		
	1301 N State Pkwy	312-787-7200
Raphael Hotel	201 E Delaware Pl	312-943-5000
Regal Knickerbocker Hotel	163 E Walton St	312-751-8100
Residence Inn	201 E Walton St	312-943-9800
Ritz Carlton Hotel	160 E Pearson St	312-266-1000
Seneca Hotel	200 E Chestnut St	312-787-8900
Sofitel Water Tower	20 E Chestnut St	312-324-4011
Sutton Place Hotel	21 E Bellevue Pl	312-266-2100
Talbott Hotel	20 E Delaware Pl	312-944-4970
Tremont Hotel	100 E Chestnut St	312-751-1900
Westin Michigan Ave	909 N Michigan Ave	312-943-7200
Whitehall Hotel	105 E Delaware Pl	312-944-6300

Map 34 • East Rogers Park

Sheraton	7300 N Sheridan Rd	773-973-7440

Map 35 • Arcadia Terrace

Guest House Motel	2600 W Bryn Mawr Ave	773-561-6811

Map 37 • Edgewater / Andersonville

Lakeside Motel	5440 N Sheridan Rd	773-275-2700
Sovereign	1040 W Granville Ave	773-274-8000
Windale Hotel	6019 N Winthrop Ave	773-907-5050

Map 40 • Uptown

Aragon Arms Hotel	4917 N Kenmore Ave	773-561-4970
Darlington Hotel	4700 N Racine Ave	773-561-1741
Northmere Hotel	4943 N Kenmore Ave	773-561-4234
Wilson Club Hotel	1124 W Wilson Ave	773-784-0691

Map 43 • Wrigleyville/ East Lakeview

Ambers Hotel	1632 W Belmont Ave	773-248-1740
Bellwood Hotel	1409 W Diversey Pkwy	773-404-6000
City Suites Hotel Chicago	933 W Belmont Ave	773-404-3400
Diplomat Hotel	3208 N Sheffield Ave	773-549-6800
Julian Hotel	924 W Belmont Ave	773-525-1221
Sheffield House	3834 N Sheffield Ave	773-248-3500

Map 44 • East Lakeview

Abbott Hotel	721 W Belmont Ave	773-248-2700
Belair Hotel	424 W Diversey Pkwy	773-248-4000
Best Western	3434 N Broadway	
Best Western	3434 N Broadway St	773-244-3434
Chateau Hotel	3838 N Broadway St	773-525-8310
Comfort Inn	601 W Diversey	
Comfort Inn	601 W Diversey Pkwy	
		773-348-2810
Days Inn	644 W Diversey Pkwy	773-525-7010
Diplomat Resort & Country Club	525 W Hawthorne Pl	773-832-1866
Hotel Majestic	528 W Brompton Ave	773-404-3499
Park Brompton	528 Brompton Place	
Willows	555 W Surf St	773-528-8400

Veterinarian

	Address	Phone	Map
Chicago Feline Medical Center	600 N Wells St	312-944-2287	2

Delivery & Messengers

	Address	Phone	Map
Deadline Express	449 N Union Ave	312-850-1200	1
On The Fly Courier	131 N Green, Ste 203	312-738-2154	4

Gyms

	Address	Phone	Map
Chicago Fitness Center	3131 N Lincoln Ave	773-549-8181	43

Locksmiths

	Address	Phone	Map
Gateway Locksmith	Multiple locations	800-964-8282	N/A
Amazing Lock Service, Inc.	739 W Belmont Ave	773-935-8900	44
AASA Locksmith	Multiple locations	773-434-4650	N/A
A-AAA Accurate Lock Service	Multiple locations	800-734-5156	N/A
A-AAround the Clock	Multiple locations	800-281-5445	N/A
Safemasters	614 W Monroe St	312-627-8209	4
Wernick Key & Lock Service	Multiple locations	888-937-6425	N/A
Abby Lock Service	Multiple locations	888-272-7435	N/A
Always Available	Multiple locations	773-478-1960	N/A
Five Star Lock & Key	N/A	773-778-2066	N/A

Plumbers

	Address	Phone	Map
Fast Service	multiple locations	773-376-6666	N/A
A Metro Plumbing & Sewer Service	N/A	877-872-3060	N/A
A-AAAA Plumbing & Sewer	N/A	773-282-2878	N/A
A Better Man Plumbing & Sewer	N/A	773-286-9351	N/A
Roto-Rooter	N/A	800-438-7686	N/A
Plumbing & Heating Inc.	N/A	773-889-1130	N/A
Sears HomeCentral	N/A	773-737-3580	N/A
Emergency Response	N/A	773-736-3247	N/A
O'Bannon Plumbing & Sewer (Northside)	N/A	773-486-5748	N/A
O'Bannon Plumbing & Sewer (Southside)	N/A	773-862-5112	N/A
Second City Plumbing & Sewer	N/A	773-581-2300	N/A
Southtown Plumbing & Sewer Service	N/A	773-779-0024	N/A
Top Quality Plumbing & Sewer	N/A	773-523-1160	N/A
Elliot Plumbing & Sewer Service	N/A	773-370-9908	N/A
Midwest Plumbing & Sewer	N/A	773-478-1000	N/A
Sunrise Plumbing & Sewer	N/A	773-960-6462	N/A

Copy Shops

	Address	Phone	Map
Kinko's	444 N Wells St	312-670-4460	2
Kinko's	128 S Canal St	312-258-8833	4
Kinko's	1242 S Canal St	312-455-0920	10
Kinko's	2300 N Clybourn Ave	773-665-7500	29
Kinko's	3524 N Southport Ave	773-975-5031	43
Kinko's	3001 N Clark St	773-528-0500	44

Pharmacies

	Address	Phone	Map
Walgreens	641 N Clark St	312-587-1416	2
Walgreens	757 N. Michigan	312-664-8686	3
Walgreens	111 S Halsted St	312-463-9142	4
Walgreens	501 W Roosevelt St	312-492-8559	7
Walgreens	3405 S King Dr	312-326-4058	14
Walgreens	1554 E 55th St	773-667-1177	19
Walgreens	1601 N Wells St	312-642-4008	31
Walgreens	1200 N Dearborn St	312-943-0973	32
Walgreens	7510 N Western St	773-764-1765	33
Osco Drug	5532 N Clark St	773-784-7348	37
Walgreens	3302 W Belmont	773-267-2328	41
Osco Drug	3572 N Elston Ave	773-583-9858	41
Osco Drug	2940 N Ashland Ave	773-348-4155	43
Walgreens	3046 N Halsted St	773-325-0413	44
Walgreens	5625 N. Ridge Ave.	773-989-7546	37
Parkway Drugs	680 N LSD	312-945-2224	3
Osco Drug	845 W. Wilson	773-275-7192	40

Areas codes are 312 unless otherwise noted.

2 • Near North / River North

Alan Koppel Gallery	210 W Chicago Ave	640-0730
Aldo Castillo Gallery	233 W Huron St	337-2536
Andrew Bae Gallery	300 W Superior St	335-8601
Ann Nathan Gallery	218 W Superior St	664-6622
Belloc-Lowndes Fine Art, Inc.	215 W Huron St	573-1157
Byron Roche Gallery	750 N Franklin, Ste 105	654-0144
Carl Hammer Gallery	740 N Wells St	266-8512
Carrie Secrist Gallery	300 W Superior St	280-4500
Catherine Edelman Gallery	300 W Superior St, Lower Level	266-2350
Douglas Dawson Gallery	222 W Huron St	751-1961
Gwenda Jay/ Addington Gallery	704 N Wells St	664-3406
Habatat Galleries	222 W Superior St	440-0288
Jean Albano Gallery	215 W Superior St	440-0770
Judy A. Saslow Gallery	300 W Superior St	943-0530
Kenneth Probst Galleries	46 E Superior St	440-1991
Lydon Fine Art	309 W Superior St	943-1133
Lyons Wier Gallery	300 W Superior St	654-8171
Marx-Saunders Gallery, Ltd	230 W Superior St	573-1400
Maya Polsky Gallery	215 W Superior St	440-0055
Melanee Cooper Gallery	740 N Franklin St	202-9305
Nicole Gallery	230 W Huron St	787-7716
Perimeter Gallery	210 W Superior St	266-9473
Peter Bartlow Gallery	44 E Superior St	337-1782
Portals Ltd	742 N Wells St	642-1066
Primitive Art Works	706 N Wells St	943-3770
R.H. Love Galleries	40 E Erie St	640-1300
Rita Bucheit, Ltd. Fine Art & Antiques	449 N Wells St	527-4080
Robert Henry Adams Fine Art	715 N Franklin St	642-8700
Roy Boyd Gallery	739 N Wells St	642-1606
Schneider Gallery	230 W Superior St	988-4033
Sonia Zaks Gallery	311 W Superior St, Ste 207	943-8440
TBA Exhibition Space	230 W Huron St	587-3300
Vale Craft Gallery	230 W Superior St	337-3525
ZG Gallery	300 W Superior St	654-9900
Zolla/Liberman Gallery	325 W Huron St	944-1990

3 • Streeterville / Mag Mile

R.S. Johnson Fine Art	645 N Michigan Ave, Ste 234	943-1661
The Arts Club of Chicago	201 E Ontario St	787-3997
The Museum of Contemporary Art	220 E Chicago Ave	280-2660

4 • West Loop Gate / Greek Town

Fassbender/ Stevens Gallery	835 W Washington St	666-4302
Jan Cicero Gallery	835 W Washington St	733-9551
Thomas McCormick Gallery	835 W Washington St	226-6800

5 • The Loop

Illinois Art Gallery	100 W Randolph St, Ste 2-100	814-5322

6 • The Loop / Grant Park

Fine Arts Building Gallery	410 S Michigan Ave, Ste 433	913-0537
The Art Institute of Chicago	111 S Michigan Ave	443-3500
The Chicago Architecture Center	224 S Michigan Ave	922-3402

8 • South Loop / Dearborn Park

Bella Vista Fine Art Gallery	746 N La Salle St	274-1490

11 • South Loop / McCormick Place

Woman Made Gallery	1900 S Prarie Ave	328-0038

21 • Wicker Park / Ukrainian Village

Axis Gallery	1542 N Milwaukee Ave	773-278-8351
Collage	1563 N Milwaukee Ave	773-252-2562
David Leonardis Gallery	1352 . Paulina St	773-278-3058
Dawning, Art the Gift	2246 W North Ave	
Feitico Gallery	1821 W North Ave.	
Gallery 203	1579 N Milwaukee Ave.	773-252-1952
The Blue Ladder Gallery	1573 N Milwaukee Ave	
Thirteenth Floor Gallery	2337 W North Ave	
Wood St. Gallery & Sculpture Garden	1239 N Wood St	

22 • Noble Square / Goose Island

1112 Gallery	1112 N Milwaukee Ave	

23 • West Town / Near West Side

Gallery 406	406 N Wood St.	
Ukrainian Institute of Art	2318 W Chicago Ave	773-227-5522

24 • River West / West Town

A.R.C. Gallery	734 N Milwaukee Ave	733-2787
Arena Gallery	311 N Sangamon St	421-0212
Aron Packer Gallery	118 N Peoria St	226-8984
Artemisia Gallery	700 N Carpenter St	226-7323
Bodybuilder & Sportsman	119 N Peoria St	492-7261
Flatfile Photography Gallery	118 N Peoria St	491-1190
G.R. N'Namdi Gallery	110 N Peoria St	587-8362
Gallery 312	312 N May St, Ste 110	942-2500
Klein Art Works	400 N Morgan St	243-0400
Peter Miller Gallery	118 N Peoria St	226-5291
Rhona Hoffman Gallery	118 N Peoria St	455-1990
Richard Milliman Fine Art	1364 Grand St	432-9900
Walsh Gallery	118 N Peoria St	829-3312

25 • Illinois Medical District

Mexican Fine Arts Center	1852 W 19th St	738-1503

28 • Bucktown

Bucktown Fine Arts	2200 N Oakley Ave	
Dawning Art the Gift	2246 W North Ave	
Eclectic Junction	1630 N Damen Ave	773-342-7865
Gallery 1633	1633 N Damen Ave	
Idao Gallery	1616 N Damen Ave	773-235-4724
Morlen Sinoway-Atelier	2035 W Wabansia	

29 • DePaul / Wrightwood / Sheffield

Havana Gallery	1139 W Webster Ave	773-549-2492

30 • Lincoln Park

Contemporary Art Workshop	542 W Grant Pl	773-472-4004

32 • Gold Coast / Mag Mile

Billy Hork Galleries	109 E Oak St	337-1199
Colletti Gallery	67 E Oak St	664-6767
Galleries Maurice Sternberg	140 E Walton	642-1700
Hildt Galleries	943 N State	255-0005
Richard Gray Gallery	875 N Michigan #2503	642-8877
Richard Reed Armstrong Fine Art	200 E Walton	664-9312
The Hart Gallery	64 E Walton	932-9646

The big ones already draw crowds and fleets of school buses. Exercise different parts of your brain at these smaller, interesting museums: David & Alfred Smart Museum, the Oriental Institute, DuSable Museum of African American History, International Museum of Surgical Science, Mexican Fine Arts Center Museum, ABA Museum of Law, Spertus Museum and the National Vietnam Veterans Art Museum.

Museum	Address	Phone	Map
A. Philip Randolph Pullman Porter Museum	10406 S Maryland Ave	773-928-3935	N/A
ABA Museum of Law	750 N Lake Shore Dr	312-988-5730	N/A
Adler Planetarium & Astronomy Museum	1300 S. Lake Shore Dr	312-922-STAR	11
Arts Club Of Chicago	201 E Ontario St	312-787-3997	3
Chicago Architecture Foundation	224 S Michigan Ave	312-922-3432	6
Chicago Athenaeum At Schamburg	225 N Michigan Ave	847-895-3950	6
Chicago Children's Museum	700 E Grand Ave	312-527-1000	3
Chicago Historical Society	1601 N Clark St	312-642-4600	32
Clarke House Museum	1827 S Indiana Ave	312-745-0040	11
Das Motorad Museum	1901 S Western Ave	312-738-2269	25
David & Alfred Smart Museum	5550 S Greenwood Ave	773-702-0200	19
Du Sable Museum-African American History	740 E 56th Pl	773-947-0600	18
Field Museum	1400 S. Lake Shore Dr	312-922-9410	11
Filipino American Historical Society Museum	3952 N Ashland Ave	773-947-8696	43
Frank Lloyd Wright Home & Studio	951 Chicago Ave, Oak Park	708-848-1976	N/A
Glessner House Museum	1800 South Prairie Ave	312-326-1480	11
Hellenic Museum & Cultural Center	168 N Michigan Ave	312-726-1234	6
Institute Museum	1341 W Fullerton Ave	773-528-1000	29
International Monetary Market	1516 N Lake Shore Dr	312-642-6502	11
International Museum of Surgical Science	1524 N Lake Shore Dr	312-642-6502	11
Jane Addams Hull House Museum	800 S Halsted St	312-413-5353	26
John G. Shedd Aquarium	1200 S Lake Shore Dr	312-939-2438	9
Leather Archives & Museum	6418 N Greenview Ave	773-761-9200	34
Mexican Fine Arts Center	1852 W 19th St	312-738-1503	25
Mimi International	56 E Oak St	312-664-6161	32
Museum Of Contemporary Art	220 E Chicago Ave	312-280-2660	3
Museum Of Holography-Chicago	1134 W Washington Blvd	312-226-1007	24
Museum Of Science & Industry	5700 S Lake Shore Dr	773-684-1414	37
Museum Shop Of The Art Institute	900 N Michigan Ave	312-482-8275	32
Museum of Contemporary Photography	600 S Michigan Ave	312-663-5554	9
Museums In The Park	104 S Michigan Ave	312-857-7136	6
National Jaz Museum	1727 S Indiana Ave	312-663-3038	11
National Vietnam Veterans Art Museum	1801 S Indiana Ave	312-326-0270	11
Oriental Institute Museum	University of Chicago - 1155 E 58th St	773-702-9514	19
Pallas Photographica Gallery	319 W Erie St	312-664-1257	2
Peggy Notebaert Natural Museum	2430 N Cannon Dr	312-652-6524	30
Peggy Notebaert Nature Museum	2060 N Clark St	773-755-5100	30
Polish Museum Of America	984 N Milwaukee Ave	773-384-3352	22
Renaissance Center	5710 N Broadway St	773-722-2900	37
Robie House	5757 S Woodlawn Ave	773-834-1847	19
Rogers Park Historical Society	6424 N Western Ave	773-764-4078	33
Smart Museum of Art	550 S Greenwood Ave	773-702-0200	19
Spertus Museum	618 S Michigan Ave	312-922-9012	9
Swedish American Museum Center	5211 N Clark St	773-728-8111	37
Terra Museum Of American Art	664 N Michigan Ave	312-664-3939	3
The Art Institute of Chicago	111 S Michigan Ave	312-443-3600	6
The Museum of Broadcast Communications	78 E Washington St	312-629-6000	5
The Peace Museum	100 N Central Park Ave	773-638-6450	N/A
Ukrainian Institute Of Art	2318 W Chicago Ave	773-227-5522	23
Ukrainian National Museum of Chicago	721 N Oakley Blvd	312-421-8020	23

While we love all bookstores, some favorites are: After-Words in River North (check out the basement's gently used books); Rain Dog Books and Savvy Traveller in the Loop; Sandmeyers in Printer's Row; 57th Street Books in Hyde Park; Barbara's in Old Town; and Unabridged Books in East Lakeview.

Areas codes are 312 unless otherwise noted.

1 • River North / Fulton Market District

N Fagin Books	459 N Milwaukee Ave	829-5252

2 • Near North / River North

Abraham Lincoln Book Shop	357 W Chicago Ave	944-3085
After-Words	23 E Illinois St	464-1110
B Dalton Bookseller	222 Merchandise Mart Plz	329-1881
Beck's Book Store	50 E Chicago Ave	944-7685
Hubbard's Street Book & Video	109 W Hubbard St	828-0953
Kendall Hunt Publishing Co	500 N Dearborn St	527-0460
Moody Bookstores	150 W Chicago Ave	329-4352
Te-Jays Book Store	53 W Hubbard St	923-9210

3 • Streeterville / Mag Mile

Barbara's Bookstore	700 E Grand Ave	222-0890
Rand Mc Nally Map & Travel	444 N Michigan Ave	321-1751
Univ Of Chicago Bookstore	450 N Cityfront Plaza Dr	464-8650

4 • West Loop Gate / Greek Town

Barbara's Bestsellers	2 N Riverside Plz	258-8007
Law Stuff USA	328 S Jefferson St	773-376-1711
National Law Resources	328 S Jefferson St	382-8282
Walden Bookstore	500 W Madison St	627-8334

5 • The Loop

Afrocentric Book Store	333 S State St	939-1956
Barbara's Bestsellers	233 S Wacker Dr	466-0223
Beck's Book Store	209 N Wabash Ave	630-9113
Borders Books & Music	150 N State St	606-0750
Brent Books & Cards	309 W Washington St	364-0126
Crown Books	105 S Wabash Ave	782-7667
Crown Books	144 S Clark St	857-0613
Cultural Book Store	100 W Randolph St	214-1314
Metropolitan Educational Inc	39 S La Salle St	641-1414
Prairie Avenue Bookshop	418 S Wabash Ave	922-8311
Psychology Bookstore	20 S Clark St	201-8789
Rand Mc Nally Map & Travel	150 S Wacker Dr Lbby	332-2009
Reading Room	112 S State St	658-0824
US Government Printing Ofc	401 S State St	353-5133
Waldenbooks	127 W Madison St	236-8446
Wells Street Books	178 N Wells St	263-9266

6 • The Loop / Grant Park

Business Savvy Inc	310 S Michigan Ave	408-0667
Chicago Architecture	224 S Michigan Ave	922-3432
Great Books-The Western World	310 S Michigan Ave	347-7000
Pauline Books & Media	172 N Michigan Ave	346-4228
Rain Dog Books	404 S Michigan Ave	922-1200
Savvy Traveller	310 S Michigan Ave	913-9800
World Book Publishing	233 N Michigan Ave	729-5800

8 • South Loop / Dearborn Park

Casterbridge Books	2 E 8th St	922-0090
Sandmeyer's Bookstore	714 S Dearborn St	922-2104

9 • South Loop / S Michigan Ave

Beck's Book Store	816 S Michigan Ave	922-2507
Bookstore	624 S Michigan Ave	344-7406
Columbia College Bookstore	624 S Michigan Ave	427-4860

10 • East Pilsen / Chinatown

Chinese Champion Book	2167 S China Pl	326-3577
Jong Mea Cultural Arts Co	217 W Cermak Rd	225-1698
World Journal Bookstore	2116 S Archer Ave	842-8005

11 • South Loop / McCormick Place

Paragon Book Gallery Ltd	1507 S Michigan Ave	663-5155

13 • Bridgeport (East)

Modern Bookstore	3118 S Halsted St	225-7911
Ram Shop	3511 1/2 S Halsted St	773-327-5324

14 • Prairie Shores / Lake Meadows

Iit Book Store	3200 S Wabash Ave	791-0770
Living Word Bookstore	3512 S King Dr	225-7500

19 • Hyde Park

57th Street Books	1301 E 57th St	773-684-1300
O'Gara & Wilson Ltd	1448 E 57th St	773-363-0993
Powell's Book Store	1501 E 57th St	773-955-7780
Reading Room	5206 S Harper Ave	773-363-1673
Scholars Bookstore	1466 E 53rd St	773-288-6565
Seminary Cooperative Inc	5757 S University Ave	773-752-4381
University-Chicago Bookstore	970 E 58th St	773-702-8729

20 • East Hyde Park / Jackson Park

Carter & Co	5400 S Hyde Park Blvd	773-363-5590

21 • Wicker Park / Ukrainian Village

Luz A La Familia	2425 W Division St	773-772-0954
Occult Book Store	1579 N Milwaukee Ave	773-292-0995
Quimby's Bookstore	1854 W North Ave	773-342-0910

22 • Noble Square / Goose Island

Pathfinder Bookstore	1212 N Ashland Ave	773-342-1780
Revolution Books	1103 N Ashland Ave	773-528-5353
Transitions Book Place	1000 W North Ave	951-7323

23 • West Town / Near West Side

Autonomous Zone	2012 W Chicago Ave	773-252-6019
Malcolm X College Book Store	1900 W Van Buren St	829-6482
Ukrainian Encyclopedia	2247 W Chicago Ave	773-489-1339
Ukranian Book Store	2315 W Chicago Ave	773-276-6373

24 • River West / West Town

Book Den	1043 Chicago Ave #B	847-864-4449
Libreria Giron	2130 W 21st St	226-1406
Login Medical Center Book Store	1910 W Harrison St	733-4544
UIC Medical Bookstore	828 S Wolcott Ave	413-5550

26 • University Village / Little Italy

Chicago Textbook	1076 W Taylor St	733-8398

27 • Logan Square (South)

New World Resource Center	2600 W Fullerton Ave	773-227-4011

28 • Bucktown

Book-Line	1958 N Damen Ave	773-862-9673
Libreria Nsra De Lourves	2346 W Fullerton Ave	773-342-8890
Minor Arcana	1852 N Damen Ave	773-252-1389

29 • DePaul / Wrightwood / Sheffield

Act I Bookstore	2540 N Lincoln Ave	773-348-6757
Barnes & Noble Booksellers	1441 W Webster Ave	773-871-3610
Crown Books	1714 N Sheffield Ave	787-4370

30 • Lincoln Park

Lincoln Park Book Shop	2423 N Clark St	773-477-7087
Tower Records/Video/Books	2301 N Clark St	773-477-5994

31 • Old Town / Near North

Barbara's Book Store	1350 N Wells St	642-5044
Over 21 Bookstore	1347 N Wells St	337-8730

32 • Gold Coast / Mag Mile

Abbott Hall Book Center	710 N Lake Shore Dr	503-8486
Adonis Inc	6 E Walton St	440-1913
Barnes & Noble Booksellers	1130 N State St	280-8155
Borders Books & Music	830 N Michigan Ave	573-0564
Chicago Rare Book Center	56 W Maple St	988-7246
Children In Paradise	909 N Rush St	951-5437
Europa Books	832 N State St	335-9677
Kabbalah Center	810 N Clark St	664-2256
Newberry Bookstore	60 W Walton St	255-3520
Waldenbooks	900 N Michigan Ave #6	337-0330

33 • West Rogers Park

India Book House & Journals	2551 W Devon Ave	773-764-6567
Interbook Russian Book Store		
	2754 W Devon Ave	773-973-5536
Iqra Book Center	2751 W Devon Ave	773-274-2665
Russian American Book Store	2746 W Devon Ave	773-761-3233

34 • East Rogers Park

Beck's Book Store	6550 N Sheridan Rd	773-743-2281
Expressway Audio Books Rental	6818 N Lakewood Ave	773-338-3008
Mustard Seed Bookstore	1143 W Sheridan Rd	773-973-7055
Telecom Movers	1740 W Albion Ave	773-761-4800
Turtle Island Books	7001 N Glenwood Ave	773-465-7212

35 • Arcadia Terrace / Peterson Park

Covenant Bookstore	3200 W Foster Ave	773-478-4676

36 • Bryn Mawr

Pathfinders Book Store	1925 W Thome Ave	773-262-3888

37 • Edgewater / Andersonville

Books Off Berwyn	5234 N Clark St	773-878-9800
Heritage Books	1135 W Granville Ave	773-262-1566
Women & Children First	5233 N Clark St	773-769-9299

39 • Ravenswood / North Center

PNA Oriental Store	2310 W Leland Ave	773-784-1797
Variety Comic Book Store	4602 N Western Ave	773-334-2550

40 • Uptown

Beck's Book Store	4520 N Broadway St	773-784-7963
Book Box	4812 N. Broadway	773-334-5311
Liberia de Hable Hispana	4441 N. Broadway	773-878-2117
Personalized Creations	5048 N Marine Dr	773-506-1040

42 • North Center / West Lakeview

Stern's Psychology Book Store	2004 W Roscoe St	773-883-5100

43 • Wrigleyville / Lakeview

Big Words Inc	3921 N Ashland Ave	773-472-7651
Healing Earth Resources	3111 N Ashland Ave	773-327-8459
Hit The Road	3758 N Southport Ave	773-388-8338
L W Sales	3237 N Ashland Ave	773-327-1000
Powell's Book Store	2850 N Lincoln Ave	773-248-1444
Stars Our Destination	1021 W Belmont Ave	773-871-2722

44 • East Lakeview

Barnes & Noble Booksellers	659 W Diversey Pkwy	773-871-9004
Bookman's Corner	2959 N Clark St	773-929-8298
Borders Books & Music	2817 N Clark St	773-935-3909
New & Used Books Inc	2928 N Broadway St	773-404-5422
Ram Book Store	3511 1/2 N Halsted St	773-525-9528
Unabridged Books	3251 N Broadway St	773-883-9119

Clubs & Cabarets · Arts & Entertainment

1 · River North / Fulton Market District

Mickey Finn's	412 N Milwaukee	312-362-6688
Q Nightlife	358 W Ontario	312-409-7772
Rednofive & Fifth Floor	440 N Halsted	312-733-6699

2 · Near North / River North

Andy's	11 . Hubbard	312-642-6805
Blue Chicago	736 N Clark	312-642-6261
Buzz Club	308 W Erie	312-475-9800
Catch 35	35 W Wacker	312-346-3500
Club 720	720 N Wells	312-397-0600
Erik & Me	1 W Illinois	630-377-9222
Excalibur	632 N Dearborn	312-266-1944
Features Bar & Grill	10 W Chicago	630-416-3310
Frankie's Blue Room	16 W Chicago	630-416-4898
Freddy's Ribhouse	26 W Hubbard	312-863-7427
Gentry	440 N State	312-836-0933
Harry's Velvet Room	56 W Illinois	312-527-5600
House Of Blues	329 N Dearborn	312-923-2000
House Of Blues Hotel	333 N Dearborn	312-245-0333
Magnum's Prime Steakhouse	225 W Ontario	312-337-8080
Minx	111 W Hubbard	312-828-9000
Mystique	157 W Ontario	312-642-2582
Palaggi's Ristorante Italiano	10 W Hubbard	312-527-1010
Redhead Piano Bar	16 W Ontario	312-640-1000
Spy Bar	646 N Franklin	312-587-8779
Vision	640 N Dearborn	312-266-2114
White Star	225 W Ontario	312-337-3223

3 · Streeterville / Mag Mile

Becco D'Oro Ristorante	160 E Huron	312-787-1300
Fitzers Pub	166 E Superior	312-787-6000
Joe's Be-Bop Cafe & Jazz Emporium	600 E Grand	312-595-5299
Navy Pier Beer Garden	600 E Grand	312-595-7437
Sayat Nova	157 E Ohio	773-381-7171

4 · West Loop Gate / Greek Town

Metro Deli & Café	210 S Canal St	312-655-0600
Snuggery Saloon & Dining Room	210 S Canal St	312-441-9334
Blonde	820 W Lake	312-226-4500
Chromium	817 W Lake	312-666-8106
Rooster Blues	811 W Lake	312-733-6577

5 · The Loop

Cal's	400 S. Wells	312-922-6392
Club Mercury	221 W Van Buren	312-427-1774
Encore	171 W Randolph	312-338-3788

6 · The Loop / Grant Park

Entre Nous	200 N Columbus	312-565-7997
Metropole Room	200 N Columbus	312-565-6665

8 · South Loop / Dearborn Park

Blackie's	755 S Clark	312-832-1806
Buddy Guy's Legends	754 S Wabash	312-427-0333
Hothouse	31 . Balbo	312-362-9707
Viking Steak House	27 W Roosevelt	630-653-2110

11 · South Loop / McCormick Place

Chicago Firehouse	1401 S Michigan	312-786-1401
Club Alphonse	1351 S Michigan	312-697-0975
Cotton Club & All That Jazz	1710 S Michigan	312-341-9787
Java Oasis	2240 S Michigan	312-328-1216
Velvet Lounge	2128 1/2 S Indiana	312-791-9050

13 · Bridgeport (East)

Puffer's	3356 S Halsted	773-927-6073

16 · Bronzeville

Checkerboard Lounge	423 E. 43rd	773-624-3240
Some Like It Black	4500 S Michigan	773-377-5004

21 · Wicker Park / Ukrainian Village

Bar Thirteen	1944 W Division	773-394-1313
Big Horse Lounge	1558 N Milwaukee	773-384-0043
Club Foot	1824 W Augusta	773-489-0379
Davenport's Piano Bar & Cabaret	1383 N Milwaukee	773-278-1830
Double Door	1572 N Milwaukee	773-489-3160
D'Vine	1950 W North	773-235-5700
Inner Town Pub	1935 W Thomas	773-235-9795
Innjoy	2051 W Division	773-394-2066
Jinx	1928 W Division	773-645-3667
Lava Lounge	859 N Damen	773-772-3355
Nick's	1516 N Milwaukee	773-252-1155
Phyllis' Musical Inn	1800 W Division	773-486-9862
Pontiac Cafe	1531 N Damen	773-252-7767
Red Dog	1958 W North	773-278-1009
Reservation Blues	1566 N Milwaukee	773-645-5200
Sinibar	1540 N Milwaukee	773-278-7797
Smoke Daddy	1804 W Division	773-772-6656
Spareroom	2416 W North	773-782-0271
Squareone	1561 N Milwaukee	773-227-7111
Subterranean Cafe & Cabaret	2011 W North	773-278-6600
Taste	1922 W North	773-276-8000
Ten56	1056 N Damen	773-227-4906
The Note	1565 N Milwaukee	773-489-0011
Zakopane Lounge	1734 W Division	773-486-1559

22 · Noble Square / Goose Island

Big Wig	1551 W Division	773-235-9100
Biology Bar	1516 N Fremont	312-266-1234
Circus	901 W Weed	312-266-1200
Crobar The Nightclub	1543 N Kingsbury	312-413-7000
Dig	1551 N Sheffield	312-377-1727
Exit	1315 W North	773-395-2700
Joe's	940 W Weed	312-337-3486
Life's Too Short	1177 N Elston	773-384-1040
Stevie B's	1401 N Ashland	773-486-7427
Zentra	923 W Weed	312-787-0400

23 · West Town / Near West Side

Bally Muck	1930 Grand	847-244-5636
6Odum	2116 W Chicago	312-666-0795

24 · River West / West Town

Babalu	1645 W Jackson	312-733-3512
Betty's Blue Star Lounge	1600 W Grand	312-243-1699
Bird's Nest	551 N Ogden	312-226-6666
Bone Daddy	551 N Ogden	312-226-6666
Carmichael's Chicago Steak House	1052 W Monroe	312-433-0025
Crab Street Saloon	1061 W Madison	312-433-0013
Moretti's	1645 W Jackson	312-850-0208
Saussy	1156 W Grand	312-491-1122

27 · Logan Square (North)

3030	3030 W Cortland	773-862-3616
Boulevard Café	3137 W Logan	773-384-8600
Club	2047 N Milwaukee	773-489-9600
El Cid	2115 N Milwaukee	773-252-4747
Fireside Bowl	2646 W Fullerton	773-486-2700
Lula Café	2537 N Kedzie	773-489-9554
Streetside Café	3201 W Armitage	773-252-9700

28 • Bucktown

Artful Dodger	1734 W Wabansia	773-227-6859
Clybar	2417 N Clybourn	773-388-1877
Danny's	1951 W Dickens	773-489-6457
Gallery Cabaret	2020 N Oakley	773-489-5471
Get Me High Lounge	1758 N Honore	773-252-4090
Liar's Club	1665 W Fullerton	773-665-1110
Quenchers Saloon	2401 N Western	773-276-9730
The Mutiny	2428 N Western	773-486-7774

29 • DePaul / Wrightwood / Sheffield

Big House	2354 N Clybourn	773-435-0130
Bistro Ultra	2239 N Clybourn	773-529-3300
Copa	1637 N Clybourn	312-642-3449
Deja Vu Bar Room	2624 N Lincoln	773-871-0205
Delilah's	2771 N Lincoln	773-472-2771
Gin Mill	2462 N Lincoln	773-549-3232
Green Dolphin Street	2200 N Ashland	773-395-0066
Hideout	1354 W Wabansia	773-227-4433
Hog Head Mcdunna's	1505 W Fullerton	773-929-0944
Irish Eyes	2519 N Lincoln	773-348-9548
Kustom	1997 N Clybourn	773-528-3400
McGee's	950 W Webster	773-549-8200
The (Prop) House	1675 N Elston	773-486-2390
U.S. Beer Co.	1801 N Clybourn	773-871-7799
Webster Wine Bar	1480 W Webster	773-868-0608

30 • Lincoln Park

Alumni Club	2251 N Lincoln	773-348-5100
B.L.U.E.S.	2519 N Halsted	773-528-1012
Bar 3	2138 N Halsted	773-348-3665
Girlbar	2625 N Halsted	773-871-4210
Griffin's Public House	2710 N Halsted	773-525-7313
Hidden Shamrock	2723 N Halsted	773-883-0304
Katacomb	1909 N Lincoln	312-337-4040
Kingston Mines	2548 N Halsted	773-477-4646
Neo	2350 N Clark	773-528-2622
Prodigal Son Bar & Grill	2626 N Halsted	773-248-3093
Wise Fools Pub	2270 N Lincoln	773-929-1300

31 • Old Town / Near North

Cucina Bella	1612 N Sedgwick	312-274-1119
Dragon Room	809 W Evergreen	312-751-2900
Glow	1615 N Clybourn	312-587-8469
Weeds	1555 N Dayton	312-943-7815

32 • Gold Coast / Mag Mile

Backroom	1007 N Rush	312-751-2433
Carton's Lounge	21 E Chestnut	312-664-5512
Dragonfly	1206 N State	312-204-9991
Hancock Observatory	875 N Michigan	312-751-3681
Jilly's Retro Club	1009 N Rush	312-664-1001
Underground Wonder Bar	10 E Walton	312-266-7761
Oakfield Charhouse	27 W North Ave	630-876-2000

33 • West Rogers Park

Cary's Lounge	2251 W Devon	773-743-5737
Chase Cafe	7301 N Sheridan	773-743-5650
Cocoabean Expressions	7007 N Glenwood	773-274-6057
Gateway Bar & Grill	7545 N Clark	773-262-5767
Heartland Cafe	7000 N Glenwood	773-465-8005
No Exit	6970 N Glenwood	773-743-3355
Red Line Tap	6970 N Glenwood	773-743-3355

37 • Edgewater / Andersonville

Edgewater Lounge	5600 N Ashland	773-878-3343
Hollywood East	5650 N Broadway	773-271-4711
Pumping Company	6157 N Broadway	773-743-7994

38 • Ravenswood / Albany Park

Candlestick Maker	4432 N Kedzie	773-463-0158

39 • Ravenswood / North Center

Club 950	2122 W Lawrence	773-878-8241

40 • Uptown

Carol's Pub	4659 N Clark	773-334-2402
Green Mill	4802 N Broadway	773-878-5552
Joy-Blue	3998 N Southport	773-477-3330
Maxwell Street Uptown Polish Sausage Restaurant	4429 N Broadway	773-989-4569
T's	5025 N Clark	773-784-6000

41 • Avondale / Logan Square

Chief O'Neill's Pub	3471 N Elston	773-473-5263

42 • North Center / West Lakeview

Hungry Brain	2319 W Belmont	773-935-2118
Kitsch'N	2005 W Roscoe	773-248-7372
Le Relais	3925 N Lincoln	773-665-8965
Martyrs'	3855 N Lincoln	773-404-9494
Seanchai	2345 W Belmont	773-549-4444
Tiny Lounge	1814 W Addison	773-296-9620

43 • Wrigleyville / East Lakeview

Bar Celona	3474 N Clark	773-244-8000
Berlin	954 W Belmont	773-348-4975
Cherry Red	2833 N Sheffield	773-477-3661
Cubby Bear	1059 W Addison	773-327-1662
Elbo Room	2871 N Lincoln	773-549-5549
Fizz Bar & Grill	3220 N Lincoln	773-348-6000
Fly Me To The Moon	3400 N Clark	773-528-4033
Fuel	3724 N Clark	773-248-3330
Goose Island Brewery	3535 N Clark	773-549-9624
Gunther Murphy's	1638 W Belmont	773-472-5139
Hi-Tops	3551 N Sheffield	773-348-0009
John Barleycorn	3524 N Clark	773-549-6000
Lakeview Links	3206 N Wilton	773-975-0505
Lithium	1124 W Belmont	773-477-6513
Metro	3730 N Clark	773-549-0203
Mullen's	3527 N Clark	773-325-2319
Pops For Champagne	2934 N Sheffield	773-472-1000
Schubas	3159 N Southport	773-525-2508
Smart Bar	3730 N Clark	773-549-4140
Strega Nona	3747 N Southport	773-244-0990
Trace	3714 N Clark	773-477-3400
Uncommon Ground Café	1214 W Grace	773-929-3680
Underground Lounge	952 W Newport	773-327-2739
Vaughan's Pub	2917 N Sheffield	773-281-8188
Wild Hare	3530 N Clark	773-327-4273

44 • East Lakeview

Angelina Ristorante	3561 N Broadway	773-935-5933
Burkhart Studios	2845 N Halsted	773-348-8536
Cocktail	3359 N Halsted	773-477-1420
Coyle's Tippling House	2843 N Halsted	773-528-7569
Gentry On Halsted	3320 N Halsted	773-348-1053
Harrigan's	2816 N Halsted	773-248-5933
Jack's	3201 N Halsted	773-244-9191
Manhole	3458 N Halsted	773-975-9244
Spin	800 W Belmont	773-327-7711

Movie Theaters • Arts & Entertainment

The impeccably restored Music Box Theatre built in 1929 features fantastic Moorish architecture and thumbs up, highbrow cinema. The Three Penny sells cheap tickets to the newest releases. The main theater at McClurg Court Theatre has one of the City's largest screens. Drunken audiences at The Vic's Brew & View nights are as entertaining as the movies.

Museum	Address	Phone	Map
Cineplex Odeon	600 N Michigan Ave	312-255-9340	3
Mc Clurg Court Theatre	330 E Ohio St	312-642-0723	3
Gene Siskel Film Center	164 N. State		5
Cineplex Odeon	826 S Wabash Ave	312-922-1090	8
Uffish Theater CO	312 N Laflin St #6R	312-243-0319	24
Logan Theater	2646 N. Milwaukee Ave.		27
Sony Theatre	1471 W Webster Ave	773-327-3100	29
Biograph Theatre	2433 N Lincoln Ave	773-348-4123	30
Sony Theatre	1616 N Wells St	312-642-7500	30
Three Penny Theatre	2424 N Lincoln Ave	773-935-5744	30
Victory Gardens Theatre	2257 N Lincoln Ave	773-549-5788	30
Piper's Alley	1608 N Wells		31
900 North Michigan Cinemas	900 N Michigan Ave	312-787-1988	32
Esquire Theater	58 E Oak St	312-280-0101	32
Village the Theater	1548 N Clark St	312-642-2403	32
Water Tower Theater	175 E Chestnut St	312-440-1554	32
Water Tower Theaters	845 N Michigan Ave	312-649-5790	32
Village North Theaters	6746 N Sheridan Rd	773-764-9100	34
Davis Theatre	4614 N Lincoln Ave	773-784-0893	39
Black Ensemble Theatre	4520 N Beacon St	773-769-5516	40
Riviera Night Club	4746 N Racine Ave	773-275-6800	40
American Blues Theatre	1909 W Byron St	773-929-1031	42
Chicago Underground Film Fstvl	3109 N Western Ave	773-327-3456	42
Brew & View At the Vic	3145 N Sheffield Ave	312-618-8439	43
Music Box Theatre Corp	3733 N Southport Ave	773-871-6604	43
Landmark Century Cinema	2828 N Clark		44

2 • Near North / River North

Mig and Tig Furniture	549 N Wells St	312-644-8277	Classic well made furniture
Montauk	223 W Erie St	312-951-5688	The most comfortable sofas
Nordstrom	55 E Grand Ave	312-464-1515	Upscale department store with the best shoe department around
Paper Source	232 W Chicago Ave	312-337-0798	Great paper and invitations
Sportmart	620 N LaSalle St	312-337-6151	Seven floors of sports merchandise with free parking

3 • Streeterville / Mag Mile

Chicago Place	700 N Michigan Ave	312-642-4811	Upscale Mall
Crate & Barrel	646 N Michigan Ave	312-787-5900	Housewares
Decoro	224 E Ontario St	312-943-4847	Fine Asian antiques and fine furnishings
Eddie Bauer	600 N Michigan Ave	312-951-5888	Yuppy clothing store
Garrett Popcorn Shop	670 N Michigan Ave	312-944-2630	Everything you could possibly think of related to popcorn!
Niketown	669 N Michigan Ave	312-642-6363	Nike label sports clothing
Rand McNally Store	444 N Michigan Ave	312-321-1751	Map store
Virgin Megastore	540 N Michigan Ave	312-645-9300	Music, books, videos, DVDs

4 • West Loop Gate / Greek Town

Athenian Candle Co.	300 S Halsted St	312-332-6988	Candles, curse breakers, greek trinkets and more
Athens Jewelry	310 S Halsted St	312-258-8018	Island gold
Greek Town Gifts	330 S Halsted St	312-263-6342	Music, tshirts, hats - everything Greek!

5 • The Loop

American Music World	333 S State St	312-786-9600	The place to go if you're looking to buy an instrument
Carson Pirie Scott	1 S State St	773-641-7000	Department Store
Gallery 37 Store	66 E Randolph St	312-744-7274	Speciality gifts
Jeweler's Mall	7 S Wabash Ave	312-460-9117	Jewelry
Marshall Field's	111 N State St	312-781-1000	Department Store
Sears	2 N State St	312-373-6000	Department Store
The Savvy Traveller	310 S Michigan Ave	312-913-9500	Travel

6 • The Loop / Grant Park

Art & Artisians	108 S Michigan Ave	312-641-0088	Art gallery
Museum Shop of the Art Institute	111 S Michigan Ave	312-443-3583	Art Institute gift shop
Poster Plus	200 S Michigan Ave	312-461-9277	Vintage posters and custom framing
Precious Possessions	28 N Michigan Ave	312-726-8118	Mineral shop

7 • South Loop / River City

Chicago Vintage Motor Carriage	700 S Des Plaines St	312-589-2708	Antique cars shown by appointment
Fishman's Fabrics	1101 S Des Plaines St	312-922-7250	Huge fabric wholesaler
Joseph Adam's Hats	544 W Roosevelt Rd	312-829-8899	Haberdashery and menswear
Lee's Foreign Car Service	727 S Jefferson St	312-663-0823	Import parts and service

8 • South Loop / Dearborn Park

Kozy's Bike Shop	600 S LaSalle St	312-360-0020	Bikes and accessories in a fun loft setting.
Mary Wolf Gallery	705 Dearborn St	312-588-1478	Unusual oils including lots of Chicago scenes
Printers Row Fine and Rare Books	715 S Dearborn St	312-583-1800	Fine and rare books
Sandmeyers Book Store	714 S Dearborn St	312-922-2104	Dream come true if you love books and atmosphere

9 • South Loop / South Michigan Ave

Bariff Shop	618 S Michigan Ave	312-322-1740	Unique Hanukkah gifts
Clancy's Market	1130 S Michigan Ave	312-922-6530	Grab snacks for a picnic in the park; new icon needed
Rain Dog Books and Café	408 S Michigan Ave	312-922-1200	Awesome used books and geek-chic clientele

10 • East Pilsen / Chinatown

Chinatown Bazaar	2221 S Wentworth Ave	312-225-1088	Part clothing store, part knick-knack shop
Chinatown Furniture	2326 S Canal St	312-236-1712	Beautiful, ornate furniture
Pacific Imports	2200 S Wentworth Ave	312-808-0456	Mostly home furnishings
Sun Sun Tong	2260 S Wentworth Ave	312-842-6398	Stock up on Chinese herbs and teas
Ten Ren Tea & Ginseng Co.	2247 S Wentworth Ave	312-842-1171	The only place to buy ginseng.
Woks 'n' Things	2234 S Wentworth Ave	312-842-0701	Stir-fry utensils and cookware

11 · South Loop / McCormick Place
Blossoms of Hawaii	1631 S Michigan Ave	312-922-0281	Florist
Blue Star Auto Stores	2001 S State St	312-225-0717	All your auto needs
Waterware	1829 S State St	312-225-4549	Designer plumbing fixtures
Y'lonn Salon	1802 S Wabash Ave	312-225-9247	Beauty salon

12 · Bridgeport (West)
Ace Bakery	3200 S Halsted St	773-225-4973	Excellent breads and pastries
Augustine's Spiritual Goods	3114 S Halsted St	312-326-3088	Mystical and religious knick knacks
Bridgeport Antiques	2963 S Archer Ave	773-927-9070	Antiques
Bridgeport News TrAvel & Tours	3252 S Halsted St	312-225-6311	Travel store
Let's Boogie Records & Tapes	3321 S Halsted St	773-254-0139	Music
Modern Bookstore	3118 S Halsted St	312-225-7911	Books

13 · Bridgeport (East)
Accutek Printing & Graphics	260 W 26th St	312-808-9903	Printing and copying needs
Chicago Technical Center	3500 S Emerald Ave	773-376-3535	Computers
Health King Enterprises Chinese Medicinals	238 W 31st St	312-567-9978	Natural remedies
Petals From HeAven Flowers	244 W 31st St	312-326-2606	Flower shop

14 · Prairie Shore / Lake Meadows
Ashley Stewart	3455 S King Dr	312-567-0405	Women's clothing
Avenue	3427 S King Dr	312-808-1492	Modern plus-size clothes
Living Word Book Store	3512 S King Dr	312-225-7500	Books
SMW Flea Market	3852 S Indiana Ave	773-624-4172	Unique gifts and housewares

16 · Bronzeville
Alvin's Watch Repair	4317 S Cottage Grove Ave	773-924-0148	Watch repair including batteries and bands
Chicago Furniture Co.	4238 S Cottage Grove Ave	773-285-3765	Furniture store
Dollar Junction	4701 S Cottage Grove Ave	773-324-2903	Lots of items for a dollar or less
Issues Barber & Beauty Salon	3958 S Cottage Grove Ave	773-924-4247	Beauty salon
Parker House Sausage Co.	4601 S State St	773-538-1112	All types of sausages
The African Hair & Weaving Center	428 E 47th St	773-285-2800	When you want your do to be fierce

17 · Kenwood
Coop's Records	1350 E 47th St	773-538-5277	Music
Footlocker	1340 E 47th St	773-924-9190	Sports store specialising in shoes and clothing
South Shore Decor	1328 E 47th St	773-373-3116	Wall coverings, paint and blinds and window treatments

19 · Hyde Park
Artisans 21	5240 S Harper Ave	773-643-8533	Art Gallery
Brush Strokes	1369 E 53rd St	773-493-3993	Paint-It-Yourself pottery
Calla Lily Gift Shop	5225 S Harper Ave	773-684-1973	Speciality gifts
Cohn & Stern For Men	1500 E 55th St	773-752-8100	Mens accessories
Dr Wax Records and Tapes	5225-d S Harper Ave	773-549-3377	Old-style vinyl
Freehling Pot & Pan Co.	1365 E 53rd St	773-643-8080	Pots and Pans
Futons N More	1370 E 53rd St	773-324-7083	Futons N More
O'Gara and Wilson, Ltd.	1448 E 57th St	773-363-0993	Rare and out of print books
Powell's Bookstore	1501 E 57th St	773-955-7780	Famous bookstore
Tony's Sports	1308 E 53rd St	773-667-7200	Sporting goods
Wesley's Shoe Corral	1506 E 55th St	773-667-7463	Shoes
Wheels and Things	5210-e S Harper Ave	773-493-4326	Bike sales and repairs

20 · East Hyde Park / Jackson Park
Art's Cycle Sales & Service	1636 E 55th St	773-363-7524	Bike sales and repairs

21 · Wicker Park / Ukrainian Village
Asrai Garden	1935 W North Ave	773-782-0680	Flowers and Garden
Brooke James, Ltd.	1460 N Milwaukee Ave	773-252-4602	Homewares
City Soles/Niche	2001 W North Ave	773-489-2001	Excellent shoe store
Fly Boutique	1472 N Milwaukee Ave	773-486-0413	Boutique clothing and accessories
Lille	1923 W North Ave	773-342-0563	Great little things for the home

Noir	1746 W Division St	773-862-9960	Upscale clothing and accessories
Paper Doll	1747 W Division St	773-227-6950	Paper and cards
Quimby's Bookstore	1854 W North Ave	773-342-0910	Books and music
Reckless Records	1532 N Milwaukee Ave	773-235-3727	Music and books
Sasabee	1849 W North Ave Unit C101	773-862-7740	For all your health and beauty needs
The Silver Room	1410 N Milwaukee Ave	773-278-7130	Clothing and accessories

22 · Noble Square / Goose Island

Arrow Vintage	1452 W Chicago Ave	312-738-2755	Antiques
Balloonz Special Event Décor	1121 N Ashland Blvd	773-342-0404	Specializing in helium balloons
Casa Loca Furniture	1130 N Milwaukee Ave	773-278-2972	Household Furniture
Crate & Barrell Outlet Store	800 W North Ave	312-787-4775	Housewares
Dusty Groove Records	1120 N Ashland Blvd	773-342-5800	Vinyl and CDS Specializes in funk, soul, rare groove, now sound and world music
Eastern Mountain Sports (EMS)	1000 W North Ave	312-337-7750	Everything for sports and outdoor fun
Home Depot	1232 W North Ave	773-486-9200	Mega-hardware store
Old Navy	1569 N Kingsbury St	312-397-0485	Everyday apparel for the family
Olga's Flower Shop	1041 N Ashland Blvd	773-645-9160	Flowers for all occasions
Restoration Hardware	938 W North Ave	312-475-9116	Fancy housewares
Right-on Futon	1184 N Milwaukee Ave	773-235-2533	Need a new bed? Check this place out!
Upgrade Cycle Works	1128 W Chicago Ave	312-226-8650	Bikes, accessories and servicing

23 · West Town / Near West Side

Alcala's	1733 W Chicago Ave	312-226-0152	Western wear emporium sells boots, jeans and cowboy hats
Decoro Studio	2000 W Carroll St	312-850-9260	Lot filled with Asian Antiques and furniture
Donofrio's Double Corona Cigars	2058 W Chicago Ave	773-342-7820	Brian Donofrio sells very fine imported cigars
Edie's	1937 W Chicago Ave	312-455-1150	Hip, vintage threads for the underground
H&R Sports	1741 W Chicago Ave	312-226-8737	Soccer gear
Salvage One Architectural Artifacts	1840 W Hubbard St	312-733-0098	Warehouse of antique, vintage and salvaged architectural pieces for home/loft restoration
Through Maria's Eyes	1953 W Chicago Ave	312-243-8983	Eclectic Vintage Store
Tomato Tattoo	1855 W Chicago Ave	312-226-6660	Every hip strip needs a tattoo parlor

24 · River West / West Town

Hollis Funk (S2)	949 W Fulton Market	773-862-2530	Cool housey stuff
Xyloform (S1)	1423 Chicago Ave	312-455-7949	

26 · University Village / Little Italy / Pilsen

Scafuri Bakery	1337 W Taylor St	312-733-8881	The secret's in the bread.

27 · Logan Square

MegaMall	2502 N Milwaukee Ave	773-489-2525	Shopping center

28 · Bucktown

Asian Essence	2025.5 W North Ave	773-782-9500	Homewares with an Asian falvor
Bleeker Street Antiques	1946 N Leavitt St	773-862-3185	Fine selection of antiques
Eclectic Junction	1630 N Damen Ave	773-342-7865	House and home
Gypsy	2131 N Damen Ave	773-395-6999	House and home
Jean Alan, Inc.	2134 Damen Ave	773-278-2345	House and home
Pagoda Red	1714 N Damen Ave	773-235-1188	House and home
Pavilion Antiques	2055 N Damen Ave	773-645-0924	Antique furniture
Red Balloon Company	2060 N Damen Ave	773-489-9800	A unique store for Children—toys, clothes & furniture
Yardifacts	1864 N Damen Ave	773-342-YARD	Flowers and Garden

29 · DePaul / Wrightwood / Sheffield

Active Endeavors	935 W Armitage Ave	312-822-0600	Playing sports or heading into the great outdoors, this is your place for gear
Bed Bath & Beyond	1800 N Clybourn Ave	312-642-6596	Health and beauty products including soaps and body creams
Best Buy	1700 N Marcey St	312-788-7213	Large volume retailer of electronics including personal computers, entertainment equipment, software, home appliances...reasonably priced CD's, video tapes, DVD's!

29 · DePaul / Wrightwood / Sheffield — continued

Cynthia Rowley	808 W Armitage Ave	773-528-6160	Apparel and accessories
Gap	1740 N Sheffield Ave	312-944-6774	Clothing for everybody
Isabella Fine Lingerie	2150 N Seminary Ave	773-281-2352	Fine after-D142hours wear
Jayson Home & Garden	1885 & 1911 N Clybourn Ave	773-248-8180	Flowers and Garden
Jolie Joli	2131 N Southport Ave	773-327-4917	Clothing and accessories
Lori's Designer Shoes	824 W Armitage Ave	773-281-5655	Designer shoes
Tabula Tua	1015 W Armitage Ave	773-525-3500	Housewares

30 · Lincoln Park

Art & Science	1971 N Halsted St	312-787-4247	Beauty salon
Coconuts Music & Movies	2747 N Clark St	773-935-3449	Music, DVDs, videos
Ethan Allen	1700 N Halsted St	312-573-2500	Furniture store
GNC	2740 N Clark St	773-528-7887	General Nutrition Center
Kwik Mart	2427 N Clark St	773-549-9576	Grocery store
Sally Beauty Supply	2723 N Clark St	773-477-6222	Cosmetics chain
Walgreens	2317 N Clark St	773-929-0706	Always reliable pharmacy

31 · Old Town / Near North

Atom Antiques	1219 N Wells St	312-867-2866	Unusual antique items, free parking!
Barbara's Bookstore	1350 N Wells St	312-642-5044	Knowledgeable, friendly staff at this great bookstore
Etre	1361 N Wells St	312-266-8101	Upscale boutique
Fleet Feet Sports	210 W North Ave	312-587-3338	The staff watches you run to make sure the shoes fit
Fudge Pot	1532 N Wells St	312-943-1777	A chocolate institution
Gallery 1756	1756 N Sedgwick St	312-642-6900	Fine art
Jumbalia	1427 N Wells St	312-335-9082	Great gift store
Old Town Gardens	1555 N Wells St	312-266-6300	Beautiful plants and flowers
See Hear Music	217 W North Ave	312-664-6285	Discount music store
Sofie	1343 N Wells St	312-255-1343	Chic boutique
The Spice House	1512 N Wells St	312-274-0378	Spice up your cooking
Triangle Gallery of Old Town	1763 N North Park Ave	312-337-1938	Don't miss their openings
Vagabonds Boutique	1357 N Wells St	312-787-8520	Reasonably priced trendy jewelry and clothes

32 · Gold Coast / Mag Mile

Anthropologie	1120 N State St	312-255-1848	Hip clothing and knick knacks
Barney's New York	25 E Oak St	312-587-1700	Upscale boutique, clothing and accessories
BCBG	103 E Oak St	312-943-5411	Apparel and accessories
Bloomingdales	900 N Michigan Ave	312-440-4460	Upscale department store
Bravco Beauty Center	43 E Oak St	312-943-4305	For those who like to be pampered
Chanel at the Drake Hotel	935 N Michigan Ave	312-787-5000	Classic, expensive clothing, accessories and fragrancies
Diesel	923 N Rush	312-255-0157	Modern clothing and accessories
Elements	102 E Oak St	312-642-6574	Cool housey stuff
Europa Books	832 N State St	312-355-9677	International Magazines
Frette	41 E Oak St	312-943-5353	European furniture and accessories
G'bani	949 N State St	312-440-1718	Shoes
Gucci	900 N Michigan Ave	312-664-5504	Tom Ford's alluring and provocative clothes and accessories
Hear Music	932 N Rush St	312-951-0242	Music and books
MAC	40 E Oak St	312-951-7310	Fabulous make up
Nicole Miller	63 E Oak St	312-664-3532	Female fashion
Portico	834 N Rush St	312-475-1307	Homewares
Prada	30 E Oak St	312-951-1113	Expensive but delightful clothing and accessories
Pratesi	67 E Oak St	312-943-8422	Linens
Tod's	121 E Oak St	312-943-0070	Clothing
Ultimate Bride	106 E Oak St, 2nd Fl	312-337-6300	Bridal gear
Ultimo	114 E Oak St	312-787-1171	Apparel and accessories
Urban Outfitters	935 N Rush St	312-640-1919	Retro clothing, nifty gifts and cool accessories
Water Tower	845 N Michigan Ave	312-440-3165	Marshall Fields

33 · West Rogers Park

Best Buy	2301 W Howard St	847-570-0450	Large volume retailer of electronics including personal computers, entertainment equipment, software, home appliances ... reasonably priced CD's, video tapes, DVD's!
Cheesecakes by JR	2841 W Howard St	773-465-6733	Over 20 flavors of cheesecakes, full bakery, retail and wholesale, same location for over 20 years, special WeSt Rogers Park treat!
Chicago Harley Davidson	6868 N Western Ave	773-338-6868	American classic motorcycles and all the gear that you need to match - leather jackets, hats, t-shirts, gifts, pet gear, etc...
Office Mart	2801 W Touhy Ave	773-262-3924	Combination office supply store and an internet coffee-shop
Office Max	2255 W Howard St	847-492-0662	Office supplies, furniture, technology, and copy services...
Snoop Shop Too, Inc.	2742 W Touhy Ave	773-262-0444	Pick out a ceramic piece and paint it! The shop will glaze and fire your work of art. Perfect for parties or just a relaxing afternoon
Target	2209 W Howard St	847-733-1144	Large volume retailer of housewares, health & beauty, clothing, etc...
Z'Afrique Ltd	7156 N California Ave	773-274-5236	Unique African art and jewelry, small neighborhood shop

35 · Arcadia Terrace / Peterson Park

Taj Sari Palace	2553 W Devon Ave	773-338-0177	Beautiful Indian clothing and accesories

37 · Edgewater / Andersonville

Broadway Antique Mart	6130 N Broadway Ave	773-743-5444	Great modern pieces as well as art deco and arts and crafts
Gethsemane Garden Center	5739 N Clark St	773-878-5915	Flowers and garden
Paper Trail	5309 N Clark St	773-275-2191	Paper and cards
Surrender	5225 N Clark St	773-784-4455	Health and beauty
The Acorn Antiques & Uniques	5241 N Clark St	773-506-9100	Antiques
Women & Children First	5233 N Clark St	773-769-9299	Women's book & music store

39 · Ravenswood / North Center

Play It Again Sports	2102 W Irving Park Rd	773-463-9900	Sporting goods
Sears	1900 W Lawrence Ave	773-561-4100	Department Store

40 · Uptown

Tai Nam Market Center	4925 N Broadway St	275-5666	Vietnamese Very Good
Wilson Broadway Mall	1114 W Wilson Dr	773-561-0300	socks, shoes, ethnic shopping, music, luggage - it's all here

42 · North Center / West Lakeview

Antique Resources	1741 W Belmont Ave	773-871-4242	Large inventory of antique furniture
Father Time Antiques	2108 W Belmont Ave	773-880-5599	Antiques store
Good Old Days Antiques	2138 W Belmont Ave	773-472-8837	Antiques and treasures
Lynn's Hallmark	3353 N Lincoln Ave	773-281-8108	Cards, stationary, and gift wrap
Serendipity	2010 W Roscoe St	773-883-1060	Gifts
Toy Town	1903 W Belmont Ave		Toys

44 · East Lakeview

Century Mall	2828 N Clark St	773-929-8100	Most notable occupants include the cinema and Bally's Fitness
Evil Clown Compact Discs	3418 N Halsted St	773-472-4761	The best hand-picked rare disc selection
Gallimaufry Gallery	3345 N Halsted St	773-348-8090	Artisan crafts inc. instruments, incense, stone fountains
GayMart	3457 N Halsted St	773-929-4272	Resources, including books and magazines, for the gay community
The Brown Elephant Resale	3651 N Halsted St	773-549-5943	Resale boutique benefits Howard Brown Health Clinic
Toyscape	2911 N Broadway St	773-665-7400	Hours of fun at this quirky toy store
Unabridged Bookstore	3251 N Broadway St	773-883-9119	Helpful bookstore with great travel, kids & gay sections

*Key: $: Under $10 / $$: $10–$20 / $$$: $20–$30 / $$$$: $30+   * : Does not accept credit cards. / † : Accepts only American Express.*

1 · River North / Fulton Market District

Chilpancingo Restaurante	358 W Ontario	312-266-9525	$$$	Gourmet Mexican madness.
Iguana Café	517 Halsted	312-432-0663	$	Internet café with bagels & such.
La Scarola	721 W Grand	312-243-1740	$$	Authentic Italian in a super-close atmosphere.
Reza's Restaurant	432 W Ontario	312-664-4500	$$	Persian food with not-so-much atmosphere.
Scoozi!	410 W Huron	312-943-5900	$$	Typical Italian.
Thyme	464 N Halsted	312-226-4300	$$$	Eclectic eating in funky atmosphere.

2 · Near North / River North

Ace Grill	71 E Wacker	312-346-7100	$$$	Low-key American fare.
Bob Chinn's Crab House	321 N LaSalle		$$$	Worth the wait.
Brett's Kitchen	233 W Superior St.	312-664-6354	$	Charming breakfast and sandwich stop.
Club Lago	331 W Superior	312-951-2849	$$	Generous servings of basic Italian.
Erawan	729 N Clark	312-642-6888	$$$$	Top shelf Thai.
Hubbard St. Grill	351 W Hubbard	312-222-0770	$$	Burgers, fries, the regular.
Kevin	9 W Hubbard St.	312-595-0055	$$$	Promising new fusion.
Kinzie Chophouse	400 N Wells St.	312-822-0191	$$$	Neighborhood steak house.
Linos	222 W Ontario St.	312-266-6159	$$$	Old school service at this classic Italian. Closed on Sunday.
Mr. Beef	666 N Orleans St.	312-337-8500	$	Get your Italian beef fix at this Chicago classic.
Naniwa	607 N Wells	312-255-8555	$$	Quality sushi. Great outdoor.
Redfish	400 N State St.	312-467-1600	$$	Fun Cajun; free beads and good drinks.
Vong's Thai Kitchen	6 W Hubbard St.	312-644-8664	$$	Thai with a satisfying kick.
Zinfandel	59 W Grand Ave	312-527-1818	$$$	Ethnic American with menu that changes monthly.

3 · Streeterville / Magnificent Mile

Bandera	535 N Michigan 2nd fl.	312-644-3524	$$	Lunch above Mag Mile.
Cambridge House Grill	162 E Ohio	312-828-0600	$	Diner; open late.
Capital Grille	633 N St. Clair	312-337-9400	$$$$	Macho steak & zin.
Cite	Lake Point Tower, 70th fl. 505 N LSD	312-644-4050	$$$$	Contemporary with a view.
Hot Diggity Dogs	251 E Ohio	312-943-5598	$*	Walk-up chicawga dawgs.
Indian Garden	247 E Ontario 2nd fl.	312-280-4910	$$	Good veggie options.
Les Nomades	222 E Ontario	312-649-9010	$$$$	Deluxe haute cuisine.
NoMI at the Hyatt Hotel	800 N Michigan Ave	312-335-1234	$$$$	Fancy-schmancy French International.
Sayat Nova	157 E Ohio	312-644-9159	$$	Armenian.
Tru	676 N St.Clair	312-202-0001	$$$$	The hottest spot in town.
Volare	201 E Grand AvE	312-410-9900	$$$	Casual Italian.

4 · West Loop Gate / Greek Town

Artopolis Café and Agora	306 S Halsted	312-559-9000	$$	Frappes to mediterranean pizza.
Athena	212 S Halsted	312-655-0000	$$$	Goddess Athena inspired outdoor & indoor.
Byzantium	232 S Halsted	312-454-1227	$$	Tapas Greek Piano Bar.
Costas	340 S Halsted	312-263-9700	$$$	Greece at its warmest.
Greek Islands	200 S Halsted	312-782-9855	$$$	Greek Heaven—not to be missed.
J and C Inn	558 W Van Buren	312-663-4114	$$$	Dingy outside—best sandwiches in town inside.
Nine Muses	315 S Halsted	312-902-9922	$$$	Brick bars and backgammon.
Parthenon	314 S Halsted	312-726-2407	$$$	Creaters of flaming saganaki!
Pegasus Restaurant and Taverna	130 S Halsted	312-226-3377	$$$	Rooftop garden—Chicago secret!
Roditys	222 S Halsted	312-454-0800	$$$	Greek lamb since 1972.
Santorini	800 W Adams	312-829-8820	$$	Fish, shellfish and roasted chicken—yum

5 · The Loop

Atwood Café	1 WWashington	312-368-1900	$$$	High tea with contemporary flair.
Berghoff Restaurant	17 W Adams	312-427-3170	$$	Chicago icon with hearty German fare.
Everest	440 S LaSalle	312-663-8920	$$$$	High fallutin' food.
Heaven On Seven	111 N Wabash	312-263-6443	$$	Cajun Chicago classic. Closed for dinner.
Italian Village	71 W Monroe	312-332-4040	$$$	Theater dining tradition.
Nick's Fishmarket & Grill	One Bank One Plaza Clark & Dearborn	312-467-9449	$$$	Power lunch.
Oasis Restaurant	21 N Wabash	312-558-1058	$$*	Middle Eastern hide-out inside of a jewelry store.

Russian Tea Time	77 E Adams	312-360-0000	$$$	Elegant Russian cuisine.
The French Quarter/ Palmer House Hilton	17 E Monroe	312-621-7363	$$$	Festive Chicago tradition.
Trattoria #10	10 N Dearborn St	312-984-1718	$$$	Authentic Italian.

6 • The Loop / Grant Park

Art Institute Restaurant On The Park	111 S Michigan Ave	312-443-3600	$$	Scenic lunch-time dining. Closes at 2:30pm.
Rain Dog Books & Café	408 S Michigan Ave	312-922-1200	$	Killer smoothies keep you from being a starving writer.

7 • South Loop / River City

Bake for Me	608 W Roosevelt	312-957-1994	$	Good coffee and pastries.
Harrison Red Hot	565 W Harrison	312-341-1979	$	Hot dog stand.
Harrison St. Grill	506 W Harrison	312-957-9100	$$	Holiday Inn burger bar.
Manny's Coffee Shop	1141 S Jefferson	312-939-2855	$	Coffee and deli sandwiches.
Nick's Grill	518 W Harrison	312-341-9163	$	Burgers and chicken.
White Palace Grill	1159 S Canal	312-939-7167	$	Greasy cabbie chow.

8 • South Loop / Dearborn Park

Bar Louie	47 W Polk	312-347-0000	$$*	Upscale Bar with one of the best bar kitchens in Chicago. Late kitchen til 1am.
Blackies	755 S Clark St.	312-786-1161	$$*	A famous Burger, lesser known best breakfast in S Loop on Fri, Sat. Sun.
Hackneys	733 S Dearborn St	312-939-3870	$$	A specialty burger and onion loaf a northshore legend since 1939 now has a little known outlet in downtown.
Prarie Restaurant	500 S Dearborn St	312-663-1143	$$$$	Stylish heartland dining.
South Loop Club	1 E Balbo	312-427-2787	$	Very casual bar restaurant with surprisingly good kitchen.
SRO	612 S Dearborn St		$	Great Kitchen boasting Chicagos #1 Turkey Burger.
Trattoria Caterina	616 S Dearborn St	312-939-7606		A little touch of Italy, and a great value for Italian.

9 • South Loop / South Michigan Ave

Artist's Café	412 S Michigan Ave	312-939-7855	$$†	Sit at the counter-the chattiest waiters in town.

10 • East Pilsen / Chinatown

Emperor's Choice	2238 S Wentworth Ave	312-225-8800	$	Start with seafood; finish with tea.
Hong Min	221 W Cermak Rd.	312-842-5026	$	Shrimp toast, Mongolian beef, dim sum. Mmm.
Lao Sze Chuan	2172 S Archer Ave	312-326-5040	$$	Authentic Chinese dishes plus evening karaoke.
Penang	2201 S Wentworth Ave	312-326-6888	$	Malaysian favorites.
The Happy Chef Dim Sum House	2164 S Archer Ave	312-808-3869	$	Entrees priced to try several dishes.
The Phoenix Café	2131 S Archer Ave	312-328-0848	$	The best Chinese breakfast in town.
Three Happiness	2130 S Wentworth Ave	312-791-1228	$	So good it has a junior restaurant nearby.
Won Kow	2237 S Wentworth Ave	312-842-7500	$	Cheap, tasty dim sum.

11 • South Loop / McCormick Place

Chef Luciano	49 East Cermak	312-326-0062	$	Walk-in restaurant with eclectic entrees; Italian/ African/Cajun influences.
Firehouse Resturant	1401 S Michigan Ave	312-786-1401	$$$$	Transformed Chicago Firehouse complete with pole and fine dining.
Giocco	1312 S Wabash	312-939-3870	$$$$	Great Italian dining.
NetWorks (at Hyatt Regency McCormick Place)	2233 S Martin Luther King Drive	312-567-1234	$$$	Contemporary American with a focus on Chicago specialties.
The FIne Print Restaurant	McCormick Place, Grand Concourse, Level 2.5		$$$	Fine dining: steaks and salads.

12 • Bridgeport (West)

Johnny O's	3461 S Morgan	773-927-1011	$*	Polish dogs and comfort food.
Mexico Steak House	2983 S Archer Ave	773-254-5151	$$	Mexican meat is the speciality.
Nicky's Carry Out Hot Dog	1734 W 35th	773-254-7852	$*	Weenies on the run.
Polo's Nut & Candy Café	3322 S Morgan	773-927-7656	$$	They even do catering.

Key: $: Under $10 / $$: $10–$20 / $$$: $20–$30 / $$$$: $30+   * : Does not accept credit cards. / † : Accepts only American Express.

13 • Bridgeport (East)

August Moon Restaurant	225 W 26th St	312-842-2951	$$	Super Indonesian.
Bridgeport Restaurant	3500 S Halsted	773-247-8977	$$	Specializing in burgers, all makes & models.
Cugino's,	300 W 26th St	312-528-1000	$*	Mmm...beef cheesie.
Dox Place	600 W Pershing Rd	773-927-0350	$$	24 hour grill.
Ferro's Homemade Italian Lemonade	200 W 31 St	312-842-0702	$*	A summer favorite.
Franco's Ristorante	300 W 31st St	312-225-9566		
Graziano's Ristorante	605 W 31st St	312-326-1399	$$	Good neighborhood fare.
Healthy Food Lithuanian Restaurant	3236 S Halsted	312-326-2724	$$	Sauerkraut soup is a must.
Kevin's Hamburger Heaven	554 W Pershing Rd	773-924-5771	$$	Hamburgers and milkshakes.
Offshore Steak House	480 W 26th St	312-842-1362	$$	Great deals, simple setting.
Phil's Pizza	3551 S Halsted	773-523-0947	$*	Pizza-rific.
Ramova Grill	3510 S Halsted	773-847-9058	$	Sure to please, American styles.
Red's Snack Shop	452 W 39th St	773-924-4750	$*	A real truck stop right in the city.
Scumaci's Italian Sandwiches	220 W 31 St	312-328-0502	$*	Go get a meatball sandwich.
Sugar Shack	630 W 26th St	312-949-1153	$*	If you need to satisfy that sweet tooth.
Wing Yip Chop Suey	537 W 26th	312-326-2822		Nader bumper sticker on window.

14 • Prairie Shore / Lake Meadows

Blue Sea Drive Inn	427 E Pershing Rd	773-285-3325	$*	Fast food and carry out.
Bronzville Market & Deli	339 E 26th St	312-225-2988	$	Simple, convenient, easy, and old fashioned.
Fisher Fish & Chicken	3901 S King Dr	773-924-4444	$*	The Catfish is worth the price.
Hong Kong Delight	327 E 35th St	312-842-2929	$$*	Not quite like being there, but close enough.
Mississippi Rick's	3351 S King Dr	312-791-0090	$*	Fish & Tips, all kinds of meat with a little on the side.
The Rib Joint	3851 S Michigan Ave	773-268-8750	$*	It is named like that for a reason. All day lunch.

15 • Back of the Yards / Canaryville

Chicago Ice Cream Cart Inc.	356 W Root St	773-538-3164	$*	Name says it all.

16 • Bronzeville

Crescent Subs	4307 S State St	773-373-0640	$*	Sub shop.
Harold's Chicken Shack #29	307 E 51st St	773-373-9016	$*	Fries, bread, and chicken.
Harold's Chicken Shack #7	364 E 47th St	773-285-8362	$*	It may say #7 but it is #1 around here.

17 • Kenwood

Kenny's Ribs & Chicken	1461 E Hyde Park Blvd	773-241-5550	$$	Cheap and good to go.
Lake Shore Café	4900 S Lake Shore Drive	773-288-5800	$$$	Good continental.

18 • Washington Park

MS Lee's Good Food	203 E Garfield Blvd.	773-752-5253	$*	It is good.
Rose's BBQ Chicken	5426 S State St.	773-268-3401	$*	Don't mind the floor, it the sauce.

19 • Hyde Park

Calypso	5211-C S Harper Ave	773-955-0229	$$	Good Caribbean Great Drinks.
Daley's Restaurant	805 E 63rd St	773-643-6670	$$*	The mayor ought to try this place.
Dixie Kitchen and Bait Shop	5225-A S Harper Ave	773-363-4943	$$	A little taste of the South.
Jarunee Thai 55 Restaurant	1607 E 55th St	773-363-7119	$$*	Good Americanized Thai.
Kikuya Japanese Restaurant	1601 E 55th St	773-667-3727	$$*	Best sushi in the neighborhood.
La Petite Folie	1504 E 55th St	773-493-1394	$$	The only Haute Cuisine in the neighborhood. The most expensive in the area—worth it.
Leona's	1228 E 53rd St	773-363-2600	$$	Huge Portions of good Italian.
Maravilla's Mexican Restaurant	5211 S Harper Ave	773-643-3155	$	Cheap, good MexicaN Stinging salsa. Open late.
Medici on 57th	1327 E 57th St	773-667-7394	$	The essence of life of U of C.
Mellow Yellow	1508-10 E 53rd St	773-667-2000	$	Comfort Food for morning and night.

Noodles Etc.	1460 E 53rd St	773-947-8787	$	Great, cheap Asian.
Rajun Cajun	1459 E 53rd St	773-955-1145	$	Cheap, good Indian and vegetarian.
Ribs N Bibs	5300 S Dorchester Ave	773-493-0400	$	Finger lickin'. Wear the bib.
Salonica Restaurant	1440 E 57th St	773-752-3899	$	Where to go the morning after.

20 · Hyde Park East / Jackson Park

Cedars of Lebanon	1618 E 53rd St	773-324-6227	$*	Good cheap Middle Eastern.
Jackson Harbor Grill	6401 S Coast Guard Dr	773-288-4442	$$	Go just for the location.
Morry's Deli	5500 S Cornell Ave	773-363-3800	$*	Good on the go.
Orly's Café	1660 E 55th St		$$*	Stick to the Mexican. Have a Margarita.
Piccolo Mondo	1642 E 56th St	773-643-1106	$$*	Best Italian in the area.
Post Link	1634 E 53rd St	773-643-0629		
The Nile Restaurant	5500 S Hyde Park Blvd		$$*	Varied Middle Eastern.

21 · Wicker Park / Ukrainian Village

Blue Fin	1952 W North Ave	773-394-7373	$$	Upscale, trendy sushi bar.
Bongo Room	1470 N Milwaukee Ave	773-489-0690	$	Great breakfast spot. Expect to wait on weekends.
Cafe Absinthe	1958 W North Ave	773-278-4488	$$$$	Outrageously expensive and chi-chi.
Cold Comfort Cafe & Deli	2211 W North Ave	773-342-1998	$$	Freshly made deli sandwiches; groceries.
Dvine	1950 W North Ave	773-235-5700	$$$$	Another place to "be seen" and blow your paycheck.
Feast	1616 N Damen Ave	773-235-6362	$$$	Popular for Sunday brunch.
Hi Ricky Noodle Shop	1825 W North Ave	773-276-8300	$	Pan-Asian.
Las Palmas	1835 W North Ave	773-289-4991	$	Great alfresco dining and atrium seating.
Lulu's Hot Dogs	1000 S Leavitt St	312-243-3444	$*	The place for ribs & Italian beef.
Mas	1670 W Division St	773-276-8700	$$	Stylish latin cooking, dinner only.
Mirai Sushi	2020 W Division St	773-862-8500	$$	Chic dining and good sushi.
MOD	1520 N Damen Ave	773-252-1500	$$	Contemporary American.
Pacific Cafe	1619 N Damen Ave	773-862-1988	$$	Inexpensive sushi/Japanese.
Piece	1927 W North Ave	773-772-4422	$$	"Designer" pizza joint.
Pontiac Café	1531 N Damen Ave	773-252-7767	$	Old pumping station, great people watching.
Smoke Daddy	1804 W Division St.	773-772-6656	$	Barbecue and blues.
Soju	1745 W North Ave	773-793-5444	$$$	Fancy Korean Barbecue.
Souk	1552 N Milwaukee Ave	773-227-9110	$$	Middle Eastern with belly dancers and hookhas.
Soul Kitchen	1576 N Milwaukee Ave	773-342-9742	$	Contemporary Soul food.
Spring	2039 W North Ave	773-395-7100	$$	Vogue, overpriced Asian.
Sultan's Market	2057 W North Ave	773-235-3072	$	Cheap Middle Eastern; groceries.
Thai Lagoon	2322 W North Ave	773-489-5747	$$	Great Thai; funky atmosphere.
The Blue Penguin	1924 W Division St	773-975-0527	$	Deli, homemade soups, and sandwiches.

22 · Noble Square / Goose Island

Corosh	1072 N Milwaukee	773-235-0600	$$	Italian and pub fare; great patio.
El Barco Mariscos Seafood	1035 N Ashland Blvd	773-486-6850	$$$	Outdoor seating; terrific ceviche.
Hilary's Urban Eatery	1500 W Division St	773-235-4327	$$	Salmon cakes to die for.
Hollywood Grill	1601 W North Ave	773-395-1818	$	Where the hipsters and drunks dry out.
Luc Thang	1524 N Ashland Blvd	773-395-3907	$	Thai with Chinese and Vietnamese touches.
Watusi	1540 W North Ave	773-862-1540	$$$$	Pan-Latin in chic environs.

23 · West Town / Near West Side

China Dragon Restaurant	2008 W Madison St.	312-666-3766	$*	Dependably fantastic Chinese.
Darkroom	2210 W Chicago Ave	773-276-1411	$$	New York strip, glazed salmon, mac and cheese and BYOB.
Dionises Restaurant & Café	510 N Western Ave	312-243-7330	$*	Rockin' Mexican.
Il Jack's Italian Restaurant	1754 W Grand Ave	312-421-7565	$$$$	Neighborhood Italian.
Munch	1800 W Grand Ave	312-226-4914	$	Laid-back, funky brunch place.
Privata Café	1936 Chicago Ave	773-394-0662	$	Eclectic Mexican-Italian cuisine, brunch buffet.
Tecalitlan Restaurant	1814 W Chicago Ave	773-384-4285	$$	Popular family-style,Mexican restaurant.

Restaurants • Arts & Entertainment

Key: $: Under $10 / $$: $10–$20 / $$$: $20–$30 / $$$$: $30+   * : Does not accept credit cards. / † : Accepts only American Express.

24 • River West / West Town

Breakfast Club	1381 W Hubbard St.	312-666-2372	$$	Brunch and then some.
Crab Street Saloon	1061 W Madison	312-433-0013	$$$	East-coast style seafood experience.
Flo	1434 W Chicago Ave	312-243-0477	$$	Mexican influenced brunch.
Hacienda Tecalitlan	820 N Ashland Blvd	312-243-1166	$$	Popular family-style, Mexican restaurant.
Jerry's Sandwiches	1045 W Madison	312-563-1008	$	Fresh and slightly gourmet concoctions.
La Borsa	375 N Morgan	312-563-1414	$$$	Not too-traditional Italian.
Moretti's	1645 W Jackson Blvd	312-850-0208	$$	Italian-American favorite.
Wishbone	1001 W Washington	312-850-2663	$$	Comfort food, comfort folks.

25 • Illinois Medical District

Carnitas Uruapan Restaurant	1725 W 18th St	312-226-2654		Carnitas muy necesitas.
El Charco Verde	2253 W Taylor St	312-738-1686	$*	A Mexican favorite.
TJ's Family Restaurant	1952 W Cermak Rd	773-927-3349	$	Neighborhood diner.

26 • University Village / Little Italy

Al's Number 1 Italian Beef	1079 W Taylor St	312-733-8896	$*	Where's the beef? Right here.
Café Viaggio	1435 W Taylor St	312-226-9009	$$	A variety of pasta, chicken and veal.
Carm's Beef and Snack Shop	1057 W Polk St	312-738-1046	$*.	Italian subs and sausages.
Chez Joel	1119 W Taylor St	312-226-6479	$$$	Delicious French cuisine in Little Italy.
Falbo's	1335 W Taylor St.	312-421-8915	$	Subs made with fresh Italian ingredients.
Francesca's	1400 W Taylor St.	312-829-2828	$$	Loud, bustling dining room.
Genarro's	1352 W Taylor St	312-243-1035	$	Standard fare served in generous portions.
New Rosebud Café	1500 W Taylor St.	312-942-1117	$	Popular with the United Center crowd.
Siam Pot	1509 Taylor St	312-733-0760	$$	Reasonable Thai in large amounts.
Taj Mahal	1512 Taylor St.	312-226-6546	$$	Affordable Indian.

27 • Logan Square (North)

Abril Mexican Restaurant	2607 N Milwaukee Ave	773-227-7252	$$	Tacos and tequila.
Boulevard Café	3137 W Logan Blvd	773-384-8600	$$	Eat, drink and be merry!
Café Bolero	2252 N Western Ave	773-227-9000	$$	Tasty Cuban fare.
Choi's Chinese Restaurant	2638 N Milwaukee Ave	773-486-8496	$$	Good, fresh Chinese food.
El Cid	2115 N Milwaukee Ave	773-252-4747	$	Authentic Mexican for the masses.
El Nandu	2731 N Fullerton Ave	773-278-0900	$$	Argentian delicacies mixed with music.
Johnny's Grill	2545 N Kedzie Blvd	773-278-2215	$*	Diner food for the grunge crowd.
Lula	2537 N Kedzie Blvd	773-489-9554	$	Pan-ethnic nouveau for hipsters.

28 • Bucktown

Café Bolero	2252 W N Western	773-227-9000	$$$	Spicy Cuban food and music.
Café Matou	1848 N Milwaukee	773-384-8911	$$$	French food; dodgy area.
Cafe De Luca	1721 N Damen Ave	773-342-6000	$$	Café and Italian sandwiches
Club Lucky	1824 W Wabansia	773-227-2300	$$	Age-old Italian joint.
Green Dolphin Street		773-395-0066	$$	Live jazz and blues, award-winning food.
Northside Tavern & Grill	1635 N Damen Ave	773-384-6337	$$	Bucktown institution; outdoor seating.
Roong Thai Restaurant	1633 N Milwaukee Ave	773-252-3488	$$	Tasty Thai.
Silver Cloud Supper Club	1700 N Damen Ave	773-489-6212	$$	Beer, sandwiches, outdoor seating,
Zoom Kitchen	1646 N Damen Ave	773-227-7000	$$	Cafeteria style dining.

29 • DePaul / Wrightwood / Sheffield

BW3's	2464 N Lincoln Ave	773-868-9453	$	Sports bar with wings.
Clarke's Pancake House & Restaurant	2441 N Lincoln Ave	773-472-3505	$	Great pancake and omelet spot.
Demon Dogs	844 W Fullerton Ave	773-281-2001	$*	Classic Chicago dogs.
Goose Island Brewing Co.	1800 N Clybourn Ave	312-915-0071	$	Pub grub at its best.
Green Dolphin Street	2200 N Ashland Ave	773-395-0066	$$$$	Live Jazz club and contemporary American.
John's Place	1202 W Webster Ave	773-525-6670	$	Healthy comfort food.
Salt & Pepper Diner	2575 N Lincoln Ave	773-525-8788	$*	Retro burger joint.
Shine/Morida	901 W Armitage Ave	773-296-0101	$$	Chinese & Japanese all-in-one.

30 • Lincoln Park

Alladin Cafe	2269 N Lincoln Ave	773-871-7327	$*	Morrocan, Lebanese, Egyptian, etc.
Asiana	2546 N Clark St	773-296-9189	$$$$	Asian HQ.
Athenian Room	807 W Webster Ave	773-348-5155	$	Casual Greek dining.
Aubriot	1962 N Halsted St	773-281-4211	$$$$	Top notch dining.
Charlie Trotter's	816 W Armitage	773-248-6228	$$$$	World renowned, dinner only.

Frances	2552 N Clark St	773-248-4580	$$*	Inventive deli.
Hi.Ma.Wa.Ri	346 W Armitage Ave	773-871-4777	$$*	Delicious Japanese and Chinese dishes.
King Crab	1816 N Halsted St	312-280-8990	$$$	Seafood experts.
L'Olive	1629 N Halsted St	312-573-1515	$$$	Great pre-theatre Marrakesh dining.
R.J. Grunts	2056 Lincoln Park West	773-929-5363	$$	Great grub.
Taco Burrito Palace #2	2441 N Halsted St	773-248-0740	$*	Speedy Mexican.
Tilli's	1952 N Halsted St	773-325-0044	$$	Cute staff and good food.
Toast	746 W Webster Ave	773-935-5600	$$	Made for brunching.
Twin Anchors	1655 N Sedgwick St	312-266-1616	$$	Regulars will vouch for the ribs.

31 • Old Town / Near North

Bistrot Margot	1437 N Wells St	312-587-3660	$$$$	Great date place.
Cucina Bella Osteria	1612 N Sedgwick Ave	312-274-1119	$$*	Solid Italian; wine bar.
Fireplace Inn	1448 N Wells St	312-664-5264	$$$	Popular spot to watch sports.
Fresh Choice	1534 N Wells St	312-664-7065	$*	Sandwich and smoothie king.
Kamehachi	1400 N Wells St	312-664-3663	$$$	Sushi favorite with upstairs lounge.
Las Pinatas	1552 N Wells St	312-664-8277	$$	Festive atmosphere; fantastic food.
O'Briens	1528 N Wells St	312-787-3131	$$$	Best outdoor in Old Town.
Old Jerusalem	1411 N Wells St	312-944-0459	$$	Cheap, good food.
Topo Gigio	1516 N Wells St	312-266-9335	$$$	Crowded reliable Italian. Big outdoor.

32 • Gold Coast / Mag Mile

Ashkenaz	12 E Cedar St	312-944-5006	$	Chicago's true Jewish deli.
Bistro 110	110 E Pearson	312-266-3110	$$$	Popular Sunday Jazz brunch.
Gibson's	1028 N Rush St	312-266-8999	$$$$	If you love steak, get a reservation.
Jilly's	1009 N Rush St	312-664-1001	$$$$	Steak and
Johnny Rockets	901 N Rush St	312-337-3900	$	Jukebox and malts—outdoor seating, late night eating.
Le Colonial	937 N Rush St	312-255-0088	$$$$	Vietnamese/French fare.
McCormick & Schmick	41 E Chestnut St	312-397-9500	$$$$	Seafood chain that outdoes itself on portions and taste.
Mike Ditka's	100 E Chestnut	312-587-8989	$$$	The place for Ditka, Chicago sports and meat.
Pane Caldo	72 E Walton St	312-649-0055	$$$$	Tucked away, genius Italian trattoria.
Spiaggia	940 N Michigan Ave	312-280-2755	$$$$	One of Chicago's best— gorgeous lake view and Italian cuisine.
Tavern on Rush	1031 N Rush St	312-664-9600	$$$$	Summer mainstay, American menu.
Tempo	6 E Chestnut St	312-943-4373	$$$	24/7 patio seating and huge menu.
The Cheesecake Factory	875 N Michigan	312-337-1101	$$	40+ kinds of cheesecake.
The Original Pancake House	22 E Bellevue Pl	312-642-7917	$$*	The apple waffle/pancake is right!
The Pump Room	1301 N State Pkwy	312-266-0360	$$$$	Chicago old school tradition. Dress code.
Tsunami	1160 N Dearborn St	312-642-9911	$$$	Sushi and sake in a club-like atmosphere.
Whiskey Bar and Grill	1015 N Rush St	312-475-0300	$$$	Great summer place. Hip and trendy folks galore.

33 • West Rogers Park

Angus	7555 N Western Ave	773-262-8844	$$	Steak & seafood. Surprisingly fancy.
Café Montenegro	6954 N Western Ave	773-761-2233	$	Greek-accented coffeeshop.
Delhi Darbar Kabab House	6403 N California Ave	773-338-1818	$	Indian/Pakastani. 24/7.
Desi Island	2401 W Devon Ave	773-465-2489	$	Think corner diner, but spicy.
Fluky's	6821 N Western Ave	773-274-3652	$*	"Famous" hot dog joint, breakfast lunch & dinner, outdoor seating.
Ghandi India Restaurant	2601 W Devon Ave	773-761-8714	$$	Family style north and south Indian fare.
Gitel's Kosher Bakery	2745 W Devon Ave	773-262-3701	$*	Baked goods and pastries, always fresh, carry-out.
Good Morgan Kosher Fish Market	2948 W Devon Ave	773-764-8115	$$$*	Fish market/restaurant in the Devon kosher strip (kosher restaurant).
HaShalom	2905 W Devon Ave	773-465-5675	$*	Israeli/Moroccan, Kosher, BYOB, closed Sat/Sun.
Sala Thai	2739 W Touhy Ave	773-743-0019	$$	Thai comfort food, generous portion/ moderately priced, dimly lit, visa only.
Tiffin, The Indian Kitchen	2536 W Devon Ave	773-338-2143	$$	A more upscale Indian restaurant.
Udupi Palace	2543 W Devon Ave	773-338-2152	$	Pure vegetarian Indian food, low-fat, not too spicy.
Viceroy of India	2518 W Devon Ave	773-743-4100	$$	Elegantly stylish Indian restaurant, separate half for fast-food / carryout, features both meat and vegetarian dishes.

Restaurants • Arts & Entertainment

*Key: $: Under $10 / $$: $10–$20 / $$$: $20–$30 / $$$$: $30+   * : Does not accept credit cards. / † : Accepts only American Express.*

34 • East Rogers Park

El Famous Burrito	7047 N Sheridan Ave	773-465-0377	$*	Mexican treats for the college crowd.
Ennui Café	6981 N Sheridan Ave	773-973-2233	$*	Tasty tidbits.
Heartland Café	7000 N Glenwood Ave	773-465-8005	$$	Eclectic health food.
Panini Panini	6764 N Sheridan Ave	773-761-7775	$$*	Italian flavor for the North Side.
Tien Tsin	7018 N Clark St	773-761-2820	$$	Great Chinese food for the family.

35 • Arcadia Terrace / Peterson Park

Charcoal Delights	3139 W Foster Ave	773-583-0056	$*	The name says it all.
Garden Buffet	5347 N Lincoln Ave	773-728-1249	$$$	Korean/Japanese buffet and sushi bar.
El Tipico 36	1836 W Foster Ave	773-878-0839	$*	Semi-authentic neighborhood Mexican.
Fireside Restaurant & Lounge	5739 N Ravenswood Ave	773-561-7433	$$	Diverse crowd and eclectic menu from ribs to pizza.
Max's Italian Beef	5754 N Western Ave	773-989-8200	$*	Chicago institution; home of the pepper and egg sandwich.
San Goo Gab San Korean Restaurant and Sushi House	5247 N Western Ave	773-334-2115	$$$	Do-it-yourself Korean BBQ at 4:00 A.M.

37 • Edgewater / Andersonville

Francesca's Bryn Mawr	1039 W Bryn Mawr	773-506-9261	$$	Dined in an SRO before?
Jin Ju	5203 N Clark St.	773-334-6377	$$$	Upscale Korean.
Moody's Pub	5910 N Broadway	773-275-2696	$*	Burgers only, but the best.
Pasteur	5525 N Broadway	773-878-1061	$$$$	Easy to imagine you're in Vietnam 50 years ago.
Pauline's	1754 W Balmoral Ave	773-561-8573	$*	Weekend breakfast hotspot; try the famous five-egg omelet.
Reza's	5255 N Clark St.	773-561-1898	$$	Many Persian options, leftovers for lunch tomorrow.
The Room	5900 N Broadway	773-989-7666	$$	Wear black, BYOB, eat fresh seafood.
Tomboy	5402 N Clark St.	773-907-0636	$$	Loud, hip and fun, BYOB.

38 • Ravenswood / Albany Park

Arun's	4156 N Kedzie Ave	773-539-1909	$$$$	Worldwide rep. for four-star prix fix Thai.
Lutz Continental Café	2458 W Montrose Ave	773-478-7785	$$	If Grandma was German, she served these pastries.
Noon O Kabab	4661 N Kedzie Ave	773-279-8899	$	Bring doggie bag for day-after lunch.
Osito Cheez	4714 N Kedzie Ave	773-509-1800	$*	Chuck-E-Cheese, except in Spanish.
Shelly's Freez	5119 N Lincoln Ave	773-271-2783	$*	Classic Italian beef and dipped soft-serve.
Thai Little Home Café	4747 N Kedzie Ave	773-478-3944	$	Two rooms + one lunch buffet = less than 10.
The Penguin	2723 W Lawrence Ave	773-271-4924	$*	High-fat, authentic Argentine ice cream (empanadas and pizza, too, but go straight for dessert).

39 • Ravenswood / North Center

Café 28	1800 W Irving Park Rd	773-528-2883	$$	Trendy Cuban.
Café Selmarie	4729 N Lincoln Ave	773-989-5595	$$	Bakery/café.
Chicago Brauhaus	4732 N Lincoln Ave	773-784-4444	$$	Live German band!
Daily Bar & Grill	4560 N Lincoln Ave	773-561-6198	$	Stylish Bar Food.
Garcia's	4749 N Western Ave	773-769-5600	$	Mexican/Tex-Mex w/ great shakes.
Grecian Taverna	4761 N Lincoln Ave	773-878-6400	$$	Greek.
Jury's Food & Drink	4337 N Lincoln Ave	773-935-2255	$	Neighborhood Pub.
La Boca della Verita	4618 N Lincoln Ave	773-784-6222	$$	Cozy Italian café.
O'Donovan's	2100 W Irving Park Rd.	773-478-2100	$	Three Words: Dollar Burger Night.
Pangea	1935 W Irving Park Rd.	773-665-1340	$$$	Contemporary American.
She She	4539 N Lincoln Ave	773-293-3690	$$$$	Upscale/Eclectic American.
Tartufo Restaurante	4601 Lincoln Ave	773-334-7820	$$	Traditional Italian.
Woody's	4160 N Lincoln Ave	773-880-1100	$$	Ribs n' Wings n' Other Sticky Eats.

40 • Uptown

Andies	1467 W Montrose Ave	773-348-0654	$$	Middle Eastern food in Babylonian surroundings.
Bale French Bakery	5018 N Broadway St	773-561-4424	$	French/Asian bakery and sandwicheS
Don Quijote	4761 N Clark St	773-769-5930	$*	Burritos as big as your head.
Frankie J's	4437 N Broadway St	773-769-2959	$$$	Laugh and eat.
Golden House Restaurant	4744 N Broadway St	773-334-0406	$	Pancakes and ambience next to the Riv.
Holiday Club	4000 N Sheridan	773-348-9600	$$*	The Rat Pack Is Back! With Food.
Magnolia Café	1224 W Wilson	773-728-8785	$$	Magnolias in an american bistro.
Smoke Country House	1465 W Irving Park	773-327-0600	$$	Great barbecue on the north side (imagine that!).

41 • Avondale / Logan Square

IHOP	2818 W Diversey Ave	773-342-8901	$	Open 24 hours.
La Finca	3361 N Elston Ave	773-478-4006	$	Servicable Mexican, margaritas.
Rancho Luna del Caribe	2554 W Diversey Ave	773-772-9333	$$	Carribean supper club.
Sunshine Grill	3523 N Elston Ave		$*	24-hour dining.
Brett's Café Americain	2011 W Roscoe St	773-248-0999	$$$	Go for brunch or dessert. Great bread basket.

42 • North Center / West Lakeview

Costello Sandwich & Sides	2015 W Roscoe St	773-929-2323	$	Yummy baked sandwiches.
El Tinajon	2054 W Roscoe St	773-525-8455	$$	Good, cheap GuatamalaN Great mango margaritas.
Four Moon Tavern	1847 W Roscoe St	773-929-6666	$	Neighborhood taverN Cozy back room. Thespian crowd.
Hot Doug's	2314 W Roscoe St	773-348-0326	$*	Gourmet "encased meat" emporium.
Kitsch'n on Roscoe	2005 W Roscoe St	773-248-7372	$$	Clever retro food and tiki bar. Friendly staff.
La Mora	2132 W Roscoe St	773-404-4555	$$	Neighborhood Mediterranean-influenced Italian.
Lee's Chop Suey	2415 W Diversey Ave	773-342-7050	$*	Chop suey and booze.
Piazza Bella Trattoria	2116 W Roscoe St	773-477-7330	$$$	Neighborhood Italian.
Riverview Tavern	1958 W Roscoe St	773-248-9523	$$	Frat food and beer.
Thai Linda Café	2022 W Roscoe St	773-868-0075	$$	Standard-issue neighborhood Thai.
The Village Tap	2055 W Roscoe St	773-883-0817	$	Beer garden and good bar food.
Victory's Banner	2100 W Roscoe St	773-665-0227	$	Best vegetarian in the city, with toga-clad waitstaff.
Wild Onion	3500 N Lincoln Ave	773-871-5555	$$	Good prairie-inspired, diverse menu.
Wishbone	3500 N Lincoln Ave	773-549-2663	$$	Southern and soul food paradise.

43 • Wrigleyville / East Lakeview

Bistro Zinc	3442 N Southport Ave	773-281-3443	$$*	Quiet elegance.
Heaven on Seven	3478 N Clark St	773-477-7818	$$*	An epicurean jaunt to N'Orleans. Yum.
Mama Desta's Red Sea	3218 N Clark St	773-935-7561	$$*	Authentic Ethiopian. No forks.
Mia Francesca	3311 N Clark St	773-281-3310	$$*	Contemporary Italian date place.
Mongolian BBQ	3330 N Clark St	773-325-2300	$$*	Stir-fry your own creations.
Shiroi Hana	3242 N Clark St	773-477-1652	$$*	Tastiest. Sushi. Ever.
Technicolor Kitchen	3210 N Lincoln Ave	773-665-2111	$$	Eclectic fusioN Try the alligator wontons.
Tombo Kitchen	3244 N Lincoln Ave	773-244-9885	$$	Modern, very good sushi. Try the eel.
Viennese Kaffee-Haus Brandt	3423 N Southport Ave	773-528-2200	$*	Breakfast and sweet things.
Wrigleyville Dog	3735 N Clark St	773-296-1500	$*	Hot dog heaven.

44 • East Lakeview

Angelina	3561 N Broadway	773-935-5933	$$	Casual, romantic Italian.
Arco de Cuchilleros	3445 N Halsted St	773-296-6046	$$$	Intimate tapas; great Sangria.
Chicago Diner	3411 N Halsted St	773-935-6696	$$	A vegetarian institutios.
Clark Street Dog	3040 N Clark St	773-281-6690	$*	24-hour hot dogs and cheese fries.
Erwin	2925 N Halsted St	773-528-7200	$$$$	Elegant.
Jack's on Halsted	3201 N Halsted St	773-244-9191	$$$$	Great wine list.
La Creperie	2845 N Clark St	773-528-9050	$$	Live French music.
Las Mananitas	3523 N Halsted St	773-528-2109	$$	Lethal margaritas.
Mark's Chop Suey	3343 N Halsted St	773-281-9090	$	The BEST eggrolls.
Nookie's Tree	3334 N Halsted St	773-248-9888	$*	24-hour diner.
The Melrose	3233 N Broadway	773-327-2060	$$	24-hour diner.
Yoshi's Café	3257 N Halsted St	773-248-6160	$$$	Franco-Japanese fusion.

Theaters • Arts & Entertainment

Chicago has a rich theatrical tradition ranging from being the birthplace of Improv at venerable Second City to creating the fiery, intense acting style known as Chicago Style spawned by John Malkovich and Gary Sinise, co-founders of Steppenwolf Theatre Company. Chicago's revitalized Loop Theater District boasts several new and renovated theaters, including the Chicago Theater, Cadillac Palace Theater, the Ford Center-Oriental Theater and the new Goodman Theater.

Museum	Address	Phone	Map
About Face Theatre	3212 N Broadway		44
Acme Theater	1444 W Chicago Ave	312-850-4069	24
Annoyance Theatre	3747 N Clark St	773-929-6200	43
Apollo Theater Ctr	2540 N Lincoln Ave	773-935-6100	29
Arie Crown Theatre	McCormick Place Lakeside Center, Level 2		11
Arts Bridges	2936 N Southport Ave # 210	773-296-0948	43
Athenaeum Theatre	2936 N Southport Ave	773-935-6860	43
Auditorium Theatre	50 E. Congress		5
Bailwick Repertory	1229 W Belmont Ave	773-883-1090	43
Beacon Street Theatre and Gallery	1145 W. Wilson	773-769-4284	40
Black Ensemble Theatre	4620 N. Beacon	773-769-4451	40
Boxer Rebellion Theater	1257 W Loyola Ave	773-465-7325	34
Breadline Theatre Group Inc	1802 W Berenice Ave	773-327-6096	42
Briar Street Theatre	3133 N Halsted		44
Broadway In Chicago	22 W Monroe St # 700	312-902-1400	5
Burnham Plaza Theater	826 S Wabash Ave	312-922-1121	8
Cadillac Place Theatre	151 W. Randolph		5
Chase Park	4701 N. Ashland	773-742-7518	40
Chicago Center-Performing Arts	777 N Green St	773-327-2040	1
Chicago Dramatists	1105 W Chicago Ave		22
Chicago Ensemble	2936 N Southport Ave	773-296-1049	43
Chicago Music & Dance Theatre	203 N La Salle St Mez	312-629-8696	5
Chicago Theatre	175 N. State		5
Chicago Theatre Restoration	175 N State St	312-372-5422	5
Child's Play Touring Theatre	2518 W Armitage Ave	773-235-8911	27
Chineese Fine Arts Society	2936 N Southport Ave	773-296-0843	43
Chopin Theater	1543 W Division St		22
City Lit Theater Co	1020 W Bryn Mawr Ave	773-293-3682	37
Civic Opera House	20 N Wacker Dr # 860	312-419-0033	5
Classics On Stage Ltd	2435 W Wilson Ave	773-989-0532	38
Comedy Sportz	2851 N Halsted		44
Congress Theatre	2135 N Milwaukee Ave	773-252-4000	27
Court Theatre	5535 S Ellis Ave	773-753-4472	19
Dance Center of Columbia College	1306 South Michigan Ave	312-344-8300	11
Emerald City Theatre Co	2936 N Southport Ave	773-529-2690	43
Emma & Oscar Getz Theatre	62 E. 11th St.		11
Equity Library Theatre	1306 W North Shore Ave	773-743-0266	34
European Repertory Theater	2936 N Southport Ave	773-248-0577	43
Factory Theatre	1257 W Loyola Ave	773-409-3247	34
Famous Door Theatre	3212 N Broadway		44
Flower Of The Dragon Prodctn	2936 N Southport Ave	773-296-0869	43
Free Street Program	1419 W Blackhawk St	773-772-7248	22
Gilead Theater Co	927 W Lawrence Ave	773-293-2829	40
Goodman Theatre	170 N. Dearborn		5
Green Light Performing Co	2014 W Belle Plaine Ave	773-935-9380	39
Griffin Theatre Co	5404 N Clark St	773-769-2228	37
H & E Partnership	645 N Michigan Ave # 530	312-280-1121	3
Healthworks Theatre Inc	3171 N Halsted St	773-929-4260	44
Imagination Theater Inc	1801 W Byron St # 2S	773-929-4100	42
Ivanhoe Theater	180 E Pearson St # 4602	773-975-7171	32
Kidworks Touring Theatre Co	3510 N Broadway St	773-883-9932	44

Museum	Address	Phone	Map
League Of Chicago Theatres	811 N Michigan Ave	312-642-2837	32
Left Eye Productions Inc	4856 N Magnolia Ave	773-275-0167	40
Lifeline Theatre	6912 N Glenwood Ave	773-761-4477	34
Lincoln Avenue Project	4545 N Lincoln Ave	773-506-0400	39
Live Bait Theater	3914 N Clark St	773-871-1212	43
Looking Glass Theatre Co	1016 N Dearborn St	312-397-0471	32
Lookinglass Theater	2936 N Southport Ave	773-477-9257	43
Lyric Opera Of Chicago	20 N Wacker Dr # 860	312-332-2244	5
Magnaverde Productions	70 E Congress Pkwy	312-939-8071	8
Mary-Arrchie Theatre Co	731 W Sheridan Rd	773-871-0442	44
Mercury Theater	3745 N Southport Ave	773-325-1700	43
Merle Reskin Theatre	60 E Balbo Ave	312-922-1999	8
National Pastime Theater	4139 N Broadway St	773-327-7077	40
Natyakalalayam Dance Co	2936 N Southport Ave	773-296-1061	43
Noble Fool Theater	8 E. Randolph		5
O'Rourke Center for the PerformingArts	1145 W. Wilson	773-878-9761	40
Orchestra Hall At Symphony Ctr	220 S Michigan Ave	312-294-3333	6
Oriental Theatre	24 W. Randolph		5
Performance Loft	656 W Barry Ave	773-529-8337	44
Performing Arts Chicago	410 S Michigan Ave # 911	312-663-1628	6
Perkins Productions	1633 N Halsted St	312-944-5626	30
Playground Improv Theatre Inc	3341 N Lincoln Ave	773-871-3793	42
Profiles Theatre	4147 N. Broadway	773-549-1815	40
Raven Theatre Co	2549 W Fargo Ave	773-338-2177	33
Red Orchid Theatre	1531 N Wells St	312-943-8722	31
Redmoon Theatre Co	2936 N Southport Ave	773-388-9031	43
Ren Hen Productions	5123 N Clark St	773-728-0599	40
Royal George Theatre	1641 N. Halsted		30
Scrap Mettle Soul	4600 N Magnolia Ave # C	773-275-3999	40
Seanachai Theatre Co	5108 N Ashland Ave	773-878-3727	40
Serendipity Theatre Co	1302 N Leavitt St # 1	773-384-4450	21
Shakespeare Reperatory	800 E Grand Ave	312-595-5656	3
Shattered Globe Theatre	2257 N. Lincoln		30
Shattered Globe Theatre	2856 N Halsted		44
Shubert Theatre	22 W Monroe St #600	312-977-1710	5
St Sebastian Players	1621 W Diversey Pkwy	773-404-7922	43
Stage Left Theatre	3408 N Sheffield Ave	773-883-8830	43
Steppenwolf Theatre Co.	1650 N. Halsted		30
Steppenwolf Theatre Co	758 W North Ave # 4	312-335-1888	31
Stolen Buick Studio	1303 W Chicago Ave		22
Storefront Theatre	66 E. Randolph		5
Strawdog Theatre Co.	3829 N Broadway		44
Symphony Center Presents	220 S Michigan Ave	312-294-3000	6
Theatre Building	1225 W Belmont Ave	773-327-5252	43
Thirsty Theater	556 W 18th St	312-491-8484	10
Thirteenth Tribe	1957 W Chicago Ave	773-252-2510	23
Time Line Theatre Co	615 W Wellington Ave	773-281-8463	44
Tmg Marketing Group	22 W Monroe St	312-920-9640	5
Tommy Gunis Garage Dinner Theatre	1239 South State St.	312-461-0102	11
Trap Door Productions	1655 W Cortland St	773-384-0494	28
Turn Around Theatre	3209 N Halsted St	773-296-1100	44
Uffish Theater Co	312 N Laflin St # 6R	312-243-0319	24
Vic Theatre	3145 N Sheffield Ave	773-472-0366	43
Victory Gardens Theatre	2257 N Lincoln Ave	773-549-5788	30
Vittum Theater	1012 N Noble St		22
WNEP Theatre	3209 N Halsted		44
Women's Theatre Alliance	407 S Dearborn St	312-408-9910	5

Essential Phone Numbers

General

All emergencies	**911**
AIDS Hotline	800-342-AIDS
Animal-Cruelty Society	312-644-8338
Chicago Dental Referral Service	312-836-7305
Chicago Department of Housing	773-285-5800
City of Chicago Board of Elections	312-269-7900
Dog Licence (City Clerk)	312-744-6875
Driver's Licences	312-793-1010
Emergency Services	312-747-7247
Employment Discrimination	312-744-7584
Gas Leaks	312-240-7000
Income Tax (Illinois)	800-732-8866
Income Tax (Federal)	800-829-3676
Legal Assistance	312-332-1624
Mayor's Office	312-744-4000
Parking (City Stickers)	312-744-6861
Parking Ticket Inquiries	312-744-7275
Report Crime in Your Neighborhood	312-372-0101
Passports	312-341-6020
Police Assistance (non-emergency)	311
Social Security	800-772-1213
Streets and Sanitation	312-744-5000
Telephone Repair Service	888-611-4466
Voter Information	312-269-7900
Water Main Leaks	312-744-7038

Helplines

Alcoholics Anonymous	312-346-1475
Alcohol, Drug and Abuse Helpline	800-234-0420
Alcoholism and Substance Abuse	312-988-7900
Domestic Violence Hotline	800-799-7233
Drug Care, St. Elizabeth's	773-278-5015
Gamblers Anonymous	312-346-1588
Illinois Child Abuse Hotline	800-252-2873
Narcotics Anonymous	708-848-4884
Parental Stress Services	312-372-7368
Runaway Switchboard	800-621-4000
Sexual Assault Hotline	888-293-2080
United Way Community Information and Referral	312-876-0010
Violence – Anti Violence Project	773-871-CARE

Complaints

Better Business Bureau of Chicago	312-832-0500
Consumer Fraud Division (Attorney General's Office)	312-814-3000
Chicago Department of Consumer Services	312-744-9400
Citizen's Utility Board	800-669-5556
Department of Housing Inspection Complaints	312-747-1500
Mayor's Office	312-744-4000
Postal Service Complaints	312-983-8400

Street	Page	Grid
E 8th St	8	B2
E 9th St	8	B2
W 9th St	8	B2
E 11th St	8	C2
W 12th Pl		
(569-646)	10	A1
(700-799)	26	B2
E 13th St	11	A1
W 13th St		
(29-49)	10	A2
(600-1725)	26	B2
(1726-2399)	25	B2
E 14th Pl	11	A1
W 14th Pl		
(530-662)	10	A1
(663-1724)	26	B2
(1725-1799)	25	B2
E 14th St	11	A1
W 14th St		
(10-535)	10	A1
(600-1726)	26	B2
(1727-2499)	25	B2
E 15th Pl	11	B1
W 15th Pl		
(700-1515)	26	B2
(2400-2559)	25	B1
W 15th St		
(1-699)	10	A1
(700-1723)	26	B2
(1724-2519)	25	B2
E 16th St	11	B1
W 16th St		
(11-649)	10	B1
(18-1748)	26	C1
(1701-2499)	25	C2
W 17th Pl	26	C2
W 17th St		
(38-499)	10	B2
(700-1705)	26	C2
(1706-2458)	25	C1
W 18th Pl		
(900-1705)	26	C2
(1706-2399)	25	C2
E 18th St	11	B1
W 18th St		
(1-649)	10	B2
(700-1705)	26	C2
(1706-2499)	25	C2
W 19th Pl	26	C2
W 19th St		
(39-749)	10	B2
(734-1714)	26	C2
(1715-2499)	25	C2
W 20th Pl		
(534-599)	10	B1
(900-1199)	26	C2
W 21st Pl		
(700-1749)	26	C2
(1750-2499)	25	C2
E 21st St	11	B1
W 21st St		
(120-699)	10	B2
(700-1749)	26	C2
(1750-2499)	25	C2
W 22nd Pl		
(200-1899)	10	C2
(2000-2399)		
W 23rd Pl	10	C1
E 23rd St	11	C1
W 23rd St	10	C2
E 24th Pl	11	C1
W 24th Pl	10	C1
E 24th St	11	C1
W 24th St	10	C2
W 25th Pl		
(500-729)	10	C1
(730-783)	13	A1
E 25th St	11	C1
W 25th St	10	C2
W 26th Pl	13	A2
E 26th St	14	A1
W 26th St		
E 27th St	14	A2
W 27th St		
(1-815)	13	A2
(816-940)	12	A2
E 28th Pl	14	A1
W 28th Pl	13	A1
E 28th St	14	A1
W 28th St	13	A2
E 29th Pl	14	A2
W 29th Pl	13	A2
E 29th St	14	A1
(1-799)	13	A2
(829-852)	12	A2
W 29th St		
(30-860)	13	A2
(861-999)	12	A2
E 30th Pl	13	A2
E 30th St	14	A1
W 30th St	13	A2
E 31st Pl	14	B1
W 31st Pl	12	B2
E 31st St	14	B1
W 31st St		
(1-813)	13	B2
(814-1499)	12	B2
E 32nd Pl	14	B2
W 32nd Pl	12	B2
E 32nd St	14	B1
W 32nd St		
(200-816)	13	B2
(817-1399)	12	B2
E 33rd St	14	B1
W 33rd Pl	12	B2
E 33rd St	14	B1
W 33rd St		
(1-811)	13	B2
(812-1599)	12	B2
W 34th Pl	12	B2
E 34th St	14	B1
W 34th St		
(68-849)	13	B2
(850-1648)	12	B2
W 35th Pl	12	C2
E 35th St	14	B1
W 35th St		
(1-40)	14	B1
(41-849)	13	B2
(850-1629)	12	B2
E 36th Pl	14	C1
W 36th Pl	12	C2
E 36th St	14	C1
W 36th St		
(500-849)	13	C1
(850-1629)	12	C1
E 37th Pl	14	C1
W 37th Pl		
(240-499)	13	C2
(800-1411)	12	C1
E 37th St	14	C1
W 37th St		
(200-849)	13	C2
(850-1649)	12	C1
E 38th Pl	14	C2
W 38th Pl		
(200-849)	13	C2
(850-999)	12	C2
E 38th St	14	C1
W 38th St		
(1-849)	13	C2
(850-1599)	12	C2
W 40th Pl	15	A2
W 40th St	15	A2
E 40th St		
(1-862)	16	A1
(863-999)	17	A1
E 41st St	17	A1
W 41st St	15	A1
E 41st St		
(38-949)	16	A1
(950-1099)	17	A1
E 42nd Pl	15	A2
E 42nd St		
(400-874)	16	A2
(875-1199)	17	A1
E 42nd St		
(38-899)	16	A1
W 42nd St	15	A2
W 43rd Pl	15	B2
W 43rd St	15	A2
E 43rd St		
(38-884)	16	B1
(885-1199)	17	B1
W 44th Pl	15	B2
E 44th Pl		
(500-599)	16	B2
(1200-1231)	17	B1
W 44th St	15	B2
E 44th St		
(1-899)	16	B1
(900-1199)	17	B1
E 45th Pl	16	B2
W 45th Pl	15	B2
W 45th St	15	B2
E 45th St		
(1-899)	16	B1
(900-1199)	17	B1
E 46th Pl	16	B2
W 46th Pl	15	B2
W 46th St	15	B2
E 46th St		
(1-899)	16	B1
(900-1299)	17	B1
W 47th Pl	15	C1
E 47th Pl		
(800-839)	16	B2
(1346-1399)	17	B2
E 47th St		
(1-899)	16	B1
(900-1420)	17	B2
W 47th St		
(1-62)	16	B1
(63-799)	15	B2
E 48th Pl	16	C1
W 48th Pl	15	C2
W 48th St	15	C1
E 48th St		
(1-899)	16	C1
(900-1450)	17	C1
W 49th Pl	15	C1
W 49th St	15	C1
E 49th St		
(1-899)	16	C2
(900-1699)	17	C1
W 50th Pl		
(401-799)	16	C2
(1600-1625)	17	C2
W 50th St	15	C2
E 50th St		
(41-886)	16	C1
(887-1699)	17	C1
E 51st St		
(39-872)	16	C1
(450-1128)	17	C1
W 51st St		
(1-66)	16	C1
(67-799)	15	C2
E 52nd Pl	19	A2
E 52nd St		
(100-199)	18	A1
(800-1539)	19	A1
E 53rd St		
(38-369)	18	A1
(370-1545)	19	A1
(1546-1799)	20	A1
E 54th Pl		
(340-1539)	19	A2
(1624-1601)	20	A1
W 54th St	18	A1
E 54th St		
(200-369)	18	A1
(370-1539)	19	A1
(1624-1799)	20	A1
E 55th Pl		
(200-399)	18	B1
(1342-1499)	19	B2
E 55th St		
(800-1605)	19	A1
(1606-1899)	20	B1
E 56th Pl		
E 56th St		
(1-370)	18	B1
(371-1573)	19	B1
(1574-1849)	20	B1
E 57th Cutoff St	20	B1
E 57th Dr	20	B1
W 57th Pl	18	B1

Street Index

Street	Page	Grid
E 57th St	20	B1
(1-399)	18	B1
(700-1523)	19	B2
W 57th St	18	B1
E 58th St		
(1-370)	18	B1
(371-1435)	19	B1
W 59th St	18	B1
E 59th St		
(1-1631)	18	B1
(369-1598)	19	B1
W 60th St	18	C1
E 60th St		
(1-750)	18	C1
(751-1599)	19	C2
E 61st Pl	19	C1
W 61st St	18	C1
E 61st St		
(1-764)	18	C1
(765-1567)	19	C1
E 62nd Pl	19	C2
E 62nd St		
(400-764)	18	C2
(765-1599)	19	C1
E 63rd St		
(334-764)	18	C1
(765-1599)	19	C1

A

Street	Page	Grid
N Aberdeen St	24	B2
S Aberdeen St		
(1-499)	24	C2
(500-1599)	26	A2
(3100-3499)	12	B2
Academy Pl	4	B1
Access Rd	11	C2
(2200-2299)	13	A2
S Ada St	26	A1
N Ada St		
(1-1624)	22	B1
(51-799)	24	B1
(1625-1699)	29	C1
E Adams St	5	B2
W Adams St		
(1-367)	5	B2
(368-864)	4	B2
(865-1647)	24	C2
(1648-2499)	23	C1
W Addison St		
(500-814)	44	A1
(815-1614)	43	A2
(1615-2473)	42	B2
(2466-3199)	41	A2
E Administration Dr	18	B2
W Agatite Ave		
(800-999)	40	B1
(2101-2199)	39	B1
(2600-2799)	38	B2
W Ainslie St		
(800-1649)	40	A2
(1650-2420)	39	A2
(2421-3199)	38	A2
N Albany Ave		
(1700-2749)	27	C1
(2750-3949)	41	C1
N Albany Ave		
(3950-5199)	38	C1
(6000-6350)	35	A1
(6351-7531)	33	A1
W Albion Ave		
(1000-6660)	34	C2
(2056-3199)	33	C2
W Aldine Ave		
(400-824)	44	B1
(825-899)	43	B2
W Alexander St	10	C2
S Allport St	26	C1
N Alta Vista Ter	43	A2
W Altgeld St		
(800-1681)	29	A2
(1682-2464)	28	A2
(2465-3217)	27	A2
W Ancona St		
(800-863)	1	A1
(864-1399)	24	A2
W Anson Pl	23	B1
W Arbor Pl	24	B1
W Arcade Pl		
(100-399)	5	B1
(530-741)	4	B2
(1000-1399)	24	C2
(1798-1734)	23	C2
S Arch St	12	A1
S Archer Ave		
(1110-2427)	10	C2
(2428-3099)	12	A2
(3100-3143)		
W Ardmore Ave		
(900-2415)	37	B2
(2416-3099)	35	B2
W Argyle St		
(821-1499)	40	A2
(1800-2398)	39	A1
(2501-3199)	38	A2
W Arlington Pl	30	A1
W Armitage Ave		
(300-864)	30	B2
(865-1659)	29	B1
(1657-2440)	28	B2
(2441-3199)	27	B1
N Armour St	24	A1
S Artesian Ave	23	C1
N Artesian Ave		
(200-599)	23	B1
(1200-1649)	21	B1
(1650-2799)	28	C1
(3600-4749)	38	B2
(4750-6349)	35	C2
(6350-7499)	33	C2
W Arthington St		
(500-517)	7	B1
(518-1399)	26	A2
(2400-2499)	25	A1
W Arthur Ave		
(1200-2064)	34	C2
(2065-3199)	33	C2
N Ashland Ave		
(400-814)	24	B1
(815-1649)	22	B1
(1650-2699)	29	C1
(2700-3949)	43	C1
N Ashland Ave		
(3950-5165)	40	C1
(5166-5729)	37	B1
(6400-7599)	34	A1
S Ashland Ave		
(1-424)	24	C1
(425-2199)	26	A1
(2604-3899)	12	A1
N Ashland Blvd	24	B1
N Astor St	32	B1
W Attrill St	27	B2
W Augusta Blvd		
(1042-1664)	22	B2
(1665-2399)	21	B2
N Avondale Ave		
(1800-2399)	28	A1
(2830-2870)	27	A2
(2871-3128)	41	C1

B

Street	Page	Grid
E Balbo Ave		
(1-99)	8	B2
(100-399)	9	B1
W Balmoral Ave		
(1000-1749)	37	C2
(1750-2414)	36	C2
(2415-5499)	35	C2
E Banks St	32	B1
W Barber St	26	B2
W Barry Ave		
(300-833)	44	C2
(834-1649)	43	C2
(1650-2455)	42	C2
(2456-3199)	41	C2
N Bauwans St	22	B1
W Beach Ave	21	A2
N Beacon St	40	B1
N Beaubien Ct	6	A1
W Belden Ave		
(300-3199)	27	B1
(325-815)	30	B1
(816-1499)	29	B2
(2200-2449)	28	B1
N Bell Ave		
(300-399)	23	B1
(1200-1649)	21	B1
(1650-2199)	28	B1
(3300-3949)	42	B1
(3950-4999)	39	C1
(5300-6364)	36	C1
(6365-7399)	33	C2
S Bell Ave		
(100-299)	23	C1
(500-1311)	25	A1
W Belle Plaine Ave		
(800-1649)	40	C2
(1650-2449)	39	C2
(2450-3199)	38	C2
E Bellevue Pl	32	B1
W Belmont Ave		
(300-809)	44	B2
(810-1649)	43	B2
(1650-2476)	42	B2
(2477-3213)	41	B1
N Belmont Harbor Dr	44	A1
S Benson St	12	B1
E Benton Pl	5	A2
W Berenice Ave	42	A2
S Berkeley Ave	17	A1
Berkeley Ave	19	A1
W Berteau Ave		
(1400-1649)	40	C1
(1650-2449)	39	C2
(2450-3199)	38	C2
W Berwyn Ave		
(998-1749)	37	C2
(1750-2399)	36	C2
(2415-3099)	35	C2
N Besly Ct	29	C1
E Best Dr	18	B2
N Bingham St	27	B2
Birchwood Ave	33	A1
W Birchwood Ave		
(1300-2065)	34	A1
(2066-3199)	33	A2
S Bishop St	26	A1
N Bishop St		
(1-803)	24	B1
(804-823)	22	C1
N Bissell St	29	C2
W Bittersweet Pl	40	C2
W Blackhawk St		
(400-864)	31	A2
(865-1699)	22	A2
S Blackstone Ave		
(4900-5149)	17	C2
(5150-6299)	19	C2
W Bliss St	22	B2
W Bloomingdale Ave		
(1401-1664)	29	C1
(1665-2464)	28	C2
(2465-3199)	27	C1
S Blue Island Ave	26	B2
S Bonaparte St	12	A1
S Bonfield St	12	A1
N Bosworth Ave		
(1200-1649)	22	B1
(1650-2774)	29	B1
(2775-3799)	43	B1
(6400-6799)	34	C2
E Bowen Ave	16	A2
E Bowen Dr	19	A1
W Bowler St	25	A1
N Bowmanville Ave	36	C1
W Bradley Pl		
(800-2199)	42	A2
(2500-2699)	41	A2
W Briar Pl	44	C2
S Broad St	12	A1
N Broadway St		
(2800-3936)	44	C1
(3937-5163)	40	C2
(5164-6399)	37	A2
W Brompton Ave	44	B1
E Browning Ave	14	C2
W Bryn Mawr Ave		
(900-1749)	37	B2
(1750-2415)	36	B2
(2416-3175)	35	B2
W Buckingham Pl	44	B1
W Buena Ave	40	C2

N Burling St
(1200-1608) 31 B1
(1609-2699) 30 C1
(2800-2999) 44 C1
E Burton Pl 32 A1
W Burton Pl
(1-99) 32 A1
(140-199) 31 A2
N Byron St
(1000-1615) 43 A2
(1616-2499) 42 A2
(2800-3199) 41 A1

C

W Cabrini St
(500-699) 7 B1
(1054-1299) 26 A2
W Calhoun Pl 5 B2
N California Ave
(1650-2724) 27 A2
(2725-3949) 41 C2
(3950-5150) 38 C2
(5151-6349) 35 C2
(6350-7549) 33 C1
W California Ter 44 C1
S Calumet Ave
(1800-2509) 11 B1
(2510-3950) 14 A1
(3951-5200) 16 A1
(5201-6299) 18 A1
N Cambridge Ave
(800-1141) 31 C1
(2300-2399) 30 B1
(2800-3199) 44 C1
N Campbell Ave
(1-199) 23 B1
(1700-2749) 27 C2
(2047-2264) 28 B1
(2750-3966) 41 C2
(3967-4749) 38 C2
(4750-6349) 35 C2
(6350-7499) 33 C2
S Campbell Ave
(100-399) 23 C1
(500-1299) 25 A1
W Campbell Park Dr 25 A1
N Canal St
(1-249) 4 B2
(250-499) 1 B2
S Canal St
(1-499) 4 B2
(600-1199) 7 A2
(1200-2549) 10 B1
(2550-3999) 13 A1
(4300-4399) 15 B1
S Canalport Ave
(1744-1963) 10 B1
(2000-2199) 26 C2
N Cannon Dr
(1917-2699) 30 B2
(2700-2799)
W Carmen Ave
(830-1699) 40 A2
(1700-2449) 39 A1
(2450-3199) 38 A2

N Carpenter St
(100-828) 24 B2
(829-899) 22 C2
S Carpenter St
(400-2199) 26 A2
(3221-3435) 12 B2
W Carroll Ave
(36-199) 2 C2
(800-863) 1 C1
(864-1649) 24 B2
(1650-2199) 23 B2
E Carver Plz 14 C1
W Castlewood Ter 40 A2
W Catalpa Ave
(1000-1799) 37 C2
(2400-2999) 35 C2
W Caton St 28 C1
E Cedar St
E Cermak Rd 11 B1
W Cermak Rd
(28-44) 11 B1
(45-655) 10 C2
(624-1749) 26 C2
(1750-2499) 25 C2
W Chalmars Pl
N Chalmers St 29 B2
S Champlain Ave
(4200-5099) 16 B2
(6000-6299) 18 C2
W Chanay St 27 B2
Channel Rd 33 A1
W Charleston St 28 B1
W Chase Ave
(1200-2049) 34 A2
(2050-3199) 33 A2
N Cherry Ave 22 A2
E Chestnut St 32 C1
W Chestnut St
(1-118) 32 C1
(119-537) 31 C2
(928-1599) 22 C2
E Chicago Ave
(1-126) 2 A2
(127-499) 3 A1
W Chicago Ave
(1-367) 2 A2
(368-841) 1 A1
(842-1664) 24 A1
(1665-2399) 23 A2
S Chicago Beach Dr 17 C2
E Chicago River Dr 6 A2
N Childrens Plz 30 B1
S China Pl 10 B2
W Churchill St 28 C1
N Cityfront Plaza Dr
S Claremont Ave 25 A1
N Claremont Ave
(239-599) 23 B1
(1300-1649) 21 B1
(1650-2299) 28 B1
(3300-3949) 42 B1
(3950-5199) 39 C1
(6000-6349) 36 A1
(6350-7499) 33 C2
N Clarendon Ave 40 C2

N Clark St
(1-261) 5 B2
(262-821) 2 C2
(822-1649) 32 B1
(1650-2749) 30 C2
(2750-3173) 44 C1
(3174-3963) 43 B2
(3964-5164) 40 C1
(5165-6363) 37 B1
(6364-7599) 34 A1
S Clark St
(1-449) 5 B2
(450-1343) 8 A1
(1344-2199) 10 B2
Clarmont Ave 23 A1
N Cleaver St 22 A1
N Cleveland Ave
(800-1649) 31 B1
(1650-2399) 30 C1
N Clifton Ave
(1930-2399) 29 C2
(3000-3899) 43 C2
(4333-4799) 40 B1
N Clinton St
(1-249) 4 B2
(250-599) 1 C2
S Clinton St
(1-420) 4 B2
(421-1214) 7 A1
(1215-1899) 10 A1
N Clybourn Ave
(1200-2799) 28 A2
(1230-1649) 31 B1
(1650-2407) 29 C2
(2800-3199) 42 C1
Coast Gd Dr Cut Off 20 C2
W Columbia Ave 34 C1
Columbia Dr 20 B1
N Columbus Dr 3 B1
S Columbus Dr 6 B1
S Columbus Dr
(100-699) 9 A1
(700-1436)
(2200-2479) 11 C2
N Columbus Dr
(298-401) 6 B1
(434-499)
N Commonwealth Ave
(2300-2399) 30 B1
(2800-2941) 44 C2
W Concord Ln 30 C2
W Concord Pl
(300-799) 30 C1
(900-2017) 29 C2
(2018-2199) 28 C1
W Congress Pkwy
(2-199) 8 A2
(530-699) 7 A1
(1000-1665) 26 A1
(1666-2499) 25 A2
Congress Pky 7 A1
Congress Pky 26 A2
E Congress Pky
(1-71) 8 A2
(72-129) 9 A1

E Congress Plaza Dr 9 A1
W Cornelia Ave
(500-814) 44 B1
(815-1617) 43 B2
(1618-2399) 42 B2
(3000-3099) 41 B1
S Cornell Ave
(4900-5199) 17 C2
(5200-6299) 20 B1
Cornell Dr 17 C2
N Cortez St 22 B1
W Cortez St
(1200-1664) 22 B1
(1665-2399) 21 B2
W Cortland St
(1200-1649) 29 C1
(1650-2449) 28 C2
(2450-3199) 27 C1
S Cottage Grove Ave
(2200-3902) 14 A2
(2250-2499) 11 C1
(3903-5120) 16 A2
(5121-6299) 19 B1
W Cottage Pl
W Couch Pl
(1-299) 5 A2
(600-799) 4 A1
W Court Pl
(1-339) 5 A2
(634-799) 4 A1
W Coyle Ave 33 B2
N Crilly Ct 30 C2
N Crosby St 31 B1
S Crowell St 12 A1
W Crystal St
(1251-1399) 22 B1
(1723-2199) 21 B2
E Cullerton St 11 B1
W Cullerton St
(1-599) 10 B2
(800-1731) 26 C2
(1712-2499) 25 C2
W Cullom Ave
(900-1649) 40 C2
(1650-2450) 39 C2
(2451-3199) 38 C2
W Cuyler Ave
(800-1499) 40 C2
(1800-2499) 39 C2
W Dakin St 43 A2

D

N Damen Ave
(1-824) 23 B2
(825-1620) 21 A2
(1621-2685) 28 C2
(2686-3949) 42 C2
(3950-5158) 39 C2
(5159-6199) 36 C2
(6400-7499) 34 C1
S Damen Ave
(1-449) 23 C2
(450-2229) 25 B2

Street Index

Street	Page	Grid
Dan Ryan Expy	13	A2
Dan Ryan Expy	15	C2
N Dayton St		
(1400-1632)	31	B1
(1633-2149)	30	C1
(2150-2749)	29	B2
(2750-4399)	43	C2
W de Koven St	7	C1
W de Saible St	13	C2
N Dean St		
N Dearborn St		
(1-250)	5	A2
(251-821)	2	C2
(822-1599)	32	C1
S Dearborn St		
(1-449)	5	B2
(450-699)	8	A2
(700-2499)	10	A2
(2500-3949)	13	B2
(3562-3501)		
(3610-3714)	14	C1
(3950-4125)	15	A2
(4639-4699)	16	B1
(5100-5499)	18	A1
E Delaware Pl	32	C1
W Delaware Pl		
(1-116)	32	C1
(117-537)	31	C1
W Deming Pl	30	A1
S Des Plaines Ave	7	A1
S Des Plaines St	10	B1
N Des Plaines St		
(1-224)	4	B1
(218-599)	1	C1
S Des Plaines St		
(1-499)	4	B1
(600-1199)	7	A1
W Devon Ave		
(1200-2064)	34	C1
(2065-3133)	33	C2
N Dewitt Pl	32	C2
W Dickens Ave		
(155-864)	30	B2
(865-1499)	29	B2
(1898-2815)	28	B2
(2816-3199)	27	B1
W Diversey Pkwy	27	A2
W Diversey Pkwy		
(100-814)	44	C2
(815-1665)	43	C2
(1666-2465)	42	C2
(2466-3199)	41	C2
W Diversey School Ct		
E Division St	32	B1
W Division St		
(1-130)	32	B1
(131-847)	31	B2
(848-1665)	22	B1
(1664-2449)	21	B2
N Dominick St	29	B1
S Dorchester Ave		
(445-5149)	17	B2
(5150-6299)	19	A2
N Dover St	40	B1
S Dr Martin Luther King Jr Dr	16	A1
(1800-3898)	14	B1
(2100-2199)	11	B1
W Draper St		
S Drexel Ave	19	A1
S Drexel Blvd		
(501-4698)	16	A2
(4700-5099)	17	B1
E Drexel Sq	19	A1
W Drummond Pl		
(526-699)	30	A1
(1100-1199)	29	A2

E

Street	Page	Grid
W Early Ave	37	B2
S East End Ave	17	C2
S East View Park	20	A1
N Eastlake Ter	34	A2
W Eastman St		
(800-850)	31	B1
(851-1129)	22	B2
Eastwood Ave	38	B2
W Eastwood Ave		
(800-2049)	40	B2
(2050-2449)	39	B1
(2450-3199)	38	B2
S Eberhart Ave		
(3130-3449)	14	B2
(6000-6299)	18	C2
W Eddy St		
(1001-1399)	43	B2
(1801-1999)	42	B2
(3100-3199)	41	B1
W Edgewater Ave	37	B1
N Edward Ct	30	B1
N Elaine Pl	44	B1
S Eleanor St	12	A1
S Elias Ct		
N Elizabeth St		
(1-799)	24	A1
(900-999)	22	C1
N Elk Grove Ave	21	A2
W Ellen St	21	B2
S Ellis Ave		
(2600-3961)	14	A2
(3962-5149)	17	A1
(5150-6299)	19	A1
E Elm St	32	B1
W Elm St		
(1-117)	32	B1
(118-699)	31	B1
W Elmdale Ave	37	A2
N Elston Ave		
(800-1629)	22	C2
(1630-2072)	29	C1
(2073-2799)	28	A1
(2800-3557)	41	C2
S Elsworth Dr	16	C1
Elsworth Dr	18	A2
S Emerald Ave		
(2500-3949)	13	A1
(3950-4699)	15	A1
W Eric St	24	A2
E Erie St		
(1-114)	2	A2
(115-499)	3	B1
W Erie St		
(1-375)	2	A2
(376-864)	1	A2
(865-1649)	24	A2
(1650-2399)	23	A2
N Ernst Ct	32	C1
W Estes Ave		
(1300-2029)	34	B1
(2030-3544)	33	B1
W Eugenie St	30	C2
S Evans Ave		
(4300-5099)	16	B2
(6100-6299)	18	C2
E Evans Ct		
S Everett Ave	20	B1
W Evergreen Ave		
(200-839)	31	B2
(840-1663)	22	B2
(1664-2199)	21	A2
W Exchange Ave	15	A1

F

Street	Page	Grid
W Fair Pl	31	B1
N Fairbanks Ct	3	B1
N Fairfield Ave		
(1700-2799)	27	A2
(2900-2999)	41	C2
(4800-4999)	38	A2
(5600-6349)	35	B2
(6350-7499)	33	C1
W Fargo Ave		
(1300-2065)	34	A1
(2066-3199)	33	A2
W Farragut Ave		
(1400-1749)	37	C1
(1750-2449)	36	C2
(2450-2999)	35	C2
S Farrell St	12	A2
W Farwell Ave		
(1100-2024)	34	B1
(2025-2999)	33	B2
S Federal St		
(300-449)	5	C2
(450-1259)	8	A1
(1260-2549)	10	A2
(2550-3987)	13	A2
(3988-5099)	15	B2
N Felton Ct	31	B1
W Ferdinand St	23	A2
N Fern Ct	30	C1
N Field Blvd	6	C2
W Fillmore St		
(1300-1599)	26	A1
(1800-2499)	25	A2
S Financial Pl		
(300-499)	5	C1
(600-999)	8	A1
W Fitch Ave	33	B2
W Fletcher Ave	43	B2
W Fletcher St		
(1200-1649)	43	B1
(1650-2449)	42	C2
(2450-3099)	41	B2
W Flournoy St		
(1205-1669)	26	A1
(1670-2499)	25	A1
S Forrestville Ave	16	B2
W Foster Ave	37	C2
W Foster Ave		
(2500-3199)	35	C2
(2997-3110)	38	A1
W Foster Dr	37	C2
W Francis Pl	27	B2
N Francisco Ave		
(1700-2749)	27	A1
(2750-3949)	41	C1
(3950-5163)	38	C1
(5164-6349)	35	C1
(6350-7599)	33	C1
N Franklin St		
(1-299)	5	B1
(400-815)	2	C1
(816-1125)	31	C2
S Franklin St		
(1-449)	5	B1
(450-599)	7	A2
N Fremont St		
(1500-1599)	22	A2
(1700-3549)	29	C2
(3550-3999)	43	A2
N Frontier Ave		
(1500-1599)	31	A1
(3900-3999)	40	C2
W Fry St	22	C1
W Fuller St	12	A1
W Fullerton Ave		
(1-823)	30	A2
(824-1676)	29	B2
(1677-2499)	28	B1
(2477-3134)	27	B1
W Fulton St		
(500-864)	1	C2
(865-1649)	24	B1
(1650-2500)	23	B2

G

Street	Page	Grid
W Garfield Blvd	18	A1
E Garfield Blvd		
(200-399)	18	A1
(749-799)		
N Garland Ct	5	B2
N Garvey Ct	5	A2
N Geneva Ter	30	B1
W George St		
(800-1599)	43	C2
(1900-2449)	42	C2
(2450-3199)	41	C2
W Germania Pl	32	A1
W Giddings St		
(2000-2399)	39	B1
(2700-2940)	38	B2
S Giles Ave	14	B1

Street	Map	Grid
W Gladys Ave		
(700-799)	4	C1
(1000-1241)	24	C2
(1242-2433)	23	C1
W Glenlake Ave		
(900-1799)	37	A2
(2300-2414)	36	A1
(2415-2960)	35	A2
N Glenwood Ave		
(4900-5165)	40	A1
(5166-6363)	37	C1
(6364-7199)	34	B2
E Goethe St	32	B1
W Goethe St		
(1-116)	32	B1
(117-799)	31	B2
W Gordon Ter	40	C2
W Grace St		
(600-849)	44	A1
(850-1614)	43	A2
(1615-2499)	42	A2
(2800-3199)	41	A1
S Grady Ct	12	A1
W Grand Ave		
(1-385)	2	B2
(386-829)	1	B2
(861-1664)	24	A2
(1665-2430)	23	A1
E Grand Ave		
(1-114)	2	B2
(115-599)	3	B1
(600-631)		
W Grant Pl	30	B1
W Granville Ave		
(900-1767)	37	A2
(1768-2415)	36	A2
(2416-3199)	35	A2
S Gratten Ave		
N Green St		
(1-249)	4	B1
(250-831)	1	B1
S Green St		
(1-499)	4	B1
(2600-3299)	12	A2
W Greenleaf Ave		
(1200-2024)	34	B1
(2025-2999)	33	B2
N Greenview Ave		
(800-1599)	22	B1
(2230-2773)	29	B1
(2774-3950)	43	C1
(3951-5964)	40	C1
(5965-6364)	37	A1
(6365-7599)	34	C2
Greenview Passage	29	A1
S Greenwood Ave		
(4200-5149)	17	B1
(5150-6299)	19	A1
W Gregory St		
(1400-1749)	37	B1
(1750-3099)	35	B2
W Grenshaw St		
(536-599)	7	C1
(1300-1399)	26	B1
(1800-2499)	25	B1

Street	Map	Grid
S Grove Ave	10	B1
S Grove St	12	A1
E Groveland Park	14	B2
W Gunnison St		
(2400-2499)	39	A1
W Gunnison St		
(2500-3099)	38	A2
W Gunnison St		
(754-1231)	40	A2

H

Street	Map	Grid
E Haddock Pl	5	A2
W Haddock Pl	5	A2
W Haddon Ave		
(1500-1664)	22	B1
(1665-2399)	21	B2
W Haines St	31	B1
N Halsted St		
(1-258)	4	B1
(259-844)	1	C1
(845-1632)	31	B1
(1629-2749)	30	C1
(2750-3799)	44	C1
S Halsted St		
(1-447)	4	B1
(448-2568)	26	A2
(2558-3924)	13	A1
(3925-5099)	15	A1
N Hamilton Ave		
(2200-2398)	28	B1
(3000-3949)	42	C1
(3950-4999)	39	B1
(6100-6199)	36	A1
(6400-7399)	33	C2
S Hamilton Ave		
(200-299)	23	C1
(1000-1799)	25	A1
N Hampden Ct	30	A1
S Harbor Dr	6	B2
N Harbour Dr	6	B2
S Harper Ave	19	A2
Harper Ct	19	B2
E Harrison St	8	A2
W Harrison St		
(1-249)	8	A2
(225-714)	7	A2
(715-1664)	26	A2
(1665-2499)	25	A2
N Hart St	23	B2
N Hartland Ct	23	A2
W Hastings St		
(1200-1724)	26	B1
(1725-2199)	25	B2
W Hawthorne Pl	44	B1
E Hayes Dr	20	C1
S Haynes Ct	12	A1
N Hazel St	40	C2
S Heath Ave	25	B1
W Henderson St		
(1200-1599)	43	B1
(1700-2925)	42	B2
W Henry Ct	27	B2

Street	Map	Grid
N Hermitage Ave		
(1-1649)	21	B2
(16-820)	23	B2
(1650-1949)	28	C2
(1950-3949)	42	B2
(3950-5032)	39	C2
(5600-6368)	37	B1
(6369-7599)	34	C1
S Hermitage Ave		
(300-399)	23	C2
(700-1199)	25	A2
N Hickory Ave	22	B2
W Highland Ave		
(1400-1766)	37	A1
(1767-2231)	36	A1
W Hill St	31	B2
S Hillock Ave		
(2556-2599)		
(2600-2899)	12	A1
W Hirsch St	21	B1
W Hobbie St	31	B1
N Hobson Ave	28	B2
S Hoey St	12	A2
N Holden Ct	5	B2
S Holden Ct	8	A2
N Holly Ave	28	B2
W Hollywood Ave		
(1000-2415)	37	B2
(2416-3056)	35	B2
W Homer St		
(1500-2049)	29	C1
(2050-2465)	28	C1
(2466-3199)	27	B2
N Honore St		
(900-1649)	21	B2
(1650-2299)	28	C2
(2900-3199)	42	C2
(4200-6764)	36	C2
(6765-7399)	34	A1
S Honore St		
(1-299)	23	C2
(500-599)	25	A2
W Hood Ave		
(1200-1599)	37	A2
(1800-2129)	36	A2
(3000-3145)	35	A1
N Hooker St		
(1000-1129)	31	B1
(1130-1505)	22	B2
Horner Park	38	C2
Howard St	33	A1
W Howard St		
(501-1933)	34	A1
(801-3199)	33	A2
N Howe St		
(1100-1899)	31	B1
(1900-2099)	30	B1
N Hoyne Ave		
(1-814)	23	B1
(815-1612)	21	C1
(1613-2699)	28	C1
(2700-3949)	42	C1
(3950-4999)	39	C1
(5200-6299)	36	C1
(6300-7599)	33	C2

Street	Map	Grid
S Hoyne Ave		
(1-399)	23	B1
(500-2229)	25	A1
E Hubbard St	2	B2
W Hubbard St		
(1-385)	2	B2
(1700-1731)		
(1732-2430)	23	B2
(386-853)	1	B1
(854-1699)	24	B1
N Hudson Ave		
(654-837)	1	A2
(838-1649)	31	C2
(1650-3199)	30	C1
N Huguelet Pl		
N Humboldt Blvd	27	B1
W Huron St		
(1-367)	2	A2
(1650-2399)	23	A2
(368-880)	1	A2
(881-1649)	24	A1
E Huron St		
(1-114)	2	A2
(115-499)	3	B1
W Hutchinson St		
(2050-2449)	39	C1
(2450-2599)	38	C2
W Hutchinson St		
(642-2049)	40	C2
S Hyde Park Blvd	20	B1
E Hyde Park Blvd		
(1125-1699)	17	C2
(5300-5499)	20	A1

I

Street	Map	Grid
E IBM Plz	2	C2
W Illinois St		
(1-385)	2	B2
(386-488)	1	B2
E Illinois St		
(1-114)	2	B2
(115-599)	3	B2
(600-699)		
S Indiana Ave		
(1200-5156)	16	A1
(1250-2549)	11	A1
(2550-3949)	14	A1
(5157-6099)	18	B1
S Ingleside Ave	19	C1
W Institute Pl	31	C2
W Iowa St		
(513-537)	31	C1
(1800-2399)	21	C2
N Irene Ave	41	B1
S Iron St	12	B1
W Irving Park Rd		
(500-1627)	40	C2
(1628-2449)	39	C2
(2450-3199)	38	C2

J

E Jackson Blvd 5 C2
W Jackson Blvd
(1-371) 5 C2
(372-914) 4 C1
(915-1649) 24 C2
(1650-2499) 23 C2
E Jackson Dr 6 C1
N Janssen Ave
(2200-2749) 29 B1
(2750-3949) 43 B1
(3950-4999) 40 A1
W Jarlath St 33 A1
W Jarvis Ave
(1200-2065) 34 A2
(2066-3199) 33 A2
S Jasper Pl 12 C1
N Jefferson St
(1-249) 4 B1
(250-499) 1 C1
S Jefferson St
(1-426) 4 B1
(427-1231) 7 A1
(1220-2199) 10 A1
W Jerome St 33 A2
N Jersey Ave 35 B1
N Jessie Ct 23 B1
N Jones St 28 A1
S Jourdan Ct 26 C2
W Julia Ct 27 B2
W Julian St 21 A2
W Junior Ter 40 C2
N Justine St 24 B1
S Justine St 12 B1

K

N Kedzie Ave
(1700-2749) 27 B1
(2750-3949) 41 B1
(3627-7599) 33 B1
(3950-5160) 38 C1
(5161-6332) 35 C1
N Kedzie Blvd 27 B1
S Keeley St 12 A2
W Kemper Pl 30 B1
N Kenmore Ave
(1836-2719) 29 C2
(2720-4199) 43 C2
(4000-5149) 40 C2
(5150-6399) 37 C2
Kennedy Expy 1 B1
S Kenwood Ave
(4700-5149) 17 C1
(5150-6299) 19 A2
S Kimbark Ave
(4737-5149) 17 C1
(5150-6299) 19 A2
S King Dr
(2200-5998) 11 C2
(2550-3918) 14 A1
(3919-5199) 16 A1
(5200-6299) 18 B2
N Kingsbury St
(394-899) 1 C2
(900-1225) 31 B1
(1436-1649) 22 B2
(1650-2064) 29 B1
E Kinzie St 2 C2
W Kinzie St
(1-374) 2 C2
(321-828) 1 C1
(829-1674) 24 B1
(1675-2331) 23 B1

L

W La Salle Dr 30 C2
N La Salle Dr
(300-821) 2 C1
(818-1649) 31 C2
(1650-1799) 30 C2
N La Salle St 5 B1
S La Salle St
(1-449) 5 B1
(450-999) 8 A1
(1816-3924) 13 A2
(2000-2599) 10 B2
(3925-4299) 15 A2
S Lafayette Ave 18 B1
S Laflin Cir 26 B1
S Laflin Pl 12 C1
N Laflin St 24 B1
S Laflin St
(1-399) 24 C1
(608-2203) 26 B1
S Lake Park Ave 11 C2
(2000-5149) 17 A1
(3500-3999) 14 C2
(5150-5599) 19 B2
N Lake Shore Dr 30 C2
(960-5801) 37 B2
S Lake Shore Dr 17 C2
(950-1249) 9 C2
(1250-2199) 11 B2
Lake Shore Dr 37 C2
Lake Shore Dr
(2600-3918) 14 A2
(3919-3999) 40 C2
N Lake Shore Dr West 44 C2
W Lake St
(1-374) 5 A2
(375-863) 4 A2
(864-1649) 24 B1
(1650-2456) 23 B2
E Lake St
(1-85) 5 A2
(86-399) 6 A1
N Lakeshore Dr 44 B1
Lakeshore Dr 44 B2
W Lakeside Ave 40 B2
N Lakeview Ave 30 A1
N Lakewood Ave
(2000-2749) 29 B1
(2750-3928) 43 C1
(3929-6349) 37 C2
(6350-6939) 34 C2
S Langley Ave
(3800-3915) 14 C2
(3916-4999) 16 A2
(6000-6299) 18 C2
W Larchmont Ave 42 A2
N Larrabee St
(600-951) 1 A1
(842-1649) 31 B1
(1650-2199) 30 C1
Lasalle St 2 C1
W Lawrence Ave
(700-1649) 40 B2
(1650-2477) 39 A2
(2478-3199) 38 A2
W Le Moyne St
(1200-1649) 22 A1
(1650-2429) 21 A2
N Leavitt St
(1-1615) 21 B1
(17-814) 23 B1
(1616-2749) 28 C1
(2750-3949) 42 C1
(3950-5176) 39 C1
(5177-6364) 36 C1
(6365-6517) 33 C2
S Leavitt St
(1-425) 23 C1
(427-2229) 25 A1
W Lee Pl
N Lehmann Ct 30 A1
W Leland Ave
(720-1649) 40 B1
(1650-2414) 39 B2
(2415-3199) 38 B2
N Lessing St
(800-825) 24 A2
(826-899) 22 C2
S Levee St 12 A1
W Lexington St
(1200-1499) 26 A1
W Lexington St
(2100-2499) 25 A1
W Lexington St
(536-599) 7 B1
W Liberty St 26 B2
W Lill Ave 29 A2
N Lincoln Ave
(1800-2429) 30 C2
(2430-26461) 29 A2
(2800-3266) 43 C1
(3267-3999) 42 B2
(4000-4883) 39 C1
(4884-5163) 38 A2
N Lincoln Park West 30 C2
N Lincoln Plz 30 C2
N Linden Pl 27 A1
S Linn White Dr
N Lister Ave 28 B2
S Lituanica Ave 12 B2
S Lloyd Ave 12 A1
S Lock St 12 A1
W Locust St 31 C2
W Logan Blvd
W Logan Blvd
(1416-3198) 27 A1
(2200-2431) 28 A1
W Lomax Pl
S Loomis Pl 12 C1
N Loomis St 24 B1
S Loomis St
(1-407) 24 C1
(408-2399) 26 A1
(2600-2999) 12 A1
(3000-3099)
S Loop Dr 18 B2
N Lover 5 B1
S Lowe Ave
(2400-2499)
(2530-3949) 13 A1
(3950-4599) 15 A1
N Lower Orleans St 2 C1
E Lower South Water 6 A1
Lower Stetson Ave 6 A1
E Lower Wacker Dr 6 A2
W Loyola Ave 34 C2
S Lumber St
(1200-1399)
(1400-2279) 10 B2
W Lunt Ave
(1100-2056) 34 B1
(2057-2999) 33 B2
W Lutz Pl 31 A1
S Lyman St 12 A2
W Lyndale St
(2030-2517) 28 B1
(2518-3399) 27 B2
S Lytle St 26 A1

M

N Macchesneyer Dr
E Madison Park 17 C1
E Madison St 5 B2
W Madison St
(1-371) 5 B2
(372-898) 4 B1
(829-1649) 24 C2
(1650-2498) 23 C1
N Magnolia Ave
(1400-1610) 22 A1
(1900-2749) 29 B1
(2750-3799) 43 A1
(4400-4999) 40 B1
(5200-6349) 37 C2
(6350-6499) 34 C2
N Malden St 40 B1
N Manor Ave 38 B2
W Maple St
(1-117) 32 B1
W Maple St
(118-199) 31 B2
N Maplewood Ave
(1700-2749) 27 A2
(2750-2921) 41 C2
(4000-4749) 38 C2
(4750-6349) 35 B2
(6350-7599) 33 C2
W Marble Pl
(1-199) 5 B2
(700-741) 4 B1
N Marcey St 29 C2
W Margate Ter 40 A2

N Marine Dr		
(2200-5199)	40	B2
(3800-3899)	44	A1
N Marion Ct	21	B2
S Marshfield Ave		
(300-3499)	26	A1
(3500-3699)		
N Marshfield Ave		
(400-820)	24	B1
(821-1649)	22	C1
(1650-2699)	29	C1
(2700-3949)	42	B2
(3950-7465)	34	A1
S Mary St	12	A2
S Maryland Ave		
(4900-4949)	16	C2
(5300-5899)	19	B1
N Maud Ave	29	C2
N Mautene Ct	22	B1
W Maxwell St		
(536-599)	10	A1
W Maxwell St		
(600-1130)	26	B2
N May St		
(1-818)	24	B2
(819-929)	22	C2
S May St		
(700-2199)	26	A2
(3100-3799)	12	B2
W Maypole Ave	23	B1
W McLean Ave	28	B1
W McLean Ave		
(1400-2815)	29	B1
(2816-2999)	27	B1
N McClurg Ct	3	B2
N McClurg Ct	3	C2
W Medill Ave		
(1200-1299)		
(1600-2449)	28	B1
(2450-3176)	27	B2
Melrose St	41	B2
W Melrose St		
(1223-1649)	43	B1
(1650-2399)	42	B2
(2500-2844)	41	B2
(400-1222)	44	B1
N Mendell St	29	B1
W Menomonee St	30	C2
W Merchandise Mart Plz	2
C1		
N Meyer Ct		
N Michigan Ave		
(1-375)	6	B1
(376-813)	3	C1
(814-999)	32	C2
S Michigan Ave		
(1-499)	6	B1
(600-1199)	9	A1
(1200-2549)	11	A1
(2550-3949)	14	A1
(3950-5156)	16	A1
(5157-6099)	18	A1
Midway Plaisance	18	B2
Midway Plaisance	19	B1
Midway Plaisance	20	B1
Mies Vander Rohe Way		

N Mildred Ave		
(2600-2749)	29	A2
(2750-2999)	43	C2
S Miller St	26	A2
N Milwaukee Ave		
(200-2608)	27	B2
(225-640)	1	C2
(482-1284)	22	C1
(641-821)	24	A2
(1255-1627)	21	B2
(1628-2061)	28	C1
W Moffat St		
(2000-2449)	28	C1
(2450-3199)	27	C2
N Mohawk St		
(800-1649)	31	C1
(1650-2099)	30	C1
W Monroe St		
(1-352)	5	B2
(1663-2499)	23	C2
(353-864)	4	B2
(865-1662)	24	C1
E Monroe St		
(1-71)	5	B2
(72-410)	6	B1
W Montana St		
(2300-2399)	28	A1
(900-1599)	29	A2
(1651-2414)	39	B2
(2415-3199)	38	B2
(552-1650)	40	B2
Montrose Dr		
N Moorman St	21	B2
Morgan Dr	18	B2
N Morgan St	24	B2
S Morgan St		
(1-424)	24	C2
(410-2199)	26	A2
(3100-3899)	12	B2
W Morse Ave		
(1100-2060)	34	B1
(2061-2999)	33	B2
N Mozart St		
(1700-2699)	27	A1
(2700-3949)	41	C1
(3950-5099)	38	C1
(5600-6349)	35	B1
(6350-6799)	33	C1
E Museum Dr	20	B1

N

W Nelson St		
(1650-2399)	42	C2
(2600-2999)	41	C2
(800-1649)	43	C2
N New St	3	B2
S Newberry Ave	26	B2
N Newgard Ave	34	C2
W Newport Ave		
(800-1399)	43	B2
(1700-1999)	42	B2
N Noble St		
(400-849)	24	B1
(850-2531)	22	B1

S Normal Ave		
(1600-2549)	10	B1
(2550-3499)	13	A1
(3950-4757)	15	A1
W North Ave		
(1-141)	32	A1
(142-884)	31	A1
(885-1664)	22	A1
(1665-2429)	21	A2
N North Branch St	22	B2
N North Park Ave		
(801-1649)	31	B2
(1744-11547)	30	C2
North Riverside Plz		
W North Shore Ave		
(1016-1799)	34	C2
(2400-3098)	33	C2
E North Water St	3	C1
W Norwood St		
(1200-1599)	37	A1
(1800-2199)	36	A2
N Nursery St	29	B1

O

W O Brien St	26	B2
E Oak St	32	B1
W Oak St		
(1-551)	32	B1
(552-1002)	31	B1
W Oakdale Ave		
(300-849)	44	C2
(850-1599)	43	C2
(1800-2299)	42	C2
S Oakenwald Ave	17	A1
S Oakland Cir	17	A1
S Oakley Ave	25	B1
N Oakley Ave		
(1600-2413)	28	B1
(2414-3949)	42	C1
(3950-5164)	39	C1
(5165-6349)	36	C1
(6350-7499)	33	C2
N Oakley Blvd		
(1-814)	23	B1
(815-1599)	21	C1
S Oakley Blvd		
(1-449)	23	C1
(438-1199)	25	A1
E Oakwood Blvd		
(400-824)	16	A2
(825-1199)	14	C2
E Oakwood St	16	A1
S Ogden Ave	25	B1
W Ogden Ave		
(1598-1663)	24	C1
(1664-1831)	23	C2
(1832-2299)	25	B1
N Ogden Ave		
(1-1599)	31	B1
(26-818)	24	B1
(819-1011)	22	C2
(1906-1931)	30	C1
W Ohio St		
(1-417)	2	B2
(1667-2448)	23	A2

W Ohio St		
(418-863)	1	B2
(864-1666)	24	A2
E Ohio St		
(1-114)	2	B2
(115-651)	3	B2
W Olive Ave	37	B1
W Ontario St		
(1-499)	2	B2
(1600-1699)		
E Ontario St		
(1-98)	2	B2
(27-499)	3	B1
N Orchard St		
(1500-1613)	31	A1
(1608-2749)	30	C1
(2750-3199)	44	C1
N Orleans St		
(300-812)	2	C1
(767-1599)	31	B2
(1700-2099)	30	C1
N Oswego St	24	B1
N Outer Lake Shore Dr		
(3138-3359)	44	B2
(3536-3859)		

P

W Palmer Sq	27	B1
W Palmer St		
(2200-2549)	28	B1
(2800-3215)	27	B1
N Park Dr	3	C1
Park Dr		
E Park Pl	19	B2
E Park Shore East Ct		
S Park Shore East Ct	19	C2
S Park Ter	8	B1
S Parnell Ave		
(2900-4318)	13	A1
(4319-4399)	15	B1
W Patterson Ave		
(600-699)	44	A1
(1100-1199)	43	A2
(1801-1999)	42	A2
N Paulina St		
(1-1649)	21	B2
(16-820)	23	B2
(1650-2770)	28	C2
(2771-3949)	42	C2
(3950-5164)	39	C2
(5165-6369)	37	C1
(6370-7447)	34	C1
S Paulina St		
(1-424)	23	C2
(425-1099)	25	A2
(1100-2199)	26	B1
Payne Dr	18	A2
E Pearson St	32	C1
W Pearson St		
(1-37)	32	C1
(501-539)	31	C1
(1500-1664)	22	C1
(1665-1799)	21	C2

W Pensacola Ave
(900-2049)	40	C1
(2050-2449)	39	B1
(2450-2599)	38	B2

N Peoria St
(1-933)	22	C2
(51-801)	24	A2

S Peoria St
(1-299)	24	C2
(300-399)		
(400-2199)	26	A2
(2600-2698)	12	A2

E Pershing Rd	14	C1

W Pershing Rd
(1-899)	13	C2
(900-1524)	12	C2

N Peshtigo Ct	3	B2
W Peterson Ave	37	A1
W Pierce Ave	21	B2
N Pine Grove Ave	44	C1
S Pitney Ct		

S Plymouth Ct
(300-449)	5	C2
(450-1250)	8	A2
(1251-1451)	10	A2

N Poe St	29	C2
N Point St	27	B2

W Polk St
(1-199)	8	B2
(300-717)	7	B2
(718-1674)	26	A1
(1675-2499)	25	A2

E Pool Dr	18	B2
S Poplar Ave	12	A2
Portland Ave	15	B2
N Post Pl	5	A1

W Potomac Ave
(1300-1499)	22	B1
(1722-2429)	21	B2

S Prairie Ave
(1441-2549)	11	B1
(2550-3949)	14	A1
(3950-5199)	16	A1
(5200-6099)	18	A1

W Pratt Blvd
(1000-2115)	34	B2
(2116-3041)	33	B2

Princeton Ave	10	C2

S Princeton Ave
(2219-2549)	10	B2
(2550-3949)	13	A2
(3950-5099)	15	A2

W Prindiville St	27	B2
Public Way	41	B2

Q

W Quincy St
(1-568)	5	C2
(569-799)	4	C1
(1000-1249)	24	C2
(1250-1711)	23	C2

S Quinn St	12	A2

R

W Race Ave
(1200-1599)	24	A1
(1800-2299)	23	A2

N Racine Ave
(1-824)	24	A2
(825-1956)	22	C2
(1957-2749)	29	B2
(2750-3899)	43	C2
(4226-4799)	40	B1

S Racine Ave
(1-424)	24	C2
(421-2199)	26	A1
(3100-3899)	12	B2

W Railroad Pl	25	C1
Rainey Dr	18	B2

W Randolph St
(1-371)	5	A2
(372-864)	4	A2
(865-2034)	24	B1
(2035-2164)	23	B1

E Randolph St
(1-84)	5	A2
(85-599)	6	B2

W Rascher Ave
(1400-1799)	37	C1
(2000-2999)	35	C2

N Ravenswood Ave
(3400-6799)	36	A2
(4200-5129)	39	A2
(6400-7099)	34	B1

N Recreation Dr		
N Reta Ave		

S Rhodes Ave
(3100-3899)	14	B2
(6000-6299)	18	C2

W Rice St	21	C2

N Richmond St
(1700-2749)	27	A1
(2750-3949)	41	C1
(3950-4599)	38	C1
(5600-6349)	35	B1
(6350-6799)	33	C1

Ridge Ave	33	B2

N Ridge Ave
(6000-6063)	37	A1
(6052-6330)	36	A2
(6331-7021)	34	C1
(7022-7599)	33	B2

N Ridge Blvd	34	B1
S Ridgewood Ct	19	A2
N Ritchie Ct	32	B1
E River Dr	3	C2
N Riverside Plz	4	B2
S Riverside Plz	4	B2

S Robinson St
(3115-3130)		
(3129-3199)	12	B1

E Rochdale Pl	19	A2
Rockwell Ave	41	B2

N Rockwell St
(1700-2749)	27	A2
(2750-3951)	41	C2
(3952-5164)	38	C2
(5165-6349)	35	B2
(6350-7599)	33	C2

N Rogers Ave	34	A1
E Roosevelt Dr	9	C1

W Roosevelt Rd
(1-299)	8	C1
(158-650)	7	C2
(651-1706)	26	B2
(1707-2498)	25	B2

E Roosevelt Rd
(1-48)	8	C2
(100-148)	9	C1

W Root St	15	A2

W Roscoe St
(400-873)	44	B1
(874-1614)	43	B2
(1615-2449)	42	B2
(2450-3199)	41	B2

W Rosedale Ave	37	B2
W Rosehill Dr	37	B1

W Rosemont Ave
(1000-1599)	37	A2
(2100-2415)	36	A1
(2416-3199)	35	A2

W Roslyn Pl	30	A1
S Ruble St	10	B1
W Rundell Pl	24	C2

N Rush St
(408-813)	2	B2
(814-1131)	32	C1

Russell Dr	18	B2

S

N Sacramento Ave
(2200-2750)	27	A1
(2751-3949)	41	B1
(3950-4899)	38	C1
(5600-6350)	35	B1
(6351-7599)	33	C1

N Sandburg Ter	32	B1

N Sangamon St
(1-930)	22	C2
(51-818)	24	B2

S Sangamon St
(1-449)	24	C2
(450-3517)	26	A2
(3518-3835)	12	C2

N Schick Pl	31	B1
E Schiller St	32	B1

W Schiller St
(1-32)		
(33-118)	32	B1
(119-768)	31	B2
(1900-2199)	21	B2

W School St
(900-1614)	43	B2
(1615-2399)	42	B2
(2925-3199)	41	B1

W Schreiber Ave	34	C2

W Schubert Ave
(600-799)	30	A1
(830-1399)	29	A2
(2300-2464)	28	A1
(2465-3199)	27	A2

E Scott St	32	B1
W Scott St	31	B1

N Sedgwick St
(644-829)	1	A2
(809-1624)	31	C2
(1625-2299)	30	C1

Seeley Ave	36	A2

N Seeley Ave
(126-419)	23	B2
(2200-2399)	28	B1
(2822-3949)	42	C1
(3950-4998)	39	B1
(6100-6350)	36	A2
(6351-7499)	34	C1

S Seeley Ave
(1-399)	23	C1
(1000-1099)	25	A1

N Seminary Ave
(1900-3999)	43	B2
(1950-2791)	29	B2

N Seneca St	32	C2
S Senour Ave	12	A2
Service Dr	11	C1
Service Rd	19	A1

W Shakespeare Ave
(1400-2049)	29	B1
(2050-2549)	28	B1
(2800-2999)	27	B1

N Sheffield Ave
(1542-1649)	22	A2
(1650-2786)	29	C2
(2787-3899)	43	C2

S Shelby Ct	26	C2

W Sheridan Rd
(600-849)	44	A1
(850-999)	43	A2
(968-1199)	34	C2

N Sheridan Rd
(1700-3798)	44	B2
(3900-3944)	43	A2
(3934-5149)	40	C2
(5150-6349)	37	C2
(6350-7599)	34	C2

W Sherwin Ave
(1190-1699)	34	A2
(2400-3199)	33	A2

S Shields Ave
(2600-3799)	13	A2
(4161-5099)	15	A2

S Short St	12	A1
N Simonds Dr	37	C2
Solidarity Dr	11	A2
S South Shore Dr	20	B1
W South Water Market	26	B2

N Southport Ave
(1900-2749)	29	B1
(2750-3949)	43	C1
(3950-4199)	40	C1

N St Clair St	3	B1
N St Claire St	3	C1
W St George Ct	27	B2
W St Helen St	27	B2
W St James Pl	30	A1

S St Lawrence Ave
(4100-5998)	16	A2
(6000-6299)	18	C2

N St Mary St	27	B2

Street	Grid		Street	Grid		Street	Grid		Street	Grid	
N St Michaels Ct	30	C1	W Taylor St			US Highway 14			S Wallace St		
W St Paul Ave			(1-199)	8	B2	(2537-4016)	14	A2	(2400-2549)	10	C1
(200-2049)	30	C2	(300-718)	7	B2	(2800-3886)	44	A1	(2550-3949)	13	A1
(2050-2399)	28	C1	(667-1652)	26	A2	(4017-5116)	17	C2	(3950-4849)	15	C1
S Stark St			(1653-2499)	25	A2	(4441-5073)	40	B2	W Wallen Ave	34	C1
N State Pky	32	B1	W Terra Cotta Pl	28	A2	(5117-6028)	35	C2	W Walnut St		
N State St			W Thomas St			(5200-6321)	20	A1	(636-699)	1	C1
(1-258)	5	B2	(1300-1599)	22	B1				(700-1649)	4	A1
(259-813)	2	C2	(1800-2399)	21	B2	**V**			(1650-2399)	23	B2
(814-1199)	32	C1	W Thome Ave						E Walton St	32	B1
S State St			(1400-1767)	37	A1	W Van Buren St			W Walton St		
(1-449)	5	B2	(1768-2231)	36	A2	(1-412)	5	C2	(1-99)	32	B1
(450-1269)	8	A2	W Thorndale Ave			(413-903)	4	C2	(140-537)	31	B2
(1270-2557)	11	A1	(900-1799)	37	B2	(871-1675)	24	C2	(1300-1664)	22	C1
(2551-6165)	18	A1	(2400-3099)	35	B2	(1676-2499)	23	C1	(1665-2399)	21	C2
(2558-3964)	14	A1	N Throop St			E Van Buren St			W Warner Ave		
(3965-5099)	16	A1	(1-799)	24	A1	(1-71)	5	C2	(1400-1499)	40	C1
N Stave St	27	B2	(1026-1626)	22	B1	(72-132)	6	C1	(1800-2499)	39	C2
N Stetson Ave	6	A1	(1627-1799)	29	C1	S Vernon Ave			W Warren Ave	4	B1
Stetson Ave	6	A1	S Throop St			(2700-3899)	14	A1	W Warren Blvd		
S Stewart St	10	A1	(1-1124)	24	C1	(3964-4320)	16	A2	(1500-1649)	24	B1
S Stewart Ave			(1000-2313)	26	A1	(6000-6299)	18	C2	(1650-2499)	23	B2
(1600-2540)	10	C1	(2600-3299)	12	A2	W Vernon Park Pl			W Washburne Ave		
(2541-3459)	13	A2	W Tilden St			(534-599)	7	B1	(1200-1724)	26	B1
(4000-4699)	15	A2	(500-629)	7	A1	(716-1199)	26	A2	(1725-2499)	25	B2
N Stockton Dr			(800-831)	4	C1	W Victoria St	37	B2	Washington Blvd	4	B2
(1700-2598)	30	B2	S Tilden St			S Vincennes Ave			W Washington Blvd		
(2401-2799)			(1000-1062)	26	A2	(3545-3916)	14	C2	(500-865)	4	B1
Stockton Dr Cut Off	30	C2	(1063-1199)	24	C2	(3917-5099)	16	B2	(866-1649)	24	B2
N Stone St	32	B1	W Tooker Pl	32	C1	N Vine St			(1650-2499)	23	B2
S Stony Island Ave	20	B1	W Touhy Ave			S Vintage Ave	12	A1	S Washington Pk Ct	16	C2
W Stratford Pl	44	B1	(1200-2029)	34	B2	N Virginia Ave			E Washington St	5	B2
Sub Lower Wacker Dr	6	A2	(2030-3199)	33	B1	(4500-4767)	38	B2	W Washington St	5	B2
E Subwacker Dr	6	A1	E Tower Ct			(4768-5999)	35	C1	N Washtenaw Ave		
W Sullivan St			N Troy St						(1700-2799)	27	A2
W Summerdale Ave			(1700-2749)	27	C1	**W**			(2800-3399)	41	C2
(1400-1749)	37	C1	(2750-3949)	41	C1				(4700-5125)	38	B2
(1750-2199)	36	C2	(3950-5165)	38	C1	W Wabansia Ave			(5200-6349)	35	C2
(2523-2999)	35	C2	(5166-6350)	35	A1	(1300-1665)	29	C1	(6350-7599)	33	C1
W Sunnyside Ave			(6351-6501)	33	C1	(1666-2464)	28	C2	S Water St	6	A1
(800-1649)	40	B2				W Wabansia Ave			N Waterloo Ct	44	C1
(1650-2414)	39	B2	**U**			(2465-3199)	27	C1	W Waveland Ave		
(2415-3199)	38	B2				N Wabash Ave			(600-849)	44	A1
W Superior St			W Ulth St	10	B1	(1-257)	5	B2	(850-1614)	43	A2
(1-367)	2	A2	N Union Ave	1	B1	(258-812)	2	C2	(1615-2499)	42	A2
(368-852)	1	A2	S Union Ave			(813-928)	32	C1	(2800-3199)	41	A1
(853-1649)	24	A2	(1200-2349)	26	A2	S Wabash Ave			W Wayman St		
(1650-2399)	23	A2	(2350-3949)	13	A1	(1-449)	5	B2	(600-864)	1	C1
E Superior St			(3950-5099)	15	A1	(450-1250)	8	A2	(865-931)	24	B2
(1-114)	2	A2	S University Ave			(1251-2549)	11	A1	N Wayne Ave		
(115-499)	3	A1	(4400-5149)	17	B1	(2550-3949)	14	C1	(2100-2749)	29	B1
W Surf St	44	C2	(5150-6299)	19	A1	(2775-6099)	18	A1	(2750-3949)	43	A1
N Surrey Ct	29	A1	Upper Randolph Dr	6	B1	(3950-5199)	16	A1	(3950-6349)	37	C2
N Sutton Pl	32	B1	US Highway 14			N Wacker Dr	5	B1	(6350-6939)	34	C2
W Swann St	15	B2	(400-828)	3	A2	W Wacker Dr	2	C2	W Webster Ave		
			(700-1699)	37	C2	E Wacker Dr			(300-814)	30	B2
T			(100-299)	6	B2	(1-87)	2	C2	(815-1625)	29	B2
			(300-1128)			(88-599)	6	A1	(1626-2199)	28	B2
Talman Ave	41	B2	(1200-1609)	32	B1	S Wacker Dr			W Weed St		
N Talman Ave			(1300-1463)	9	C2	(1-411)	5	B1	(613-829)	31	A1
(1700-2699)	27	A2	(1600-2799)	11	A2	(412-599)	7	A2	(900-1099)	22	A2
(2800-4749)	41	C2	(1701-5999)	37	B2	E Wacker Pl			W Wellington Ave		
(4750-4999)	38	A2	(1758-2424)	36	B2	(4-84)	2	C2	(300-824)	44	C2
(5600-6349)	35	B2	(1800-2399)	36	C2	(85-123)	6	A1	(822-1649)	43	C2
(6350-7429)	33	C1	(2000-2449)	30	C2	E Waldron Dr	11	B2			
S Tan Ct	10	B2	(2425-3199)	35	A2						

Street	Page	Grid
W Wellington Ave		
(1650-2299)	42	C2
(2500-3199)	41	C2
S Wells	13	B2
Wells St	10	B2
N Wells St		
(1-258)	5	B1
(259-813)	2	C1
(814-1617)	31	C2
(1618-1826)	30	C2
S Wells St		
(1-449)	5	B1
(450-999)	8	A1
(2609-3949)	13	A2
(3950-5098)	15	C2
W Wendell St	31	B2
S Wentworth Ave		
(1600-2567)	10	B2
(2450-5099)	15	A2
(2568-4339)	13	A2
N Western Ave		
(1-814)	23	B1
(815-1649)	21	C1
(1633-2749)	28	A1
(2750-3965)	42	B1
(3966-5162)	39	A1
(5163-6349)	36	C1
(6350-7549)	33	C2
S Western Ave		
(1-449)	23	C1
(450-2248)	25	A1
W Westgate Ter	26	A1
N Whipple St		
(1700-2749)	27	A1
(2750-3949)	41	C1
(3950-4999)	38	C1
(5800-6350)	35	B1
(6351-6899)	33	C1
N Wicker Park Ave	21	B2
N Wieland St		
N Wilcox St	23	C1
N Willard Ct		
(100-949)	24	B2
(950-1051)	22	B1
N Willetts Ct	27	A1
W Willow St		
(200-864)	30	C1
(865-2099)	29	C2
N Wilmot Ave	28	C1
W Wilson Ave		
(700-1649)	40	B2
(1650-2414)	39	B2
(2415-3199)	38	B1
W Wilson Dr Ct	40	B2
N Wilton Ave		
(2600-2784)	29	A2
(2785-3899)	43	C2
N Winchester Ave		
(400-899)	23	B2
(900-1649)	21	B2
(1650-2399)	28	C2
(4200-5149)	39	C2
(5150-6299)	36	C2
(6598-7599)	34	C1
S Winchester Ave		
(1-299)	23	C2
(600-799)	25	A2
W Windsor Ave		
(800-999)	40	B2
(2140-2199)	39	B1
(2600-2799)	38	B2
N Winnebago Ave	28	C1
W Winnemac Ave		
(1200-1649)	40	A1
(1650-2449)	39	A2
(2450-2799)	38	A2
N Winona	38	A1
W Winona St		
(840-1649)	40	A2
(1650-2449)	39	A2
(2450-2899)	38	A2
N Winthrop Ave		
(4600-5149)	40	B1
(5150-6349)	37	C2
(6350-6599)	34	C2
W Wisconsin St		
(200-864)	30	C1
(865-1199)	29	C2
N Wolcott Ave		
(1-817)	23	B2
(818-1399)	21	C2
(1600-2758)	28	C2
(2759-3965)	42	C2
(3966-5149)	39	C2
(5150-6764)	36	C2
(6765-7599)	34	B1
S Wolcott Ave		
(1-299)	23	C2
(800-2225)	25	A2
W Wolfram St		
(800-1649)	43	C2
(1650-2399)	42	C2
N Wood St		
(1-1649)	21	B2
(16-815)	23	B2
(1650-2399)	28	C2
S Wood St		
(1-399)	23	C2
(600-2223)	25	B2
E Woodland Park Ave	14	B2
S Woodlawn Ave		
(4427-5149)	17	B1
(5150-6299)	19	B2
W Wrightwood Ave		
(400-817)	30	A1
(818-1663)	29	A2
(1664-1831)	28	A2